Y0-CFS-223

DISCARDED

The North Sea
Challenge and Opportunity

The North Sea
Challenge and Opportunity

Report of a Study Group of
The David Davies Memorial Institute
of International Studies

Edited by
M M Sibthorp

Published for
The David Davies Memorial Institute of International Studies
by
EUROPA PUBLICATIONS
LONDON

Europa Publications Limited
18 Bedford Square, London, WC1B 3JN

© The David Davies Memorial Institute
of International Studies, 1975

ISBN: 0 900 36276 6

Printed and bound in England by
Staples Printers Limited
at The Stanhope Press, Rochester, Kent

Contents

Foreword, by the Rt. Hon. George Thomson — vii

Introduction, by Professor R. B. Clark — ix

I   Uses of the North Sea — 1
    A. The Extraction of Resources
      1. Living Resources
      2. Mineral Resources
    B. The Addition of Alien Substances

II   The Sea and Coastline as a Supporting Medium — 41
    1. Marine Transport and Navigation
    2. Marine Installations
    3. Coastal Development
    4. Ocean Support Facilities

III   Competing Uses and Interests in the North Sea — 67
    1. Introduction
    2. Competition between Different Uses and Interests
    3. Summary

IV   The Present Legal Regime of the North Sea: International Law — 85
    Introduction
    Jurisdiction
    Regulation of Particular Activities
    Conclusions

V   The Present Legal Regime of the North Sea: National Law — 158
    Introduction
    Jurisdictional Zones
    Regulation of Particular Activities
    Conclusions

VI   Summary and Recommendations — 210
    1. Resource Management
    2. Some Specific Problems
    3. Policy Questions
    4. International and National Control of Activities
    5. The Problem of Enforcement
    6. Regional Regimes
    7. Recommendations

Appendix I — 247
Treaties and Conventions covering the North Sea

Appendix II   252
ICES Map of the North Sea

Appendix III   253
Extract (and map) on Petroleum and Natural Gas in the North
　Sea, from *Keesing's Contemporary Archives*

Appendix IV   270
Selected Belgian, Danish, Netherlands and Norwegian legal
　documents, covering aspects of North Sea exploitation

Index   317

Tables
1. Fish landings by species, 1947–1973   5–8
2. Recorded catch of demersal and pelagic fish landed by each
　　country from the North Sea in 1970   9
3. Estimates of vessels fishing the North Sea   10–11
4. North Sea shellfish landings by species   12
5. Estimates of deposition rates over the North Sea   38
6. Displacement of merchant fleets; number of large oil tankers
　　and bulk carriers   42
7. North Sea container ports   46

Figures
A. Domestic sewage discharges from the English coast   26
B. Displacement of merchant fleets   43
C. Mean size of merchant ships   44
D. Number of large oil tankers and bulk carriers   45
E. Man's impact on the sea   71
F. Jurisdictional zones   89

Foreword

One of the most striking developments of our time has been the radical change in the use of the seabed round our shores. Not only has the discovery of oil and natural gas introduced an entirely new element, but their exploitation inevitably entails far-reaching changes affecting traditional ways of life in our coastal communities as well as at sea.

In these circumstances, conflicts between the interests involved are inevitable since, in some cases, these are incompatible and a choice of uses has to be made. It was in view of this situation that the David Davies Memorial Institute of International Studies decided to undertake a comprehensive study of the waters round the United Kingdom, of which this on the North Sea is the first. The study has been carried out over a period of some two years but every effort has been made to bring the facts up to date as of November 1974.

We have been fortunate enough to secure the help of a wide range of experts in the various fields covered and I feel that the work will make a valuable contribution to discussion on a subject of immense importance for our future.

George Thomson
Commissioner of the European Communities

Abbreviations

BP	British Petroleum.
CCMS	Committee on Challenges of Modern Society (NATO).
CRISTAL	Contract Regarding an Interim Supplement to Tanker Liability for Oil Pollution.
DAFS	Department of Agriculture and Fisheries for Scotland.
EURATOM	European Atomic Energy Community.
FAO	Food and Agriculture Organization of the United Nations.
IAEA	International Atomic Energy Agency.
ICES	International Council for the Exploration of the Sea.
ICJ	International Court of Justice.
IGS	Institute of Geological Sciences.
IMCO	Inter-Governmental Maritime Consultative Organization.
IMER	Institute for Marine Environmental Research.
MAFF	Ministry of Agriculture, Fisheries and Food (England and Wales).
NATO	North Atlantic Treaty Organization.
NEAFC	North-East Atlantic Fisheries Commission.
NERC	Natural Environment Research Council.
OECD	Organisation for Economic Co-operation and Development.
SOLAS	Safety of Life at Sea (Convention/Regulations).
TOVALOP	Tanker Owners' Voluntary Agreement Concerning Liability for Oil Pollution.
UKAEA	United Kingdom Atomic Energy Authority.
UNITAR	United Nations Institute for Training and Research.

Introduction

The North Sea and its coasts are a vast natural resource, used intensively and in a great variety of ways by the coastal states and the international community at large. The Strait of Dover and the southern North Sea are among the most heavily trafficked sea routes in the world, while the central and northern North Sea are the site of important gas and oil fields. The whole area contains one of the most productive fisheries in the world and it is an important source of sand and gravel for the building industry. At the same time the North Sea receives much of the domestic and industrial effluent from the countries surrounding it; much of its coastline is used for enjoyment and relaxation by the urban population; its rich coastal waters, marshes and estuaries provide winter refuge for large numbers of Arctic birds and are staging posts for migrants travelling farther south, and in its more northerly part there are large permanent seabird colonies. Several coastal areas are of exceptional scientific interest and have been designated as nature reserves.

Before the present century human activity in the North Sea was on such a scale that it had little widespread impact on so great a resource and one activity interfered very little with others. This has now changed. The increased population, increased industrial activity and, above all, the vastly expanded technological capabilities of states using the North Sea have led to a situation where it is possible to overexploit a resource – whether it be fisheries or tourist beaches – to the point where it is seriously damaged and no longer serves its original purpose. Furthermore, each separate activity is now potentially, and sometimes actually, in conflict with others: the industrial and municipal need to discharge effluents impinges on the need for clean, healthy water in amenity areas; a proliferation of oil rigs impinges on the rights of freedom of movement for shipping on the high seas.

The great and multifarious natural resource of the North Sea is already exploited intensively and this will continue for the foreseeable future. To make the best use of it in the aesthetic and recreational sense as well as commercially, rational management is vital to ensure both that each activity is conducted at such a rate and in such a way as to serve the best long-term interest, and that the prosecution of one activity is harmonized, so far as possible, with that of another. The problem is essentially one of environmental management, a concept which is familiar enough on land in a country as densely populated as England, where almost any change or development has repercussions on most other facets of life and regulation down to a very detailed level has been found necessary.

Some of the commercially exploitable resources of the North Sea, such as petroleum, gas and gravel, are finite. They are a wasting asset from the moment exploitation of them begins. Unless they are to be viewed as an untouchable museum piece, there is no question of leaving the asset in the same state as we found it and the principle that the environment should not be altered to our immediate advantage if that is to the detriment of future generations cannot apply in any absolute sense. In a rational world, the rate at which the asset is used would be governed by a decision about where the balance of advantage lay between high yield/short life and low yield/long life. This, in turn, involves prediction about future needs. Thus the high rate of utilization of fossil fuels in this century is accepted partly because we have no immediate alternative, partly because of the belief that alternative fuel sources, such as nuclear energy, solar energy and tidal power, can replace them as the need to do so arises.

Management of the renewable resources, such as fish, is now a science. Providing sufficient is known about the biology of an organism it is possible, through the control of fishing techniques, total annual catch, close seasons, etc., to maintain a certain annual yield indefinitely. There is an optimum intensity of cropping that will produce the "maximum sustainable yield". More intense cropping or "overfishing" will gradually deplete the stock, less intense cropping will allow older members of the species to survive longer but at some point this may become detrimental to the species because larger numbers subsist on the same food supply.

The aesthetic, amenity and recreational value of the North Sea and, in part, its value as a shipping route can be indefinitely sustained at an extremely high level of use and, in one sense, the North Sea provides an inexhaustible resource for these users. Regulation of them is necessary, however, partly because at some point use of this resource becomes self-defeating, e.g. when the density of traffic is such as to introduce severe navigation hazards, as with shipping in the English Channel and southern North Sea; or tourist beaches, where the amenity which people are trying to enjoy is lost because too many people visit one area at the same time. Regulation is also needed because of the interaction between these and other users of this environment.

It may be possible to regulate an activity to the level at which it does not impinge on others, but in most cases this "innocuous" level will be so low as to be unattainable and it is realistic to think in other terms.

It is important to recognize that the North Sea is not a homogeneous body of water. The shallows off the Dutch coast are a vital nursery ground for young fish and the priorities there are quite different from those in the Norwegian Trench and its adjacent oil field. Thus the interests which are in conflict in one area are quite different from those in another. Furthermore, some have local significance (mineral resources exist only in certain places; shipping routes are related to the position of major ports) but others have general significance for a considerable part, or even the whole of the North Sea (plaice spawned and growing off the Dutch coast are cropped as adults in the central North Sea; an area of particular scentific interest may be unique). While some comprehensive regulation may be justified, a simplistic approach to the problem which ignores the immense variety of the North Sea is valueless.

In assessing the relative importance of such disparate activities as navigation, fishing, waste disposal or tourism, it is convenient to use a monetary yardstick to provide a common denominator of their interest or stake in the resource. This is already being accepted as a means of deciding priorities: oil stranded on the coast of Britain is removed with detergent where beaches are important for tourism, but not where there are shellfisheries or sites of scientific importance because of the risk of damage to marine organisms by the dispersant. Although administratively convenient, this approach has its dangers. It is relatively easy to evaluate in monetary terms the cost of waste disposal into the sea or the value of a fishery, and to balance one against the other. At present there is no way of evaluating the aesthetic value of an area or the scientific importance of a geological structure or biological community, which may be unique, in equivalent terms. The economists' equation is therefore incomplete and, if not valueless, is at least dependent upon purely subjective judgement. Public reaction to pollution or disfigurement of the landscape may be uninformed and emotional, but is an indication that non-commercial and therefore unquantifiable considerations have not been given adequate weighting.

For the solution of the problems of good management of the North Sea, regulation is needed to ensure that each separate activity is conducted at an intensity which is not self-defeating and, so far as that can be achieved, which is in harmony with other conflicting interests. Since the North Sea is an international resource, the common good will best be served if international law is strengthened while national law is harmonized and related to the management needs of this relatively enclosed body of water.

The problem is not an easy one to solve. While the general principles of management of a multifaceted resource are reasonably clear, the scientific knowledge needed for detailed management decisions is often grossly inadequate and, in most cases, legislation lags far behind even what is known. This report gives an outline of the sort of technical and scientific considerations that must be taken into account in framing the problem, and reviews the present national legislation of North Sea states which is directed towards the management of the natural resource which the North Sea represents. The difficulty experienced in drawing together this body of information is some indication of the lack of an adequate approach to the subject and of the machinery to deal with it.

It only remains for me to say something about the Study Group itself. The members, under the Chairmanship, initially, of Mr. J. E. S. Fawcett, later replaced by myself, were: Mr. Basil Boothby; Dr. Derek Bowett*;

* Later resigned.

Mr. Tom Busha; Mr. Ian Drummond; Mr. J. E. S. Fawcett; Professor J. Garner; Dr. Maurice Mendelson; Professor J. Mitchell; Mr. A. J. O'Sullivan; Colonel J. Sheppard; Professor Sir Francis Vallat; the Director of the Institute, Miss M. M. Sibthorp; and Mrs. J. Unwin, who acted as Rapporteur and for whose dedicated work the members of the Group are most grateful. The Group is also collectively most grateful to Miss Esme Allen, whose shouldering of the immense task of typing and re-typing the manuscripts is beyond praise.

The Group began its deliberations in May 1972. Sections dealing with various aspects of the Report were drafted by members of the Working Party appointed by the Group, discussed and amended by the whole Group and referred, as appropriate, to other authorities for comment and criticism. The initial working draft was prepared by Mr. Tony Loftas, while Chapter IV (on the prevailing situation under international law) was researched and written entirely by Dr. Maurice Mendelson, and Chapter V (on the national law of the United Kingdom) was prepared by Dr. Maurice Mendelson with the collaboration of Miss Elizabeth Wilmshurst. The Group agreed the final version of the work and the concluding recommendations.

For providing information or making most helpful comments and suggestions during the course of the Study we are particularly indebted to: Mr. A. A. Archer, Institute of Geological Sciences; Mr. Jeffrey Archer; the Lord Ashby, The Master, Clare College, Cambridge; Commander P. Beazley, Hydrographic Department, Ministry of Defence; Mr. R. J. H. Beverton, Secretary, Natural Environment Research Council; Mr. Colin Bibby, Royal Society for the Protection of Birds; Dr. John Blair, Legal Department, Shell Petroleum Co.; Mr. Robert Boote, Director, The Nature Conservancy; Mr. A. Bos, Assistant Legal Adviser, Ministry of Foreign Affairs, The Netherlands; Dr. E. D. Brown, Reader in International Law, University of London; Dr. Ian Brownlie, Wadham College, Oxford; Dr. W. R. P. Bourne, Department of Zoology, University of Aberdeen; Dr. Jean Carroz, Senior Legal Officer, Fisheries Department, FAO; Dr. H. A. Cole, Fisheries Laboratory, MAFF; Dr. L. H. N. Cooper, Marine Biological Association of the United Kingdom; Professor J. Erickson, Director, Defence Studies, University of Edinburgh; Sir Vincent Evans, Foreign and Commonwealth Office; Sir Frank Fraser Darling; Dr. D. J. Garrod, Lowestoft Laboratory, MAFF; Dr. J. A. Gulland, Chief, Fishery Statistics and Economic Data Branch, Fishery Economics and Institutions Division, FAO; Mr. Graham Harrison, Assistant Clerk, Trent River Authority; Mr. H. Hill, Fisheries Laboratory, MAFF; Captain J. R. Hill, Ministry of Defence; Dr. Martin Holdgate, Institute for Terrestrial Ecology, NERC; Dr. Sidney Holt, International Ocean Institute, Malta; Mr. C. W. Ingram, Department of Industry; M. Jacquet, Netherlands Foundation for International Research; Professor R. Y. Jennings, Q.C.; Dr. Alexander King, Director-General for Scientific Affairs, OECD; Admiral W. Langeraar, Director-General, Association Européenne Océanique; Mr. A. J. Lee, Fishery Laboratory, MAFF; Captain D. E. Macey; Mr. C. Maestripieri, Legal Department, Commission of the European Communities; Dr. A. Nelson-Smith, University College of Swansea; Mr. Ogden, Shell Petroleum Co.; Dr. B. B. Parrish, Department of Agriculture and Fisheries for Scotland; M. Jacques Piccard, Lausanne; Mr. A. Preston, Fisheries Laboratory, MAFF; Mr. Laurance Reed; Dr. Ian Richardson, Fisheries Development Ltd.; Mr. Sands, Meteorological Office, Bracknell; Dr. Oscar Schachter, UNITAR; Mr. I. M. Sinclair, Senior Legal Adviser, Foreign and Commonwealth Office; Dr. J. E. Smith, Director, Marine Biological Association of the United Kingdom; Mr. Hans Tambs-Lyche, General Secretary, ICES; Mr. David Thomas, Department of Politics, University of Southampton; Mr. Russell Train, Chairman, Council on Environmental Quality, U.S.A.; Dame Joan Vickers; Dr. Peter Victor, University of Kent at Canterbury; Mr. J. Wardley Smith, International Tankers Owners' Pollution Federation; Mr. Carl Wilms-Wright, Commission of the European Communities.

We hope that the Report may make a useful contribution to the continuing study of the problems it considers. I would, however, emphasize that the views expressed are the responsibility of the Study Group alone.

R. B. Clark
Professor of Zoology
University of Newcastle upon Tyne

I
Uses of the North Sea

A. THE EXTRACTION OF RESOURCES

1. Living Resources

For the purposes of this study the northern and southern limits of the North Sea are taken to be 61°00′ N and 51°32′ N respectively. These limits are based on the ICES Report on Pollution of the North Sea (*Co-operative Research Report*, Series A, No. 13). However, the geographical boundaries do not fall conveniently into degrees of latitude and the consensus would probably fix the boundaries north of the Pentland Firth on the western side and south of Belgium on the east as far as Dunkirk (See Appendix I).

(a) The Resource Base

The biological productivity of the sea depends overwhelmingly on the abundance and rate of growth of floating, microscopic plants – the phytoplankton. As with land plants, the phytoplankton have basic needs for adequate supplies of nutrients (e.g. nitrates, phosphates, carbon dioxide) and sunlight. In the presence of sunlight, carbon dioxide and water are converted by the process of photosynthesis into more complex materials, and the growth and multiplication of phytoplankton are directly related to this.

The phytoplankton are consumed by small planktonic animals and these, in turn, are eaten by larger animals, including fish. The dead bodies of animals and plants in the plankton sink to the bottom where they support a community of organisms living on or in the seabed. Directly or indirectly, nearly all life in the sea, including all commercial fish species, is dependent upon the growth and production of phytoplankton.

The availability of nutrients, especially nitrates and phosphates, and the amount of sunlight both vary seasonally in temperate and boreal waters, resulting in an annual cycle of plankton abundance with a peak in spring and a second, smaller peak in the autumn. During the winter, storms stir up nutrients from the sea bottom, enriching the surface waters. As spring approaches the increase in daylight allows these nutrients to be utilized by phytoplankton populations which grow very rapidly.

This sudden outburst of phytoplankton production lasts only a few weeks, however. Phytoplankton are confined to surface waters where the light is strong enough to allow photosynthesis and, as these waters warm during late spring and summer, the water often becomes stratified into relatively stable layers differing in temperature and salinity. This reduces considerably the movement of nutrients between the water layers, and the continual sinking of dead organisms towards the seabed results in a rapid depletion of nutrients at the surface where photosynthesis is possible. There is consequently a reduction in the abundance of phytoplankton as summer proceeds.

In late summer and autumn, cooling of the surface waters breaks down the stratification of water and this allows water mixing and the replenishment of nutrients in the surface layers. There is then a second peak in phytoplankton production, which is brought to an end by the reduction in the amount of sunlight, and in winter the abundance of phytoplankton is at its minimum level.

In the turbid waters of the North Sea, sunlight is able to penetrate only a short distance, restricting phytosynthesis to the top few metres, but in the relatively shallow areas, especially near coasts and over submerged banks, the summer water stratification is easily broken down and phytoplankton production is high. The nutrient level around the coasts is further enhanced by the discharge of rivers and run-off from the land. These rich shallow areas form the spawning and nursery grounds for many commercially important species of fish.

The productivity of the North Sea, as measured by the amount of carbon fixed by the phytoplankton, gives an average value of 100 gm.C/m^2/year. This is high when compared with oceanic sites of similar latitude – North Atlantic, 21 gm.C/m^2/year; North Pacific, 50–70 gm.C/m^2/year.[1] Coastal regions where nutrient-rich water from the depths of the ocean emerges at the surface provide sites of very high productivity – for example, St. Margaret's Bay, Nova Scotia, 190 gm.C/m^2/year[1]; off the coast of Peru, 120 gm.C/m^2/year; and the Canary Islands, 145 gm.C/m^2/year.[2]

Since 1950 the seasonal occurrence of plankton species in the North Sea has been monitored by the Oceanographic Laboratory, Edinburgh (incorporated in the Institute for Marine Environmental Research in 1970). During this period there has been a downward trend in the abundance of many species of zooplankton and phytoplankton in the North Sea and North-east Atlantic, together with a progressive delay in the time of the spring outbursts of phytoplankton production. In the English Channel and Celtic Sea, on the other hand, the spring phytoplankton outburst has tended to come earlier. The causes of these changes are unknown but are

[1] NERC Report, 1971/72 (NCP411), HMSO.
[2] D. H. Cutling, Fisheries technical paper 84, FAO, Rome, 1969.

suspected of being related to natural long-term climatic and oceanographic conditions; pollution is thought unlikely to be responsible.[3]

In order to obtain a better understanding of any future changes of this nature, physical and chemical factors known to affect planktonic organisms are to be monitored in the North Atlantic by IMER as part of its routine programme. An informal group of North Sea nations (the United Kingdom, Belgium, the Netherlands and West Germany) plan to develop a network of moored data stations to record a number of oceanographic and meteorological variables. A pilot network was already in operation in June 1971.

The direct harvesting of plant and animal plankton has often been suggested as a source of protein-rich livestock feed. It is theoretically more efficient to harvest plankton which is at the base of the food chain than to harvest fish which are near the top of it because at each stage in the food chain only a small percentage of the food intake is utilized in growth and the rest is lost to the system. While the Soviet Union has experimented with harvesting planktonic crustaceans (krill) in the Antarctic, evidently with promising results[4], it is generally thought extremely unlikely that plankton will be harvested in the North Sea because of the enormous quantities of water that need to be filtered to produce a worthwhile yield, even when plankton is at its most abundant.[5]

(b) Commercial Fisheries

The fisheries and shellfisheries are, for man, the most important of the sea's biological resources. The total world catch (including freshwater fish) increased from 20 million metric tons in 1950 to 70 million metric tons in 1971, when almost 3 million metric tons were landed from the North Sea.

The North Sea fisheries include pelagic and demersal fisheries, together with fisheries for shellfish.

(i) *Pelagic and demersal fisheries*

The pelagic fisheries catch species such as mackerel, herring, pilchard and sprat, which occur in large shoals in mid-water between the surface and the bottom, whereas the demersal fisheries catch species such as cod, haddock, rays, plaice, sole, turbot and whiting, which live or feed on or near the sea bottom. In 1971 the demersal and pelagic fisheries landed 1,560,000 metric tons and 1,383,000 metric tons respectively from the North Sea.[6]

The total annual landings, and landings by species, for the North Sea

[3] Sir A. Hardy, *The open sea, its natural history: I, The world of plankton*, Collins.
[4] "Harvesting of krill in the Antarctic", *Pravda*, 12 Oct. 1973.
[5] Sir A. Hardy, *ibid.*
[6] G. S. Saetersdal, in Churchill, Simmonds and Welch (eds.), *New Directions in the Law of the Sea*, Vol. III, pp. 36–45, 1973.

during the period 1947–1973 are shown in Tables 1 and 2.[7] From 1961 there was an upward trend in the total weight of fish landed from the North Sea, reaching a peak in 1968. The 1970 catch of 3.2 million metric tons was valued at around £280 million (United Kingdom landing prices).

The total landings are affected by the production and survival of the young of each fish species, the nature and scale of the fishing effort, and, indirectly, by consumer preference. The increase in landings from the North Sea in recent years can be partly explained by the exploitation of previously unfished species which are now being used industrially for the preparation of fishmeal; for example, the Norway pout[8] and sand-eel[9] have been fished by Norway and Denmark since 1960, and each gave a catch exceeding 300,000 metric tons in 1972. Although industrial fish species command a relatively low price, the industrial fisheries are carried out on a large scale, and lend themselves well to modern techniques of mechanization and mass handling.[10] The decline of the East Anglian herring stocks is attributed partly to increased fishing of adult spawning fish on the East Anglian ground, but principally to the development of an industrial fishery of juvenile herring. In 1945 Denmark began exploiting juvenile herring on and around the Bløden grounds. From 1,300 tons landed in 1948, the total catch rose to 64,000 tons in 1954. In 1953 Germany also began to fish juvenile herring for this purpose. The result of this gross over-exploitation was a decline in herring landings in the 1950s and failure of the fishery in the 1960s.[11] The recent increased catches of other fish species result largely from an increase in the fishing effort.

About 40,000 fishing vessels are involved in the North Sea fisheries, although the majority of vessels are small, with only about 1,500 having a displacement greater than 100 gross registered tons. The smaller vessels of those countries which have only a North Sea coastline probably restrict their activities to local waters, but this does not apply to many of the countries whose fleets are known to be active in the North Sea. Part of Norway, for example, is adjacent to the North Sea, but further north it falls into one of the Atlantic ICES areas, and the Faeroes fleet, part of which fishes the North Sea, is based on islands outside the North Sea area. An analysis of the North Sea catch by countries exploiting the fishery in 1970 is shown in Table 2.

A combination of increases in investment in fishing fleets, and technical innovations in fishing methods and technology has resulted in a great expansion in total effort within the fisheries.[10] The commercial fleets of

[7] ICES, Fisheries tables.
[8] FAO, Fisheries synopsis, No. 33.
[9] FAO, Fisheries synopsis, No. 82.
[10] J. R. Coull, *The Fishing Economy*, "The Fisheries of Europe", G. Bell, 1972.
[11] W. C. Hodgson, *The Herring and Its Fishery*, Routledge & Kegan Paul, London, 1959.

TABLE 1

Landings by Species, 1947-73*
('000 metric tons)

	River eels	Atlantic salmon	Other salmonids	Common dab	Lemon sole	European plaice	Common sole
1947	1.6	1.3	0.2	7.4	1.3	82.5	7.7
1948	1.4	1.4	0.3	10.1	1.8	84.1	4.7
1949	1.4	1.8	0.2	8.9	2.2	81.2	8.4
1950	1.4	1.4	0.6	5.8	3.8	67.4	16.5
1951	1.5	1.5	0.6	8.1	4.7	66.5	18.4
1952	1.0	1.6	0.5	7.7	4.9	70.8	16.4
1953	1.1	1.4	0.4	5.7	5.4	78.9	18.8
1954	1.1	1.5	0.5	5.5	4.0	67.0	18.5
1955	1.4	1.6	0.5	6.5	4.0	63.3	14.6
1956	1.0	1.2	0.4	5.3	3.5	63.9	12.4
1957	1.2	1.5	0.7	6.0	3.6	69.3	11.7
1958	1.1	1.5	0.6	6.2	3.3	72.4	14.2
1959	1.4	1.5	0.7	5.1	3.8	78.3	13.7
1960	1.3	1.4	0.6	5.0	4.2	86.3	18.5
1961	1.3	1.3	0.5	4.4	5.1	85.8	23.9
1962	1.2	2.0	0.8	4.1	4.6	87.4	26.8
1963	1.3	1.6	0.6	4.6	3.8	107.1	26.1
1964	1.4	2.1	1.2	4.3	4.8	110.4	11.3
1965	1.5	1.6	1.9	4.8	5.7	96.9	17.0
1966	1.7	1.6	0.7	5.1	6.1	100.1	31.8
1967	1.8	2.0	0.7	3.6	6.9	100.6	21.6
1968	2.2	1.5	0.7	3.6	6.6	108.8	29.4
1969	2.3	2.0	0.5	4.1	4.5	121.7	27.6
1970	1.8	1.5	0.8	5.2	3.5	130.3	19.7
1971	1.8	1.6	0.7	6.5	4.0	113.9	23.7
1972	1.5	2.1	0.5	8.0	3.7	123.2	21.1
1973†	1.6	2.4	0.8	8.6	4.6	129.7	19.3
Change in total Landings 1947-73	0	+1.1	+0.6	+1.2	+3.3	+47.2	+11.6

(continued)

TABLE 1 (continued)

	Turbot	Atlantic cod	Haddock	European hake	Ling	Norway pout	Pollack
1947	8.5	92.9	93.8	7.5	11.6	0	1.1
1948	6.8	70.4	71.1	7.5	9.2	0	1.1
1949	6.2	80.1	55.2	5.2	6.9	0	2.1
1950	6.0	66.8	56.4	5.4	9.2	0	2.6
1951	5.9	68.4	56.5	6.4	8.0	0	2.6
1952	5.8	76.4	57.4	5.8	7.2	0	3.1
1953	5.9	81.1	63.8	5.0	6.7	0	2.5
1954	5.6	80.6	70.1	4.5	8.0	0	3.3
1955	6.0	83.4	87.7	5.6	8.6	0	4.3
1956	6.3	80.3	93.9	4.5	8.8	0	3.8
1957	5.9	95.0	105.3	4.3	15.1	0	3.4
1958	6.0	103.7	96.2	3.9	15.9	0	3.1
1959	5.2	109.5	79.7	3.7	9.7	0	2.6
1960	5.5	104.4	66.4	4.0	9.3	0	2.0
1961	5.7	105.8	67.2	6.1	6.6	33.8	1.6
1962	5.0	89.6	52.8	4.7	4.5	157.0	2.2
1963	5.7	105.9	59.4	5.0	8.1	166.8	2.1
1964	4.9	121.6	198.7	4.8	10.2	82.7	3.1
1965	4.2	179.5	221.7	3.4	10.0	59.3	2.7
1966	4.3	219.7	269.0	2.5	9.8	52.7	2.9
1967	3.4	249.8	167.4	2.0	7.8	180.2	3.3
1968	4.2	285.3	139.5	3.1	6.3	468.7	2.7
1969	4.7	199.0	639.2	3.3	7.8	134.5	2.6
1970	4.0	224.7	671.8	3.1	5.9	273.6	2.1
1971	4.3	320.0	257.9	3.3	10.4	358.9	1.8
1972	4.4	346.3	213.2	2.9	12.3	492.5	1.6
1973†	4.2	233.6	189.1	3.3	8.8	448.0	1.6
Change in total Landings 1947–73	−4.3	+140.7	+95.3	−4.2	−2.8	+448.0	+0.5

(continued)

TABLE 1 (continued)

	Saithe	Tusk	Whiting	Sand eels	Horse mackerel	Atlantic herring	Sprat
1947	27.3	1.5	45.8	0	0.2	989.1	8.6
1948	28.1	1.0	59.1	0	0.3	1,290.5	9.9
1949	24.7	0.9	35.7	0	0.3	1,057.2	13.2
1950	19.7	1.1	45.4	0	0.2	1,107.5	9.7
1951	20.6	1.5	73.4	0	0.4	1,220.2	11.7
1952	21.6	1.5	73.3	0	0.5	1,145.1	16.8
1953	21.3	1.4	62.5	0	0.5	1,211.4	21.5
1954	33.3	1.3	64.8	0	0.3	1,297.3	17.4
1955	40.9	1.5	72.4	0	0.3	1,411.2	23.5
1956	46.6	1.5	74.9	0	0.4	1,364.1	18.0
1957	51.9	2.7	84.3	0	0.5	1,047.8	22.4
1958	47.8	3.6	77.5	0	0.4	804.6	24.3
1959	46.7	2.2	80.5	0	0.8	903.7	32.4
1960	29.0	2.7	53.1	0	0.2	787.0	16.5
1961	31.0	1.5	83.3	83.7	1.0	689.8	19.7
1962	22.3	2.0	69.0	110.0	3.7	678.5	31.3
1963	27.6	3.3	98.7	162.1	4.5	805.3	67.7
1964	55.1	2.3	91.5	128.5	1.2	932.0	70.8
1965	68.9	2.5	106.7	130.8	5.7	1,230.3	76.2
1966	86.9	1.8	155.2	161.1	2.1	1,038.9	106.6
1967	72.5	1.2	91.2	188.8	0.1	819.3	69.5
1968	97.4	1.4	144.9	194.2	0.1	850.1	65.4
1969	106.0	3.3	199.0	112.9	1.2	724.9	65.3
1970	169.5	1.6	181.5	191.4	12.0	748.8	51.0
1971	206.3	1.6	112.2	382.1	32.1	644.4	89.2
1972	198.6	2.7	108.8	358.4	8.0	604.8	92.4
1973†	90.5	3.6	141.4	296.9	42.0	598.4	228.2
Change in total Landings 1947–73	+63.2	+2.1	+95.6	+296.9	+41.8	−390.7	+219.6

(continued)

TABLE 1 (continued)

	Atlantic mackerel	Picked Dogfish	Dogfish and hounds	Rays and skates	Total
1947	13.4	8.4		14.4	1,458.7
1948	31.0	10.9		14.8	1,762.9
1949	35.4	11.7		10.8	1,500.7
1950	31.8	12.0		10.5	1,529.7
1951	48.4	10.4		17.8	1,758.7
1952	39.7	18.8		10.6	1,678.3
1953	41.3	19.6		11.5	1,716.9
1954	45.3	22.3		12.3	1,889.1
1955	53.2	24.2		12.7	2,018.2
1956	43.7	28.1		11.9	2,013.1
1957	68.9	26.4		11.5	1,819.1
1958	68.8	31.3		11.6	1,586.0
1959	70.1	29.6		12.1	1,798.4
1960	72.9	31.8		11.0	1,553.1
1961	85.8	33.8	2.7	12.3	1,451.0
1962	66.3	27.5	3.0	9.6	1,515.0
1963	55.4	31.9	2.4	10.7	1,840.3
1964	79.4	16.9	4.7	11.0	2,146.3
1965	151.7	21.9	4.2	10.0	2,597.2
1966	505.1	20.0	3.4	8.2	2,886.3
1967	909.9	21.7	4.6	7.5	3,030.0
1968	808.6	29.3	7.1	7.7	3,352.7
1969	713.9	31.3	6.7	7.7	3,237.0
1970	290.0	22.9	4.9	5.7	3,172.9
1971	227.9	18.1	6.1	5.8	2,951.8
1972	182.2	30.7	6.3	5.5	2,907.0
1973†	318.1	26.0	6.6	5.2	2,986.5
Change in total Landings 1947–73	+304.7	+24.2		−9.2	+1,527.8

* Figures cover each species of which the total catch was at least 1,500 metric tons in 1970.

† The 1973 figures are preliminary. The Finnish catch is not included, and the Norwegian numbers are incomplete. The figures for herring, cod and Norway pout will definitely increase, as should some of the other categories.

Source: ICES, *Fisheries Tables.*

TABLE 2

Recorded catch of demersal and pelagic fish landed by each country from the North Sea in 1970

Country	Catch ('000 metric tons)
Denmark	941.1
Norway	612.1
U.S.S.R.	482.2
United Kingdom	362.5
Sweden	220.8
Netherlands	181.2
France	112.7
Faeroe Islands	107.7
Federal Republic of Germany	96.1
Belgium	26.3
Iceland	23.6
Poland	6.7
Total	3,173.1

Source: ICES, *Fisheries Tables.*

Europe have tended to become concentrated at fewer and fewer ports, and this trend has been accompanied by a switch to larger and more specialized vessels (see Table 3). This has often had important consequences for in-shore fisheries. For example, Denmark built large vessels to exploit a local industrial fishery which proved inadequate and rapidly declined. These vessels now operate on the north-east coast of England, to the detriment of local fishermen with small boats, who cannot fish elsewhere. This resulted in friction in 1972, when three of the four U.K. fishery protection vessels had to be posted to the area.

(ii) *Shellfisheries*

The shellfisheries include a rather heterogeneous group of molluscan and crustacean species, which comprise only about 6 per cent by weight (1970) of the total fisheries landings from the North Sea. The annual landings for some species are difficult to assess, since many of the fisheries are essentially local. However, Table 4 gives comparative figures for shellfish landings in 1950, 1960 and 1970.

The Netherlands is the chief producer of bivalve molluscs. Virtually nothing remains of the deep-sea oyster beds of the North Sea, as a result of the combined action of overfishing, pests and parasites. The majority of European oyster fisheries rely on relaid seed (young oysters), most of which originates from the Oosterschelde,[12] although seed produced at Conway (U.K.) supplies many of the U.K. east coast fisheries. The U.K. has recently placed restrictions on the importation of foreign oyster seed, in an attempt to prevent outbreaks of particular diseases and parasites.

[12] P. Korringa, "Shellfish of the North Sea", *Ser. Atl. Mar. Envir.*, 1969.

TABLE 3

Estimates of vessels fishing the North Sea
These estimates are very approximate and are based on various assumptions made about the published figures.

United Kingdom

Trawlers	*Number*
Inshore Trawlers under 79.9'	750
Near-Water Trawlers 80'–109.9'	125
Middle-Water Trawlers 110'–140'	150
Seiners	
Seiners under 79.9'	605
Liners	
Liners under 79.9'	406
Liners 80'–109.9'	6
Ringnetters under 79.9'	60
Others	
Under 40'	1,000
40'–79.9'	100

Belgium

Inshore Vessels (0–239 h.p. engines)	134
Near-Water Vessels (240–349 h.p. engines)	75
Middle-Water Vessels (350–499 h.p. engines)	69

Belgium has some distant-water vessels and these are assumed to catch the third of the Belgian catch taken in waters other than the North Sea.

Iceland

Trawlers of more than 100 g.r.t.	13

Most of Iceland's catch is, of course, taken locally, but 13 vessels have been allocated to the North Sea to account for 3 per cent (1969) taken from North Sea grounds.

Poland
Poland's North Sea catch was low in 1969 and it is assumed that 8 middle and distant water trawlers could account for it.

Sweden
About 77 per cent of Sweden's catch in 1969 came from the North Sea. This is assumed largely from the effort of her larger vessels.

Displacement (g.r.t.)	*Number of vessels*
(a) 26–50	283
(b) 51–150	411
(c) 151–500	50

(1969 ICES tables give Sweden 6,615 vessels in the 0–25 g.r.t. group in addition to those numbered above. But it should be pointed out that only the largest vessels of the second group (b) and all of group (c) would fall into the British near- and middle-water classification.)

USES OF THE NORTH SEA

Denmark

Displacement (g.r.t.)	Number of vessels
Over 100	209
50–100	204
15–50	1,883
5–15	1,369
Under 5	3,628

Denmark has 3,615 vessels without motors.

Faeroe Islands

The Faeroese catch a lot of fish in the North Sea (63,360 tons in 1969, equivalent to the annual catch of 30 or 40 distant-water trawlers). It is quite difficult to see how they catch this amount. It has been assumed that 25 small trawlers (average displacement 200 g.r.t.) operate for at least some of the time in the North Sea, likewise the 20 purse seiners, 75 of the 102 long-liners and 4 distant-water trawlers. In other words, probably around 30 vessels of an appreciable size (near- and middle-water trawlers) and a number of smaller vessels fish there.

France

	Number
Middle-water trawlers	83

Federal Republic of Germany

Luggers (average displacement 313 g.r.t.)	14
Cutters (average displacement 40 g.r.t.)	921

Netherlands*

Motor Vessels (average displacement 39 g.r.t.)	187
Cutters (average displacement 56 g.r.t.)	607

* Includes vessels fishing Lake Ijssel.

Norway

About 40 per cent of Norway's catch in 1969 came from the North Sea but this is assumed to be accounted for more by the larger vessels than by the smaller. There were 22,873 open craft, but most of these probably fished the Northern coastal fisheries. Perhaps 20 per cent of the next size group (26–50 g.r.t.) fished the North Sea, and 50 per cent of the remaining vessels would have fished the North Sea either during part of the year or for the whole of the year, except perhaps for the largest factory trawlers.

Displacement (g.r.t.)	Number of vessels
0–25	1,226
26–50	396
51–100	154
101–200	106
201–500	159

U.S.S.R.

200 distant-water trawlers. This figure must be a very rough approximation. It is estimated from the known catch of the Soviet Union in 1969.

German Democratic Republic

Unknown – possibly 50 (?)

TABLE 4

Total North Sea shellfish landings by species
(metric tons)

	1950	1960	1970
Shrimp (*Crangon*)	35,939	39,660	50,870
Prawn (*Pandalus*)	966	3,334	7,421
Edible crab	4,420	5,232	3,944
Lobster	1,431	1,321	699
Norway lobster	310	1,576	3,864
Various crustaceans	0	78	83
Total crustaceans	43,066	51,201	66,881
Mussel	54,496	107,961	114,483
Cockle	7,172	7,716	10,793
Oyster	2,143	3,038	912
Periwinkle	703	516	685
Portuguese oyster	0	0	54
Scallop	57	0	3,382
Squids	0	0	190
Whelk	2,927	1,931	2,540
Various molluscs	470	0	131
Total molluscs	67,968	121,162	133,170
Starfish	0	0	4,712
Total shellfish	111,034	172,363	204,763

Source: ICES, *Bulletin Statistique.*

The Netherlands has the highest shellfish production and the highest mussel and oyster landings. The United Kingdom has the highest edible crab, lobster, Norway lobster, cockle, periwinkle, scallop, squid and whelk landings. The Federal Republic of Germany has the highest shrimp and starfish landings. Norway has the highest prawn landings.

During 1971, Conway hatcheries produced, for the first time, commercial quantities of seed of *Crassostrea gigas*, a hatchery-reared Japanese oyster. The majority of British fisheries have been reluctant to try this new species, and most of the seed produced was exported to France.[13]

Since 1950, mussel farming has become more remunerative with the increased mechanization of the industry. The most productive area is in the Waddenzee (Netherlands), but fisheries also exist in England, West Germany, Belgium and Norway.

Cockles are consumed chiefly in England, and are fished in the North Sea area on the south-east coast of England and in the Waddensee. On the south-east coast of England, the Wash and the Thames estuary are the two major cockle producing areas. In recent years, the continuous-lift hydraulic dredge, developed by the United Kingdom's White Fish Authority, has revolutionized the fishery in the Thames estuary, enabling the utilization of low density cockle beds which could not previously be fished profitably.[14]

On the completion of the "Delta project" in the near future, some of the rich bivalve producing areas of the Oosterschelde will be lost. The area is also used as a cleaning bed for mussels produced in the Waddensee. The closure of the area will necessitate the building of cleaning tanks in the Waddensee area.[15]

Small local fisheries exist for exploiting whelks, periwinkles and scallops. The scallop fishery on the north-east coast of England and south-east coast of Scotland is probably capable of further growth.

Of crustaceans, lobsters, Norway lobsters, edible crabs, shrimps (*Crangon*) and prawns (*Pandalus*) are fished in the North Sea. Lobsters are fished on a commercial scale only on the U.K. and Norwegian coasts. The Norway lobster is often caught as a by-catch with demersal fish, and the fishery was not exploited commercially until 1950. The most important fishing area for the Norway lobster in the North Sea occurs off the coast of Northumberland (U.K.). Since 1965, North Sea stocks have been monitored, and it has been shown that, in the last few years, the proportion of small Norway lobsters in landings has increased. This is thought to be partly due to a change in the fishing pattern, with a concentration on fishing early in the season, when small Norway lobsters are usually more abundant. It does not appear at the moment that the stock is being overfished.[16]

As a general rule, crustaceans such as lobsters, crabs and the Norway lobster command a high unit value, but the small quantities involved

---

[13] MAFF, Shellfish Information Leaflet, No. 23, "A review of some of the shellfish research undertaken at the fisheries laboratories in 1971" (P. C. Wood & P. R. Walne), 1972.
[14] MAFF, Shellfish Information Leaflet, No. 23, 1972.
[15] P. Korringa, "Shellfish of the North Sea", *Ser. Atl. Mar. Envir.*, 1969.
[16] MAFF, Shellfish Information Leaflet, No. 23, 1972.

usually restrict their total value to 5 per cent or less of the total fish landings value. Molluscs, on the other hand, include a much wider value range. In the North Sea, shellfish production is dominated by mussels, for which prices are low, whereas scallops and oysters command a much higher price.

(iii) *Fisheries management*

Up to a point, the greater the fishing effort, the more fish are caught, but, beyond that point, fish become sufficiently scarce that greater and greater fishing effort is needed simply to maintain the size of the total catch. Depletion of the breeding stock results in a reduction in the number of young fish being produced each year and the fishery may then go into serious decline to the point where it is no longer worth exploiting commercially.

The aim of fisheries management is to regulate fishing to produce the largest harvest that can be sustained indefinitely. This concept of a Maximum Sustained Yield (MSY) is used as a guiding principle but is often not achieved in practice because of economic or social pressures, or market preferences. A fully exploited fishery contains few large, old fish (which consume food but add weight slowly); satisfying a demand for large specimens could be achieved only by under-exploiting the fishery. More commonly, however, economic pressures tend towards overfishing, and fishery management is concerned chiefly with restricting catches and protecting breeding stocks. This is done in several ways: by limiting the size or nature of fish landed; by closing certain areas to fishing vessels; by establishing closed seasons; by limitations on the type of fishing gear that may be used; by limiting the size or power of fishing vessels; by limiting the size of the total catch; and by limiting the total fishing effort.[17]

Resource management to achieve or approach the MSY in a particular fishery is not easy. The size of the fish stocks and the recruitment of young fish to them vary year by year, depending on the success of spawning and other natural variables, and regulatory measures should ideally be flexible enough to relate the intensity and type of fishing to the current state of the fish stocks. Furthermore, each of the practicable types of regulatory measure affects the fish population in a different way.

The scientific basis for rational management of the North Sea fisheries is known and, despite the difficulties, adequate management programmes have in many cases been brought into operation at the national level. However, the North Sea provides one of the most productive fisheries in the world and the fleets of many countries exploit it. International co-operation is essential if the stocks are to be fished efficiently. Nearly all stocks of high value fish are now heavily fished and many are overfished,

---

[17] "Conservation and management of sea fisheries in coastal waters", *Sinews for Survival: A Report on Management of Natural Resources*, H.M.S.O., 1972.

resulting in reduction of yield, wasted fishing effort and the risk of reduced potential for reproduction of the stock. Lack of international co-operation which has led to overfishing has been shown most spectacularly in the decline of the East Anglian herring fishery and, more recently, in the decline of herring stocks in the northern North Sea.

There are two main intergovernmental bodies concerned with promoting international co-operation in the field of fisheries. The International Council for the Exploration of the Sea (ICES) is an old-established research organization, based in Copenhagen, whose aims are to encourage all research connected with exploration of the sea and to co-ordinate the activities of participating governments. It publishes, *inter alia*, valuable comparative data on fisheries. The North-East Atlantic Fisheries Commission is concerned with the conservation of the fish stocks and the rational exploitation of the fisheries of the North-East Atlantic Ocean and adjacent waters, and bases its recommendations on ICES information. Its role is described more fully in the chapter on the international legal regime.[18]

(iv) *Aquaculture*

Major developments in marine fish farming have occurred only in the past ten years or so, although experiments aimed at increasing fishing stocks by breeding fish species in hatcheries, with subsequent release of the young fish, were carried out in the late nineteenth century. Later, in the early part of this century, Dutch and British scientists considered the possibilities of transplanting fish from coastal nursery grounds to more fertile fishing grounds. Young plaice transplanted from the breeding grounds off the Dutch coast to the Dogger Bank were found to grow three to four times as fast as those which remained in the breeding grounds. Coastal states have been reluctant to act on the results of these experiments, since it would involve the investment of large sums of money in improving fishing for other countries which are free to fish these waters.

Aquaculture may simply involve the fattening of transplanted animals, or include the breeding and rearing of the subsequent juveniles to a marketable size. Both methods are employed with oysters and mussels in the Oosterschelde and Waddenzee (Netherlands).[19]

Many technical difficulties are yet to be overcome in the farming of marine species of fish. These include enclosure design,[20] the rearing of fish larvae, cheap sources of food, the control of parasites and diseases, and genetic selection and the breeding of more suitable fish stocks.[21]

At the present time, only high value species are being considered for aquaculture, since this is necessary to offset the present cost of production.

[18] See chapter IV.
[19] P. Korringa, "Shellfish of the North Sea", *Ser. Atl. Mar. Envir.*, 1969.
[20] *Marine Research*, 1970: No. 1, "Fish Farming".
[21] FAO, Fisheries Report, 119.

Research of the White Fish Authority indicates that the production of turbot is worthwhile, but problems still exist in the rearing of the larval fish.[22] The White Fish Authority also suggests that mixed cultures of, for example, oysters, clams and fish (e.g. plaice, sole or saithe), might prove commercially viable. Recent experiments have been carried out at Conway (U.K.) on the culture of different species of prawn and shrimp. To date, experiments with the jumbo tiger prawn (*Panaeus marodon*), a native of the Philippines, have provided the best results with a yield of 1.96 kg/m^2 in four months.[23]

Although, in future years, aquaculture will no doubt become more important, it appears that, in the foreseeable future at least, it will be largely restricted to the production of high cost species (sole, turbot, lobster).

(c) Trends in Development

The total world fisheries landings are capable of doubling without over-exploiting fish populations.[24] In the North Sea, however, the majority of fish stocks are already fully exploited, or overfished. The only under-exploited major resource in the region is the poutassou or blue whiting (*Micromesistius poutassou*), which occurs principally in the Norwegian Sea, and west of Scotland, but extends into the northern North Sea. Some possibilities of increasing crustacean and shellfish production may exist – for example, the deep-water prawn (*Pandalus borealis*) and scallops.

Trends in the North Sea must be directed towards effective international conservation and management of fish stocks, rather than an expansion of production. It has been calculated that cod and herring landings should be fished at about half their present level if stocks are not to be overfished.[25]

In general, the number of vessels fishing the North Sea will gradually decline, with the catch stabilizing at around the present level. The total landings from the North Sea will probably fall as a result of the Icelandic government's efforts to extend the country's fishing limits to include grounds fished by European nations, especially the United Kingdom and West Germany. This may result in increased fishing effort being centred on the North Sea, unless effective management measures are taken.

This reduction in total landings may be counteracted to some extent by the joint actions of the members of the enlarged European Economic Community (EEC). Since the governments of member countries already have effective control of the seabed mineral rights in the North Sea, they might seek to extend their jurisdiction to include the living resources,

[22] White Fish Authority, Ann. Rep., HMSO, 1972.
[23] MAFF, Shellfish Information Leaflet, No. 23, 1972.
[24] J. R. Coull, *The Fishing Economy*, "The Fisheries of Europe", G. Bell, 1972.
[25] G. S. Saetersdal, in Churchill, Simmonds and Welch (eds.), *New Directions in the Law of the Sea*, Vol. III, pp. 36–45, 1973.

perhaps forming a European fishing "pool" based on some kind of quota system; studies of this kind are known to be in hand. Should such a move be made, in the absence of new international legislation, it would probably affect some East European fishing fleets and, paradoxically enough, some Icelandic vessels.

Marine aquaculture is, at present, only in the developmental stage and, in the near future, should be of use only in the production of high-cost species.

2. Mineral Resources

(a) Technology

Unlike biological resources, which are usually renewed annually, mineral resources are, for practical purposes, non-renewable. Known or indicated reserves of some minerals on land are sufficient to support the present rate of extraction and use for only a few more decades. At the present rate of consumption, for example, world copper reserves may have been exhausted in about 30 years' time. At the same time, world consumption of nearly all minerals is growing rapidly.

The term "reserves" is applied to deposits that are believed to be commercially workable under the current, locally prevailing economic circumstances. Resources, on the other hand, are deposits that are likely to be workable in the future in response, for example, to higher prices or lower costs. The work involved in establishing whether or not a mineral deposit should be classified as reserves, that is whether they are currently workable, is substantial and expensive. For this reason, it is unusual for reserves to be proved for many more than 15 or 20 years in advance of planned production. Nevertheless, the projections of the growth in demand for some minerals accepted by many mineral economists are such as to give rise to concern about the availability of these commodities from traditional sources in the longer term future. Increasing attention is, therefore, being directed towards the seas as an alternative source, principally by the development of undersea mining, but also, to a much lesser extent, by direct extraction from sea water.

It is possible that new techniques for mining below the seabed, including structures for shaft sinking, hoisting, mineral treatment, living quarters and underwater transport facilities will be developed in due course. The cost and period of development, however, will both be very great and it is very unlikely that such operations will function in this century. Similarly, extraction of minerals not already being recovered from sea water presents serious economic difficulties. In the foreseeable future, increased exploitation of minerals from the seabed is likely, therefore, to be restricted to recovery by dredging or by boreholes.

It is now clear that much of the North Sea's floor has been covered by the sea for millions of years, resulting in the formation of thick sedimentary deposits. In this geological environment only three groups of minerals are likely to be present in sufficient quantity to allow them to be economically worked: (i) superficial, unconsolidated, deposits such as sand and gravel and, perhaps, so-called "heavy minerals" (notably including sources of titanium); (ii) bedded deposits such as coal, evaporites (e.g. halite (salt), potash and anhydrite) and (iii) petroleum and natural gas.

(b) Sea Water

No information is available on desalination plants using water from the North Sea. The only mineral being extracted on a substantial scale is magnesium, at Hartlepool (U.K.) and in Norway. Production figures are not available, although it is known that 61–65 per cent of the world production of magnesium is extracted from seawater. Salt is being recovered on a very small scale at Malden in Essex (U.K.).

(c) Superficial Deposits

Difficulty in obtaining sufficient building aggregate on land has led to the increasing use of marine aggregates since the early 1960s; by 1972 this source was contributing about 12 per cent of total production in Great Britain. At present, about 6 million tons of sharp sand and gravel are dredged annually from the North Sea. For economic working, ideally deposits should be several feet thick and composed of about 60 per cent gravel and 40 per cent sand, with less than 5 per cent silt and organic matter. Most suitable deposits are in the British sector of the North Sea, 7–20 miles off-shore at various sites from the Humber to the Thames. To the north, the sea shelves rapidly from the shore and most of the bottom is rocky or too deep for current dredging techniques. The continental side of the North Sea is sandy with exceptionally rare gravel deposits. As a result, dredged aggregate is delivered from the British areas to Rotterdam, Dordrecht, Bruges, Dunkirk and Calais.

Although the growth of marine aggregate extraction has more than doubled during the last 10 years, it is doubtful if there will be much further increase in the rate of extraction in the future. Exhaustion of satisfactory deposits may even make it difficult to maintain the present rate of extraction indefinitely, but the reserves of aggregate in the North Sea have not yet been reliably assessed because of the cost and difficulty of sampling the deposits.

Technological developments and the building of very large dredgers of up to 10,000 tons, carrying complete treatment plants, may enable low-grade areas containing as much as 20 per cent clay to be worked. But there are formidable difficulties, not least the disposal of large quantities of clay in suspension in such a manner as not to contaminate the deposit or cause siltation elsewhere.

(d) Evaporites

Strata containing salt, anhydrite (calcium sulphate) and potash extend beneath the North Sea off the Yorkshire and Durham coasts.

(i) *Salt*

Salt is extracted near the Tees Estuary from depths between about 275 and 365 metres by controlled pumping of a saturated brine solution through a network of boreholes. The bed in places is up to 45 metres in thickness but pumping is controlled in such a way as to extract only a small proportion of the salt bed, and subsidence is avoided. Although enormous deposits of salt have been found beneath the North Sea during the search for hydrocarbons, there are very large reserves of salt on land in Britain and it is most unlikely that salt will ever be extracted from beneath the sea.

(ii) *Anhydrite*

Anhydrite was mined by conventional methods at Billingham for many years but this has now ceased. Even if workings were restarted in this area it is very unlikely that they would extend beneath the sea or have any deleterious effect on the marine environment.

(iii) *Potash*

Potash occurs in an extensive bed at a depth of about 4,000 feet over a very large area in Yorkshire from the Durham border to Scarborough and for a considerable distance out to sea.

The technical problems have deterred would-be operators until recently, but Imperial Chemical Industries, in partnership with Charter Consolidated Company, have recently completed shafts near Saltburn-by-the-Sea, about a mile from the coast. Only a small proportion of the deposit will be mined, as a precaution against subsidence, and it is planned to extend the mine beneath the sea unless prevented by geological faults, reduction in the grade, or thickness, or other factors.

The deposit contains considerable quantities of salt and a little anhydrite as well as potash. Treatment of the extracted mineral will remove the extraneous materials which will be pumped through tunnels which have been driven out to sea and discharged three miles offshore. Since the effluent consists of about 90 per cent salt, a little anhydrite and 2–3 per cent inert solids, it is not expected to harm marine life. Nevertheless, the effects of this effluent will be closely monitored and planning permission for this operation has been granted for only five years, after which consent will be reviewed.

Effluent from a French potash mine discharged into the Rhine is at present causing concern because the impact of a discharge of concentrated brine into a river is clearly far greater than that of a similar discharge to the sea, where most organisms tolerate locally elevated salt concentrations without difficulty.

(e) Coal

Coal measures extend beneath the sea off the Northumberland and Durham coasts. Several mines immediately adjacent to the coast extend beneath the sea and the National Coal Board considers that it would be possible, using conventional mining techniques, to extend the workings 10 miles offshore. Since the coal measures are 1,000 feet or more beneath the seabed, with impervious layers above, these mining operations should have no direct impact on the marine environment.

It has been the practice for many years for colliery waste, composed largely of shale but with some coal, to be tipped into the sea. Many thousands of tons of this material are tipped into the sea from concrete towers or jetties. The coastal currents then sort minerals of different density and particulate size, with fine coal being deposited on sandy beaches miles to the south of each dumping point. So much coal has accumulated on these beaches that some small operators have found it worth their while to collect it, using mechanical excavators, for sale to local power stations as low-grade coal.

This practice destroys the amenity value of these beaches which, if they were not polluted, would be of fine sand.

(f) Petroleum and Natural Gas

Petroleum and gas are the most important mineral products of the North Sea, both in terms of investment and potential value. In the southern North Sea, east of Yorkshire, Lincolnshire and Norfolk (U.K.), only gas has been found, but considerable concentrations of mineral oil exist in the deeper water off the coast of Scotland.

By the end of 1974, 442 exploration or appraisal wells and 219 production wells had been drilled in the U.K. sector. Seven gas fields and 13 oil fields had been declared commercial. The cost of drilling in the North Sea is very high, being approximately six times that of on-shore drilling, at an average cost per well of £1 million.

(i) *Natural Gas*

By the end of 1974, seven proved fields and a further 24 significant discoveries of gas and gas liquids (ethane, propane, butane and pentane) had been made in the southern North Sea. Among the major fields proved during this extensive exploration programme is Leman Bank, which is among the largest off-shore gas fields so far discovered. More recently, promising finds have been made in the northern North Sea during the search for petroleum. However, so far only the large southern gas fields have been brought into production – the first natural gas came ashore in

1967. Since then, production has increased and it is expected that by 1975–76 these fields will provide between 5,000 million and 6,000 million cubic feet per day – five to six times the total sales of the United Kingdom gas industry prior to North Sea production.

A complete assessment of recoverable reserves of natural gas is not possible. The gas fields in the British sector in the southern part of the North Sea dominate the picture with reserves of about 26.5×10^{12} cubic feet. However, new reserves continue to be found in the North. In April 1974, Norwegian gas reserves, largely in the Ekofisk, Cod and Frigg fields, were estimated to be 17.5×10^{12} cubic feet. However, with the recent discovery of the very large Statfjord field, near the British Brent field, it is thought likely that this amount might be doubled. The Dan field in the Danish sector may contain up to 1,000 million cubic feet of gas. And the search continues.

(ii) Petroleum

Considerable quantities of mineral oil have been found in the northern North Sea, off the coast of Scotland. Although the full extent of the fields has not, as yet, been ascertained, it has been estimated that the annual oil yield in the British sector will be between 100 and 140 million tons by 1980.

North Sea crude oil is high quality, low in sulphur and "light", and therefore suitable for the production of petrol and diesel fuel, but unsuitable for heating fuel.

By the end of 1974, 13 commercial fields had been proved in the United Kingdom sector of the North Sea, three or four off Norway and one each off the Netherlands and Denmark. Of these, the Ekofisk field in the Norwegian sector was the first to be brought into production (in July 1971), followed by the Danish Dan field. By December 1974 Ekofisk had yielded about 38 million barrels of oil, which has been pumped directly into tankers. Pipelines from the various major fields to Aberdeen and the Shetland Islands are now being laid or are at the planning stage. (See map in Appendix III.)

Although the final reserves to be proved beneath the North Sea will be small compared with the Middle East, production will make a very significant contribution to meet the demand from neighbouring countries. In 1973 the expanded EEC's consumption of crude petroleum was 617 million metric tons. The initial forecast of EEC needs in 1985 was 1,160 million metric tons, though the aim is to reduce the requirement to 650 million metric tons. It is therefore unlikely that the production of local crude will prevent Europe from importing more distant crude than is bought at present. In 1973 the United Kingdom demand was more than 110 million tons: by 1980, production from the United Kingdom sector of the North Sea should more than cover the country's internal needs for the next 20 years or so, even allowing for some increase in demand. The cost of extracting the oil, however, is rising steadily. In the Forties development costs have escalated (at 9 October 1974) from £350 million to a suggested total cost of over £600 million. Presumably costs will rise in other fields *pari passu*.

B. THE ADDITION OF ALIEN SUBSTANCES

1. Introduction

The wastes created by human societies always have been, and for the most part still are, discharged into the natural environment: into middens, into rivers and streams, and into the seas. There the wastes provide food for scavenging animals, or they may rot and be broken down into chemically simple substances by bacterial action, or they may corrode and fragment. Some wastes decay quickly, others may take a very long time to do so, but, whatever the time-scale, the result is generally part of the cycle of growth, death, decay and re-use which is the basis of all life on this planet. The ultimate products of decay nourish plant life – in the sea as much as on the land – on which, in the last resort, all animal life depends.

All wastes, whether they are in the form of the carcass of a dead animal or the effluent from a chemical factory, have some impact on the immediate environment. Whether the ecological change that results is local or widespread, brief or prolonged, trivial or major, it is an inevitable and perfectly natural concomitant of death, decay and waste disposal. If man-induced changes are of such an extent, nature and duration that they are environmentally damaging they become a matter of concern, but it must not be forgotten that waste disposal is as vital a human activity as any other.

The development of sewage and water transport systems in the late 18th and 19th centuries, to combat insanitary conditions in towns, transferred the greater part of the domestic sewage load from the land to rivers which then, for the first time, began to suffer gross pollution. Moreover, the building of industrial cities on and near estuaries resulted in the discharge of large volumes of domestic and industrial waste into tidal waters.

The recent increasingly strict control of waste discharge into inland waters has stimulated the tendency for industry to move to the coast where liquid wastes can be piped directly into the sea. This process is likely to continue and the need to safeguard both drinking water supplies and trade patterns within the EEC may also be expected to further encourage the siting of industry on the shores and estuaries of the North Sea. However, this is not the only industrial sector whose wastes enter the sea: the long-lived wastes still discharged into rivers are carried there and a service industry has recently grown up which specializes in the shipment of waste material from inland industries to off-shore dumping grounds.

While the volume of waste entering the sea has steadily been increasing, its nature has changed. Initially, although it comes from the land it was composed of naturally occurring materials such as organic wastes, bacteria, silt, nutrients, etc. Now a large number of synthetic chemical by-products produced by industrial processes are discharged as waste. Such new chemical products are estimated to be increasing at about 400 to 500 per annum, and more than 3,000 chemical products or their derivatives have been identified in the atmosphere.[26] Many enter the sea through conventional outfalls but pollutants in the air are washed out by rain to the land and thence to the sea, often in important quantities. Many of these new products – the organochlorine pesticides and various halogenated aliphatic and aromatic compounds used as degreasing or cleansing agents and plasticisers – are both toxic and long-lived in the environment. Even non-toxic products, such as plastics and synthetic polymers, constitute an environmental hazard because of their virtual indestructibility.

Because they cannot be digested or broken down, and often cannot be eliminated once they enter the tissues of a plant or animal, they tend to accumulate in the body and so reach much higher concentrations than are found in the surrounding seawater. Animals feeding on these primary accumulators of the pollutant thus have an enriched diet of the substance and themselves accumulate even higher concentrations.

Thus animals at the top of a food chain, such as fish-eating seals, birds and humans, may be exposed to, and acquire very large doses of, substances which are present only in traces in the sea water. Products of even low toxicity can then cause damage.

The distribution and dilution of toxic additives to the water depends chiefly on the mixing of water masses rather than on diffusion, but in many areas the rate of mixing is slow and discrete bodies of water may retain their identity for some considerable time. There is also a separation of water masses on a larger, more permanent scale. In the North Sea there are several distinguishable bodies of water each characterized by different planktonic species.[27]

The consequences of these hydrographic conditions for marine pollution were illustrated by an incident on the Dutch coast after the illegal dumping of copper sulphate near Nordwijk in 1965. The polluted water remained in a narrow coastal strip during the following two weeks as it spread 80 kilometres northwards towards the Waddensee, and its concentration at the end of that time was still 20 per cent of what it had been at the beginning.[28]

[26] L. C. Cole, "Playing Russian roulette with biogeochemical cycles", *The Environmental Crisis* (ed. H. W. Helfrich), pp. 1–14, Yale University Press, 1970.
[27] T. Laevastu, FAO Fisheries Division Project No. 2 (21/3), Rome, 1960.
[28] R. T. Roskam, "A case of copper pollution along the Dutch shore", CM ICES, C:44, Near Northern Seas Committee, 1965; *Wat. Bodem Lucht*, 56: 19–21, 1966.

Radioactive caesium, included in wastes discharged from the Windscale nuclear fuel reprocessing plant, labels the receiving water uniquely and the subsequent distribution and dilution of this waste can therefore be followed over a wide area. An important discovery in a recent survey is that the receiving waters hug the coast as they travel around the north of Scotland into the North Sea.[29]

Both this and the Dutch incident illustrate the relatively slow rate of mixing of in-shore waters, which receive the bulk of effluent discharges, with the general body of North Sea water.

2. Polluting Agents

Although almost all effluents discharged into oceans or the sea are complicated mixtures and therefore have multiple effects on the environment, it is convenient to give characteristics of different classes of pollutants separately.

(a) Urban, Domestic and Agricultural Waste

The constituents of domestic waste include suspended, colloidal and dissolved organic matter, nutrient salts and bacteria derived from sewage together with further quantities of organic material and detergents, which arise from other household activities. Agricultural waste is of two kinds: natural organic waste, which normally finds its way into the sea in combination with domestic sewage, and run-off from agricultural land, which is an important source of persistent insecticides, fungicides, mercuric compounds used in seed dressings, etc. It is necessary to distinguish between them, since the latter category might equally be regarded as industrial waste. Urban waste, that is the effluent from town sewers, contains, in addition to sewage, silt, oil and tarry materials from road drainage. Agricultural effluent may be increasing in volume and in polluting load as intensive farming begins to play a greater role in agricultural production. Changing patterns in agriculture and urbanization are also making it more difficult to dispose of the resulting wastes.

About 50 per cent of the volume may be made up of industrial wastes derived from the discharge to local authority sewers of industrial effluents.[30] The presence of organic matter as a major constituent distinguishes urban, domestic and agricultural wastes from those derived from other sources.

These wastes enter the marine environment either by discharge from coastal outfalls or via rivers and estuaries into which they are initially discharged. They are not normally dumped from ships either in treated

[29] D. F. Jefferies, A. Preston, A. K. Steele, *Marine Pollution Bulletin*, 4 (8): 118–121, 1973.
[30] Jeger Committee, *Report of the Working Party on Sewage Disposal*, London, HMSO, 65 pp., 1970.

or raw form but the residue of primary sludge remaining after settlement or humus sludge (after digestion has taken place) is frequently dumped off-shore.

It is difficult to estimate the total volume of either sewage or urban waste entering the sea. An appreciation of some of these difficulties may be gained by attempting to assess the volume of sewage entering the North Sea from Great Britain.

The Jeger Committee (1970) estimated that the sewage and trade waste from a population of about 6 million is discharged directly to the sea or to estuaries but the Committee's report stressed that this figure did not include discharges independent of local authority main drainage systems; thus many hotels, holiday camps and caravan sites, which are extensive on the east coast of England, would have been excluded. Assuming an average flow of 204.6 litres per person per day (45 gallons per head per day) this population would yield about 1,230,000 cubic metres per day. The most recent estimate currently available, which is provided by the ICES Working Group on Pollution of the North Sea (1969), indicated that the total quantity of sewage discharged from England and Wales directly to the sea is 2,500,000 cubic metres per day. Assessing the proportion of this which goes to the North Sea is not easy but, from one of these figures in the ICES report (reproduced as figure A), it is possible to estimate the total amount of both direct and indirect discharges as 4,780,000 cubic metres per day. Making allowances for growth it is likely that the daily total may now be in the region of 6,000,000 cubic metres. The ICES report estimated the total quantity of sewage discharged to the sea in Scotland to be in the region of 1,300,000 cubic metres per day. A true total, therefore, for the whole of the British coast may lie somewhere in the region of 8,000,000 cubic metres per day.

Estimates are equally difficult to obtain for countries on the European mainland; the ICES report estimated that 2,300,000 cubic metres of sewage per day was discharged directly to the sea from Belgium, and 10,000 cubic metres per day from Denmark. The total figure of sewage discharged from the Federal Republic of Germany is reported to be small and insignificant compared with that carried by the rivers. Unfortunately, no figures appear to be yet available for the pollution load carried by the rivers. France is reported as discharging approximately 85,000 cubic metres of sewage per day, while the data for the Netherlands are given in terms of the pollution load of phosphorus, nitrogen and BOD (biological oxygen demand) which, in the absence of accurate figures for the polluting strength of Dutch sewage, cannot be compared with the volumetric data from other European countries. The total quantity of sewage discharged directly to the sea from Norway is estimated at 380,000 cubic metres per day but, surprisingly, no figures are available for the total quantity of sewage discharged from Sweden.

THE NORTH SEA

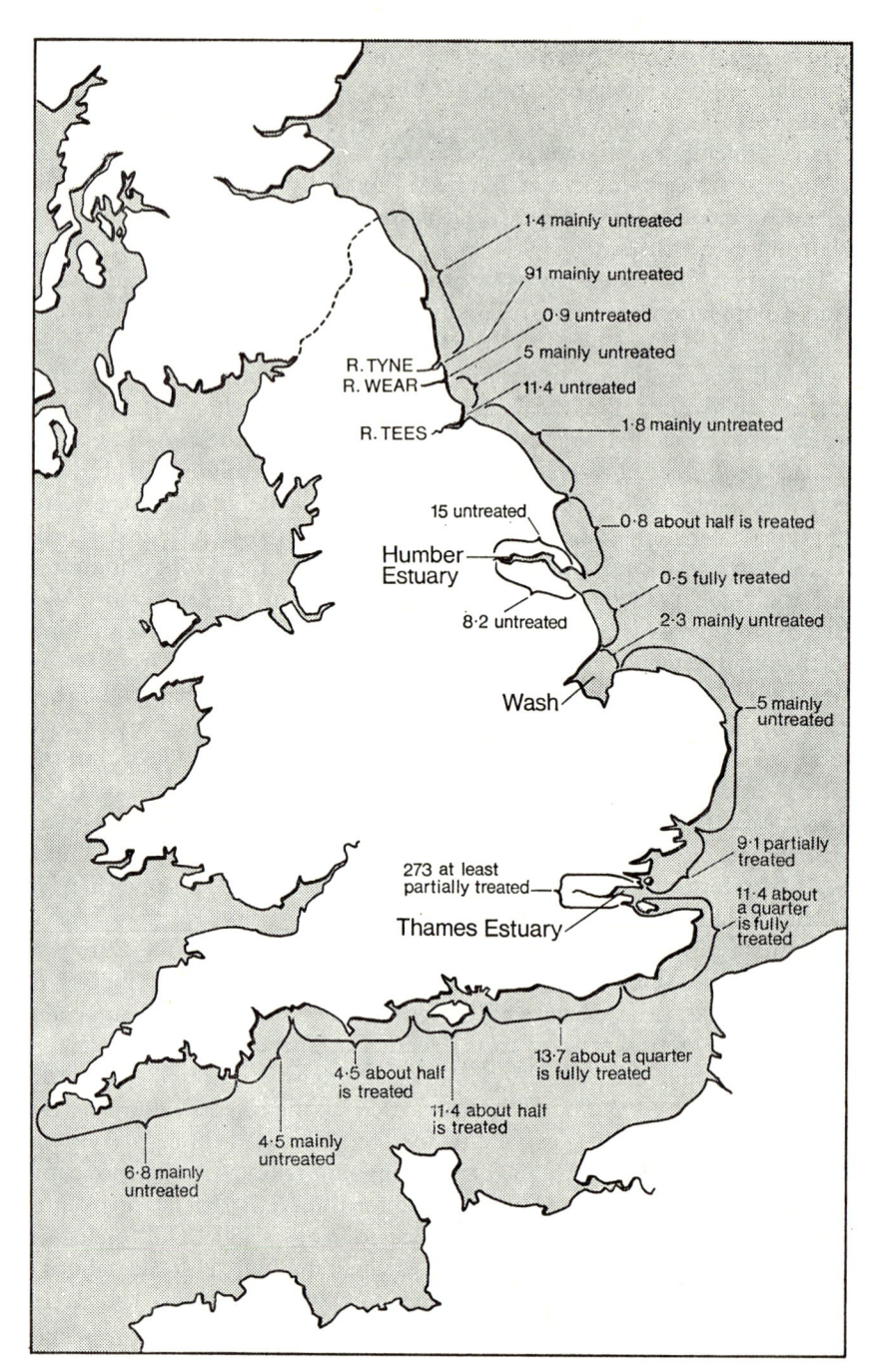

Fig. A: Domestic sewage discharges (10^4 cubic metres per day) from the English coast (ICES report, 1969).

Labels on map:
- 1·4 mainly untreated
- 91 mainly untreated
- 0·9 untreated
- 5 mainly untreated (R. TYNE)
- 11·4 untreated (R. WEAR)
- 1·8 mainly untreated (R. TEES)
- 15 untreated
- 0·8 about half is treated
- Humber Estuary
- 0·5 fully treated
- 8·2 untreated
- 2·3 mainly untreated
- Wash
- 5 mainly untreated
- 9·1 partially treated
- 273 at least partially treated
- Thames Estuary
- 11·4 about a quarter is fully treated
- 13·7 about a quarter is fully treated
- 4·5 about half is treated
- 11·4 about half is treated
- 4·5 mainly untreated
- 6·8 mainly untreated

Addition of these quoted figures gives a sum of 10,755,000 cubic metres of sewage per day discharged to the North Sea though it will be realized that the real total must be well in excess of this. The off-shore disposal of sewage sludge adds a small but significant fraction to these figures. From the London area about 5 million tons per annum are dumped in the outer Thames estuary and it is also reported that some sewage sludge is dumped seaward of Oslo Fjord. No data on the composition of this Norwegian sludge are available but the sludge dumped from England and Scotland (both east and west coasts) contains between 3 and 8 per cent of solids and has a BOD ranging from 12,000 to 37,000 parts per million.[31]

Treatment

Untreated sewage contains an enormous number of bacteria but a large proportion of these is removed if the sewage is treated. During the treatment process the numbers of other bacteria may have built up and the effluent, therefore, acquires a population of micro-organisms which may continue to increase in number until the point of discharge into sea water is reached. When mixing with seawater has taken place many species of bacteria, and coliforms in particular, are subject to severe mortalities though as yet there seems no clear idea of what the major factors affecting this mortality are. The effects of sunlight and the presence of phytoplankton have been suggested, and a recent study finds a close correlation between mortality and increasing salinity.[32] Only rough estimates appear to be available for the proportion of sewage which is treated on the various countries bordering the North Sea. Sewage can be either fully or partially treated. In the former case (see above), most of the organic matter and bacteria are removed, while partial treatment is usually understood to involve only screening and settling. Belgium discharges largely untreated sewage though some sewage receives partial treatment; from Denmark both treated and partially treated sewage is discharged; in Germany the large quantities of wastes carried by the main river systems are treated but it is not known whether any treatment is given to the smaller quantities of sewage discharged directly to the sea. About half of the sewage discharged from France receives some form of treatment while in the Netherlands most of the sewage is discharged through long sea outfalls with little or no treatment. Prior to the passing of a pollution control law in 1968, few Norwegian towns treated their sewage but the present situation is not known. Rapid progress towards the treatment of sewage and other wastes

[31] D. W. Mackay & G. Topping, "Preliminary report of the effects of sludge disposal at sea", *Effl. Wat. Treat. J.*, 10, 641–649, 1970; R. G. J. Shelton, "Sludge dumping in the Thames Estuary", *Marine Pollution Bulletin*, 2 (2), 24–27, 1971.
[32] A. Guelin and M. L. Cabioch, "Sur l'utilisation du phénoméne de bactériolyse spontanée pour la connaissance de l'état sanitaire des eaux douces et marines", *Comptes Rendus Acad. Sc. Paris*, 271, Série D, 137–140, 1970.

is believed to have been made in Sweden but there are no actual figures available. The situation may radically change when the 1974 Helsinki and Stockholm Conventions, covering the Baltic Sea, come into force. On the east coast of England and Scotland sewage is discharged mainly untreated except from a number of holiday resorts and estuaries where some partial treatment is given.

Silt from land run-off and road drainage is partially settled out even if primary treatment is given to the sewage; nevertheless the quantities discharged may have important effects on coastal and estuarine fauna. No estimate of these quantities is available; to obtain such an estimate would be very difficult because the silt content of sewage varies with the rates of flow and the amount of silt reaching the sea by rivers and estuaries is masked by the greater quantities of naturally-derived river-borne silt.

Inorganic salts containing nitrogen and phosphate, commonly termed nutrient salts, are ordinarily present in solution in sewage but further quantities are liberated when organic matter is broken down. Even where full biological treatment is given to the sewage, only a proportion of the nutrients is removed; this proportion varies from about 30 to 70 per cent. If the sludge remaining from treatment is digested or disposed of separately to an estuary or the sea, the remaining nutrients eventually reach the marine environment. Other sources of nutrients include wastes from food processing industries and run-off from land, particularly agricultural land to which chemical fertilizers have been heavily applied. Household detergents also provide an important source of phosphate.

While most of the phosphorus discharged to sewers and rivers eventually reaches the sea, some of the nitrogen may be converted to its gaseous form by denitrifying bacteria and hence lost to the atmosphere. Unfortunately there are very few quantitative data regarding this process in various rivers and estuaries, though Head[33] does give data for the amount of nitrogen deposited in the sediments and lost to the atmosphere from the Tyne and Thames. He also notes that the amounts of nitrogen discharged to the North Sea by each river are vastly different. The Tyne discharges 6-7 tons of nitrogen per day, while the Thames discharges 89-90 tons per day. Thus an estimate of the total quantities discharged to the North Sea is impossible without the benefit of further information.

The nutrient contributions to the sea from sewage and run-off have been calculated at some 1.548 nitrogen tons per day and 256 phosphorus tons per day.[34] The bulk of these nutrients (80 per cent) is discharged into the shallow southern section of the North Sea which receives most of the drainage of North-Western Europe and a considerable portion of

[33] P. C. Head, "Discharge of nutrients from estuaries", *Marine Pollution Bulletin*, 1, (9), 138-140, 1970.
[34] James and Head, "The Discharge of Nutrients from Estuaries and Their Effect on Primary Productivity", *Marine Pollution and Sea Life*, pp. 163-165, 1972.

that from the United Kingdom. To some extent the anticlockwise circulation of currents and salinity distribution in the North Sea reduces this high concentration of nutrients to levels more typical of the North Sea as a whole – which at present are also fairly typical of northern temperate waters. Nonetheless further increases in the supply from land run-off might produce a serious build-up of nutrients in the southern sector; since, as indicated above, the rate of mixing is relatively slow.

As already indicated, agricultural waste contains not only organic material and nutrients but also highly toxic organochlorine pesticides such as DDT, dieldrin, aldrin and endrin. Over the past few years the use of such pesticides has declined and the level of pesticide residue found in North Sea fish, though high, is apparently not increasing. However, seals and sea-birds – which, of course, feed on fish – have been found to contain substantially higher levels. Generally speaking, when pesticides are screened against related forms of plant and animal life, marine forms are not included. However, tests show that crustaceans, e.g. shrimps and prawns, are highly susceptible. Also, there may well be effects on physiology, behaviour and breeding success produced by pesticide concentration levels well below those which respond to "acute toxicity" tests.

(b) Industrial Wastes

In dealing with this aspect of the problem it is easier to handle it on a country by country basis since much of the statistical material is available in this form.

Many industrial wastes contain large amounts of organic matter but the feature that is used to distinguish them from sewage is the presence of highly toxic or non-biodegradable material such as heavy metals and synthetic chemicals. Some trade wastes, e.g. those from food processing and natural fibre industries, contain mainly organic matter, while urban sewage from industrial areas may contain toxic substances. Thus, in practice, the distinction made above cannot be applied too rigorously.

Industrial waste enters the marine environment through pathways similar to those for sewage, that is via coastal outfalls, via rivers and estuaries or by direct dumping from ships at sea. The following details of industrial discharges from the countries surrounding the North Sea are taken mainly from the ICES report,[35] with additions where indicated.

Belgium: A large number of industrial wastes are discharged to the rivers and, although some work is in progress on the effect of the wastes of fisheries, very little is at present known about their effects or composition. The Schelde is affected by industrial pollution from higher up the river and from Antwerp but this river's contribution to the North Sea is

[35] Report of the ICES Working Group on Pollution of the North Sea, *Co-operative Research Report*, Series A (13), ICES, Charlottenlund, Denmark, 1969.

only 10 per cent of that of the Rhine. Only one major industrial waste is discharged directly to the sea and this consists of a liquid containing on average 10 per cent sulphuric acid and 2–3 per cent iron sulphate. About 200 tons per day are dumped in an area about 40 miles WSW of the Hook of Holland.

Denmark: There is very little heavy industry in Denmark and therefore very little direct pollution of the sea from industrial sources. The only major problem mentioned occurs at a factory producing weed-killers. Some phenols were being discharged to the sea and some fish, particularly eels, cod and flounders, were affected by tainting but this problem has now been eliminated.

France: Industrial pollution along the north-east coast of France, that is from east of the Pas de Calais, comes primarily from an oil refinery at Dunkirk, a factory treating titanium minerals, a paper mill and a small distillery at Calais. No detrimental effects from these discharges have been reported and no discharges of wastes other than dredgings are made from ships. The Rhine, however, is very heavily polluted.

West Germany: The Federal Republic of Germany has very little industry near the coast, and there are no important discharges to the sea. The main industries of the Federal Republic at present discharge their effluents to inland waters and a considerable raising of standards is taking place. As a result many industries are turning to sea disposal beyond territorial waters as an alternative. Waste materials for which application has been made to carry out disposal at sea include sulphuric acid, iron sulphate, gypsum, chromate, hydrocarbons, polyethylene, creosote, pyrites cinders, calcium arsenate and arsenic residues. It is understood that the proposed application to discharge sulphuric acid and iron sulphate was granted and that the proposal to dump polyethylene was turned down. The disposal area designated for the arsenic residues, calcium arsenate, chlorohydrocarbons and gypsum is in the north Atlantic beyond the continental shelf and hence outside the scope of this review.

Great Britain: The north-east coastal area of England around the estuaries of the rivers Tyne, Wear and Tees is by far the most important and contributes the greatest variety of chemical wastes. In the river Tees over 90 per cent of the 1.4×10^6 m^3/d is waste from the chemical industry complex which discharges a wide variety of chemicals including sulphuric acid, metals, cyanide, ammonia and phenol. Just north of Teesmouth a factory which extracts magnesium from sea water discharges 2.3×10^6 m^3/d of spent sea water containing about 35 tons of suspended solids. Coal washings and coal wastes dumped directly onto the shoreline amount to 1.8×10^4 m^3/d and 4 million tons per year, respectively.

1.4×10^6 m³/d of treated wastes are discharged into the Humber estuary. They include 1,000 tons per day of sulphuric acid, 250 tons per day of iron sulphate, 2,500 tons per day of gypsum, 7.2 tons of zinc, 3 tons of phenols and many other chemicals. Until very recently the Thames estuary carried 2.8×10^6 m³/d of mixed trade waste and sewage and was devoid of oxygen along a 5-mile length at certain times of the year. The situation is slowly being rectified by sewage purification and treatment of wastes.

In Scotland the industries which give rise to the majority of industrial wastes are iron and steel manufacture, coal-mining, pulp and paper or board production, and whisky distilling. Paper and board production in Scotland give rise to about 2.4×10^3 m³/d of effluent but most of the mills discharge their waste to inland waters. The annual production of whisky in Scotland is reported to be around 6×10^6 m³ (80 million gallons). In the Moray Firth alone over 4,450m³/week of "spent ale" are discharged with a BOD equivalent of 112.5 tons of oxygen. This is one fourteenth of the sewage BOD for the whole of Scotland. In some areas road tankers dump hot spent liquor directly into the sea from harbour jetties. Whisky wastes can cause the death of lobsters near the point of discharge and they have also been blamed for the mortalities of salmon held in bag nets.

Dumping of wastes from ships has increased in recent years and now includes 1 million tons of power station ash and 2 million tons of colliery wastes. Some industrial wastes are also dumped into the Thames estuary. Dumping of wastes in Scottish waters is confined mainly to the Firth of Forth and the Clyde. Approximately 250,000 tons of fly ash are dumped annually in the Clyde and explosives are dumped both in the Clyde and the Forth; these explosives are claimed to cause tainting or colouring of fish.

The exploitation of North Sea oil can be expected to add substantially to the amount of waste to be dealt with in the area generally.

Netherlands: The major source of industrial pollution in the Netherlands is the Rhine. This river, as well as carrying the effluents discharged to it in the Netherlands, also carries the effluents discharged in the other countries through which it passes. An account of existing pollution of the Rhine has been given by Tinker[36] who showed that, in spite of extensive expenditure and treatment of pollutants, the oxygen content of both upper and lower Rhine is declining, and the BOD of the river water is increasing.

The extensive industrial area of Rotterdam discharges wastes into the same area as the Rhine. Other important sources of pollution are the river Schelde and Antwerp, although these are considerably less polluted than the Rhine. There is also some dumping from the North Pier (Hook of Holland) of industrial wastes, which include 1,500 tons per year of nitric

[36] J. Tinker, "Europe's Majestic Sewer", *New Scientist*, 26 Oct. 1972.

acid and lower fatty acids, a total of 1,700 tons per year of pickling bath wastes from three sources which contain a variety of metals such as aluminium, iron and chromium together with sulphuric and hydrochloric acids and cyanide.

Shipping contributes a variety of wastes, of which oil is the most important, to the general pollution load. International disposal of wastes at sea from ships outside territorial waters has been increasing. Among the wastes at present being discharged each year are 1,200 tons of mixed salt and sulphates; 3,600 tons of sulphuric acid containing aromatic sulphur compounds; and 750,000 tons of titanium residue containing 20 per cent sulphuric acid and 5 per cent iron sulphate. The number of new proposals for discharge by this method is still increasing and they include proposals to dump 700,000 tons per year of gypsum waste, 60,000 tons per year of iron sulphate, 700 tons per year of pickling wastes containing cyanide and 10 per cent metals, and 4,000 tons per day of sewage sludge and quantities of chlorinated hydrocarbons. Many of these new proposals have come from other countries, for example Germany, as a result of increased pollution control measures in inland waters.

There have been a number of incidents at pesticide plants which have resulted in fairly extensive fish mortalities. A case of pollution by copper sulphate in coastal waters caused locally extensive fish mortalities in 1965.[37]

Norway: In 1968 industrial pollution in Norway had not reached levels of very great importance but the growth rate of industry was very rapid and pollution was on the increase. The principal sources are the timber and paper pulp industries which discharge fibres; fish processing industries which discharge nearly 2,000 tons of 40 per cent formalin solution annually (half of this directly to the sea), and the aluminium industry which produces a waste containing aluminium oxide, hydrofluoric and sulphuric acid and large quantities of "red mud". In addition to the formalin waste, the fish curing industry can give rise to wastes containing fish oils and soluble materials; and these can create pollution problems up to several kilometres from the outfall. Mining activities, mainly in southern Norway, for iron, copper, sulphur and niobium have also caused local problems but their effects on the marine environment are believed to be negligible.

Sweden: The principal Swedish industry causing marine pollution is the timber and forestry industry which, taken as a whole, imposes a BOD loading of 20,000 tons per year on the waters to which it discharges its waste. By comparison, sewage from Sweden has a total BOD loading of

---

[37] R. T. Roskam, "A case of copper pollution along the Dutch shore", CM ICES, C:44, Near Northern Seas Committee, 1965.

50,000 tons per year and the total contribution for other Swedish industries is 25,000 tons per year. Most of the discharges are, however, to the Baltic Sea. Pollution problems arising as a result of forest industry are much worse in Sweden than in Norway, and fishing has been affected in many coastal areas. Pollution by mercury compounds is very serious in Sweden;[38] the metal being present in sediment, fish and birds from both freshwater and marine areas. The problem has now reached the stage where commercial fishing has had to be prohibited in certain lakes and some coastal areas. Mercury is a cumulative poison and its uptake and transformation into dangerous compounds by aquatic organisms is now beginning to be understood.

Other industries such as metallurgy, engineering, food and chemicals are situated primarily in southern Sweden and some of the biggest factories are on the coast. Generally their wastes are controlled and only local trouble may be caused.

Some dumping of wastes from effluent disposal ships is carried out. The materials dumped include harbour dredgings, sodium sulphide, chemicals in drums and paper mill fibre sludges which interfere with fishing and cause tainting of fish.

(c) Oil

River discharges and shipping activities are at present the major sources of oil entering the North Sea; but increasingly in the future, as undersea oil fields already located become commercially exploited, drilling operations and pipelines will provide additional sources. Few quantitative data are available regarding the contribution of oil from rivers though there is some evidence that the amount is still growing, as a result, to a considerable extent, of spillages in road transit or in garages.

Oil discharged as a result of shipping activities or the transport of crude oil and petroleum products may be either accidental or deliberate. Bulk transport of both crude oil and refined products has increased immensely in recent years and with this trend – which has been examined in more detail in the previous section of this report – has come increasingly frequent incidents of pollution. Total movements of oil by tanker around the coasts of the British Isles now exceed 350×10^6 tons per year, and these are increasing annually by 10 per cent.[39] The introduction of the "load-on-top" system has lessened the need to discharge oil in tank washings yet the extent of pollution appears to continue unabated. The series of annual reports produced by the Advisory Committee on Oil Pollution of the Sea indicate the severity of the problem; in its report for 1971 the Advisory Committee was concerned that the length of coastline

[38] H. Ackefors, "Mercury pollution in Sweden with special reference to conditions in the water habitat", *Proc. Roy. Soc.*, London, B, 177, 365–387, 1971.
[39] Jeger Report, 1970.

polluted by oil increased by a third compared with that in 1970. Beaches surrounding a semi-enclosed sea such as the North Sea are particularly liable to pollution for the oil has little chance to disperse or degrade naturally before being blown ashore. An additional cause for concern is the number of oil slicks which may, despite the apparent density of shipping in the North Sea, remain unobserved for considerable periods and whose existence is not suspected until large numbers of dead seabirds are washed ashore.

(d) Radioactive Materials

The principal sources of radioactive discharges are nuclear power stations and fuel processing plants; other sources such as the use of radioactive isotopes in hospitals, science and industry are believed to contribute little to the environment. The testing of nuclear weapons is also generally held to be an important source. Pollution from weapon-testing occurs on a global scale and can be considered as affecting the marine environment through fallout from the upper atmosphere. Over the North Sea, which is geographically far removed from the major testing sites, radioactivity from these sources is generally considered to cause only a slight increase in the natural background radiation.

Existing nuclear power stations on the coast of the North Sea are reported to have a good safety record. Around the whole of Britain, nine stations are operating, four are at the planning stage and another four are under construction.

No nuclear fuel processing plants are believed to be situated on any of the coasts of the North Sea at present, though one is planned for the west coast of Sweden. In Britain the chief fuel processing plant (believed to be the largest in Europe) is at Windscale on the Cumberland coast bordering the Irish Sea; other UKAEA stations dealing with radioactive substances are mostly in the west of the country, at Salwick (near Preston), Harwell, Chapel Cross and Capenhurst. However, radioactive waste from Windscale, albeit in low concentrations, eventually reaches the North Sea via the north coast of Scotland. Only the long-lived, low-level wastes, that is effluents having low concentrations of radioactive isotopes, are released from these plants; the high level wastes are stored until the radioactivity dies down. This storage must continue in some cases for thousands of years. The latest estimates put the period at from 6,000 to 250,000 years for some wastes. Marine dumping of solid wastes has been carried out, but the dumping sites are beyond the continental shelf and it is generally presumed that no material of this type has been dumped in the North Sea.

(e) Heat

The need to dispose of waste heat arises from the basic inefficiency of the energy cycle used to extract power from fossil fuels or nuclear sources.

This inefficiency is considerable. For example, in a modern coal- or oil-fired plant, the amount of heat rejected to the condenser from the turbine exhaust steam is about 50 per cent of the heat input to the boiler. This is equivalent to about 1.33 kilowatts of heat rejected for each kilowatt of electric power generated. For a plant operating on nuclear fuel, about 66 per cent of the heat input to the boiler is rejected to the condenser; this is equivalent to about 2.0 kilowatts of heat for each kilowatt of electric power generated.[40]

The main sources are therefore power stations. Other sources, such as steel plants and oil refineries which require water for cooling purposes, release smaller quantities of waste heat, having only local effects. Older power stations, particularly those on inland sites, get rid of waste heat in many cases to the atmosphere by means of cooling towers; modern nuclear stations, because of the greater quantities of heat to be disposed of, are nearly all situated on the coast where direct cooling by seawater is the cheapest system of heat removal.

Thermal pollution from power stations is all the more significant because many stations are situated on estuaries where a build-up of the heated effluent may occur. For example, the recent application by the Central Electricity Generating Board in Britain to build two more nuclear power stations on the shores of the upper part of the Bristol Channel will make a total of six nuclear generating stations operating, under construction or planned in the upper Bristol Channel and Severn estuary. Despite this concentration of generating capacity, thermal pollution of seawater is not yet a major problem in Britain apart from a few specific localities such as enclosed docks and basins.[41]

The North Sea's major source of thermal pollution may again be the Rhine. The difficulties of controlling the amount of waste heat discharged to the river have been described by Tinker.[42] A joint working group of the German states calculated recently that if existing and projected nuclear power plants were cooled directly from the river, the peak temperature of the Rhine would rise in summer to 28°C in 1975 and to 35°C in 1985. At Fessenheim in southern Alsace, France has two reactors, totalling 2,100 megawatts, under construction and four more reactors are planned. They have no cooling towers and could raise river temperatures in winter by 15–18°C. If such a temperature rise above ambient is maintained all the way to Rotterdam by a succession of thermal additions, the amount of heat discharged to the North Sea by the Rhine's average flow of 1,451 cubic

---

[40] R. D. Woodson, "Cooling Towers", *Scientific American*, 224, (5), 70–78, May 1971.
[41] E. Naylor, "Effects of heated effluents upon marine and estuarine organisms", *Advanced Mar. Biol.*, 3, 63–103, 1965.
[42] J. Tinker, "Europe's Majestic Sewer", *New Sci.*, 56, (817), 194–199, 26 Oct. 1972.

metres per second (1971) would be very large indeed. Other nuclear power stations using the North Sea for cooling are on the west coast of Sweden and at Hamburg on the Elbe estuary.

3. Pollution: Air-Sea Interaction

An important but relatively unconsidered source of pollution of the sea is by deposition from the air. It is, of course, not possible to deal with air-sea pollution on a regional basis since "the wind bloweth where it listeth" save in very particular instances. Pollutants discharged into the air or entering the atmosphere in other ways may subsequently be washed out by rain or be deposited directly by a process known as "dry deposition".

The greatest concentration of contaminants is generally to be found close to the source of pollution but once they have been discharged into the atmosphere (particularly if they reach the upper atmosphere), long-lived substances may be distributed to virtually all parts of the world. It is difficult to quantify this input to the sea but it is certainly very considerable and, for some substances, preponderant.

The pattern and distribution of fall-out are governed by meteorological factors and local human activities. Lead, derived from leaded anti-knock petrol additives, released in car exhausts, may amount to 200,000 tons per annum globally, equal to the input of lead into the sea from all other polluting sources.[43] Elevated lead concentrations in seawater and marine organisms in the sea near Los Angeles is related to the enormous concentration of petrol-driven vehicles there and the concentration declines offshore until background levels are reached. It is possible to measure the lead concentration at various depths in the snow cap in northern Greenland.[44] At the greatest depths, representing snow that fell more than two millennia ago, there is no lead, but there is an increase in the lead concentrations at levels representing the period 1750–1950, coinciding with the industrial revolution in the northern hemisphere. The most dramatic increase has taken place since 1940, coinciding with the enormous increase in lead emissions from internal combustion engines. A comparable increase in lead concentration has not been found in Antarctic snow, suggesting that industrial sources have been responsible for the increase in the northern hemisphere and, since coal burning has increased by only 40 per cent since 1940 but the production of lead alkyls (i.e. anti-knock petrol additives) has increased 20 or 30 times, it is likely that the steep

[43] Report of 3rd Session IMCO/FAO/UNESCO/WMO/WHO/IAEA/UN Joint Group of Experts on the Scientific Aspects of Marine Pollution (GESAMP); FAO Fisheries Reports, No. 102, 1971.

[44] M. Murozumi, T. J. Chow and C. Patterson, "Chemical concentrations of pollutant lead aerosols, terrestrial dusts, and sea salts in Greenland and Antarctic snow strata", *Geochim. Cosmochim. Acta*, 33: 1247–1294, 1969.

rise in global lead pollution in recent years is due to air pollution from automobile exhausts. There is, however, some recent evidence to support the view that the lead peak may have passed.[45]

An unknown but possibly very large part of hydrocarbon pollution in the sea may be from unburned petroleum hydrocarbons released to the air in vehicle exhausts.

Organochlorine pesticide residues have made a substantial addition to marine pollution from the air. Dry conditions in the fruit- and vegetable-growing regions of central California, coupled with the practice of aerial spraying of crops with D.D.T. (now largely discontinued) and other organochlorine pesticides, result in a considerable windborne transport of these materials in dust to the adjacent Pacific Ocean. The accumulation of these residues in Antarctic penguins far from places where these substances have been used may be in part due to transport by ocean currents and migrating marine organisms, but aerial transport is certainly an important and perhaps a dominant factor.

Mercury reaches the sea via the general de-gassing of the earth's surface including volcanic eruptions, but here the combustion of fossil fuels may also contribute mercury to the wash-out from the air.[46] The acidification of lakes in southern and central Sweden is probably largely due to the precipitation of acidic sulphurous compounds derived from air pollution in the industrial Ruhr or windborne deposit from the industrial Midlands of England.

The input of pollutants to the North Sea from the air, given the prevailing westerly airflow over the region, is derived partly from global pollution, partly from the industrial areas of the Continent, but chiefly from the United Kingdom. Estimates of deposition rates over the North Sea are given in Table 5.

These estimates are, on the whole, very crude and are often very little better than an informed guess. To get a realistic view of the significance of atmospheric deposition of pollutants in the North Sea it will be necessary to monitor fall-out in a comprehensive way for a number of years. More reliable estimates of the total deposition over the whole area are certainly needed but, in view of the fact that separate bodies of water exist in the North Sea, it will be important to measure the geographical distributions and seasonal and annual variation in the amounts of pollutants that are deposited.

It should, however, be noted that the distribution of most metals in North Sea water is influenced, in so far as higher concentrations are concerned, by input from rivers and pipelines, creating a picture of enhanced

[45] R. Chester and J. H. Stoner, "Pb particulates from the lower atmosphere of the eastern Atlantic", *Nature*, Vol. 245, pp. 27–28, 1973.
[46] *Marine Environmental Quality* (National Academy of Sciences, Washington, D.C.), pp. 12–14, 1971.

TABLE 5

Estimate of Deposition Rates over the North Sea

	Deposition Rate per Unit Surface (kg/km²/yr)	Total Deposition on the North Sea (metric tons/yr)
1. Dissolved organic matter	10,000	5×10^6
2. Sulphur* as SO_2	5,000	3×10^6
3. Particulates*	3,000	1.5×10^6
4. Nitrogen (fixed)	2,000	1×10^6
5. Lead	3	1.5×10
6. DDT residues	0.5	3×10
7. Other chlorinated hydrocarbons	(at least as much as preceding entry)	
8. Mercury	0.05	30

1. Based on the general finding that organic matter in precipitation is roughly equal to the total dissolved inorganic matter.
2. Based on a world SO_2 emission of 10^8 metric tons/yr with an enhancement factor of 25 allowing for the geographical distribution of the sources.
3. Based on an average atmospheric dust content of 10 microgrammes/std m³ and a deposition velocity of 1 cm/sec.
4. Based on values from the West European Precipitation Chemistry Network.
5. Based on a lead emission by automobile exhaust of 300 g/km²/yr on the global average with an enhancement factor of 10, which is considered to be a lower limit.
6. Based on a world production figure of 300 g/km²/yr assuming worldwide dispersion due to a relatively large atmospheric residence time.
8. Based on an average concentration of 0.1 microgramme/litre of precipitation and an average yearly precipitation of 500 mm. It is likely that this deposition is, in part, balanced by an escape of organic mercury compounds.

* An additional 1 ton of dust per km²/yr on the average is likely to be deposited during 15 years in one century due to volcanic eruptions. These eruptions would also lead to an increase in the sulphur depositions.

water concentrations.[47] With the possible exception of lead, it would seem that the atmosphere is not a very important route for most metals.

So far, the only serious programme to have been mounted is one by ten countries in north and west Europe, under the auspices of the OECD, to measure concentrations of sulphur dioxide. This programme began in July 1972. Some 40 monitoring stations measure daily sulphur dioxide and particulate sulphur in the air and the acidity and sulphate content in rain. The Norwegian Institute for Air Research is acting as the data centre for this research. In addition to this programme, the British Meteorological Office and the Warren Spring Laboratory of the Department of Industry are sampling the sulphur dioxide content of the atmosphere off the east coast of Britain by regular aircraft flights. A programme of research into the importance of the atmosphere as a pathway is being carried out under the auspices of the United Kingdom Government fisheries laboratories (MAFF and DAFS) in which metals are to be evaluated and to which organohalogen compounds are to be added.

This international investigation is largely in response to the Swedish complaint, mentioned above, that sulphur dioxide from north-west and central Europe acidifies their rain, causing lakes and soil in parts of Sweden to become substantially more acid. Sweden argued powerfully at the 1972 UN Conference on the Human Environment that emissions into the atmosphere should be subject to international control on this account. However, the results of the recent surveys indicate that a considerable fraction of sulphur dioxide emissions from Britain has been deposited or converted to sulphate by the time it passes the east coast. If, as now seems likely, acidified rain and sulphate deposition is largely confined to areas close to the point of emission, controls are largely a matter for national policy rather than international agreement. Deposition of sulphates and oxides of sulphurs into the sea are, as far as is known, of little present consequence since, unlike the lakes and soils of Sweden, the sea is strongly buffered and can readily neutralize such additions.

The same is not necessarily true, unfortunately, of other aerial pollutants which may be entering the North Sea in considerable quantities. An international investigation of one type of polluting aerial fall-out has been embarked on and it is vital that comparable studies be made of others which may be potentially more damaging in the marine environment.

The NATO Science Committee Conference on the North Sea drew attention to the fact that the North Sea provided an accessible laboratory which had some of the features of the global oceanic situation and was

[47] T. J. Chow, K. W. Bruland, K. Bertine, A. Soutar, M. Koide and E. D. Goldberg, "Lead pollution records in Southern California coastal sediments", *Science*, Vol. 181, pp. 551–552, 1973; A. Preston, "Heavy metals in British waters", *Nature*, Vol. 242, pp. 95–97, 1973.

ideal for observations and pilot studies of air-sea interactions.[48] Meteorological and oceanographic investigations are, of course, an integral part of any such programme.

4. Environmental Effects

The effects of the environmental additions listed above will, in this report, be considered in terms of how they increase or diminish the value of other resources in the North Sea. Adding materials to the sea or using the sea's capacity to dilute, disperse or oxidize mankind's waste products may be considered as a legitimate use of the marine environment. Such a use carries with it the responsibility for careful and adequate control. Materials added should be confined to those which the sea is capable of "metabolizing". Only in exceptional cases should substances be added at a rate greater than that at which they can be oxidized or dispersed without adverse effects, even if there is a resulting beneficial effect on other resources, e.g. when controlled fertilization improves the yield of fish. More frequent or heavier additions, however, will bring about further changes as the ecosystem adapts to the excess; such changes are frequently undesirable and diminish the value of the other resources. In Chapter III the deliberate or accidental addition of wastes will be considered in terms of its effects on other resources.

---

[48] "North Sea Science", Recommendations of NATO Science Committee Conference, Aviemore, Scotland, 15–20 November 1971.

II
The Sea and Coastline as a Supporting Medium

1. Marine Transport and Navigation

(a) Introduction

Since the beginning of the century the world's merchant fleet has grown three times in number and twelve times in tonnage. In 1973 Lloyd's Register of Shipping listed nearly 60,000 steam and motor ships of 100 gross tons and over, and in recent years the average annual growth of tonnage has exceeded eight per cent. (See Table 6 and figs. B, C and D.) If this rate of growth continues the total tonnage will double by the end of the decade. However, this growth has not been uniform in all sectors. There has been a marked decline in passenger services, with the exception of short-distance ferry boats which are prospering, whereas increasing amounts of cargo are now moved by sea. Between 1960 and 1972 the amount of international cargo transported by sea more than doubled from 1,110 million metric tons to 2,860 million metric tons. The greatest proportion of the cargo trade is now accounted for by tankers.[1] Although tankers represent less than half the tonnage of the world fleet, they carried nearly 60 per cent of world trade in 1972.

The increased demand for cargo space has resulted in an increase in the size and efficiency of ships and also in improvements to port facilities to allow more intensive use of cargo vessels. Many changes have been made with the aim of improving the speed of cargo handling and thus reducing the time spent idle in port. For example, tankers now have a very rapid turn-round at their terminals. Another important change has been the switch to unitized cargo, typified by the use of containers. Other developments along these lines include the roll-on/roll-off ship and the LASH (lighter aboard ship) system in which a mother ship lifts aboard and transports loaded barges, exchanging them for others, either en route or at the final destination.

---

[1] The main reason is that tankers spend much less time in port than other forms of cargo transport and carry more cargo per unit ton of displacement.

TABLE 6

1. Displacement of Merchant Fleets*
(at 30 June each year)

Year	World Total (million gross registered tons)	Average Displacement ('000 gross registered tons)
1948	80.3	2.74
1949	82.6	2.73
1950	84.6	2.74
1951	87.2	2.79
1952	90.2	2.87
1953	93.4	2.94
1954	97.4	3.01
1955	100.6	3.10
1956	105.2	3.18
1957	110.3	3.26
1958	118.0	3.35
1959	124.9	3.45
1960	129.8	3.58
1961	135.9	3.60
1962	140.0	3.62
1963	145.9	3.69
1964	153.0	3.74
1965	160.4	3.83
1966	171.1	3.98
1967	182.1	4.10
1968	194.2	4.09
1969	211.7	4.21
1970	227.5	4.34
1971	247.2	4.49
1972	268.3	4.67
1973	289.9	4.86

2. Number of Large Oil Tankers and Bulk Carriers

Year	Number over 50,000 g.r.t.	Number over 100,000 g.r.t.
(a) *Oil Tankers*		
1964	34	0
1965	44	0
1966	67	0
1967	105	0
1968	163	12
1969	231	51
1970	316	98
1971	406	162
1972	431	239
1973	506	322
(b) *Ore and Bulk Carriers*		
1964	0	0
1965	0	0
1966	0	0
1967	9	0
1968	23	0
1969	49	0
1970	75	0
1971	121	2

* Figures refer to steam and motor vessels of more than 100 gross tons, excluding ships trading on the Caspian Sea.

Source: Lloyd's Register of Shipping (London).

SEA AND COASTLINE AS A SUPPORTING MEDIUM

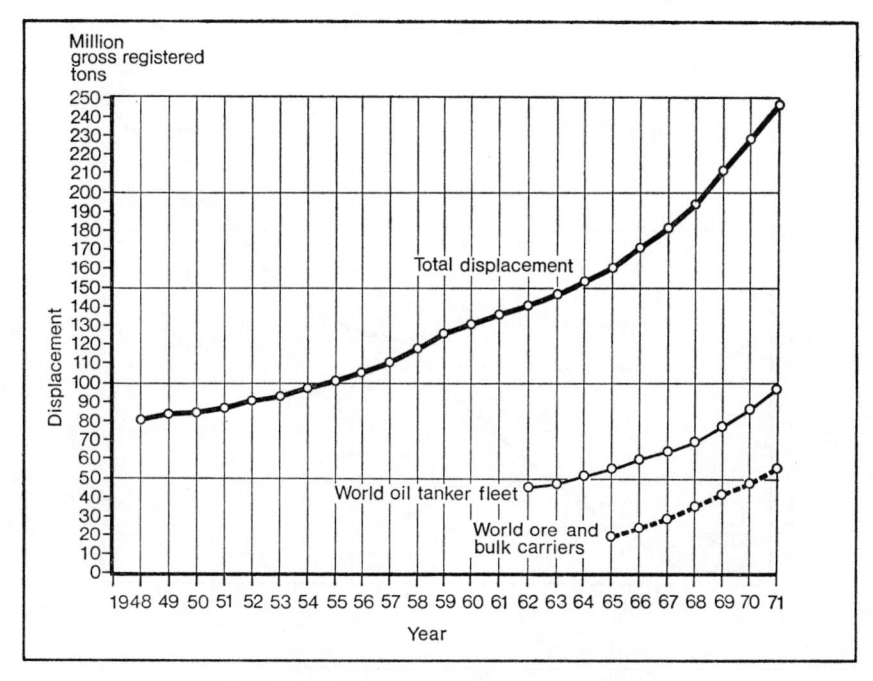

Fig. B: Displacement of merchant fleets.

With the increased traffic on the world's seaways and the attendant increase in accidents and collisions, it is necessary to improve navigation and this may, in turn, entail some curtailment of the traditional freedom of the sea. The accuracy of position-fixing systems using radio waves, satellites and internal devices has increased dramatically, but the equipment is often costly. Accurate charts are indispensable. Unfortunately, the increased number of ships, and their greater average speed due to economic pressures, combine to produce convergence areas of high density traffic – in narrow straits and in the approaches to large ports and off-shore oil and gas fields. Traffic separation schemes have been evolved to prevent accidents in these congested areas. About 60 such schemes have been developed by the Inter-Governmental Maritime Consultative Organization (IMCO). In 1971 the 1960 Convention for the Safety of Life at Sea was amended to make them mandatory.[2]

(b) North Sea Traffic and Trade

Figures are not available on the amount of shipping traffic in the North Sea. There is even some discrepancy in estimates of the vessels passing through the Dover Strait, the most important route to North Sea ports.

[2] See chapter III, Part A, para. 67.

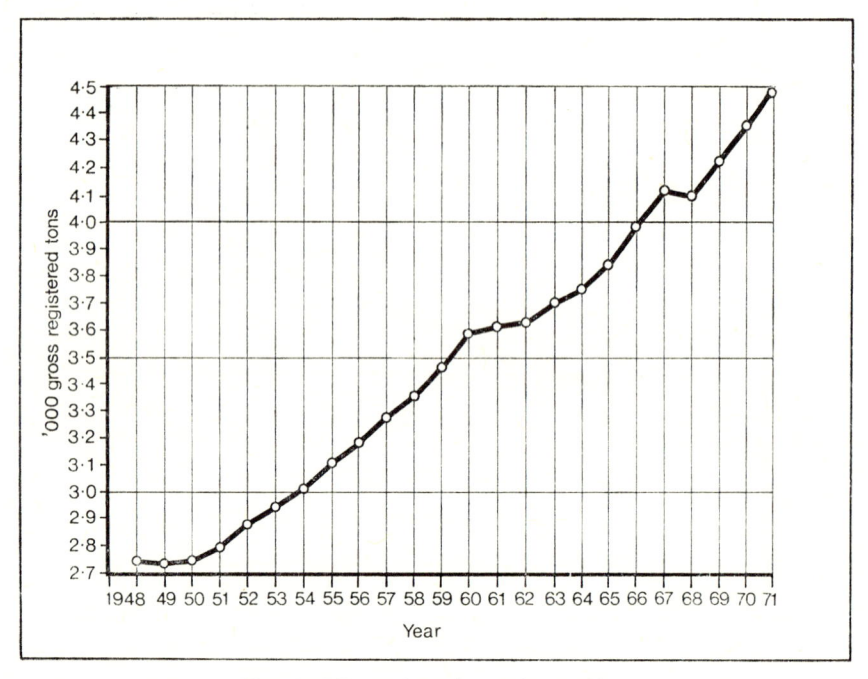

Fig. C: Mean size of merchant ships.

Recent surveys indicate a figure of 300 ships per day. Accurate estimates are made difficult by the fact that, unlike many countries, the United Kingdom, Belgium, Denmark, the Netherlands and Norway do not reserve their coastal trade to ships of the national flag and, of course, as a major area of commerce Europe receives deep-sea vessels from countries all over the world. However, no grounds exist for contradicting the widely held belief that this is one of the busiest sea areas in the world. About a third of the world's gross tonnage is registered in the countries (including France) that border on the North Sea. In 1972 Europe (including the U.S.S.R.) accounted for 35 per cent of the world's sea-borne international dry cargo trade (by weight) compared with North America's 19 per cent, Asia's 24 per cent, South America's 9 per cent, Africa's 7 per cent and Oceania's 6 per cent.[3] Certainly Western European fleets and ports reflect the changes and developments outlined in the introduction.

The trend towards even larger ships (see fig. D), has resulted in a greater need for ports nearer deep water. Already many upstream dock complexes are closing or contracting and new docks are being built elsewhere. In the Port of London, for example, the upper reaches are being abandoned in favour of Tilbury which is being expanded as a

[3] United Nations, *Statistical Yearbook 1973*.

SEA AND COASTLINE AS A SUPPORTING MEDIUM

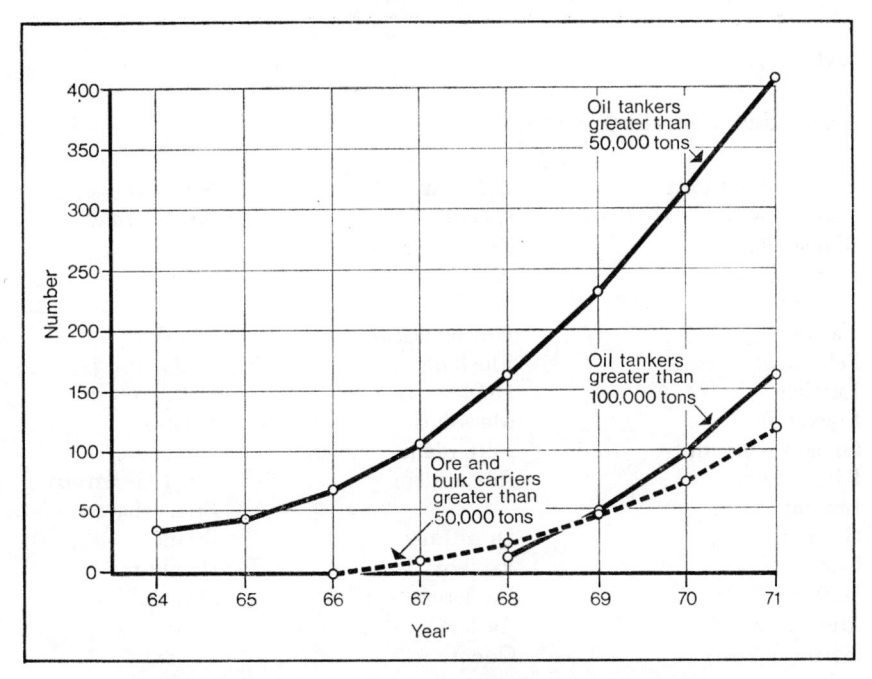

Fig. D: Number of large oil tankers and bulk carriers.

container and bulk cargo port as well as for general cargo. Ports elsewhere on the North Sea have also had to invest considerable sums of money to provide deep berths. For example, since the war the Port of Amsterdam has spent some £40 million on enlarging and deepening the North Sea Canal, the main entry to the Port. Even so, it is unlikely that Amsterdam or any major port in Europe, such as Europoort–Rotterdam, Zeebrugge or Dunkirk, will be able to accommodate the largest oil tankers. These tankers will need to use terminals off-shore. At present, most British tanker terminals cannot handle fully laden 250,000 d.w.t. ships while a third of world tanker capacity is composed of ships greater than 200,000 d.w.t. The Humber can take ships of 250,000 d.w.t. whereas the English Channel is limited to 200,000 d.w.t. A two-tier system is in use whereby oil is delivered to a deep water terminal (e.g. Bantry, Milford Haven) and then distributed to ports (Europoort, Zeebrugge) using smaller tankers.

Large container ships also require deep ports and channels, but unit load systems efficiency is determined by the efficiency of port handling services. Table 7 (based on an OECD report[4]) lists North Sea container ports.

[4] *Developments and Problems of Seaborne Container Transport, 1970*, OECD, 1971.

TABLE 7

North Sea Container Ports.

United Kingdom	**Belgium**	**Norway**
(East Coast)	Ostend	Kristiansand
Whitstable	Zeebrugge	Brevik
Rochester	Antwerp	Oslo
Tilbury		
Harwich	**Netherlands**	**Sweden**
Felixstowe	Flushing	Gothenburg
Ipswich	Hook	Helsingborg
Lowestoft	Maassluis	Malmö
Great Yarmouth	Rotterdam	
King's Lynn	Amsterdam	**West Germany**
Immingham		Bremerhaven
Gunnes	**Denmark**	Bremen
Goole	Esbjerg	Hamburg
Hull	Fredericia	Lübeck
Middlesbrough	Aarhus	Kiel
Hartlepool	Odense	
Leith	Copenhagen	
Grangemouth	Hirtshals	

N.B. Lists do not include the Swedish ports of Norrköping, Oxelosund, Stockholm and Gävle, or Finnish, Soviet, Polish and East German ports on the Baltic.

In many of these ports there have recently been increases in annual throughput of between 50 per cent and 100 per cent, but competition between them is growing and creating problems. To maximize the economies of containerization, and to justify the high speed and high capital investment of container ships, port calls should theoretically be kept to a minimum. Competition of a possibly self-defeating nature therefore becomes almost inevitable when several ports in a region are equipped to handle high volumes of container traffic.

Some of these ports provide facilities for European ferry services. In Europe the carriage of passengers on short sea routes has expanded significantly in recent years. Between 1958 and 1968 the numbers carried between the United Kingdom and the Republic of Ireland, the Continent and Mediterranean Sea area increased by over half to nearly 9 million, in spite of the spectacular growth in air travel. The number of accompanied cars carried by sea has been increasing even more rapidly and now exceeds

SEA AND COASTLINE AS A SUPPORTING MEDIUM

one million per year.[5] In fact, the number of cars transported by air has declined as more efficient facilities have been introduced on sea routes, including the introduction of the SRN-4 type hovercraft capable of carrying 250 passengers and 30 cars between the United Kingdom and the Continent in a third of the time taken by the conventional car ferries.

The increase in size of ships, particularly oil tankers (see fig. D), has given a new urgency to accident prevention. One tenth of all accidents at sea occur in the North Sea and its approaches, and half the world's collisions take place between Dover and the Elbe. The primary cause of all accidents at sea is human failure of judgement or failure to obey rules or recommendations aimed at ensuring safety for all ships. In 90 per cent of collisions in the Dover Strait where actions were known, the International Regulations for Preventing Collisions at Sea[6] appear to have been contravened. In the final analysis, many of these human failures can be traced back to a lack of training, generally of the crews of ships of countries that do not exercise a strict control on the certification of ships' officers. Thus Liberia, a flag-of-convenience country, with the largest fleet in the world, has a very bad accident record. The United Kingdom, which has the third largest fleet, has a relatively good record. However, as a result of recent events, in particular a series of accidents in the Channel,[7] the Liberian authorities are beginning to show concern about the control of their essentially foreign fleet.

In association with the International Labour Office, IMCO has a joint committee on training which has, amongst other things, the task of introducing minimum standards for training and certification. In addition, IMCO has agreed to a number of major extensions and improvements to the separation schemes in the English Channel and the southern North Sea. The changes, which came into effect from 3 April 1972, can be summarized as follows:

(i) the existing schemes for the Dover Strait and southern North Sea have been extended so that they form a continuous system from the Greenwich Meridian to the North Hinder at a longitude of approximately 2°45′ E;

(ii) the English Inshore Zone has been widened by up to one nautical mile between Dungeness and the South Foreland. The French Inshore Zone has also been widened off Cap Gris Nez. These inshore zones are intended for coastal shipping and vessels may travel in either direction;

---

[5] *Report of the Committee of Inquiry into Shipping* (Cmnd. 4337), HMSO, 1970.
[6] See chapter IV, paras. 66 and 67.
[7] In January and February 1971 three ships were sunk, the third one because it ignored wreck buoys and a light-ship indicating the danger area.

(iii) separation zones have been introduced between the English Inshore Zone and the westbound lane, from off Folkestone to the Greenwich Meridian; between the traffic lanes for westbound and eastbound vessels; and, finally, between the French Inshore Zone and the eastbound lane, from off north of Boulogne to the Greenwich Meridian;

(iv) the eastbound lane has been widened on its southerly side between Les Ridens and the Greenwich Meridian;

(v) a deep-draught route has been introduced north-west of the Sandettie Bank for use by vessels bound for North European ports which need deeper water than is available on the south side of the bank.

The advent of the large deep-draught ship has made collision and stranding more difficult to prevent. These ships are difficult to halt while their deep draught limits the ability to take avoiding action in narrow sea lanes. It also becomes necessary to know accurately the minimum depth at all points. Particularly in the shallow North Sea Channel, variations occur due to fluctuations in predicted tide levels and in the seabed itself due to sand waves. In the Southern Bight (depth about 30 metres) sand waves are usually less than 6 metres high; but some are 10 metres. An Anglo-Dutch team is at present in operation to produce a survey showing minimum depths at every point. In other words, safe margins of bottom clearance based on charts and tidal predictions can be eroded to the point of disaster by conditions which are quite beyond the present ability of either tanker operators, or hydrographers who provide the information, to foresee. (See Section 4 (b).) There are, unfortunately, strong commercial pressures for accepting minimum clearances from the seabed: an extra foot of draught on a modern tanker means another £25,000 a year to the oil company.

The growth in port traffic and the increases in size and draught of ships has stimulated dredging activities, both capital dredging (the creation of new channels and berths) and maintenance dredging (maintaining these facilities at or near their design depth). Maintenance dredging involves the removal of recently deposited material. Capital dredging, on the other hand, generally involves the removal of older seabed deposits ranging from sands and fairly soft clays through mudstones, marls and sandstones to hard rock. In the United Kingdom, the largest capital dredging projects up to the time of writing were on the River Tees (£5.3 million over $2\frac{1}{2}$ years) and in Milford Haven (about £7.5 million over 3 years). Elsewhere in the North Sea there are plans to build an outer port to Amsterdam at Ijmuiden, and the development of Europoort–Rotterdam and the associated Maasvlakte are continuing. The latter two projects have already cost an estimated £3,000 million. The total area of land reclaimed for port-based industrial development in Rotterdam since 1947 amounts to nearly 20,000 acres, involving the dredging of some 400 million cubic yards of material. The French also have plans for the development of Dunkirk.

Once again, strong economic pressures exist to accept the minimum depth for approach channels and hence minimum under-keel clearance. In 1970 the cost of capital dredging for an extra foot depth over a length of one mile and width of 1,000 feet could range from between £50,000 in soft material through £200,000 in, say, a hard claystone to perhaps £2 million in hard rock.[8] In addition, material would also have to be removed from the sides of the channel to maintain a stable profile, involving 50 per cent or more dredging. Some savings are possible using precision position-fixing systems to cover approach channels: the installation of Decca Hi-fix, for example, enabled a saving of 500 feet in width of the 8½-mile-long entrance channel to Europoort. With the present trends in shipping, however, the demand for capital and maintenance dredging is likely to continue in order to accommodate large vessels with draughts of 100 feet or more.

(c) Trends in Development

The changes already apparent in shipping are likely to continue altering the pattern of North Sea traffic and trade. The closer political and commercial association of the United Kingdom with continental Europe is likely to stimulate coastal and short sea trade as well as lead to increased competition between major ports for the role of "gateways" into Europe. These events will take place in the context of a world trade situation in which the weight of goods traded internationally will continue to grow, perhaps to well over three times its present level by the end of the century.[9]

Eventually, constraints of a purely physical nature are likely to intervene: the shallowness of the southern North Sea must set a limit, even allowing for some capital dredging, to the size of vessels capable of entering these waters. This will encourage new port and terminal developments in the northern North Sea. Feasibility studies have been completed of the possibilities of deepening the approach channel to the Humber so that it could handle bulk carriers of 250,000 tons drawing 66 feet of water. The cost of dredging 10½ miles of the 18-mile approach from Spurn Point was estimated in 1972 at about £2 million. Eventually, 500,000 d.w.t. oil tankers may come to northern parts taking a route around Scotland.

The technological changes now so evident in both shipping and ports are leading to increased productivity and thus reductions in the real cost of transport; although the rocketing price of oil since 1971 has more than offset this increased productivity. Between 1971 and the end of 1974 the payment to host governments on a barrel of crude oil rose from about

[8] Committee of Marine Technology, *Report on a Survey of Dredging Technology* (CMT Publication No. 1), 1970.
[9] *Report of the Committee of Inquiry into Shipping* (Cmnd. 4337), HMSO, 1970.

U.S. $1.25 (a price which had been static for some time) to nearly $10. The basic trend towards increased automation and specialization is, on present showing, likely to continue. However, the advantages of this technological revolution can be secured only as long as ships can operate safely and unimpeded. The tremendous unit capital investment often means that critical factors, such as operating depths or port facilities, can exert a basic influence on the economic viability of vessel operations, productivity being raised at the expense of versatility. As a result, modern fleets require greater support facilities (see section 4) than in the past. Thus the future pattern of development may well be determined, at least as far as the North Sea is concerned, by advances in support activities such as hydrographic surveying and meteorological services.

The traffic routeing scheme in the Channel and southern approaches to the North Sea provides an example of another important trend – the increasing control and policing of shipping. At the regional level, this control will involve demarcating routes across the North Sea and will no doubt include areas where gas and oil production rigs are installed. At a local level, it will involve the extension of pilotage services to govern entry into ports and harbours.[10] Already there is a trend towards a system more akin to airspace control than traditional navigation with ships being "talked in" to the port along a channel covered by complicated position-fixing equipment and control radar. It is not impossible that eventually the equivalent of a "blind-landing" system will be devised which will remove all responsibility for approach and berthing procedures from the bridge of the ship. Investigations of the causes of collisions and shipping accidents certainly provide support for this development since, as already stressed, human factors such as negligence or simple carelessness, rather than instrument failure or faults in the vessels themselves, are the chief causes of accidents.

[10] According to a recent United Kingdom Report (*Safety in British Ports*, Conservative Central Office, August 1974), the arrangements for ships entering or leaving ports need considerable improvement; ships can enter or leave ports without prior notice and without a pilot. "In general any ship is allowed to arrive without giving any notice of its arrival; unless a pilot is ready waiting for it, it is allowed to enter port without one. It may use whatever channel it pleases, so long as it keeps to the starboard side (if it can). When it leaves it may do so as soon as it is ready, again without warning." Most ships do, of course, both give prior warning and take a pilot. It is recommended, *inter alia*, that there should be a Port Traffic Bill requiring all ships of more than 500 tons to carry electronic equipment and to contact the Port authority when entering or leaving. Port authorities would be required to draft strict regulations covering traffic control in their area. Masters and owners of ships would subsequently be liable to fines of from £1,000 to £10,000 and a year in prison should they be caught breaking the regulations. There is also need to bring up to date the organization of shipping pilots. The Report adds "The dangers from the mammoth vessels with potentially vicious cargoes are indeed immense".

2. Marine Installations

(a) Petroleum and Natural Gas

In recent years as many as 24 drilling rigs have been operating in the North Sea. These rigs are involved in exploratory drilling for new petroleum and gas reservoirs, evaluating discoveries or drilling production boreholes. As yet, comparatively few companies are involved in the preparation of production platforms. By the end of 1974 four oil platforms had been erected in the British sector. In the southern sector 44 gas platforms were operational and 13 more under construction. The Frigg field had a further four platforms but these are 30 times as large as those in the southern sector. Constructing rigs and platforms provides an engineering challenge in the difficult conditions of the northern North Sea.

All types of rig are still to be found around the world. About half of the world's drilling rigs are of the jack-up type, i.e. the legs of the drilling platform can be jacked up to enable it to be moved, but for deep-water drilling either semi-submersibles or drilling ships are generally used. On the whole the semi-submersible, because of its greater stability, has been favoured – 35 rigs of this type were on order in September 1972. By October 1974 there were 161 off-shore drilling rigs on order; of these 75 were semi-submersibles, 50 jack-up units and 36 drill-ships. The latter are gaining ground as is shown by the figures for orders between January and October 1974, i.e. jack-ups and semi-submersibles total 25 each and drill-ships number 29. The semi-submersibles tend to be large and expensive: the largest costs between £15 million and £25 million to build and in the region of £20,000 to £25,000 a day to hire. They can operate in depths of up to 500 metres, although 200 metres is more common. The record for deep drilling is held by a drilling ship, the *Glomar Challenger*, which is taking part in the Deep Sea Drilling Project (part of the U.S. National Science Foundation's JOIDES Program). *Glomar Challenger* has worked in 3,710 metres of water and has found traces of oil at a depth of 4,000 metres of water in the Gulf of Mexico.

Experience gained in an area where wind speeds can exceed 100 m.p.h. and wave heights in excess of 30 feet are to be expected, resulting in loss of the rigs *Sea Gem* and *Ocean Prince*, has led to the production of "second generation" semi-submersibles with improved clearance from the surface of the sea as the search moves northwards. These structures have some 20,000 tons displacement as against STAFLO's 12,000 tons. For example, there is now a form of self-propelling semi-submersible rig destined for use in the North Sea, the *Ocean Victory*.

Independence from the seafloor presents the semi-submersible and the drilling ship with problems of maintaining station. The flexibility of the drilling pipe allows some leeway, but this is generally limited to about 5 per cent of the length of the pipe in the water in any one direction. Movement in the vertical plane must also be restricted; otherwise drilling has to be abandoned in anything but the calmest weather. Various systems exist for anchoring semi-submersibles to the seafloor. These are usually supplemented by computer-controlled devices such as powered winches for the moorings, or thrusters in the submerged floats (one of the latest rigs has four 1,600 h.p. thrusters). Dynamic positioning reaches its peak in the drilling ship. The *Glomar Challenger* lowers a sonar beacon at the drilling site. The signals from this are picked up by three hydrophones projecting below the ship's hull and the information is fed into a shipboard computer which, in turn, controls two pairs of thrusters fore and aft and the vessel's two main propellers to maintain station. The need for such complicated equipment has encouraged the maximum development of the jack-up rig, the latest version of which, the *Zapata Nordic*, can drill in up to 100 metres of water.

Once exploratory and evaluation drilling are completed, a rig moves on to a new site either under its own power, in the case of drilling ships and the latest types of semi-submersible, or under tow. The next phase in the development of an oil or gas field is the installation of a drilling and production platform or platforms. So far, the only large permanently fixed production platforms in the North Sea are those in the large southern gas fields. Typical of these are the Shell/Esso Leman Field drilling and production platforms.[11] The gas is fed from the production platform to the onshore terminal at Bacton by pipeline (see section 2 (b)).

Existing platforms have been installed in shallow waters up to 50 metres deep, a depth which presents few problems compared with the depths of 130 metres or more found in the northern North Sea. For example, *Graythorpe I* and *Highland I*, the BP platforms in the Forties Field, stand approximately 240 metres from the seabed to the tip of their drilling masts and are fixed in water 140 metres deep. Shell and Esso have considered several types of structure for Scottish waters.[12] Designs in hand include a template type of platform and a "tower" structure.

The hazardous environment of the North Sea and the tremendous costs and difficulties of installing fixed platforms in deep waters have led oil companies to consider the possibilities of undersea production systems. According to a recent comparative study,[13] underwater systems have considerable economic as well as practical value for oil production in deep waters and for exploiting small peripheral accumulations. Several systems

[11] K. H. Davison, "The Leman Field – from Discovery to Production", *World Petroleum*, November 1968.
[12] George Williams, "Technology of Operating in the North Sea", in U.K. Offshore Exploration supplement, *Financial Times*, 22 May 1972.
[13] E. L. Dougherty, R. D. Goodknight, R. B. Oldaker, "A Comparative Study of the Economics of a Subsea and Platform Oil Producing System", *Proceedings of Oceanology International, 72*, 1972.

are under study and at least three are undergoing trials. At its simplest level, a subsea system consists of underwater well-heads which are completed from the surface, possibly with diver assistance. At their highest technical level, they involve a large underwater chamber or base with a "shirt sleeve" environment – in effect an underwater production platform. The largest group in the field is Subsea Equipment Associates Limited (SEAL) which has two subsea systems under development.[14] The first phase in an operational trial of one system devised by Lockheed, placing a well-head collar on the seafloor, began in 1972 in 126 metres of water off Louisiana. Major refinements would be necessary to enable the system to work in the stormy waters of the North Sea; and the necessary modifications are being planned.

The possibility of oil's escaping from an off-shore well clearly must be guarded against. On-shore, a "blow-out preventer", a special valve, is inserted into the hole which closes automatically if there is a sudden increase in pressure of oil or drilling fluid coming to the surface. In off-shore works there are several such valves, so that if a ship were to collide with a drill rig and the whole rig be carried away, the valve would close and no oil would escape. Of the thousands of holes drilled off-shore in the world, only a handful have given rise to spillages.

(b) Pipelines and Storage

Undersea pipelines link many off-shore oil and gas fields around the world to distribution facilities ashore. In recent years a spectacular increase has occurred as a result of the expansion of off-shore exploitation and, to a lesser extent, to provide tankers with facilities for loading and discharging crude oil and other materials where port facilities are lacking or navigational channels are too shallow for large bulk carriers. The need for off-shore storage facilities combined with tanker mooring buoys is also growing, once again because of the deep draughts of modern tankers, but also because off-shore production is moving further and further from the shore and into deep waters. The first seabed storage tank, with a 500,000 barrel capacity, was installed in the Persian Gulf off Dubai in 1969. Now the North Sea has become the site for a massive concrete storage tank with a one million barrel capacity standing in 75 metres of seawater in the Ekofisk oilfield. This latest tank is probably more accurately described as a man-made concrete island since, unlike that in the Persian Gulf, it is approximately 90 metres in height and 92 metres in diameter. It consists of a

[14] The original parent companies of SEAL were British Petroleum, Compagnie Française de Pétroles, Westinghouse Electric Corporation and Groupe DEEP (a group of 14 engineering companies). In 1971, SEAL bought all North American Rockwell rights to a subsea production system developed by Mobil Oil and North American Rockwell, and Mobil became a partner. Other companies have also become associated with SEAL's development programmes.

group of nine cylindrical storage vessels surrounded by a nearly circular wall to withstand the swells of the North Sea. It will be used not only as a storage vessel but also as a platform for production equipment, etc. when oil-gas pipelines come into operation.

The first major pipeline was laid in the North Sea in 1966 to carry natural gas from BP's West Sole Field to a processing plant about 40 nautical miles away near Easington on the Yorkshire coast. The line, which is 16 inches in diameter, was laid in an average water depth of 26 metres. The maximum depth encountered was 35 metres. Others quickly followed: Shell/Esso's 30-inch diameter line (with a 4-inch methanol line strapped piggy-back fashion to it) from Complex A in the Leman Field to Bacton, Norfolk, 30 nautical miles away, in 1967; the Phillips/Arpet Line from Hewett to Bacton in 1968; and Amoco/Gas Council's line from the Leman Field to Bacton, also in 1968. These formed main trunk-lines to which smaller diameter pipelines were constructed from other production platforms. During the 1970–71 winter the first oil pipelines were laid in the North Sea in the Phillips Ekofisk Field. These lines, at a depth of 80 metres of water (twice the depth of previous pipelines), brought oil from four subsea well-head completion systems to two single buoy moorings for tankers. Much longer pipelines to bring the oil and gas to the shore in West Germany and the United Kingdom are due to be built. Plans are under consideration to bring Norwegian oil to Teesside (see map in Appendix III).

In general, pipelines have considerable advantages over tankers, particularly in the North Sea. They are not affected by surface congestion or climatic conditions. They follow a relatively straight route. They are capable of operating continuously and their high degree of remote operation and automation keep operating costs to a minimum. Design methods for submarine lines do not differ greatly from those for use on land as regards determining the most economic diameter, the safe working pressure, grade of steel pipe and flow conditions inside the line. However, submarine lines are much more difficult to construct, inspect and repair. They are therefore three to five times as expensive to build as comparable land lines. Like land lines, the North Sea pipelines are trenched into the seabed. As far as possible they are laid in areas where there is a "static environment", that is where there is no movement of unconsolidated sediments on the seabed. They are laid on average about 2.3 metres deep to avoid damage from ships' anchors. Even so, they have not in the past escaped damage: the Shell/Esso line was dented by a deep-draught vessel passing only about 130 metres off the Bacton shore approach; and the Amoco/Gas Council line was holed some 15 miles from shore, apparently by a ship's anchor, just after completion.

Experience over six years of operations in the North Sea has led to advances in pipelaying techniques and technology, for example to the stage of designing a large pipe-laying barge for deep-water work. One particular problem, now overcome by a dredger built specifically for the North Sea, was the hard boulder clay found in some areas. This North Sea dredge has more than twice the hydraulic power possessed by those used in the Gulf of Mexico. Elsewhere mobile sand ridges (submarine sand dunes) created serious difficulties. The practice now is to use a modified dredger to smooth the proposed route of the pipeline just prior to laying. Other developments include advances in automatic welding, a remote controlled X-ray machine that travels inside the pipe, improved dredging techniques which enable only a narrow trench to be made beneath the pipe, and in general, the adaptation of gear and techniques to the rigorous conditions of the North Sea.

(c) Trends in Development

The story of the development of the North Sea resources is one of increasing difficulties and dangers for both explorer and exploiter. As production moves from the comparatively sheltered southern coastal gas fields to the oil fields of the northern North Sea and perhaps eventually to the open Atlantic, existing technology becomes increasingly inadequate. The northern North Sea has therefore become a trial area for advanced marine technology. It is here that commercial rather than scientific deep drilling is taking place; where deep pipelines will be laid; and where sub-sea completion systems of the most advanced kind will probably be in demand. Islands of an unprecedented size, each with a complete community of people perhaps living out an appreciable part of their working life on them, may be built. One is now being considered for the shallow southern North Sea off the Dutch coast. Here solidly built-up multi-purpose artificial islands are projected, ranging from 50 to 1,000 hectares in area. These could be utilized for extensive oil installations, power and chemical plants, and possibly airports. There is equally no reason why they should not be built for amenity or residential purposes. Given present technology, the building of such islands would take, it is estimated, from 4 to 14 years, depending on size. One thing that seems certain is that, once the problems of the northern North Sea and North Atlantic have been conquered, few off-shore areas cannot then be exploited.

The immediate developments in the northern North Sea will centre on major oil fields that have been discovered recently (see Appendix III). BP is already well advanced with its £360 million programme to develop the Forties Field, and a pipeline to Cruden Bay is being laid. The Montrose Field may be linked to this pipeline. Most of the other large fields will eventually be connected to the land by pipelines. Small fields or those far out to sea are likely to be serviced by tankers. In some cases production may be taken initially by tankers until a pipeline is installed as is the case with the Norwegian Ekofisk Field. For example, Shell/Esso plans to start production at the Brent Field using tankers but eventually a pipeline to south Shetland will probably be laid. The decision *vis-à-vis* tankers and pipelines will be very much influenced by the results of current exploratory drilling in promising areas.

In the long term much will depend upon advances in technology for deep-water activities. Conventional pipe-laying technology is probably capable of being developed to work in depths down to 500 feet in North Sea conditions. Beyond this depth a new generation of equipment and methods will be required. It may be that beyond these depths subsea production systems and underwater storage will come into their own. Subsea production systems are also likely to figure prominently in small peripheral fields or areas where weather conditions are extreme. Elsewhere conventional production platforms can probably hold their own. However, with much of the exploratory work still to be done, it is difficult to envisage the future pattern of development. One point is clear: the ultimate brake on exploitation will arise from economic factors rather than the limits of production systems or exploratory drilling technology.

3. Coastal Development

(a) Coastal Construction and Engineering

Throughout the world, populations have tended to move towards, and to be increasingly concentrated in, coastal areas. In the United States of America, for example, about half of the population lives within 100 miles of the coast and 29 per cent within a 50-mile wide coastal belt. Until recently, this trend has not been apparent in countries bordering on the North Sea, partly because of the ease of access in the United Kingdom, as a result of its geographical shape, and the existence of major rivers, in particular the Rhine, in Western Europe. The only real exception to this has been the Netherlands where the pressure for land, coupled with a fear of inundation by the sea, has prompted unique reclamation of salt marsh and shallow sea areas. In the process, maritime activities have been enhanced by the creation of deep-water berths and channels during the dredging for landfill. Nevertheless, apart from sparsely populated Norway, demographic maps of the North Sea countries do show generally high densities of population in coastal areas and these are apparently increasing.

Undoubtedly, the exploitation of North Sea oil and gas is helping to stimulate settlement in coastal areas, but many other factors are probably involved: the desirability of siting many industrial complexes near major ports or coastal power stations; the desire to live, or at least holiday, away from traditional inland industrial conurbations; the increased leisure time and money available for aquatic pastimes; the social pressures against further deterioration of inland environments; and simply the fact that the coast offers the possibility of virtually unrestricted development on the seaward side. This movement towards the coast and sea is further assisted by advances in dredging and the design of off-shore structures (both floating and those supported from the seabed) which enable off-shore airports, power stations and refineries, and possibly one day floating cities, to be considered as outlined above.

(b) Domestic and Amenity Development

The increasing concentration of domestic dwellings, temporary holiday homes, camp-sites and commercial and state-controlled leisure centres along the coast is something that can be seen by the most casual observer. Yet these developments tend to remain un-analysed on anything but a local level. Coastal zone management, an activity that has come very much into vogue in the U.S.A., has been largely neglected in the United Kingdom and Western Europe. Developments, with the exception of major national projects, tend to be considered at a local level. Thus the value of recreation in and around the North Sea is not known in either monetary or social terms.

Recreational uses include sailing, swimming, skin diving, sports-fishing, water-skiing, scuba-diving, speed-boating, sun-bathing, cruising, nature-watching and walking or driving through areas of scenic beauty. To accommodate the growing number of people wanting to live and to relax by the sea, property developments have mushroomed along the coasts. Originally, this expansion started with existing holiday spots, but now untouched areas are being invaded, partly as an overspill from crowded resorts and partly because of the deliberate policies of tourist boards and agencies. The trend is further encouraged by the increasing desire of people, disenchanted with existing resorts, to travel farther afield in search of "unspoiled" holiday and recreational places. The net result has been a gradual deterioration of the natural seascape, and some coastal environments, particularly salt marshes, are disappearing rapidly.

The threats to natural habitats and areas of scenic beauty have caused concern to naturalists, scientists and agencies, both private and governmental, with an interest in environmental matters. The result has been that some coastal areas have been made nature reserves or national parks. The United Kingdom has six such areas on its North Sea coast; Norway has one; Denmark has three; the Netherlands has five; and Belgium has two. In addition to these main reserves, a number of others are owned and managed by natural history societies and similar organizations. A particular problem is the conservation of extensive estuarine areas. There are only a few major ones in the North Sea – all of them important feeding and wintering grounds for wildfowl. All are undergoing development or reclamation on the assumption that the birds will go to one of the others.

However, as far as can be determined, the North Sea does lack one category of national park found elsewhere – an underwater marine park catering specifically for scuba divers or small submersibles. So far, protection of the North Sea environment tends to stop at low water mark and is concerned principally with preservation of coastal lands.

North Sea coastal areas have considerable innate protection, at least as far as holiday and amenity development is concerned, in the unreliable weather and coldness of the water. There is little doubt that the ease and, in recent years, cheapness of travel to the warm, sunny Mediterranean shores have slowed down the development of North Sea coastal areas. The Mediterranean has become the playground of Europe. Whether it will remain so is debatable as resorts become overcrowded, the sea polluted and holidays expensive. Moreover a brake is being put on further development. In 1971 nearly 26.8 million foreign residents visited Spain, in 1972 the total exceeded 32.5 million, and in 1973 passed 34.5 million. But the concentration of tourism round the Costa del Sol, the Costa Blanca and the Costa Brava is beginning to provoke an adverse reaction which may act as a brake on the growing tourist trade, the most important economic activity in Spain. The main causes of discontent are:

(i) The natural beauty of the coastline has been irreparably damaged by a frenzied and, to a large extent, uncontrolled building spree.

(ii) The millions of foreigners who "clog the roads, cover the beaches and jam the hotels, restaurants and cafés" are giving the Spaniards the feeling of being foreigners in their own country.

(iii) The industry is dependent on foreign tour operators who keep rates low and encourage a form of proletarian tourism; little is spent locally except marginally.

(iv) Spanish culture has virtually disappeared, replaced by every form of national "kitsch". The local fishermen have become barbers or waiters, wholly dependent on the tourist trade.[15]

On the credit side, the National Association of Hotels and Tourist Activities announced recently that tourism had earned U.S. $20,000 million in foreign currency in 20 years, covering the persistent trade deficit and paying for the import of capital equipment that has permitted rapid industrial development. In spite of this, there is a growing public feeling that the price paid is becoming too high.

This trend can be seen elsewhere and is gradually becoming widespread. For instance, as a result of the growing influx into London there have recently been suggestions that a tourist tax should be imposed. In the United Kingdom the impact of mass tourism upon resorts in western and south-eastern England are plain for all to see and must be paralleled

[15] Abstracted from a report in the *Herald Tribune*, Paris, 28 August 1973.

in the other countries of the European Community. Under these circumstances it is difficult to foresee to what extent air travel will continue its present expansion rate.

(c) Commercial and Industrial Development

Major industrial and commercial complexes are associated with North Sea ports and oil terminals (see 1 (b)). With oil production from the North Sea only just under way, further development is obviously taking place. It will centre mainly on existing complexes and refineries but new centres, particularly in the Shetland Islands, will probably be created if the promise of present exploration is fulfilled. The largest single off-shore construction programme at present under way in Europe is the Dutch Delta Plan. It represents the only true example of total environmental planned change.

The Netherlands has a long history of land reclamation. Originally the country occupied the delta of the Rivers Rhine, Maas and Scheldt – an area subject to frequent river flooding and inundation by the sea. The Dutch built dykes and made polders in their country as far back as the 10th century, but the great step forward in their battle against the North Sea came with the construction of the Barrier Dam (Afsluitdijk) which was completed on 28 May 1932. When, by about 1980, the reclamation work is finished, the Netherlands will have added 550,000 acres (about 10 per cent) to its arable land area. Not all of the Zuyder Zee will have been drained: a large freshwater lake, over 300,000 acres in extent, will remain as a reservoir providing water for domestic and industrial consumption as well as for agricultural use.

The United Kingdom has carried out studies of several similar but far less ambitious projects at Morecambe Bay, the Solway Firth and the Wash. Follow-up investigations have been carried out in Morecambe Bay but proposals for the Wash appear to be in abeyance.

In the future, the pressure on coastal and in-shore areas seems likely to increase. The expansion of the North Sea oil and gas industry, coupled with the increased size of ships, will help to ensure this. Other factors are likely to intrude, e.g. transport costs. Taking the Dutch example it is becoming increasingly attractive with the present cost of land to reclaim marginal areas and also to annex suitable bays and estuaries for freshwater storage. Sea-based storage of oil and liquefied natural gas is another real possibility for which precedents already exist. Finally, there are more remote possibilities such as the construction of enclosures for fish farms. Most of the experiments in fish farm engineering have taken place on the west coast of Scotland. So far, the enclosures have not involved any large permanent structures, with the exception of the fish pond at Ardtoe which involved the construction of two sea walls and a rockfill dam.[16]

[16] P. H. Milne, "Fish Farm Engineering", *Proceedings of Oceanology 72 Conference*, 1972.

4. Ocean Support Facilities

(a) Introduction

The multiple use of the North Sea demands numerous support services from charting to oceanographic forecasting. Throughout the preceding sections reference has been made to the extreme, and often dangerous, conditions confronting exploiters and users of this sea area. A detailed knowledge of these conditions is essential for both the design and construction of structures ranging from sea walls to production platforms. Already the example has been given of changes in rig specifications by classification societies as a result of improved oceanographic data. Mention has also been made of the dangers inherent in operating deep-draught vessels with only a few feet of clearance in an area where meteorological and oceanographic conditions can combine to produce unpredictable changes in depth. Therefore, this section reviews a miscellany of activities which help to make operations in the North Sea successful and, perhaps above all, safe.

It is difficult to place ocean support facilities or activities in any particular category. Many of them are as useful to oil companies as they are to shipping lines. These same services may also assist amenity use and recreation. Thus air-sea rescue activities can range from assisting bathers or yachtsmen in difficulties to air-lifting crews from a foundering or endangered drilling rig. However, for the purpose of this section a division has been attempted between those services of general use and those related to one specific use, even though the division is often an arbitrary one. These activities also represent an area where international co-operation can be seen to be in everybody's interest.

(b) General Services

(i) *Surveying and Charting*

The first stage in the preparation of a nautical chart is a hydrographic survey. The chart, which is the end product, is an essential part of the equipment for any maritime activity whether it be fishing, locating drilling rigs, laying pipelines or safe navigation. To a very great extent, the need for charts has been dependent on the draught of ships: when the greatest draught was not more than 20 feet, any depth greater than 60 feet or 10 fathoms could be considered "safe" and the areas that needed to be surveyed were therefore comparatively limited.

The responsibility for providing very high-precision surveys of the North Sea is not confined to one country alone: a North Sea Hydrographic Commission has been established, consisting of hydrographers from the United Kingdom, the Netherlands, West Germany, Denmark, Sweden and Norway. National programmes are co-ordinated to ensure that mariners have the best possible charts and to avoid any unnecessary duplication of effort. At the same time, the Commission organizes the sharing of some of the highly expensive and complicated equipment essential for these surveys.

For example, one of the most important Hi-fix (navigational) chains in the southern North Sea has its transmitting stations in the Netherlands and England. Unfortunately, no matter what the level of co-operation, basic doubts exist as to whether surveys can at present achieve the accuracy demanded of them. For example, although the Hi-fix system provides precise position-fixing in the southern North Sea, precise measurement of depth relative to tidal and meteorological conditions still presents a problem.[17]

Hydrographic maps are an important starting point for geophysical surveys. The search for hydrocarbons and other mineral resources in offshore areas has spurred activity in this area. Ideally, any company wishing to consider marine mineral operations should be able to consult the results of surveys and geological maps of sea areas as detailed as those available for the land. The United Kingdom's Institute of Geological Sciences (IGS) is at present engaged in creating a comprehensive picture of the continental shelf around the British Isles. The IGS survey is carried out on 1:100,000 base maps; geological and geophysical data are now becoming available on this scale for specialist users, but primary publication is to take the form of 1:250,000 maps, each covering an area of 1° of latitude by 2° of longitude. The maps will include available information from all sources, including IGS, university and other government-financed studies and commercial surveys where the results of these can be released.[18]

Government-financed bodies are not normally engaged in prospecting for specific minerals, but the British survey does include a preliminary assessment of resources that might be worth further consideration by developers. However, in general, geological and geophysical maps have potential value to a wide number of users. These include engineers concerned with assessment of the best sites to survey in detail for pipelines and towers; geochemists studying seabed pollution which cannot be assessed without a knowledge of the geological age of seabed minerals under review; fisheries research workers; sedimentologists; and planning authorities concerned with the rational exploitation of raw materials. Most important, where governments are concerned, accumulated geological data are valuable in determining future policies on licensing and the control of exploitation. In spite of such value, considerable areas of the North Sea still have to be surveyed. In fact, before the detailed exploration of the North Sea

[17] Tony Loftas, "Tanker peril in shallow seas", *New Scientist*, 3 November 1970.
[18] R. A. Eden, J. E. Wright, R. McQuillan, "The Geological Survey of the U.K. Continental Shelf", *NERC Newsjournal* No. 4, November 1971.

could begin, oil companies had to band together to share the cost – over £350,000 – of a magnetic survey over the entire area from southern Norway to the Straits of Dover – a total of 144,000 square miles.

(ii) Ocean Forecasting and Studies

Most marine activities rely on some form of ocean forecasting or detailed information relating to winds, waves, tides and currents. Oceanographic data are essential also to the designers of marine structures, particularly those that are fixed or are sufficiently mobile to avoid extreme conditions arising at sea. The needs for accurate data and forecasting have already been mentioned with respect to chart preparation and shipping. A major factor in this is the influence of storm surges. A storm surge occurs when meteorological conditions cause a change in sea level; a rise in sea level is a positive surge, a lowering is a negative one. The effects extend to coastal areas and beyond, where sea defences are breached – or estuaries flood. The extensive and disastrous flooding of 31 January and 1 February 1953 on the coasts of the Netherlands and eastern England is a case in point. Finally, oceanographic studies have a significant bearing on weather forecasting and meteorology generally.

A pilot programme, Project Jonsnap, for an oceanographic buoy array in the North Sea was proposed by United Kingdom, German, Dutch and Belgian scientists. Their proposed Pilot Network would have consisted of 24 stations in the North Sea and 16 in the Baltic, some of which were established as part of an ICES project which ended in 1971. The stations would be concentrated in the southern North Sea. The eventual goal of the group, as outlined at an informal meeting in London in 1970, was to set up a network of permanent ocean data stations in the North Sea consisting in part of large telemetering buoys, one of which is now under construction,[19] which would provide data relevant to a number of oceanographic and meteorological problems. It proved, however, impossible to get the agreement of the nations concerned to such an ambitious scheme. It has therefore been agreed that, in the first instance, there shall be 6 to 8 such buoys, the first of which is planned to begin operating on 1 September 1976. The oceanographic problems studied under the ICES project, and which would be continued, included hydrographic studies relating to fisheries, storm surge prediction in connection with coastal engineering and flood warning schemes for navigational purposes, predicting the transport and dispersal of pollutants, and more general scientific subjects concerned with variability, sea level and tidal prediction.[20]

The British Meteorological Office already operates a storm surge warning system. Its work and the causes and occurrence of storm surges

---

[19] By a consortium consisting of EMI and Green, Filey and Weir, shipbuilders.
[20] H. W. Hill, "A Report on the U.K.–German–Dutch–Belgian Pilot Ocean Data Station Network for the North Sea".

in the North Sea have been described recently.[21] Surges frequently accompany the passage of a depression over or near to a sea area and can last for a period of between one or two hours and a few days. The two meteorological forces most important for their development are the tractive force of the wind and the effects of changes in atmospheric pressure on the water surface. The definition of surges is based on the difference between predicted levels as a result of astronomically generated tides and actual levels observed at stations forming part of the Storm Tide Warning Service (STWS). A storm surge occurs when the difference is two feet or more at high water at more than one reference station. Generally speaking, storm surges move anti-clockwise in the North Sea, affecting the east coast of Britain first as they travel southwards and then moving on to the Belgian and Dutch coasts. Obviously, even a few hours' advance warning of the surge is invaluable, either to lessen the effect of flooding in the case of a positive surge, or to alter the course of ships in the case of a negative one.

The STWS endeavours to give a preliminary high-water forecast one tidal period ahead for each of eight reference ports and then a final surge height estimate some hours later. On the whole, the emphasis has been on the predictions of positive surges in the past, since these are relevant to many coastal areas. The average number of positive surges per STWS operational season (which runs from September to April – the period when nearly all the surge producing conditions arise) has been just over 15 since regular data collecting began in 1953. Fewer data are available on negative surges, the effects of which have become important to shipping in the shallow southern North Sea. However, in the 1970–71 season, there were 10 negative surges. Eventually, it is hoped that frequent forecasts of negative surge conditions (included in daily forecasts of tidal heights – both low and high) will be possible for all critical shipping areas. However, progress in this respect is hampered by lack of information on changes in sea level away from coastal areas as a result of surge conditions.

Apart from storm surge warnings, conventional weather and sea state forecasts are provided for the North Sea. These forecasts are particularly important for ships operating in the area, but they may also be vital to the organization of rigs and related off-shore operations.

Oceanographic studies are not limited to surface and meteorological influences; they extend down through the water column to include the nature and behaviour of the seabed itself. Occurrences at the surface and on the sea floor are often related in shallow water areas. For example, the profile of the sea floor helps to determine the path of the tidal wave in the North Sea. Events at the two levels can be even more specifically related, e.g. vibrations set up by wave action on a rig's support columns can cause

[21] R. D. Hunt, "North Sea Storm Surges", *The Marine Observer*, No. 237, July 1972.

a loss of the bearing strength of sand or mud from around rigs or pipes. Finally, migrating sand waves, now known to exist in parts of the North Sea, may hazard shipping or once again hinder drilling and pipeline operations. Therefore a complete environmental profile of the North Sea is required, based at least on the result of prolonged study and eventually providing data on a "real-time" rather than retrospective basis.

(iii) Rescue and Safety at Sea

A variety of rescue services operate in the North Sea for the protection of mariners, yachtsmen, bathers and the like. In addition, there is the maritime tradition of responding to those in distress. Principal rescue organizations in the United Kingdom, for example, are the Coastguard Service and the Royal National Lifeboat Institution. There are over 50 lifeboat stations, all manned by volunteers, on the North Sea coast of the British Isles. The Coastguards maintain a constant watch at certain stations and many others are manned for limited periods, especially during the holiday season or when weather conditions are bad. Rescue and safety at sea are further covered by regulations on the provision of life-saving equipment and training on vessels and rigs.

Another important factor in ensuring safety at sea is the major lights situated in strategic areas. Major lights are those automatic or manned lights (including lightships) that are visible from the main shipping lanes and are used by navigators to check their position. To aid identification the lights usually have distinguishing characteristics. For example they may emit flashes (or revolve) at fixed intervals. A light station usually has an audible signal that can be used in times of poor visibility; some have radio and radar beacons. There are over 100 major lights situated around the North Sea, with the greatest density in the southern North Sea.

(c) Special Facilities

(i) Diving, Salvage and Underwater Working

In an area where accidents to shipping are frequent, salvage operations are common and often lucrative, sufficiently so for some ocean-going salvage tugs to be kept in a constant state of readiness. However, most salvage and underwater work is of a far less dramatic nature. Most interesting in this respect has been the increasingly important part played by the diver in North Sea operations and the evolution of systems and techniques suited to work in these cold and difficult waters. Initially, much of the diving support for drilling rigs was in the hands of United States operators, but British and other European companies have now gained useful experience and can offer advanced systems, designed to operate to depths of 600 feet or more, bringing the entire continental shelf within the diver's ambit.

The diver has many tasks to perform to support the operations of drilling rigs, such as underwater exploration and surveying sites for drilling operations; measuring the degree of scouring around rigs resting on the seabed; inspecting underwater structures for fatigue, fractures and damage; and assisting in underwater completions of well-heads. As drilling rigs have moved to deeper waters, diving techniques have been advanced so that divers can continue to provide their services. As a result, the time lag between experimental descents to depths beyond normal working dives and the commercial follow-up of these practices has been shortened to a few years or less. Working dives can now be made safely on air to 60 metres, or for very short periods to as low as 80 metres, while dives are made regularly to 120-135 metres and occasionally to 200 metres, using breathing mixtures in which the nitrogen and some of the oxygen in air are replaced by the inert, light gas helium. The use of submersibles will probably be extended but, at the present time, they do not play a large part in developments.

Finally, there is the possibility of using underwater work bases or habitats for work in the North Sea. The German experience with the underwater habitat, Heligoland, has shown that prolonged stays in the North Sea are feasible. In addition, some welding and pipeline repair has been carried out in the North Sea using canopies. The present experiments with well-head chambers for subsea systems are also relevant here. However, for the most part, working dives in the North Sea remain difficult, dangerous and uncomfortable, particularly as there are few divers used to the great depths involved, and the lack of expertise in young divers, attracted by the money paid by American oil companies, has resulted in diving fatalities.

(ii) Surface Support for Oil and Gas Operations

A feature of recent developments in the North Sea has been the need to set up shore bases to support drilling activities. Apart from transferring personnel and supplies to rigs, these bases must provide storage and transport for a wide range of materials from drilling equipment and spares to drilling mud (a heavy fluid containing a high percentage of barium sulphate). As the search moves north, new bases are being established, bringing employment and investment to previously under-developed areas. In fact, the provision of support services (including, of course, diving and oceanographic research) is a major growth area for investment. It is at present the subject of detailed studies by the United Kingdom Departments of Trade, Energy and Employment. On the other hand, the changes that these support bases bring are not universally welcomed. For example, rising land prices and the diversion of labour from less lucrative, but traditional, employment (such as in-shore fisheries) are claimed to be having a socially disruptive influence as well as leading to deterioration of the coastal environment. The Norwegian Government is particularly concerned about the possibly destructive impact of off-shore oil development on the traditional life-structure of Norwegian coastal areas, especially in the north of the country. This also formed the subject of a 1974 report by a Committee of the Oil Development Council for Scotland, "North Sea Oil and the Environment".

(iii) Advisory Services

Many of the activities that take place in the North Sea are dependent upon specialist advisory services, most of them supplied by Government-sponsored or controlled agencies. Examples of these have been given in several of the preceding sections. There is already, for instance, a long history of fishery research in the area. Since 1932 there has been a widespread survey of marine plankton. The work is exceptional in that the collections are made by instruments (continuous plankton recorders) which are towed behind merchant ships, ocean weather ships and fishing vessels in the normal course of operation. Until recently, these machines were restricted both to the sampling depth – 10 metres – and in taking only plankton samples. New instruments are now becoming available which can undulate between depths of 10 and 100 metres as they move along. At the same time, they record other oceanographic data, enabling a more complete survey of the zone of the sea populated by plankton.

The indications are that specialist advisory services will increase in importance and complexity. In particular, there must be more co-operative research, such as that carried out by ICES on fisheries and related matters. Ultimately, the development of the North Sea and its conservation will rely on the quality of the advice and support in terms of scientific and technical data.

III
Competing Uses and Interests in the North Sea

1. Introduction

This section sets out some elements in the conflicts which can arise from the uses discussed in earlier chapters.

In attempting to deal with this section of the Report it must be acknowledged initially that the information on which to base assessments of the full extent of these conflicts is, to a very large extent, still lacking. The realization that the activities of man can be a real threat to his environment, the quality of his life and even, eventually, to his survival, is so recent that it is only since the early 1960s that the studies which are essential to establish the factual situation have begun to be undertaken.

In this context, the first step is to make a distinction between those factors which can be more or less clearly defined, and so dealt with, and those which constitute the more difficult areas where the component elements are not easily quantifiable. In the first category one can place extraction of sand and gravel and oil, navigation and transport (including air transport), installations, commercial fisheries, additions of substances and, to a very great extent, protection of the organic and inorganic resources of the sea and the seabed. To the second belong the protection of coastal amenities, marine wildlife, recreation and tourism.

When it comes to questions of how the various activities affect each other, data are even more scanty and often contradictory.

In circumstances, such as the present, when we have a rapid development and application of advanced technology, but at the same time no certain knowledge of what is taking place in and under the sea or of the precise effects of many of man's marine activities, this study questions the goal of *maximum* exploitation of any one resource. Instead it assumes there is a need to regulate activities in the North Sea to harmonize with one another as far as possible so as to give an *optimal* exploitation of resources: that is, that the various interacting activities are managed to give the greatest benefit on balance.

There are a number of major difficulties in this approach, not least the problem of assigning values to the different activities. In assessing the relative importance of such disparate activities as navigation, fishing, waste disposal or tourism it is convenient to use a monetary yardstick to provide a common denominator of interest. For example, calculations were made by FAO in 1972 to assess marine products and services as sources of income on a world scale. These gave a 1970 figure of $8,200 million for the landing value of the world nominal catch from all commercial fisheries. Ocean freight shipment costs were practically double fishing revenues; world oil and gas production were worth roughly half commercial fishing at a slightly earlier date (1966), with extraction of remaining minerals adding another $250 million.

The recreational value of the oceans is not, predictably, well documented except to a limited extent for the United States of America. The U.S. estimates suggest that in 1964 all leisure activities along the continental shelf regions entailed expenditures of $3,900 million.[1] Swimming was the most popular activity at $1,500 million, followed by sports fishing ($800 million) and pleasure boating ($700 million). With the increase in demand for outdoor recreation calculated at approximately 10 per cent each year, the 1970 equivalent of total recreational expenditures could have exceeded $6,000 million.

So it can be seen that there are problems in putting really accurate comparative figures even to highly organized commercial activities such as oil extraction or fisheries; it is far more difficult to assess the value of natural amenities – i.e. beautiful scenery – even considering them in terms of a commercial asset to tourism; and it is possible to put a value to, for example, the preservation of marine birdlife only by such rough and ready devices as calculating the number of people who visit bird sanctuaries. At present there is really no way of evaluating, in commercial terms, the aesthetic value of an area or the scientific importance of a geological formation or a biological community, such as a sea-bird colony which may be unique. Public reaction to disfigurement of the landscape may be uninformed and emotional, but it is an indication that non-commercial and unquantifiable considerations somehow have to be taken into account.

In practice, too, the financial yardstick is not the only one that is applied. For example, oil stranded on the coast of Britain is removed with detergent where beaches are important for tourism, but not in scientifically important areas, even though these may be adjacent to the tourist beaches. It may, of course, be argued that the potential financial advantages to be derived from the results of scientific research are likely to be greater than the actual financial benefits of tourism. This raises the second major difficulty in considering conflicts of interest with a view to the optimal exploitation of resources: that is, the time dimension.

[1] Battelle Memorial Institute, 1966.

The more that is known about conservation of biological resources, the foreseeable exhaustion of non-renewable mineral resources, and the long-term effects of discharged chemical substances, the more it becomes a responsibility to decide what use to make of this knowledge. Present activities, naturally seen in terms of immediate commercial interest and based on a long period when there seemed to be no limits to natural resources, are undertaken on an essentially short-term view. Forecasts and future planning, whether by industry or government, make the assumption that our use of various resources will continue at present rates, or increase in line with expected growth rates, without necessarily giving as careful thought to what happens when supplies run out. Thus North Sea oil is to make the United Kingdom self-sufficient by the 1980s – assuming the oil is available for consumption in this country and allowing for a continued import of heavy oil to give the right refining structure – with the implication that this state of affairs will continue indefinitely, so that there is no debate on regulating its use. The finite nature of oil as a resource is recognized by the oil companies, who are diversifying into nuclear power and more vaguely admitted by everyone else on a "but it won't happen yet" basis. Governments are by their nature committed to acting on short-term considerations (witness the decision to rely on imported oil rather than home-produced coal on grounds of economy). Finally, there is no place in contemporary economic, social or political thinking for the idea of forgoing consumption. Even if there were, the problem would persist – forgoing for how long? Do we aim to benefit the next generation or the generation after that? The fact that these are extraordinarily difficult questions to answer does not remove the need for some sort of management decision: if the decision is to continue using up resources at top speed, let it at least be acknowledged that this is what we are doing. The problem of management is considered in the following chapter, but it should be recognized that the long-term versus the short-term problem is a hidden conflict inherent in almost every use of the North Sea.

Finally, it goes without saying that conditions vary in different parts of the North Sea. The shallows off the Dutch coast are a vital nursery ground for young fish and the priorities there are quite different from those in the Norwegian Trench and its adjacent oilfield. The interests which are in conflict in one area are quite different from those in another. Furthermore, some have local significance (mineral resources exist only in certain places; shipping routes are related to the position of major ports), others have general significance for a considerable part, or even the whole of the North Sea (plaice spawned and growing off the Dutch coast are cropped as adults in the central North Sea; an area of particular scientific interest may be unique). While some comprehensive regulation may be justified, a simplistic approach to the problem, which ignores the immense variety of the North Sea, is valueless.

2. Competition between Different Uses and Interests in the North Sea

It is possible to set out the interactions of the main uses described in Chapter I in some such diagram as Figure E, opposite.

One important point which this brings out is the inequality of interaction. Some activities cause effects elsewhere and are themselves affected by different activities: others cause effects without themselves being interfered with and still others only suffer interference without themselves causing any effects on other activities. Of course, any human activity will cause change both in the immediate circumstance of the activity and indirectly for many other activities in the same environment. The change may be damaging to some interests but beneficial to others. To talk of "conflicts" therefore does not do justice to the full complexity of the situation; the major interactions, however, do represent conflicts of interest.

Activities which fall into the first category are fisheries, the extraction of minerals, transport, installations and coastal development, and some recreational activities (such as boating). Though not a human activity, marine wildlife also has repercussions elsewhere as well as being affected by various human activities. Seals are in conflict with the salmon industry in eastern Scotland, and seals also harbour codworm, which is an important parasite of fish in the North Sea and causes considerable concern to fishing authorities. There is also the marginal case of sea-birds taking fish from trawlers. On the other hand, additions to the sea, whether in the form of sewage, oil discharges from ships or solid waste, can only cause ill effects without suffering any in return, while the enjoyment of natural coastal amenities can only suffer ill effects without causing any. The last category is the one whose value is most difficult to assess in commercial terms, and it also opens up the question of the general interest in protecting and conserving the resources of the sea, subject to necessary uses. This, as a general principle, is allowed by everyone to be of great importance, but it is not readily perceived as sufficiently in any one particular interest for any measure to be taken. In practice, this is likely to be a source of conflict between science and commercial exploitation.

Apart from the conflicts between different uses of the sea, there is also, of course, competition between users of the same or closely related resources, which does not appear on the chart opposite. This is essentially a problem of congestion and arises chiefly over fisheries, transport and recreation.

(a) Sea Fisheries

International competition over fisheries in the North Sea, which is a major fishing area, is well-known and well-documented. It is the activity where

COMPETING USES AND INTERESTS

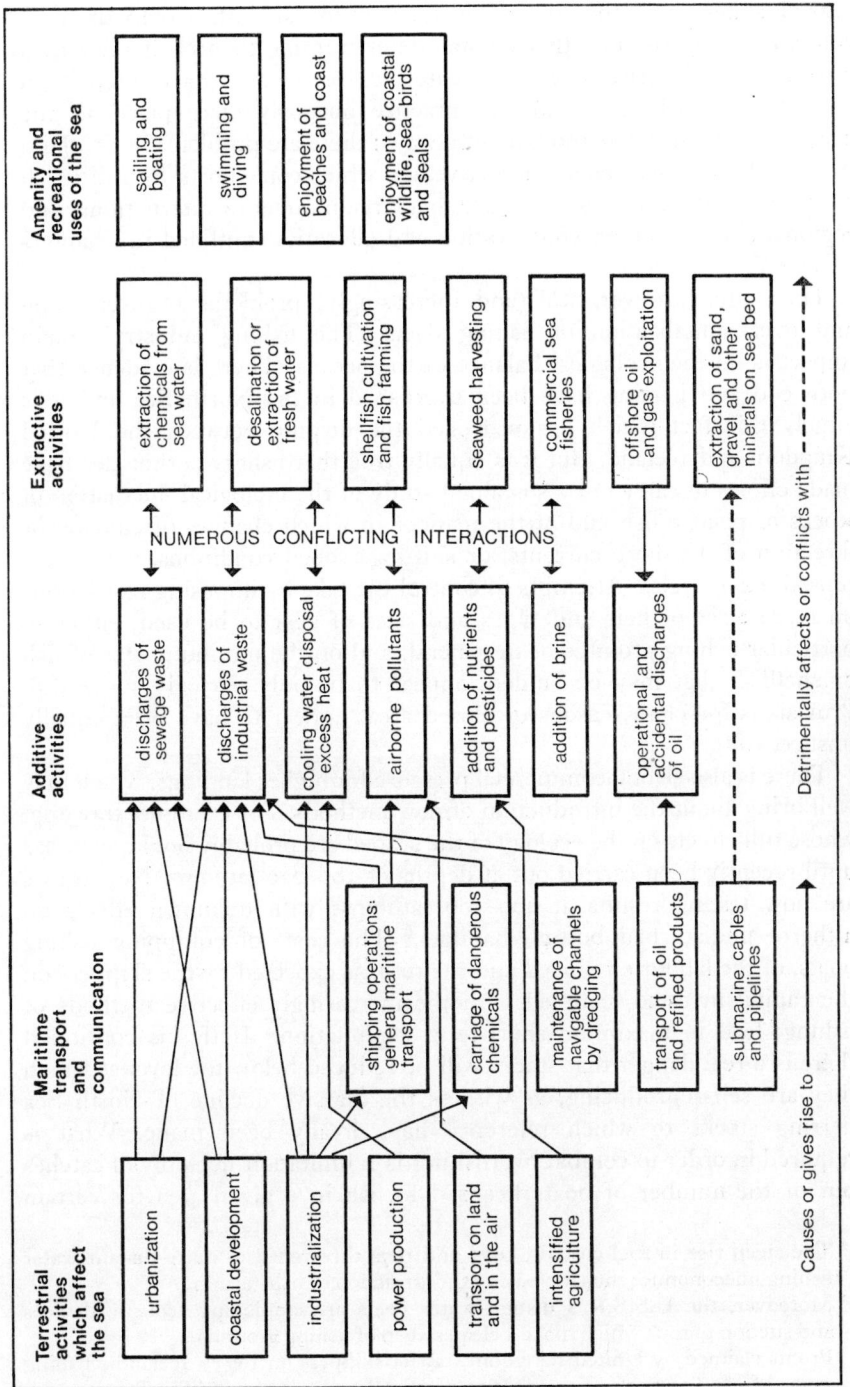

Fig. E: Man's impact on the sea.

coastal states have the longest history of investment. Competition is complicated by the fact that coastal states wanting to protect their own coastal home fisheries may to a greater or lesser extent have interests in distant-water fishing[2] – which in practice normally takes place off the coasts of foreign states, though not always: there are problems in Scotland between local fishermen and larger vessels which come north from English ports. This situation has given rise to a large number of international and regional agreements on conservation and allocation, outlined in Chapters IV and V.

There are, however, still (and increasingly) problems of overfishing and over-capitalization of fishing fleets. The fishing industry's main impact is on the ecological balance of the oceans. There is evidence that both cod and herring have been overfished in the North Sea and it is largely this fact which has provoked the dispute between the United Kingdom and Iceland. But it is equally true that fishery authorities have made efforts to carry out a sustained study of the biological fluctuation of stocks of pelagic fish and of the manner in which changes of climate, or direction of off-shore currents, or shifting seabed conditions, may affect reproductive cycles. Attempts to control the take by imposing restrictions on mesh sizes of nets and types and sizes of gear to be used, either in particular fishing grounds or in general, and on the minimum size of fish or shellfish that may be landed, appear to be only partially successful. Provisions for close seasons or closed areas appear to have been equally unsuccessful.

There is also strong commercial pressure for higher landings, which may well bring about the introduction of new methods. For example, trawling, whose full effects on the ecology of the seabed are probably not known, has until recently been carried out at depths of 200–250 fathoms. New trawls are now testing results at 300–500 fathoms; with unknown effects on hitherto undisturbed bottom habitats.[3] The costs of equipping fishing boats, of the labour employed and the returns expected by the skippers on the capital invested, coupled with the increasingly effective methods of fishing, lead to maximum short-term exploitation.[4] If this is continued there is a real danger that stocks will be reduced below the level at which they are self-reproducing, as witness the massive decline of North Sea herring stocks to which reference has already been made. What is required in order to combat overfishing is a limitation not only of catches but of the number of boats licensed to fish in a given area for certain

---

[2] The steep rise in fuel costs in 1973 and 1974 threatened to make distant-water fishing uneconomic; thus increasing the attraction of fish-farming.

[3] Moreover, the U.S.S.R.'s distant-water fleets are employing acoustic devices and suction pumps which make a clean sweep of fishing grounds.

[4] Profits claimed by United Kingdom trawler skippers on 1973's Icelandic fishing ranged from £20,000 to £27,000/£30,000 for the average catch (*The Times*).

species; and, again, this entails agreement between competing national interests.

Further problems of accommodation are conflicts arising primarily from the uses of different harvesting techniques and/or the destruction by one technique of the other use, such as trawling over shellfish beds, or the case where an existing fishery extends its range into an area traditionally used by another, different fishery.

The only way in which fishing can interfere with another "man-made" activity is that trawling might possibly damage underwater communication cables and pipelines.

(b) Amenity Uses

The competition for recreational use of the North Sea is not well documented. One problem is that the favourite word "amenity" is used to describe very different things, largely because its basic meaning of pleasantness, particularly of places, raises all the difficulties of definition consequent upon beauty's being in the eyes of the beholder. For the most part "amenity" is now used to refer to man-made conveniences in every sense of the word; but in occasional phrases, such as "the amenity of a situation", the original meaning persists. In densely populated Western Europe underdeveloped natural coastline is becoming scarce. Any extensive recreational use of such an area conflicts with its maintenance as an unspoilt region of natural beauty; this is a case where the amenity of coastline *qua* coastline is lost if too many people seek to enjoy it at the same time. But, even assuming that recreation implies tourism (with the development of investment that the latter entails), there is acute competition for available resources in the form of beaches, marinas, hotels, road access and so forth; and different opinions – for example between chambers of commerce and year-round private residents at tourist resorts – concerning the extent to which use of these resources can be expanded. It has been seen in an earlier chapter that tourism can altogether cease to be commercially attractive from the point of view of the local inhabitants. In practice, up to now, the only limiting factor appears to be pure physical capacity, and at this end of the scale recreational uses find themselves in conflict with other forms of commercial development in coastal areas. There is also, of course, a question of competition between different recreational activities, notably between powered boats on the one hand and sailing boats and swimmers on the other.

(c) Extraction of Sand and Gravel

The extraction of sand and gravel from the North Sea, which has taken place only since the early 1960s, poses dangers to fishery interests and to the ecological balance by causing damage to the seabed and by increasing the turbidity of the surface waters, thus reducing light penetration. The chief complaints from the fishery industry have been of hazards to trawl nets, disturbance of spawning grounds, burial of shellfish beds, and direct disturbance to fish from dredging. It can also cause changes in navigable channels which in the shallow North Sea may be situated far out to sea; and may affect recreational and amenity interests by causing coastal erosion. The classic case of accelerated erosion in the United Kingdom following dredging is that of the village of Hallsands in Devon. The dredging of some 650,000 tons of shingle off-shore for harbour works at nearby Plymouth led to a lowering of its beach. Dredging was halted but, within twenty years of the onset of dredging operations there, the village had been destroyed by wave action. Material from a working can be carried along by the current and silt up a neighbouring harbour. On the other hand, areas for sand and gravel extraction on shore are becoming scarce – the obvious necessity is to discover substitutes which can take their place in the building of roads and for use as aggregates.

These dangers are well recognized and the Crown Estate Commissioners – in whom control of all mineral exploitation (other than coal, oil or natural gas) is vested – have evolved a procedure of consultation to ensure that no such damage will be produced before dredging licences are granted. In addition, the Marine Division of the Department of Trade ensures that marine operations do not present a navigational hazard.

Nevertheless, however good the licensing provisions, there are problems in their enforcement. Illegal dredging or poaching of United Kingdom off-shore gravel resources reportedly amounts to some millions of tons annually (total annual production could approach as much as 20,000,000 tons, which would be nearly 50 per cent more than the 14,000,000 tons reported for 1970) and illegal dredging is unlikely to respect the boundaries of licensed areas.

Moreover, with dredging restricted to a relatively small area of the southern North Sea, and a growing demand for sand aggregate, production is increasing at a rate which probably averages around 8 per cent per annum. The exhaustion of satisfactory deposits, both on land and at sea, may well lead to pressure for the working of low-grade areas containing, say, 20 per cent of clay. This would create formidable difficulties over the disposal of the clay.

(d) Off-shore Dredging and Mining

The effects of these activities are, to all intents, similar to those cited immediately above. Coastal coal mines, the shafts of which run under the sea, can have a destructive influence on the shore life and the tailings can, as in Durham, totally destroy beaches by overlaying them with a skin of coal or black mud. Again, at a cost, such destruction could be avoided by forbidding the discharge of mining waste into the sea.

(e) Deep Sea Mining

This is likely to be confined to dredging from super-tankers for nodules on the seafloor. Unfortunately, there are no agreed rules in sight to govern such dredging operations beyond the bounds of national jurisdiction. It is, however, unlikely that such activities will be of major importance in the North Sea. It must, however, be appreciated that – thanks to the recent advances in technology – it is now possible to exploit the seabed at whatever depth may be required. Dredging and mining can hamper recreational uses of the beach and sea as a result of restrictions on access imposed by the operating companies. Structures associated with mineral exploitation can interfere with sailing and water skiing. Large areas inland may be occupied by storage and processing plant which can totally destroy their amenity use; the processing plant will cause pollution of the water, thus precluding swimming. The remedy may lie partly in purification of waste before it is discharged.

(f) Coastal Construction

The replacement of natural coastlines by concrete quays, terraces and housing developments can interfere with biological productivity. Not only can property development completely alter the littoral fringe, but construction work, such as dynamiting and excavating, can cause serious damage to marine life, either directly as the result of the use of explosives, or indirectly when excessive sediments pollute the water.

The construction of barrages and dams can destroy marine fisheries. Estuaries are commonly the nursery grounds of commercially important fish and regions of high productivity because of the supply of nutrients carried by the river water; lessening the flow can have adverse effects and the tendency to enclose them for other uses is growing.

(g) Oil and Natural Gas Extraction

Exploration and drilling for oil and natural gas in the North Sea are, in economic terms, by far the most important activities in these waters. They are at present confined to the northern areas. The activity with which they most seriously interfere is navigation – drilling rigs may not only lie in the path of shipping, but obstruct marker buoys and other navigational aids. Obviously precautions are taken to ensure that rigs and pipelines do not present a navigational hazard, but the risks of accident and poor weather conditions cannot be eliminated. The presence of rigs limits fishing activities within a half-mile radius: this may be bad for the immediate interests of fishermen but good for fish stocks. These immediate conflicts are, however, probably of less importance than the impact of the shore-based support for North Sea drilling on the coastal areas where it is sited. These may not be of major tourist importance, yet be areas of great natural beauty – the Shetland Islands are the most obvious example of an area which may be changed beyond recognition as the result of North Sea drilling.[5]

The above are ways in which the search for oil and natural gas are bound to affect other activities, regardless of whether any wells go into production. The chief potential danger, and one which would have incalculable effects on every form of marine life, is of course that of a major oil leak.

The greatest safeguard from disaster is that, in this instance, commercial interests are on the side of the most stringent safety precautions: the beaches in oil producing areas in the Middle East are remarkably oil-free. It is also arguable that the discovery of oil in the North Sea will reduce the numbers of tankers entering European ports which present a greater likelihood of oil pollution. Nevertheless, however unlikely, the risk of oil leaks from the North Sea wells exists, and has somehow to be allowed for although, like the risk of a leak from a nuclear reactor, it tends to be dismissed as a practical possibility.

(h) Traffic Congestion

Competition for space between commercial shipping arises only in certain areas but where it exists it is an acute problem. The southern North Sea contains the approaches to a number of large ports as well as to the highly congested Strait of Dover, and both the number of ships and port developments are on the increase. There is at present a lack of compulsory international regulation of traffic movements[6] and, although this is on its way, it is possible that the limits of transport development have not yet been fully realized and may indeed need more far-reaching measures. Furthermore, almost unbelievably, there is at present no international regulation requiring the captain and officers of a merchant vessel to have any qualifications at all. Of course, the major maritime nations lay down strict requirements for the training of merchant navy crews. By the time, for instance, that a British Merchant captain becomes master of a vessel he will have reached at least B.Sc. standard and will have had some 15 years' training and experience. Ships sailing under flags of convenience are likely to have very mixed crews whose training varies from the vestigial to the sophisticated, a fact which does not emerge until after a major catastrophe. A further hazard is the ever-increasing delicacy and complexity of navigational equipment which, unless given the requisite care, can either malfunction or cease to function with possibly disastrous consequences.

---

[5] See the Report of a Committee of the Oil Development Council for Scotland, *North Sea Oil and the Environment*, 1974.
[6] See Chapter II.

(i) Navigation and Transport

In general terms the major impact of marine transport is via its land-based support, i.e. port developments which compete for coastal space with other uses such as recreation, housing, etc. Problems of traffic congestion are discussed immediately above.

The most important single aspect of marine transport, in terms of its effects on other parts of the marine environment, is undoubtedly the carriage of oil. Most of the oil pollution found on beaches, and much of that at sea, is caused by the deliberate discharge of oil as ships wash out their empty tanks after unloading, or else by accidents to tankers. However, the tanker which grounded at Milford Haven in 1973 demonstrated another hazard. Its cargo was not crude oil but petrol which, in this case (owing to surrounding circumstances, rough seas and slow leakage), had not evaporated sufficiently quickly to prevent its influx into the water. Because petrol is more toxic than oil its effects, if it manages to reach the shore line, are far more damaging. Dr. Janet Baker, of the Oriellton Field Centre, Pembroke, has emphasized that the forms of oil pollution which were potentially most damaging were successive spillages, such as those at oil terminals, and oil-containing effluents pumped from the refineries. More oil went into the sea through effluents than through accidents and problems arose where the same stretches of coastline were continually affected by either minor spillage or effluent. International efforts to control discharges from ships, as the scale of their effects has become more widely appreciated, are set out in Chapter II above.

The effects of oil on the living resources of the sea are extremely difficult to assess. The most obvious effects of oil pollution are damage to beaches and the death of sea-birds in particularly distressing circumstances. It also seems possible, and even likely, that the marine environment in general – i.e. fish, plankton, etc. – suffers damage from oil pollution, but this is more difficult to demonstrate since there are many different types of oil; there are erratic natural changes in the marine environment against which changes caused by pollution have to be read; the extent to which petroleum hydrocarbons may be biodegradable in the marine environment is not known; and there are technical difficulties in determining the toxicity to aquatic animals of materials that are not mixable with water. Consequently, there may be concealed effects which are not easily detected. Also, when there is a major spill a proportion of the oil may sink to the seafloor and remain there, coating it for an indefinite period.

One obvious effect of oil pollution is tainting of the flesh of marine animals. It therefore clearly affects fisheries, more particularly shellfisheries since tainted fish acquire an unpleasant taste and become unmarketable. Nor is it clear whether, even after the oily taste and smell have disappeared, the fish may be free from all the polluting components.

Further interference with fishing activities can occur if the oil is dispersed by sinking: it is then liable to interfere with fishing gear which, in turn, can lead to tainting of the whole catch.

As against the difficulty of positively demonstrating long-lasting damage to marine populations, it should be pointed out that these changes can often turn out to be more far-reaching than was originally thought. There is growing evidence that oil pollution may affect the reproduction success of breeding populations of sea-birds even when it does not affect the adults. At present little is known about the mortality among larval forms of marine animals: greater knowledge may produce similar conclusions here. It is possible that low-level pollution may interfere with the natural behaviour of commercially important fish, disrupting breeding, selection of habitats, feeding and homing.

Reverting to the obvious damage to sea-birds and beaches: in spite of the considerable publicity when this occurs as a result of a direct oil spillage, there is no evidence that the public at large puts any great value on avoiding such damage. Surveys of tourism in affected areas have come up with the estimate that, given proper information, a tourist would be prepared to pay only some minute proportion of his holiday expenditure as "insurance" to prevent himself being affected by oil pollution. A British report in 1973 showed, for example, that on total seaside expenditure and relative pollution levels throughout the United Kingdom, tourists would pay a total of £750,000 to safeguard themselves against oil pollution, out of a total seaside expenditure of £870 million per annum. Sea-birds in strictly economic terms have no value at all, unless they are used for food which is not now common in this country.[7] However, on the not very adequate basis of what people were willing to pay to travel to a bird reserve in the United Kingdom, it was estimated that the population would pay between £350,000 and £750,000 to maintain birds in their present environment.

(j) Waste Disposal

While it is generally acknowledged that disposal of wastes into the sea is essential and, therefore, acceptable, such disposal must be kept within limits which fall short of inflicting lasting damage or destroying other uses of the area. Moreover, it must constantly be remembered that the seas and the oceans form a closed system; once waste is discharged it has nowhere else to go and unless it is biodegradable it forms an increasing load on the environment. A further consideration is that the movement of wastes by tides and off-shore currents is not so far adequately plotted. In actual fact, the circularization and stratification of the waters, as well as the pattern of flow or current movements, present major problems for

[7] This assessment, of course, ignores the role of sea-birds in the general ecological balance of a given area.

scientific study. The main discharges of waste products are from sewage works, industrial processes, agricultural run-off and oil discharges from ships and refineries.

The disposal of waste matter into the sea – particularly the North Sea, surrounded by some of the most heavily industrialized states in the world – has a wide variety of sources, as indicated in Chapter I. Where a particular substance has adverse effects on different forms of marine activity it is often very difficult to trace its origin. There are a large number of diverse interests which derive benefit from using the sea as a dustbin and/or a sink, and to a large extent they are land based. These activities affect most forms of marine life, recreational pursuits and, to a lesser extent, fishing.

(k) Solid Waste

Solid objects dumped into the sea consist of both floating and sunken articles – drums, wire, bottles, timber and plastic articles, ropes and fishing nets. Many of these are initially indestructible and can cause serious problems for fishermen; for example, pieces of synthetic rope and fishing nets can immobilize fishing vessels by getting wound round propeller shafts. Containers of waste and bottom roughening waste also interfere directly with trawling. Significant areas of the North Sea are said to be untrawlable because of the debris dumped on the sea floor, and there is pressure from ICES as well as from states bordering on the North Sea for a complete ban on dumping.[8] The 1972 Oslo Convention on dumping[9] goes some way to control this sort of activity as its contracting parties have agreed to ban certain substances altogether and to put others under severe restrictions.

(l) Sewage Disposal

The release of untreated sewage into coastal waters conflicts with their use as spawning and fish nursery grounds and for shellfish cultivation. Although depuration techniques can cleanse molluscs of bacteria, shellfish in heavily polluted waters become either so tainted or so contaminated that it is no longer safe to consider them for human consumption. The transmission of a viral disease, infectious hepatitis, by the consumption of raw shellfish taken from contaminated waters is well documented. As a result of the desire to avoid contamination of estuaries and tourist beaches, large volumes of waste with high BOD content may be discharged offshore into fish nursery and spawning grounds. (It is established that fish are more susceptible to pollution in their early stages.) Unfortunately, the

[8] See "The disposal of containers with Industrial Waste into the North Sea is a problem for Fisheries", Experience Paper 73, FAO Technical Conference on "Marine Pollution and Its Effects on Living Resources and Fishing", December 1970.
[9] See Chapter IV, para. 105.

positions of spawning grounds and nursery areas in the North Sea are not fully documented, although the more important ones are certainly quite well known.

Infectious micro-organisms released into the sea with untreated sewage present a health hazard to bathers. Although seawater can kill these pathogens within a few hours, this natural cleansing action begins to fail as the water becomes heavily polluted and the system overloaded. Numerous minor ailments, such as ear infections, can be traced back to swimming in polluted waters. Increasingly, parts of the Mediterranean are considered unsafe for bathing as a result of water pollution and it is possible there may be a discernible effect on tourism in future years. In parts of Italy bathing has been banned by the authorities. In the more open North Sea no health risk from bathing has yet been recognized.

Apart from any health danger, however, sewage and other forms of waste disposal cause filth, smell and reduction of water transparency. This reduction of amenity value affects all those wishing to enjoy beaches, not merely swimmers and boaters.

(m) Excess Nutrients

The release of nutrients such as treated sewage, food processing and other biological wastes, and chemical fertilizers, into coastal waters can lead to widespread changes in the phytoplankton which, in turn, have repercussions on higher members of the marine food web. If there is an unnatural balance caused by injected nutrients it may encourage blooms of toxic plankton as well as excessive growth of unwanted algae which deprives the water of oxygen as it decays. The result can be very large kills of fish, as well as contamination of shellfish with marine biotoxins, although these effects have not so far occurred in the North Sea on any appreciable scale.

The effects of over-fertilization can be particularly serious in estuaries which are permanent nurseries and passage zones for about 90 per cent of commercially important fish. Equally, it has been suggested that the supply of nutrients can have a beneficial effect on phytoplankton in the immediate vicinity of a polluted estuary.

(n) Industrial Wastes

The release of toxic industrial wastes, whether by design or accident (such as spillage of lethal chemicals in transport), can lead to contamination of marine organisms and large fish kills. However, the greatest danger to marine life comes from the release of heavy metals such as mercury, copper, zinc, lead and cadmium, which can accumulate in and spread throughout the marine food web. The classic example of this is the mercury waste which has contaminated the shellfish and fish of Minimata Bay, Japan, and led the Japanese Government to fix limits for the amounts of fish that can be safely consumed. About half the world's production of mercury –

4,000 to 5,000 tons – is believed to enter the oceans each year from industrial sources.

Bulky organic wastes, such as those from pulp and paper mills, may give rise to deoxygenation and the destruction of bottom animals by smothering. Inert materials in suspension (e.g. coal dust, china clay, fly ash from power stations, gypsum) may cause marked changes in the character of the bottom. In some cases these changes may bring about an increased production of soft-bottom animals suitable as fish food. However, by cutting down light penetration, materials in suspension may affect the growth of bottom algae and reduce phytoplankton production.

The most urgent task is to separate sewage waste from industrial waste since this would enable sewage sludge to be used as manure with a much diminished risk of soil contamination. Under the present system this is, of course, impracticable since a great deal of industrial waste is discharged directly into main drains. Another possibllity is to utilize the waste products for the production of methane gas.

As was stressed again at the conference organized by the British Society for the Advancement of Science in July 1973, many of the problems posed by industrial wastes could be solved by extraction and recycling. But this would require the installation of appropriate machinery in the factory. Since recycled metals are in general easier to rework, long-term benefits should balance short-term financial outlay; in such a highly competitive market, however, the first steps are always the most difficult to take.

The present dilemma is highlighted by the developments in Rotterdam – Europoort. This is now becoming a huge storage and distributing centre for crude oil, but further development of the immense oil refineries already operating have been largely precluded on grounds of unacceptable pollution of the environment. It appears that pollution has now reached such a level that it is becoming intolerable. The key to immediate trends can be seen in the fact that across the Belgian border, only 80 kilometres (50 miles) away, stringent anti-pollution measures do not apply and both the industrial climate and subsidy provisions are more attractive. This, in the long run, simply means that the problem is taken one remove further into the future. Another aspect is the economic and environmental cost of providing channels sufficiently wide and deep to accommodate the new generation of tankers, some of which will be unable to negotiate the English Channel. Plans are already afoot for the construction of artificial islands built up from the seafloor which could be used for oil terminals and refineries and, possibly, chemical works. These, on a large scale, would pose a number of problems varying with their situation. It would be essential to control the resulting pollution of the sea which could affect fisheries. Careful study of the prevailing currents would be essential to avoid possible fouling of the shore line and such islands could also affect navigation if placed on the continental shelf.

The Dutch Waddenzee is one of the most polluted areas; the terns in this area are heavily polluted by chemical wastes. Off the Hebrides and Aberdeen concentrations of mercury ranging from 0.7 ppm to 1.22 ppm in young guillemots and red-breasted mergansers have been found.

The main sources of pollution of the North Sea are the rivers discharging into it. In this connection the Rhine is notorious and bids fair to become an even greater menace if the French plans for siting a number of nuclear power stations on its banks materialize.

(o) Waste Heat

Waste heat released from electric power plants, both conventional and nuclear, and industrial processes can heat in-shore waters and cause changes in marine fauna and flora. Most damage to fish stocks so far has occurred in rivers. However, it is likely that more nuclear plants will be sited on the coast in future and the standards proposed in various countries have so far resulted only in rather general guidelines for disposal of heat, which require to become more detailed.

(p) Radioactive Waste

Although the continuous trickle of low-level radioactive waste into the ocean is slight, marine organisms (including shellfish) can retain and accumulate radioactive elements and, in spite of careful control of the concentration of radioactive materials at the point of discharge to coastal waters, high-level radioisotopes have been discovered in aquatic organisms in areas where there has been discharge from atomic plants. This does not have an immediate application to the North Sea.

The disposal of low-level radioactive waste in the North Sea is very carefully monitored and so far cannot be shown to have had any very adverse effects. Where high-level waste has been disposed of at sea there has been a number of minor incidents: the problem of the safe disposal of wastes, some of which may retain their radioactivity for 30,000 – or on other estimates up to 250,000 – years, is very far from a solution.

(q) Agricultural Run-off

This can give rise to two hazards affecting both fisheries and bird life: the injection of excess nutrients which may deprive the water of sufficient oxygen, and the effects of pesticides. Minute quantities of DDT can reduce photosynthesis by as much as 75 per cent in marine plants, thus building up residues in the marine food chain. Organo-chlorine pesticides are in process of phasing out in the countries bordering the North Sea, but this process should be speeded up and research directed to their replacement. Mercury seed dressing is another source of pollution, as are fertilizers with a high nitrogenous content. Here research is being carried out into the possibility of increasing the range of plants which concentrate nitrogen and introduce it into the soil on their root systems. Some success has already been achieved, though as yet on only a small scale. Another hazard can be caused by leakage of poisons from storage tanks into streams running into the sea.

(r) Commercial Exploitation versus Scientific Management

Exploitation commonly moves ahead of scientific knowledge and information, just as much of early technology was devised largely on the basis of trial and error. This situation is particularly true of fisheries. The greater interest shown by the nations in this source of food and income has led to the need for some form of scientific management. However, considerable conflict can arise between commercial interests – which are largely, at first blush, short-term – and those of the scientist who, to the businessman or the statesman, does not seem to be aware of economic or political realities. The position is further confused by a general lack of data and knowledge which enables competing factions to persist among scientific advisers.

The same considerations apply to the erection of "sea cities". Not enough attention would seem to be directed to estimating their impact upon the environment as distinct from the feasibility of building the structures.

(s) Communications

The only foreseeable conflict of uses in this regard is that of trawling and dredging combined with large-scale movements of sand and scouring by currents, both of which can damage cables.

3. Summary

From the preceding survey it can be concluded that overfishing of the main stocks in the North Sea is an established fact. The remedy is, however, much more difficult to forecast since it entails co-operation to an unprecedented extent between competing nation-states. The fact that deeper trawling is not only advocated but already being practised is an indication of the situation. There is, so far, no indication that the European Economic Community has any intention of administering its fishing interests in the North Sea as an interlocking whole. The indication is that there will be every effort to increase fishing in those areas which were reserved for coastal states prior to the formation of the Community. States which have destroyed or greatly impaired the productivity of their coastal fishing will now transfer their fishing fleets to more rewarding grounds.

Again, the temporary destruction of shellfish (molluscs and crustaceans) in a given area, as a result of pollution by oil or chemical waste, means greater pressure on the remaining areas. In one incident quoted the area concerned will take from three to five years to recover and this will, in turn, entail greater pressure on other areas. A trend is already apparent for the catch to consist of a larger proportion of immature specimens, which again will affect breeding successes.

So far as is known, extraction of chemicals from the sea, including salt, has had no adverse effects on the ecological balance. But it must be remembered that so far such extraction has taken place to only a very limited extent.

The control of dumping at sea under the Oslo Convention[10] is totally inadequate, partly because there are no means of enforcing its provisions. The North Sea carries the greatest density of commercial traffic (relative to its size) of any sea area and the ships using it fly every known flag. The observation by crews of international regulations vary very considerably and the application of the penalties incurred can only be described as haphazard, depending upon whether a ship is caught in *flagrante delicto*. A possible form of initial control might be for air force training to include *sea* patrols which could report on ships seen to be contravening agreed restrictions. Swedish newspapers have reported that 40,000 to 60,000 steel drums filled with "poisonous substances" have been dumped into the North Sea fishing areas in recent years. In April 1971 a Danish trawler hauled up 72 barrels of waste material that had been caught in its nets. Significant areas of the North Sea are said to be untrawlable because of the debris of waste and containers dumped on the seafloor and, as has already been stressed, there is pressure from, *inter alia*, ICES as well as from states bordering on the North Sea for a complete ban on dumping.

Navigation requires much closer consideration of the rules governing movements of ships and traffic separation schemes, and much more uniform requirements for the qualifications of crews and skippers. With the ever-increasing number of installations which can be expected to be erected in the North Sea, both as a result of intensive oil and gas extraction and the necessity to provide off-shore berths for the enormous tankers coming off the slipways, navigation will become still more difficult. Again, the problem will be to enforce the rules which are generally agreed and embodied in conventions and codes by, *inter alia*, IMCO. Too often such an agreement remains a dead letter because either its provisions are ignored or the number of countries accepting them is too small to effect its purposes. The penalties for breach of an agreement should be made commensurate with the damage caused, or threatened, as a result of the breach.

The impact of air navigation on the North Sea comes mainly from the effect of aircraft exhaust gases on sea-air exchange and from the provision of new airports which encroach upon the coastline. The effect of sonic boom upon marine life in terms of vibration cannot yet be estimated: should supersonic travel become the rule rather than the exception, it may become a problem which has to be considered.

[10] See Chapter IV, para. 105.

IV
The Present Legal Regime of the North Sea: International Law*

INTRODUCTION

1. The purpose of this Chapter is to present an account of the current[1] rules of public international law relating to the North Sea.[2] Being intended for lawyers and laymen alike, it aims to provide a reasonably comprehensive[3] account of the legal position without excessive technicality.

2. As its title suggests, the scope of this Chapter is largely confined to the existing rules on the subject (*lex lata*) although reference will be made to treaties which, though adopted, have not yet entered into force. Proposals for new rules (*lex ferenda*) are beyond the scope of this Chapter. A very large number of different proposals for reform have been made and it is difficult to predict with complete confidence which, if any, of them will be ultimately adopted; consequently their inclusion here would tend to confuse the exposition of the existing law. Moreover, the Study Group's own proposals will be found in Chapter VI.

3. However, one set of proposals for the reform of the existing law must be mentioned from the outset. The Third United Nations Conference on the Law of the Sea has an agenda covering almost the entire law of the sea and it must accordingly be borne in mind that the law expounded here is subject to revision within the next few years. This does not mean, however,

---

* This chapter was researched and written by Dr. Maurice Mendelson, Fellow and Tutor, St. John's College, Oxford.

[1] Unless otherwise indicated, the present account is based on information available to the writer up to 1 June 1974.

[2] For the purposes of this Chapter and unless otherwise indicated, latitudes 61°00′N and 51°32′N will be taken to be respectively the northern and southern limits of the North Sea, and the United Kingdom, Belgium, the Netherlands, the Federal Republic of Germany, Denmark and Norway as the North Sea coastal states. Use of the superjacent air space will not be discussed.

[3] Limitations of space make a completely exhaustive account impossible, especially when it is borne in mind that there are more than 100 relevant treaties in force and that the permutations of parties vary considerably.

that the present study is inopportune, for the following reasons. First, it is against the background of the present law that proposals for reform are to be considered. Secondly, the Conference may well go on for some years. Thirdly, it is by no means certain that the Conference will reach a successful conclusion, and, fourthly, even if it does, the treaty or treaties which emerge are unlikely to come into force for some time. Finally, many of the subjects to be considered at the Conference (such as the regime of the ocean floor and of mid-ocean archipelagos) are of little or no direct relevance to the North Sea.[4] However, where particular proposals do appear to have good prospects of being adopted and to have particular relevance to the present study, reference will, of course, be made to them, either in this Chapter or in the Chapter containing the Study Group's own proposals.

4. In earlier times, the law of the sea was based on so-called customary international law, which evolved from the practice of states. Today it is increasingly to be found in treaties – multilateral treaties of general application, "plurilateral" treaties (i.e. those confined to a relatively small number of states) and bilateral treaties.[5] Among the reasons for the increasing role of treaties are the inability of customary law to evolve rapidly in response to new problems (e.g. pollution) and the increasing desire of states to limit possible causes of friction, to the extent that they can do so without jeopardizing what they perceive to be their vital interests.[6]

5. The purpose of some treaties is to redistribute rights. For example, coastal states may agree in treaties of commerce, navigation and friendship to restrict their right to prohibit entry to their ports, or states may agree – on the basis of reciprocity – to leave fishing rights in a particular area of the high seas to nationals of the adjacent coastal state. Other treaties are more concerned with securing joint action by states with a common interest. Collision regulations are one example of this, and jointly agreed fishery conservation schemes another. In the first, "redistribution" type of agreement, governments tend to deal with one another as representatives of self-contained units (sovereign states), jealously guarding the national patrimony and making concessions only in return for a *quid pro quo*. In the second class of treaty, the real confrontation may be between the individual on the one hand, and the institution of Government on the other, and the purpose of the agreement is to ensure that the uncooperative individual

---

[4] Cf. *infra*, para. 20.

[5] Even in the context of public international law it may also be necessary to consider questions of national law (including uniform national law and the conflict of laws).

[6] The utility of the treaty approach is limited by one important factor, however. Broadly speaking, a state can be bound by a treaty only if it expressly consents thereto. A state may, by contrast, sometimes find itself bound by rules of customary law without any conscious act of volition or great effort on its part.

does not slip through the jurisdictional net. There is a substantial degree of overlap between these two classes.

6. Any study of the law of the sea must begin with an examination of the different types and bases of jurisdiction, for it is only through, or by limitation of, the jurisdiction of states to prohibit or prescribe that conflicting interests can be reconciled. Having considered the jurisdictional question, it will then be possible to explore the law relating to particular activities or problems, and more particularly those which, like fishing and pollution, are not limited to one particular jurisdictional zone.

I JURISDICTION

A. Flag Jurisdiction

7. The Geneva Convention on the High Seas, 1958,[7] deals, *inter alia*, with the legal connection between ships[8] and the countries in which they are registered. Subject to agreed limitations, the state whose flag the ship is entitled to fly has exclusive jurisdiction over the ship on the high seas,[9] and its jurisdiction is not completely ousted even when the ship enters waters subject to the jurisdiction of another state (e.g. the territorial sea).

8. The jurisdiction of the flag state has both a negative and a positive aspect. In a negative sense, it means that – at any rate on the high seas – other states are not normally entitled to exercise control over the ship's activities unless they have obtained the assent of the flag state. This can often cause difficulties, e.g. in relation to the policing of a fishery conservation scheme.[10] The positive aspect of flag jurisdiction is that, even on the high seas, a ship is not beyond the reach of the law, for the flag state may exercise jurisdiction over it to prevent unacceptable conduct if it wishes. Indeed, under the High Seas Convention it is *obliged* effectively to exercise its jurisdiction and control in administrative, technical and social matters, and in particular must take steps to ensure compliance with rules relating to the safety of life at sea and certain other matters.[11] However, this obligation, even if respected, does not seem to go far enough and, in particular, there have been complaints that "flag-of-convenience"

[7] 29 April 1958 (entered into force 30 September 1962); 450 UNTS 82; 13 UST 2312; TIAS 5200; UKTS No. 60 of 1963 (Cmnd. 1929): hereinafter referred to as the "High Seas Convention". Of the six North Sea states, Norway is the only non-party. In general, the Convention codifies the existing customary law.

[8] Definitions of "ship" vary from treaty to treaty and domestic statute to statute. See Lazaratos, "The Definition of Ship in National and International Law", *Revue hellénique de Droit International*, 1969, p. 57.

[9] Those on board may also be subject to the jurisdiction of their respective states of nationality, but in the present context this head of jurisdiction can be ignored.

[10] Cf. *infra*, para. 60.

[11] Cf. esp. Arts. 5, 10, 11, 12 and 13.

states have not been co-operative in accepting or enforcing internationally agreed standards.[12]

B. Zonal Jurisdiction

9. As we shall see, the high seas are, in general, open to all, and no state except that of the flag has the right to exercise jurisdiction over a ship on the high seas. On the other hand, states are concerned to restrict access to, or regulate conduct in, sea areas adjacent to their coast, inasmuch as such activities may pose a threat to their security, economic well-being or other interests. The solution adopted by international law is to permit various derogations from the principle of the freedom of the seas in a series of limited off-shore zones. This we may call "zonal" jurisdiction. In general, the exclusiveness and comprehensiveness of the jurisdiction increases the closer one approaches to the shore.[13] There are thus two main areas of the sea: what we shall call "national waters", over which the coastal state exercises complete or almost complete control, and the high seas, which are regarded as common property and so are not generally subject to special claims by coastal states. Both areas can be further sub-divided into zones, each of which has a different juridical status from the others.[14] The main geographically delimited zones are as follows: (a) national waters: internal waters and territorial sea; (b) high seas: "high seas proper", contiguous zone and continental shelf.[15]

[12] Although Article 5 of the Convention requires a "genuine link" to exist between the ship and its flag states, the meaning of "genuine link" is not defined. It would seem to require a less close connection than the "genuine and effective link" applied in certain cases concerning the nationality of individuals. In its Advisory Opinion on the *Constitution of the Maritime Safety Committee of the Inter-Governmental Maritime Consultative Organisation*, ICJ Rep. 1960, p. 150, the International Court of Justice declined to agree that flag-of-convenience states could be ignored when determining which were the "eight largest ship-owning nations" for the purpose of constituting the Maritime Safety Committee of IMCO. In practice, it would be unwise for a state to treat a ship as having a nationality other than that of the state whose flag it flies, or no nationality – cf. Boczek, *Flags of Convenience* (1962).

Certain flags-of-convenience states have recently begun to take a closer interest in the ships bearing their registration, particularly as regards maritime safety, but a still more active participation by these states in the various treaty arrangements is highly desirable.

[13] Cf. McDougal and Burke, *The Public Order of the Oceans* (1962), pp. 28–51.
[14] See figure F.
[15] There is constantly increasing support for the idea that states should be able to claim rights over the living and mineral resources of the sea and seabed for a distance of 200 miles from base-lines – the so-called Exclusive Economic Zone. If this right receives general recognition at the Third United Nations Conference on the Law of the Sea and is adopted by the North Sea coastal states, it will enable those states to divide up virtually the whole of the resources of the North Sea between them, and the only significant activity which will remain open to states from outside the area will be navigation.

PRESENT LEGAL REGIME: INTERNATIONAL LAW

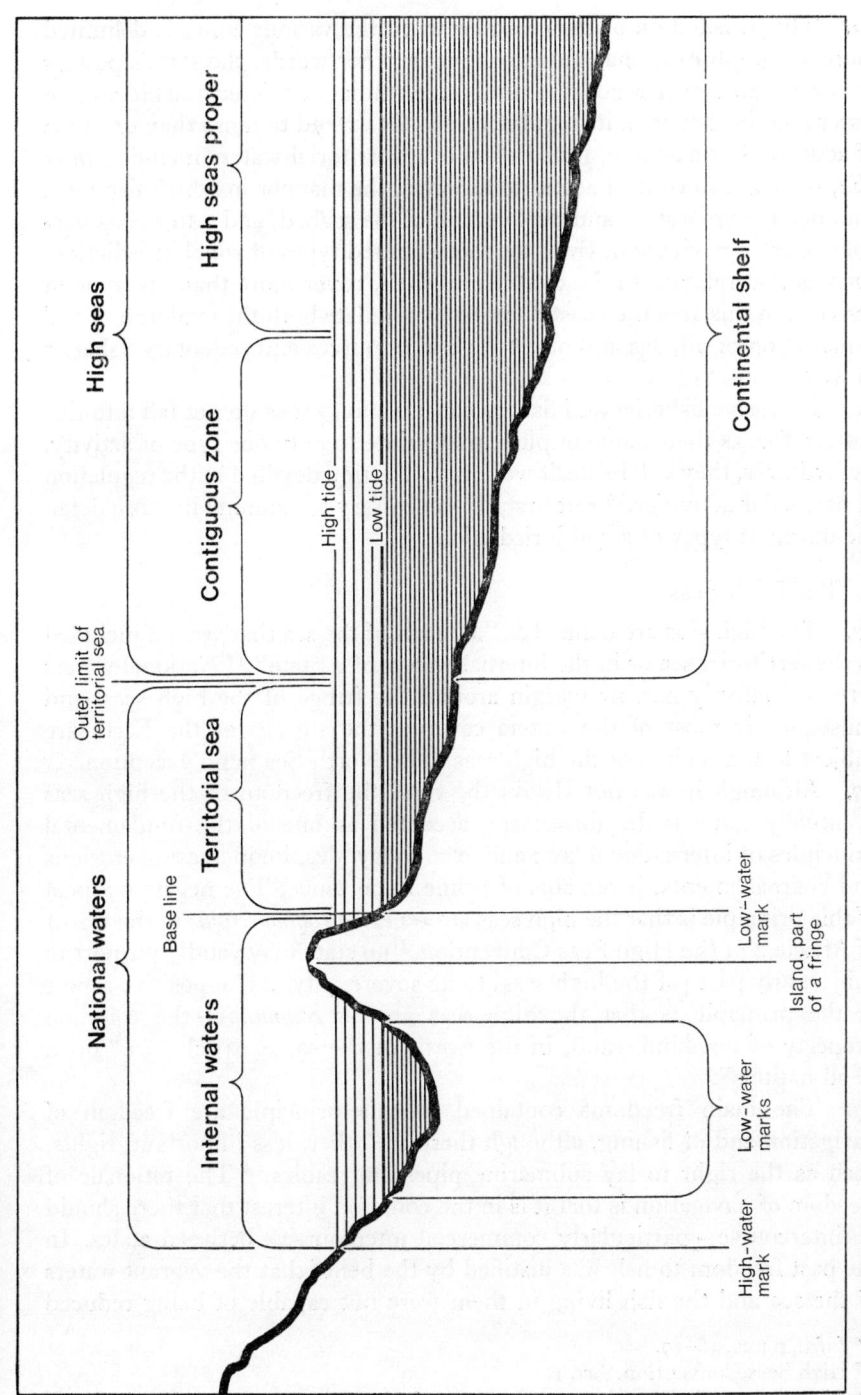

Fig. F: Jurisdictional zones, cross-section (based on Bin Cheng's diagram in Schwarzenberger, *A Manual of International Law*)

10. The jurisdiction of the coastal state in the various zones is delimited more geographically than functionally; in other words, the state's powers are exercisable over a geographically determinate or determinable area of water and, in that area, its regulatory powers extend to more than one type of activity. For example, jurisdiction over territorial waters includes, *inter alia*, the right to control access to fisheries, the manner in which fishing is conducted, exploration and exploitation of the seabed, and – to a considerable extent – navigation. Even the more limited types of zonal jurisdiction, such as that relating to the continental shelf, cover more than one type of activity: in this area the coastal state may regulate both the exploration and exploitation of oil, gas and other mineral resources and sedentary fisheries as well.

11. Exclusive fisheries and fishery conservation zones do not fall into this pattern for, as their name implies, they relate to only one type of activity. Accordingly, they will be dealt with in the Section devoted to the regulation of particular activities.[16] But first, it is necessary to examine in more detail the different types of zonal jurisdiction.

1. The High Seas

12. The high seas are defined as "all parts of the sea that are not included in the territorial sea or in the internal waters of a State".[17] National waters form a relatively narrow margin around the fringe of the high seas, and consequently most of the waters covering the surface of the Earth are subject to the regime of the high seas. The North Sea is no exception.

13. Although it was not always the case, the freedom of the high seas eventually came to be universally accepted as one of the fundamental principles of international law; and even today, despite increasing erosions and encroachments, it remains of prime importance. The negative aspect of this principle is that the high seas are *res extra commercium*; in the words of Article 2 of the High Seas Convention, "no state may validly purport to subject any part [of the high seas] to its sovereignty". The positive aspect of the principle is that the high seas are *res communis* – the common property of mankind – and, in the words of the same Article, are "open to all nations".

14. The main freedoms contained in this principle are freedom of navigation and of fishing, although there are other, less important, rights, such as the right to lay submarine pipes and cables.[18] The rationale of freedom of navigation is that it is in the common interest that there should be intercourse – particularly commercial intercourse – between states. In the past freedom to fish was justified by the belief that the vagrant waters of the sea and the fish living in them were not capable of being reduced

---

[16] *Infra*, paras. 46–59.
[17] High Seas Convention, Art. 1.
[18] Rights of overflight are beyond the scope of this study.

into possession, and that the fisheries represented an inexhaustible common resource.[19]

15. Since the high seas are not, in general, susceptible of claims of national sovereignty, and since their extent is defined only negatively (i.e. as areas outside the territorial or internal waters of states), we shall not be surprised to find that there are no treaties delimiting the high seas regions of the North Sea as such or apportioning *general* jurisdictional rights among the littoral states. However, precisely because the high seas are beyond both the control and the responsibility of any one state, it has been particularly necessary to develop a body of law (now mainly treaty-based) regulating particular activities – such as navigation – in those waters. These treaties will be considered in the Section dealing with specific activities and problems (*infra*, Section II).

16. Although the general principle is, then, that the high seas are beyond states' territorial jurisdiction, there are two areas of the high seas over which littoral states *are* accorded a measure of jurisdiction, although it does not amount to comprehensive sovereignty. They are the continental shelf and the contiguous zone.

The Continental Shelf

17. Oceanographers' definitions of the continental shelf vary, but for present purposes it can be defined as "The zone around the continent extending from the low water-line to the depth at which there is usually a marked increase of declivity to greater depth".[20] Around the world, this change of gradient ("the shelf break") begins at a depth of anything from less than 60 to more than 500 metres, though it averages 130 metres.

18. The *legal* definition of the continental shelf, contained in the Geneva Convention on the Continental Shelf, 1958,[21] is different. Article 1 provides:

"For the purpose of these articles, the term 'continental shelf' is used as referring (a) to the seabed and subsoil of the submarine areas adjacent to the coast but outside the area of the territorial sea, to a depth of 200 metres or, beyond that point, to where the depth of the superjacent water admits of the exploitation of the natural resources of the said areas; (b) to the seabed and subsoil of similar submarine areas adjacent to the coasts of islands."

19. One difference is that, although from an oceanographer's point of

---

[19] Cf. Oppenheim, *International Law* (8th ed., 1955), Vol. I, p. 593. Some of these assumptions are no longer tenable.

[20] Cf. Guilcher, "Geo-Physical Characteristics [of the Seabed and Ocean Floor]" in Churchill, Simmonds & Welch (eds.), *New Directions in the Law of the Sea*, III (1973), p. 109.

[21] Hereinafter referred to as "the Continental Shelf Convention": 29 April 1958 (entered into force 10 June 1964); 499 UNTS 311; 15 UST 471; TIAS 5578; UKTS No. 39 of 1964 (Cmnd. 2422). Of the North Sea States, Belgium and the Federal Republic of Germany are not parties to the Convention.

view the continental shelf begins at the coast, for a lawyer it technically begins at the outer limit of territorial waters. As Article 2 of the Territorial Sea Convention recognizes,[22] the coastal state has complete and exclusive rights over the seabed and subsoil underlying its territorial sea, not by virtue of the comparatively new law of the continental shelf, but by virtue of the ancient rule that, in its territory, the sovereignty of the state extends *usque ad caelum et ad inferos* (up to the heavens and down to the depths).[23]

20. Although there is at present considerable controversy regarding the outer limit of a state's continental shelf jurisdiction,[24] the position with regard to the North Sea is more or less settled, for two reasons.

(a) In the first place, with the possible exception of the Norwegian Trough,[25] the entire bed of the North Sea outside the territorial waters plainly forms a single continuous shelf, in both the legal and the geological senses. Nowhere (except again in the Norwegian Trough) does the depth exceed 200 metres, so that the vexed problems of the shelf's "movable outer limit"[26] and of the regime of the seabed beyond the shelf do not arise in this region.

(b) How continental shelves should be delimited between opposite and adjacent states in the absence of agreement is controversial; indeed the question has been the subject of proceedings by Federal Germany against both the Netherlands and Denmark in the International Court of Justice.[27] Fortunately, however, in the case of the North Sea these problems now belong largely to the past because, apart from a

---

[22] Geneva Convention on the Territorial Sea and Contiguous Zone (hereinafter referred to as the "Territorial Sea Convention"), 29 April 1958 (entered into force 10 September 1964); 516 UNTS 205; 15 UST 1606; TIAS 5639; UKTS No. 3 of 1965 (Cmnd. 2511). Of the North Sea states, only Norway and the Federal Republic of Germany are non-parties. On the other hand, the total number of parties is not high, and several of the parties have made far-reaching reservations.

[23] Cf. e.g. Oppenheim, *International Law*, Vol. I, pp. 501–502.

[24] Cf. Brown, *The Legal Regime of Hydrospace* (1971), Part I.

[25] It has been suggested that the Norwegian Trough does not constitute a true shelf edge, but is merely a deep gorge in the continental shelf – cf. UN Conference on the Law of the Sea (1958), Prep. Doc. No. 2, "Scientific Considerations relating to the Continental Shelf", 1 Official Records, p. 39 at paras. 20, 34.

[26] Brown, *op. cit.*, Chap. 2.

[27] I.C.J. Reports, 1969, p. 3. The dispute arose out of the unwillingness of Federal Germany to accept a delimitation based on the equidistance principle laid down in Art. 6 (2) of the Continental Shelf Convention (to which she is not a party), because she considered that this principle, when applied to her concave coastline, would give her an unduly small section of the shelf. The Court upheld her claim, decreeing that the delimitation should be effected "by agreement in accordance with equitable principles, and taking account of all the relevant circumstances in such a way as to leave as much as possible to each party of all those parts of the Continental Shelf that constitute a natural prolongation of its land territory into and under the sea, without encroachment on the natural

relatively small part adjacent to Belgium, the entire continental shelf has been apportioned in a series of bilateral agreements.[28] Under these arrangements the United Kingdom has obtained rights over approximately one-half of the total shelf area.

prolongation of the land territory of the other". Agreement was in fact reached between the parties: cf. (a) Denmark–Federal Germany, Treaty relating to the Delimitation of the Continental Shelf under the North Sea, Copenhagen, 28 January 1971 (entered into force 7 December 1972), 10 *Int. Legal Materials* (1971), p. 603; (b) Federal Germany–Netherlands, Treaty relating to the Delimitation of the Continental Shelf under the North Sea, Copenhagen, 28 January 1971 (entered into force 7 December 1972), *ibid.*, p. 607; (c) Denmark–Federal Germany–Netherlands, Protocol to the Agreements Delimiting the Continental Shelf in the North Sea, Copenhagen, 28 January 1971, *ibid.*, p. 600.

[28] Cf. the treaties referred to in note 27 *supra* and the following further agreements: (a) Denmark–Federal Germany, Agreement and Protocol concerning the Delimitation in Coastal Areas of the Continental Shelf of the North Sea, Bonn, 9 June 1965 (entered into force 27 May 1966), 570 UNTS 96; (b) Federal Germany–Netherlands, Treaty concerning the Lateral Delimitation of the Continental Shelf in the Vicinity of the Coast, Bonn, 1 December 1964 (entered into force 18 September 1965), 550 UNTS 128; (c) Denmark–United Kingdom, Agreement relating to the Delimitation of the Continental Shelf between the Two Countries, London, 25 November 1971 (entered into force 7 December 1972), UKTS No. 6 of 1973 (Cmnd. 5193); (d) Federal Germany–United Kingdom, Agreement relating to the Delimitation of the Continental Shelf under the North Sea between the Two Countries, London, 25 November 1971 (entered into force 7 December 1972), UKTS No. 7 of 1973 (Cmnd. 5192); (e) Netherlands–United Kingdom, Agreement relating to the Delimitation of the Continental Shelf under the North Sea between the Two Countries, London, 6 October 1965 (entered into force 23 December 1966), UKTS No. 23 of 1967 (Cmnd. 3253); (f) Netherlands–United Kingdom, Protocol Amending the Agreement of 6 October 1965 relating to the Delimitation of the Continental Shelf under the North Sea between the Two Countries, London, 25 November 1971 (entered into force 7 December 1972), UKTS No. 130 of 1972 (Cmnd. 5173); (g) Netherlands–United Kingdom, Agreement relating to the Exploitation of Single Geological Structures Extending across the Dividing Line on the Continental Shelf under the North Sea, London, 6 October 1965 (entered into force 23 December 1966), UKTS No. 24 of 1967 (Cmnd. 3254); (h) Norway–United Kingdom, Agreement relating to the Delimitation of the North Sea between the Two Countries, London, 10 March 1965 (entered into force 29 June 1965), UKTS No. 71 of 1965 (Cmnd. 2757); (i) Norway–United Kingdom, Agreement relating to the Transmission of Petroleum from the Ekofisk Field and Neighbouring Areas to the U.K., Oslo, 22 May 1973 (entered into force on same date), UKTS No. 101 of 1973 (Cmnd. 5423); (j) Denmark–Norway, Agreement on the Delimitation of the Continental Shelf between Denmark and Norway, Oslo, 8 December 1965 (entered into force 22 June 1966), 634 UNTS 71; (k) Denmark–Norway, Exchange of Notes Constituting an Agreement Amending the Agreement of 8 December 1965, Copenhagen, 24 April 1968 (entered into force same date), *ibid.*, p. 414; (l) Norway–Sweden, Agreement on the Delimitation of the Continental Shelf, Stockholm, 24 July 1968 (entered into force 18 March 1969), (1968) Overenskomster med Fremmede Stater 324.

21. The continental shelf rights of states are not unlimited. In the first place, the coastal state has no special rights in the superjacent waters, which retain their character as high seas (Art. 3). Secondly, the exclusive "sovereign rights" over the shelf recognized by the Convention are confined to the exploration and exploitation of the shelf's natural resources (minerals and sedentary living organisms); nothing in the Convention authorizes states to claim exclusive rights over "their" shelf for other purposes (e.g. military installations).[29] Thirdly, even the "sovereign rights" of exploration and exploitation are restricted in certain respects, in order to accommodate the reasonable interests of the other users of the high seas:

(a) subject to the coastal state's right to take reasonable measures in the exercise of its sovereign rights, the establishment or maintenance of submarine cables or pipelines on the shelf is not to be impeded (Art. 4);[30]

(b) there is to be no "unjustifiable" interference with navigation, fishing or the conservation of the living resources of the sea, nor any interference at all with fundamental oceanographic or other scientific research carried out with the intention of open publication (Art. 5(1));

(c) devices and installations necessary for exploration and exploitation, with surrounding safety zones to a distance of 500 metres, may be established, but not where interference might be caused to the use of recognized sea lanes essential to international navigation. The devices and installations do not possess the status of islands, have no territorial sea of their own, and do not affect the delimitation of the territorial sea of the coastal state. Due notice must be given of the construction of installations, and permanent means for giving warning of their presence maintained; abandoned or disused installations must be entirely removed. The coastal state is obliged to undertake, in the safety zones, all appropriate measures for the protection of the living resources of the sea from harmful agents (Art. 5);

(d) although the consent of the coastal state is needed before research concerning the shelf can be undertaken there, the state is not normally entitled to withhold its consent where *bona fide* scientific work is involved (Art. 5(8)).

The coastal state also retains the unimpaired right to exploit the subsoil by means of tunnelling (Art. 7).

---

[29] Art. 2. This is not to say that coastal states are prohibited from using the shelf for non-Convention purposes, but rather that, if they do so, they can claim no exclusive rights in connection therewith. Cf. Bowett, *The Law of the Sea* (1967), p. 49, and *infra*, paras. 127 & 131.

[30] Cf. also the Convention for the Protection of Submarine Cables, Paris, 1884 (75 B.F.S.P. 356; 2 Malloy 1949; 2 M.N.R.G. (2ème sér.) 281).

22. The exact status of the continental shelf in the law of the European Communities has not yet been resolved. On 18 September 1970 the Commission issued a memorandum[31] maintaining that the Treaty of Rome, and in particular the directives on freedom of establishment and the rendering of services relating to mining and quarrying[32] and to prospecting and drilling for oil and natural gas,[33] was applicable to the shelf of the member states. Reference was also made, in relation to the customs union between the member states, to the Council Regulation of 28 June 1968 on the common definition of the concept of the origin of goods.[34] This definition treats as obtained in a member state "products taken from the seabed or beneath the seabed outside territorial waters, if that country has, for the purposes of exploitation, exclusive rights to such soil or subsoil". It should be noted, however, that the significance of this provision is substantially diminished by the fact that it does not apply to petroleum products. In support of its claim, the Commission in its Memorandum seeks to assimilate the continental shelf with the territory of member states. As we have already seen, claiming such an assimilation is somewhat dubious.[35] The Commission may be on stronger ground legally when it argues that the field of application of the Treaty extends to all activities within the control of the member states which have economic effects in the different spheres to which the Treaty relates.[36] The fact remains, however, that this whole question is politically very sensitive and, so far, the Council of Ministers of the Communities has refrained from expressing its approval of the Commission's stance.

The Contiguous Zone

23. Although the territorial sea forms a kind of buffer zone around the state, the security that this has afforded has not been enough to satisfy all states, and especially those with a narrow territorial sea.[37] Accordingly, for some years certain states (including, most notably, the U.S.A.) have claimed certain additional rights in limited areas of the high seas contiguous to their territorial waters, principally with a view to preventing infringements of their customs and sanitary regulations and the like. This practice has now been recognized in Article 24 of the 1958 Geneva Convention on the Territorial Sea and Contiguous Zone.

---

[31] Memorandum concernant l'application du Traité de la Communauté Economique Européenne au plateau Continental, SEC (70) 3095 Final; English translation in 10 *International Legal Materials* (1971) 202.
[32] 64/428, J.O. 1964, p. 1871.
[33] 69/82, J.O. 1969, L68/4.
[34] 802/68, J.O. 1968, L148.
[35] Cf. paragraph 21 above.
[36] Cf. e.g. Wenger, "La CEE et le plateau continental", 143 *Revue du Marché Commun* (1971), p. 184, esp. at p. 189.
[37] Cf. McDougal and Burke, *The Public Order of the Oceans*, pp. 565–575.

24. Article 24 describes the contiguous zone as "a zone of the high seas contiguous to [the] territorial sea". Since it may not extend beyond twelve miles from the baseline from which the breadth of the territorial sea is measured,[38] the breadth of states' contiguous zones varies with the breadth of their territorial seas. Thus, a state claiming a three-mile territorial sea could claim a nine-mile contiguous zone, while a state claiming a territorial sea of twelve miles or more would be entitled to no contiguous zone at all.[39]

25. It is important to note that the language of Article 24 is permissive: unlike the territorial sea,[40] the contiguous zone is not automatically appurtenant to the coastal state, and the appropriate rights must be claimed before they can be enjoyed.[41] Among the North Sea states, the United Kingdom, Federal Germany and the Netherlands have not claimed any contiguous zone rights as such, and the claims of the other states are not as extensive as the Convention permits.

26. Within the contiguous zone, according to the Convention, the coastal state may exercise the control necessary to: (a) prevent infringement of its customs, fiscal, immigration or sanitary regulations within its territory or territorial sea; and (b) punish infringements of those regulations committed within its territory or territorial sea. Additional rights in zones adjacent to the territorial sea are sometimes claimed by states, but are invalid unless authorized by customary law or express agreement. Such additional claims as may be relevant will be dealt with in the appropriate sections of this report.[42]

27. Since the contiguous zone retains its character as high seas, the presumption is that the coastal state is *not* entitled to exercise jurisdiction over foreign ships or devices in this zone unless it can show that the rights it is purporting to exercise fall within the recognized exceptions. Unlike the position in the territorial sea, the coastal state's jurisdiction in the contiguous zone is thus limited and occasional.[43]

2. National Waters

28. The national waters of states fall into two categories. Internal waters include, as well as lakes and rivers inside the land territory of the state, ports, harbours, historic bays, and all other waters on the landward side of the baseline of the territorial sea. The territorial sea (or territorial waters)

---

[38] Cf. *infra*, para. 29.
[39] Para. (3) of Art. 24 provides: "Where the coasts of two states are opposite or adjacent to each other, neither of the two states is entitled, failing agreement between them to the contrary, to extend its contiguous zone beyond the median line every point of which is equidistant from the nearest points on the baselines from which the breadth of the territorial sea is measured."
[40] Cf. *infra*, paras. 30–31.
[41] Cf. Brownlie, *Principles of Public International Law* (2nd ed., 1973), p. 210.
[42] *Infra*, paras. 46–59, 125–127.
[43] Cf. McDougal and Burke, *The Public Order of the Oceans*, p. 629.

is the body of water to the seaward of the baseline, up to the point where the high seas begin. Before examining the rights exercisable in these two zones, it will be convenient to consider how the baseline is drawn.

The Baseline

29. The normal baseline from which the territorial sea is measured is "the low-water line along the coast as marked on large-scale charts officially recognized by the coastal State".[44] However, as the Territorial Sea Convention goes on to recognize, following the lead given by the International Court of Justice in the *Anglo-Norwegian Fisheries* case,[45] certain exceptional (primarily geographic) circumstances justify the employment of *straight* baselines across water. Precisely when and how straight baselines may be drawn is a highly technical and often controversial question, and much may turn on the facts of the particular case. The following are the main principles set out in the Territorial Sea Convention:

(a) *Localities where the coastline is deeply indented or bordered by an archipelago*
Here the baseline may be constructed by drawing straight lines between appropriate points.[46] The drawing of such baselines must not depart from the general direction of the coast, and the sea areas lying within the baselines must be sufficiently closely linked with the land domain to be subject to the regime of internal waters. Certain other limitations and criteria are set out in Article 4 of the Convention, which also requires the coastal state clearly to indicate straight baselines on charts, to which due publicity must be given. A typical coastline to which the straight baseline system may properly be applied is the west coast of Norway, which is both deeply indented and fringed with islands, as was recognized by the International Court of Justice in the above-mentioned *Anglo-Norwegian Fisheries* case.[47] Denmark and West Germany have also drawn straight baselines along parts of their North Sea coasts.

---

[44] Territorial Sea Convention, Art. 3. This Article codifies existing law. In point of fact, hydrographers recognize a variety of low-water marks, as the International Law Commission recognized in the Commentary to Art. 4 of its 1956 Draft Articles – Report of the International Law Commission on the work of its 8th Sess., *YBILC* 1956-II, pp. 266–267. However, these differences do not result in very significant variations on the horizontal plane, at any rate in the North Sea area.

[45] ICJ Rep. 1951, p. 116.

[46] Article 4.

[47] Another such area is the west coast of Scotland, to which the system has been applied by the Territorial Waters Order in Council, 1964, cf. *infra*, Chapter V.

(b) Bays

Article 7 of the Convention also enables straight lines to be used to enclose as internal waters bays (or parts of bays) the coasts of which belong to a single state. A bay is defined as "a well-marked indentation whose penetration is in such proportion to the width of its mouth as to contain landlocked waters and constitute more than a mere curvature of the coast". To be regarded as more than a "mere curvature", the indentation must be at least as large in area as the semi-circle, the diameter of which is the line drawn across its mouth.[48] The closing-line of such a bay may be taken as the baseline, provided that its length does not exceed 24 miles. If it does exceed this figure, the baseline should be the 24-mile line so drawn within the bay as to enclose the maximum area of water. This system, which is arguably more generous to coastal states than the previous law, has been adopted by a number of North Sea states.[49] These provisions do not derogate from the right of states to treat "historic bays" as national waters, whether or not the criteria set out in paragraphs (1) to (5) of Article 7 are met. On the other hand, the right set out in Article 7 cannot be invoked where states employ the straight baseline system provided for in Article 4.[50] There are a number of "historic bays" in the North Sea region.[51]

The Territorial Sea

30. As stated above, the territorial sea is a belt of sea located between the coast and internal waters of the state and the high seas. Its maximum permissible breadth is controversial. By about the beginning of the present century, it seemed as if the three-mile limit, supported by such important maritime powers as the United Kingdom and the U.S.A., would prevail. However, there was never unanimity on the subject, and the 1958 Geneva Conference on the Law of the Sea failed to achieve an agreed solution, although the provision in Article 24 of the Territorial Sea Convention fixing the maximum breadth of the contiguous zone at 12 miles from the baseline of the territorial sea seems to recognize implicitly that the territorial sea can be no wider than 12 miles.[52] A second Conference was

---

[48] Para. (3) defines what constitutes the area of an indentation, and how the diameter is to be drawn.

[49] E.g. the United Kingdom, in the Territorial Waters Order in Council, 1964. Unlike Art. 4 of the Convention, Article 7 does not require publication of details, and it is in fact not always easy to ascertain how the delimitation has been effected. For example, Art. 3 of the Order in Council only lays down the test, but does not identify the bays to which it applies.

[50] Article 7(6).

[51] For a useful discussion of some further baseline problems, cf. Brownlie, *Principles of Public International Law*, pp. 200–203.

[52] In the commentary to its Draft Articles (Art. 3), the International Law Commission firmly stated its views that extensions beyond 12 miles are not permissible: *YBILC* 1956–II, pp. 265–266.

held in 1960 to settle the question, but again no agreement could be reached. Since then, the three-mile limit has been steadily eroded. Many newly-independent states have claimed 12 miles, and many others have extended their claims to the 12-mile limit.[53]

31. At the moment, the territorial sea claims of the North Sea states are modest: Belgium, Denmark, Federal Germany, the Netherlands and the United Kingdom all claim only three miles, while Norway historically claims four. As will be seen, however, several of them claim more extensive fishing zones,[54] and they may extend their territorial waters to the 12-mile limit if, as seems probable, a consensus on this limit emerges from the UN Conference on the Law of the Sea.

Regime of the Territorial Sea

32. According to Article 1 of the Territorial Sea Convention, states have sovereignty over their territorial sea. There is some doctrinal debate as to the precise juridical nature of the regime,[55] but the substance is that the coastal state has, subject to certain important exceptions to be considered below, the same rights over its territorial waters as it has over its land territory and internal waters – an exclusive, comprehensive and continuing competence.[56]

33. In the first place, the coastal state may reserve fisheries for its own nationals, subject to such customary or treaty rights as may be enjoyed by foreign nationals; this subject will be examined further in a subsequent Section.[57] Secondly, the coastal state may exclude foreign vessels from trading along its coast (*cabotage*).[58] Thirdly, under Article 2, the littoral state has complete control over the seabed and subsoil of its territorial sea, and consequently wider powers than over its continental shelf. Fourthly, there is a general power of police in such matters as security, customs and

---

[53] In 1960, according to Brown, 26 states claimed 3 miles, 10 claimed 6 miles and 13 claimed 12 (with a handful of other assorted claims); in October 1972 27 claimed 3 miles, 12 claimed 6 miles and 50 claimed 12 miles (again, with a few other assorted claims) – "Maritime Zones: a Survey of Claims" in Churchill, Simmonds and Welch (eds.), *New Directions in the Law of the Sea*, III, p. 157 at p. 161.

[54] *Infra*, paras. 50–52.

[55] Cf. e.g. O'Connell, *International Law* (2nd ed., 1970), Vol. I, pp. 467–475; Brownlie, *Principles of Public International Law*, pp. 183–185.

[56] Cf. McDougal and Burke, *The Public Order of the Oceans*, pp. 179–304.

[57] *Infra*, Section IIB – Fisheries.

[58] Again, subject to agreement; cf. e.g. the Exchange of Notes Constituting an Agreement between Norway and Sweden Regarding the Coasting Trade, Oslo, 9 June 1958, 427 UNTS 223 (also in UN Legislative Series, *National Legislation Relating to the Territorial Sea, the Contiguous Zone, the Continental Shelf, the High Seas and to Fishing and Conservation of the Living Resources of the Seas*, ST/LEG/SER.B/15 – hereinafter referred to as *National Legislation and Treaties* – p. 749).

fiscal regulation, and sanitary, pollution and health controls.[59] This last right is, however, subject to the right of innocent passage and to certain jurisdictional rights of flag states.

34. With certain exceptions, Section III of the Territorial Sea Convention codifies the customary law relating to innocent passage. Passage is defined as navigation through the territorial sea for the purpose either of traversing that sea without entering internal waters, or of proceeding to internal waters, or of making for the high seas from internal waters.[60] Passage is innocent as long as it is not prejudicial to the peace, good order or security of the coastal state. Some controversy exists as to whether, and on what terms, the Convention (or customary law) permits foreign warships to invoke the right of innocent passage. With regard to foreign fishing vessels, however, the Convention is more explicit: Article 14(5) provides that their passage is not to be considered innocent if they do not observe such laws and regulations as the coastal state may make and publish in order to prevent such vessels from fishing in the territorial sea. Submarines must navigate on the surface and show their flag. The coastal state must not hamper innocent passage and must give appropriate publicity to navigational hazards known to it. It may, on the other hand, take the necessary steps to prevent passage which is not innocent, and may suspend, temporarily and on a non-discriminatory basis, the right of innocent passage in certain areas if this is essential for the protection of its security. Such suspension must be duly publicized, and may not extend to international straits.

35. In exercising the right of innocent passage, foreign ships must comply with the laws and regulations made by the coastal state, and particularly those relating to transport and navigation, in conformity with the Convention and any other relevant rules of international law. The Convention does, however, seek to strike a reasonable balance between the territorial jurisdiction of the coastal state and the interest of the flag state in innocent passage and in applying its own laws to the ship in question. Thus, the coastal state may levy no charges on foreign merchant ships (including state-owned ships operated for commercial purposes) in respect of innocent passage, but only as payment for specific services rendered to the ship: these charges must be levied without discrimination. The *criminal* jurisdiction of the coastal state should not be exercised over the ship in connection with any crime committed on board during its passage through the territorial sea, save only in cases where the consequences of

---

[59] In support of this power, states have a right of "hot pursuit" of vessels suspected of breaking national laws and regulations. Provided that pursuit is commenced in national waters or the contiguous zone, it may continue, and arrest may be effected, on the high seas. For details, cf. High Seas Convention, Art. 23.

[60] Art. 14. Ships may stop and anchor only if such actions are incidental to ordinary navigation or rendered necessary by *force majeure*.

the crime extend to the coastal state, where the crime is of a kind liable to disturb the peace of the state or the good order of the territorial sea, where the assistance of the local authorities has been requested by the captain or by the consul of the flag state, or where it is necessary for the suppression of illicit traffic in narcotic drugs. The coastal state may not take any action on board a foreign ship passing through the territorial sea to arrest any person, or to conduct any investigation in connection with any crime committed *before* the ship entered the territorial sea if the ship, proceeding from a foreign port, is only passing through the territorial sea without entering internal waters. On the other hand, the coastal state may take the steps authorized by its laws for the purpose of an arrest or investigation on board a ship passing through the territorial sea from internal waters. The rules for the exercise of *civil* jurisdiction provide that the coastal state may levy execution against, or arrest, the ship only in respect of obligations assumed or liabilities incurred by the ship itself in the course of, or for the purpose of, its voyage through the territorial or internal waters of that state.[61]

36. As stated above, all of these rules apply to government-owned ships operated for commercial purposes. Government ships operated for non-commercial purposes are subject only to the general rules of navigation. They are also exempt from charges and enjoy the immunities conferred by the rules of general international law. If a warship does not comply with the regulations of the coastal state concerning passage through the territorial sea and disregards any request for compliance, the coastal state may ask it to leave the territorial sea.[62]

Regime of Internal Waters

37. The internal waters of the state are as much part of its sovereign territory as the land itself. Unlike the position with respect to the territorial sea, there is in general no right of innocent passage through, or of entry into, internal waters.[63] Other rules relating to jurisdiction over foreign vessels also differ.

38. There are certain exceptions to the principle that foreign ships have no right to enter internal waters. First, a ship in distress may

---

[61] For a possible conflict between these provisions and the Brussels Convention relating to the Arrest of Sea-going Ships, 1952, cf. Brownlie, *Principles of Public International Law*, p. 209. The ships may not be stopped or diverted for the purpose of exercising civil jurisdiction in respect of a person on board.

[62] For a more comprehensive examination of jurisdictional problems, cf. O'Connell, *International Law*, Vol. II, pp. 630–639.

[63] Some writers – e.g. Colombos, *International Law of the Sea* (6th ed., 1967), p. 176 – maintain that there exists a customary right of access to ports by merchant ships. This view is not generally accepted, however, and seems to be belied by the practice.

enter.[64] Secondly, Article 5(2) of the Territorial Sea Convention provides: "Where the establishment of a straight baseline in accordance with Article 4 has the effect of enclosing as internal waters areas which previously had been considered as part of the territorial sea or of the high seas, a right of innocent passage, as provided in Articles 14 to 23, shall exist in those waters." And thirdly, states may by treaty confer the right of entry on ships flying each other's flags, for example by treaties of friendship, commerce and navigation.[65] In addition to these bilateral treaties, the subject is also dealt with in the Geneva Convention and Statute on the International Regime of Maritime Ports, 1923,[66] which provides for equality of treatment of foreign and national vessels in regard to access to ports normally frequented by seagoing vessels and used for foreign trade. The right is granted on a basis of reciprocity, and is extended to all publicly or privately owned or controlled vessels other than fishing vessels, warships and vessels "exercising any kind of public authority".[67]

39. In internal waters, including ports, the coastal state's territorial jurisdiction is to some extent tempered in favour of what has been termed the "extraterritoriality" of foreign vessels. The practice in this regard varies from one state to another, but in general it may be said that the coastal state will refrain from exercising jurisdiction in matters purely internal to the ship, and that warships are accorded complete immunity. Space does not permit a more detailed exposition here.[68]

II REGULATION OF PARTICULAR ACTIVITIES

A. Exploration and exploitation of mineral resources

40. As indicated above,[69] the sovereignty of the coastal state extends to the seabed in internal waters and the territorial sea. The coastal state, therefore, has the exclusive jurisdiction to determine whether, and on what

---

[64] Cf. McDougal and Burke, *The Public Order of the Oceans*, p. 110.

[65] E.g. Treaty of Friendship, Commerce and Navigation between the Federal Republic of Germany and Italy, 21 November 1957, BGB 1959-II, p. 949 (reproduced UN Leg. Ser. *National Legislation and Treaties*, p. 747). In the case of warships, any consent must normally be obtained *ad hoc*.

[66] 58 LNTS 287, reproduced in UN Leg. Ser. *Laws and Regulations on the Regime of the Territorial Sea* (1956), UN Doc. ST/LEG/SER. B/6 (hereinafter referred to as *Laws and Regulations on the Territorial Sea*), p. 706; entered into force 26 July 1926. All of the North Sea states are parties.

[67] Cf. also High Seas Convention, Art. 3, and the Barcelona Convention and Statute on Freedom of Transit, 20 April 1921 (entered into force 31 October 1922), to which all of the North Sea states are party, 7 LNTS, p. 11; UKTS No. 27 of 1923 (Cmnd. 1992); (reproduced in UN Leg. Ser. *Laws and Regulations on the Territorial Sea*, p. 702).

[68] For a fuller discussion, cf. O'Connell, *International Law*, Vol. II, pp. 612–627; McDougal and Burke, *The Public Order of the Oceans*, pp. 126–173.

[69] Paras. 33–37.

terms, the mineral resources of the seabed should be exploited, subject only to its obligation not to create a danger to shipping exercising the right of innocent passage and, it would seem, not to permit the creation of an international nuisance.[70] Beyond the outer limit of the territorial sea, the exploration and exploitation of seabed mineral resources come under the regime of the continental shelf.[71] Apart from sedentary fisheries – relatively unimportant in the North Sea – that regime is concerned exclusively with rights and duties relating to the exploration and exploitation of mineral resources. Since this has already been described in the sub-Section on Zonal Jurisdiction,[72] it is unnecessary to elaborate further here.[73]

B. Fisheries[74]

41. If fish stocks were inexhaustible, there would be little need for coastal states to attempt to regulate fishing by foreign nationals.[75] However, it has become increasingly clear that even the extremely rich North Sea fisheries are not inexhaustible, and with this realization has come mounting pressure on governments, particularly on behalf of home-waters fishermen, to regulate fishing in areas adjacent to their coasts. On the other hand, extensive jurisdictional claims may result in similar claims by other states, and consequently there has also been counter-pressure from distant-water fishermen, who often operate close to foreign coasts. In a country like the United Kingdom, whose nationals operate in home, middle and distant waters, the interplay of pressures can be very complex indeed.

42. Measures concerned with the regulation of fishing relate mainly to conservation or allocation. Conservation measures pure and simple are concerned not so much with who catches the fish (nationals of the coastal state or others) as with the quantities or species of fish that may be taken; the aim is to prevent the depletion of stocks below the level at which the optimum yield can be sustained.[76] By allocation, on the other hand, is

---

[70] Cf. para. 96 *infra*.
[71] For the reasons indicated above (para. 20) a study restricted to the North Sea need not concern itself with the regime of the seabed beyond the continental shelf.
[72] Paras. 21 and 22 *supra*.
[73] For a consideration of the legal status of installations for the exploration and exploitation of these resources, cf. *infra*, paras. 129–131. Recently, steps have been taken with a view to the establishment of internationally agreed safety standards for drilling rigs and associated equipment.
[74] For an excellent "contextual" study of the general law of fisheries, see Johnston, *International Law of Fisheries* (1965).
[75] Though it might still be felt to be desirable to protect local fishermen from foreign competition, e.g. by restricting the right of foreign nationals to land fish locally.
[76] For a discussion of the concept "maximum sustainable yield", cf. Coull, "The Economics of Fishing" in Churchill, Simmonds and Welch (eds.), *New Directions in the Law of the Sea*, III, p. 52.

meant control over *who* may fish, defined in terms of nationality (or, more precisely, of the nationality of the fishing vessel). Theoretically the two topics are distinct, but in practice they are often closely connected. For example, in national waters states have, as will be seen, jurisdiction both to prescribe conservation measures and to exclude foreign vessels. Again, there is an increasing tendency on the part of states to extend their territorial waters, or to claim exclusive fishery zones, on the grounds that foreign nationals are depleting traditional fisheries.

43. In this sub-Section, the right of the North Sea states to regulate fishing operations in the "normal" zones, described in paragraphs 12 to 39 above, will be considered before turning to special fishery zones.

1. National Waters

44. As has already been indicated,[77] for all relevant purposes the jurisdiction of the coastal state over its internal and territorial waters is as full as on land. It follows, therefore, that the state has inherent authority to exclude foreign vessels from fishing in these waters, and to prescribe measures of conservation.[78] This power is, however, subject to such concessions or treaty rights as may exist in favour of foreign states or nationals.[79]

2. The High Seas

45. As has also been seen, the freedom to fish is one of the fundamental freedoms of the high seas; derogations from it must be founded on common consent. The contiguous zone is no exception to this principle; although the coastal state has certain powers with respect to customs and sanitary matters and the like, these do not extend to the regulation of fishing, which remains subject to the regime of the high seas.[80] It is otherwise with the continental shelf under the high seas; as has been indicated,[81] the Continental Shelf Convention recognizes the exclusive right of the coastal state to regulate the exploitation of such sedentary species as may be found there.[82] It should be noted, however, that this

---

[77] *Supra*, paras. 30–39.

[78] Cf. Jessup, *The Territorial Waters and Maritime Jurisdiction* (1927), pp. 115–208; Riesenfeld, *The Protection of Coastal Fisheries in International Law* (1928), p. 3.

[79] Cf. Windley, "International Practice Regarding Traditional Fishing Privileges of Foreign Fishermen in Zones of Extended Maritime Jurisdiction", 63 *American Jl. of Int. Law* (1969), p. 490.

[80] Cf. *supra*, paras. 26–27.

[81] *Supra*, para. 21.

[82] Art. 2(4) of the Convention defines "organisms belonging to sedentary species" as "organisms which, at the harvestable stage, either are immobile on or under the seabed or are unable to move except in constant physical contact with the seabed or subsoil". Certain difficulties have arisen regarding the classification of certain species, but in the context of a study of the North Sea the matter is not of sufficient importance to merit discussion.

Convention gives the state to which the shelf "belongs" no rights regarding fishing in the superjacent waters. Moreover, although the coastal state has the power to construct and maintain or operate devices or installations for the exploitation of shelf resources, and to establish limited safety zones around them, these measures must not result in unjustifiable interference with fishing or conservation.[83] In general it remains true, then, that high seas fisheries can be regulated only by special agreement.

3. Special Agreements

46. Special agreements fall into two main categories; those relating to conservation, and those relating to allocation.[84] Typically, such agreements authorize the creation of special conservation or exploitation zones and regulate the rights of nationals of the different states parties to fish in them. Sometimes these zones straddle national waters and high seas, and cannot conveniently be subsumed under either heading. For example, part of the "inner six-mile" exclusive fisheries zone granted to parties to the European Fisheries Convention[85] falls within their three-mile territorial sea, but the other part is in what is technically high seas.

(a) Conservation regimes[86]

47. The key instrument in this field is the Geneva Convention on Fishing and Conservation of the Living Resources of the High Seas, 1958.[87] The Convention established the obligation of states to adopt, or co-operate in adopting, conservation measures, defined as "the aggregate of the measures rendering possible the optimum sustainable yield from [the sea's living] resources so as to secure a maximum supply of food and other marine products", priority being given to food for human consumption (Arts. 1 & 2). Where necessary, conservation measures are to be adopted by the state whose nationals are the only ones concerned with a particular fishery; where nationals of different states are involved, the states must negotiate; "newcomers" are bound by these arrangements (Arts. 3, 4 & 5). The special interest of the coastal state in adjacent fisheries, even if its nationals do not fish there, is recognized in several ways. It has the right to participate

---

[83] Art. 5(1). How seriously this prohibition is taken is another matter; cf. Young, "Offshore Claims and Problems in the North Sea", 59 *American Jl. of Int. Law* (1965), p. 505 at p. 519.

[84] These terms are used here in the sense indicated above, at para. 42.

[85] See below, paras. 50–52.

[86] Cf. e.g. Garcia Amador, *The Exploitation and Conservation of the Resources of the Sea* (2nd ed., 1963); Oda, *International Control of Sea Resources* (1963).

[87] 29 April 1958 (entered into force 20 March 1966), hereinafter referred to as "the Geneva Conservation Convention"; 559 UNTS 285; 17 UST 138; TIAS 5969; UKTS No. 39 of 1966 (Cmnd. 3028); text in UN Legislative Series *National Legislation and Treaties*, p. 847. Of the North Sea states, Federal Germany and Norway have not become parties.

in research and any regulatory regime, and may call for negotiations for an agreed conservation regime (Art. 6). If no such agreement is reached within 12 months, the coastal state may unilaterally adopt conservation measures, provided that there is an urgent need, that the measures adopted are based on appropriate scientific findings, *and that they do not discriminate in form or in fact against foreign fishermen* (Art. 7). States whose nationals are not engaged in fishing in areas not adjacent to their coast, but which nevertheless have a special interest in a fishery, can call on states whose nationals do fish there to adopt conservation measures (Art. 8). Disputes are to be referred to a special commission of five members, with the power to make binding decisions (Arts. 9–12). By its emphasis on negotiation and non-discrimination, the Convention has not gone far enough for some coastal states, who would prefer to have a *preferential* right to the permissible catch. However, the Convention has provided something of an impetus for the conclusion of conservation agreements, either on a regional or sub-regional basis, or with reference to particular species or genera.[88]

48. In relation to the North Sea, the most important regional arrangement is the 1959 North-East Atlantic Fisheries Convention,[89] which established the North-East Atlantic Fisheries Commission (NEAFC). The Commission has regulatory functions, being responsible for making recommendations to member states for the purpose of achieving "rational exploitation" based on information received from the International Council for the Exploration of the Sea (ICES). Article 7 enables the Commission and its Regional Committees to make recommendations on (a) mesh sizes; (b) fish sizes; (c) closed seasons; (d) closed areas; (e) regulation of fishing gear (other than mesh sizes); (f) any measures for the improvement and increase of marine resources, including artificial propagation and transplantation of organs or young. If all Contracting States agree, there may be added to this list: (g) measures for regulating the amount of total catch, or the amount of fishing effort in any period, or any other kinds of conservation measures. Under Article 8 of the Convention, recommendations of the Commission adopted by a two-thirds majority of delegations present or voting are binding on each of the parties, unless the party in question objects within a certain time, or three or more others

---

[88] For an example of an agreement of the latter type, cf. Denmark–Norway–Sweden, Agreement Concerning Measures for the Protection of the Stock of Deep Sea Prawns (*Pandalus borealis*), European Lobsters (*Homarus vulgaris*), Norway Lobsters (*Nephrops norvegicus*) and Crabs (*Cancer pagarus*), Oslo, 7 March 1952 (entered into force 26 January 1953), 175 UNTS 208, as amended by Protocol, Oslo, 14 October 1959 (entered into force 14 October 1959), 427 UNTS 336; UN Leg. Ser. *National Legislation and Treaties*, p. 839.

[89] London, 24 January 1959 (entered into force 27 June 1963); 486 UNTS 158; UKTS No. 68 of 1963 (Cmnd. 2190); UN Leg. Ser. *National Legislation and Treaties*, p. 853. All six North Sea states are parties, as are other states with important fishing interests in the area, such as the U.S.S.R. and Poland.

do so.[90] So far, most of the recommendations adopted have concerned minimum mesh and fish sizes but, although these have in general made substantial contributions to the conservation effort, some species have still been considerably depleted.[91] This is partly due to the reluctance of parties to accept really strong regulatory measures, and partly to the fact that, until the Contracting States unanimously agreed, the Commission had no powers to make recommendations on the important subjects referred to in (g) above. In 1970 the Commission sought these additional powers,[92] but it is only recently that they have been granted. Until then the Commission had sought to persuade states to accept national quota arrangements outside the framework of the Convention. The Convention suffers from a further inherent limitation, however; it does not bind non-parties, whose vessels remain free in law to enter the area and reap the benefit of the conservation measures adopted (though at present it is relatively rare for them to do so). The fishing industries of the North Sea states are not likely to acquiesce readily in the adoption of strict conservation measures within the NEAFC system if they find that outsiders are failing to comply with those measures. This is the ever-present drawback of regional schemes under present-day international law.[93]

49. Finally, it should be noted that to date the question of the legal protection and conservation of marine species for purely scientific or tourist/amenity purposes has been virtually ignored.[94]

(b) *Allocation regimes: The European Fisheries Convention and related agreements*

50. All over the world, the intensification and increasing efficiency of distant-water fishing has produced a reaction on the part of coastal states anxious to protect their traditional coastal fisheries from depletion and their in-shore fishermen from foreign competition. The response of many states has been to extend the limits of the territorial sea to 12 miles, or even beyond, thereby acquiring the jurisdiction to exclude or regulate foreign fishing boats.[95] The North Sea states, on the other hand, have so far resisted this temptation, mainly, it would appear, because they did not

---

[90] Art. 10 also contains provisions for opting out at a later stage.
[91] Cf. Koers, "The Freedom of Fishing in Decline: the case of the North-East Atlantic" in Churchill, Simmonds and Welch (eds.), *New Directions in the Law of the Sea*, III, p. 19.
[92] NEAFC, *Report of 8th Meeting* (London, 1970), p. 12.
[93] For other "structural" difficulties, cf. Koers, *op. cit.*
[94] Cf. Starke, *Introduction to International Law* (7th ed., 1972), p. 230.
[95] An examination of the practice reveals a fairly general acceptance of the coastal state's right to extend its territorial sea, and *a fortiori* to create an exclusive fisheries zone, up to the 12-mile limit, possibly subject to a duty to respect the "vested rights" of those who have traditionally fished in a particular area of what was formerly high seas, at least for a transitional period.

wish to encourage encroachments upon the high seas which would interfere with other maritime interests. However, they felt that they had to do something to protect their coastal fisheries and the 1882 North Sea Fisheries Convention, based on three-mile limits, was clearly inadequate. Accordingly, it was replaced by the European Fisheries Convention, which authorizes the creation of adjacent fishery zones.[96]

51. Under the Convention, each party may establish in the waters outside the baseline of its territorial sea two zones (Art. 1). In the first, which extends six miles from the baseline (the "inner six"), the coastal state has exclusive jurisdiction over fisheries and the exclusive right to fish (Art. 2).[97] The second zone is a belt between six and twelve miles from the baseline (the "outer six"); in this zone, the right to fish is confined to the coastal state and those other Contracting Parties whose nationals habitually fished in that belt between 1 January 1953 and 31 December 1962 (Art. 3). However, such non-coastal states "shall not direct their fishing effort towards stocks of fish or fishing grounds substantially different from those which they have habitually exploited" (Art. 4).[98] Within the "outer six" the coastal state has the power to regulate the fisheries and to enforce these regulations (including *internationally agreed* conservation measures), provided that there is no discrimination against other Contracting Parties (Art. 5). In addition, if the local population is "overwhelmingly dependent upon coastal fisheries", a coastal state may make particular areas in the "outer six" completely exclusive, subject to the approval of the other Contracting States (Art. 11). The Convention adopts the principles laid down in the Geneva Convention on the Territorial Sea and the Contiguous Zone, 1958, as regards straight baselines, bay closing lines, and median lines (Arts. 6 & 7). Disputes are to be arbitrated by a Tribunal of five members, who have power to give a binding award (Art. 13 and Annex II).

52. To date, 11 European states have ratified the Convention.[99] This represents a substantial proportion of the states involved in fishing in the North Sea, but does not include the U.S.S.R. (which has a large fleet

---

[96] London, 9 March 1964 (entered into force 15 March 1966); 581 UNTS 57; UKTS No. 35 of 1966 (Cmnd. 3011); UN Leg. Ser. *National Legislation and Treaties*, p. 862.

[97] Art. 9(1) provided for agreement to be reached regarding the phasing out of fishing by nationals of other Contracting Parties who had habitually fished in that belt. Two such agreements were concluded but, as the "phase-out" period has now expired, there is no need to consider them here.

[98] On the basis of this provision and subsequent agreement, the Hydrographer of the Royal Navy published in 1971 an illustrative map (Q.6385) of "Foreign Fishing Rights and Concessions within the Fishery Limits of the British Islands", which showed which countries were entitled to catch which species in the "outer six". The situation has, however, changed somewhat in consequence of the expansion of the EEC; see below, paras. 53–59.

[99] Belgium, Denmark, France, Ireland, Italy, the Netherlands, Poland, Portugal, Spain, Sweden and the United Kingdom.

operating in these waters), nor two of the littoral states – Norway and West Germany. (Norway, in fact, unilaterally claimed a 12-mile exclusive fishery zone in 1961.) To some extent, these gaps have been filled by bilateral treaties; in addition, a number of bilateral agreements have been concluded among the parties to the Convention itself.[100] However, the whole picture has been significantly altered by the expansion on 1 January 1973 of the European Economic Community, to which reference must now be made.[101]

(c) The EEC regime[102]

53. Article 38(1) of the EEC Treaty[103] provides:
"The Common Market shall extend to agriculture and trade in agricultural products. 'Agricultural products' means the products of the soil, of stockfarming and of fisheries and products of first-stage processing directly related to these products."
On 20 October 1970, acting under this and other provisions,[104] the Council of Ministers of the Communities adopted the two regulations which established the original Common Fisheries Policy, as well as a series of further implementing regulations.[105]

54. The first of these regulations is Regulation 2141/70 on the Establishment of a Common Structural Policy for the Fishing Industry ("the Structure Regulation"). This Regulation recognizes the need to complement the establishment of a common market for products of the fishing industry. In the first place, recognizing the fact that, to achieve a common market, it is necessary to remove not only trade barriers but production barriers too, it establishes the principle of *equal access to fishing grounds*. Article 2(1) of the Regulation provides:
"The system applied by each Member State in respect of fishing in the maritime waters coming under its sovereignty or within its jurisdiction must not lead to differences in treatment with regard to other Member States.

[100] Useful tables showing the arrangements up to the date of the expansion of the EEC are to be found in Lay, Churchill and Nordquist (eds.), *New Directions in the Law of the Sea: Documents* (1973), II, pp. 875–879. The chart dealing with the post-Accession situation is not entirely accurate.
[101] Art. 10 of the European Fisheries Convention provides: "Nothing in the present Convention shall prevent the maintenance or establishment of a special regime in matters of fisheries ... as between States Members ... of the European Economic Community."
[102] Cf. esp. Brown, "British Fisheries and the Common Market", 25 *Current Legal Problems* (1972), p. 37, on which paras. 54–58 below are largely based. Cf. also Garron, *Le marché commun de la pêche maritime* (1971).
[103] 298 UNTS 11; Cmnd. 4864.
[104] Articles 7, 43 and 235. References to Article 52 on Freedom of Establishment were deliberately omitted.
[105] HMSO, *European Communities Secondary Legislation, Part 24: Fisheries* (1972).

"In particular, Member States shall ensure equal conditions of access to, and exploitation of, the fishing grounds situated in the waters referred to in the preceding paragraph, for all fishing vessels flying the flag of a Member State and registered in Community territory."[106]

The Regulation does not attempt to deprive coastal states of all jurisdiction; they remain free to subject the waters in question to their own regime (including conservation measures), provided that this is done on a non-discriminatory basis. What Article 2(1) does seek to ensure, however, is equality of access to national waters and to other – especially fishery – zones. The principle of equal access is subject to limited exceptions intended to protect in-shore fishermen, who are especially vulnerable to competition from foreign and more efficient deep-water fleets. Article 4 empowers the Council, acting by qualified majority on a proposal from the Commission, to reserve areas within a limit of three nautical miles from the baseline of the territorial sea for certain types of fishing by the local population of the coastal region concerned, if that population depends primarily on in-shore fishing. However, the period of exception cannot extend beyond 31 October 1975. In addition, the Regulation provides a framework for the restructuring and rationalization of the industry and the co-ordination of national structural policies.

55. The "Market Regulation" of the same date (Regulation 2142/70) deals with the common organization of the market in products of the fishing industry. Its aim is to achieve the adaptation of supply to the demands of the market and to achieve a fair return for producers, and accordingly Article 1 establishes a common organization of the market in products of the fishing industry, including a price and trade system as well as common rules on competition.[107] Although this Regulation is perhaps of less interest to the international lawyer than the Structure Regulation, it should be remembered that there is a very important relationship between market conditions, on the one hand, and questions of the allocation and conservation of fishery resources, on the other.[108]

56. For the six original members of the EEC, the mutual concessions embodied in the Common Fisheries Policy were not particularly great, for

---

[106] Art. 5, however, empowers the Council, acting by a qualified majority on a proposal from the Commission, to adopt the necessary conservation measures if there is a risk of over-intensive exploitation.

[107] Article 4(f) of Regulation 802/68 on the common definition of the concept of the origin of goods (OJ No. L148 of June 1968) applies the definition of "a product originating in a member State" to fish taken from the sea by vessels registered in that country, irrespective of the place where the fishing took place.

[108] Cf. Johnson, "European Fishery Limits", in British Institute of International and Comparative Law, *Developments in the Law of the Sea 1958–1964* (International Law Series No. 3, 1965), p. 48 at pp. 57–61. Both Regulations refer to the objective of the conservation and rational exploitation of the living resources of the sea.

their in-shore fishing activities are relatively limited. Not surprisingly, however, the Policy did not entirely commend itself to the United Kingdom, Denmark, Ireland and Norway, who had in fact applied for membership of the Community before the two Regulations were adopted. In particular, having achieved a measure of protection for coastal fisheries up to a distance of 12 miles in the European Fisheries Convention (or, in the case of Norway, by unilateral declaration), they did not relish the prospect of fishing by the vessels of other Community Members right up to their shoreline. Accordingly they sought, and to some extent achieved, a derogation from the access provisions of the Structure Regulation.

57. The compromise is spelled out in Articles 100 to 103 of the 1972 Brussels Treaty of Accession.[109] On fishery limits and freedom of access, the Treaty features yet another "six-plus-six" formula. (a) With regard to the "inner six", and in derogation from Article 2 of the Structure Regulation, Article 100(1) of the Treaty authorizes Member States "until 31 December 1982, to restrict fishing in waters under their sovereignty or jurisdiction, situated within a limit of six nautical miles, calculated from the baselines of the coastal Member State, to vessels which fish traditionally in those waters and which operate from ports in that geographical coastal area ...". In other words, for the first ten years of the expanded Community, fishing can in effect be reserved for local fishermen in the "inner six".[110] This restriction is subject to the proviso that the local fishermen may not be permitted to fish under conditions "which are less restrictive than those applied in practice at the time of accession" – in other words, they may not exhaust the fishery. The remainder of Article 100 contains other qualifications; in particular, paragraph (2) provides: "The provisions laid down in the preceding paragraph and in Article 101 shall not prejudice the special fishing rights which each of the original Member States and the new Nember States might have enjoyed on 31 January 1971 in regard to one or more other Member States; the Member States may exercise these rights for such time as derogations continue to apply in the areas concerned. ..." (b) In addition, this qualified and temporary right to exclude other Community Members from the "inner six" is extended by Article 101 to the "outer six" belt in a few specified areas. As far as the North Sea is concerned, the areas in question are the west coast of Denmark from Thyborøn to Blaavandshuk, the Shetlands and the Orkneys, the north and east of Scotland from Cape Wrath to Berwick, and the north-east of England from the river Coquet to Flamborough Head.[111] In the remainder

[109] Brussels, 22 January 1972 (entered into force 1 January 1973), U.K. Misc. No. 3 (1972) – Part I (Cmnd. 4862–I).
[110] Under the terms of the Benelux Treaty, fishing boats flying the Belgian flag may fish in all Netherlands waters, and *vice versa*.
[111] The concessions accorded to Norway in this Article and in Protocol No. 21 need not be considered here, in view of that country's failure to ratify the Treaty of Accession.

of the "outer six" areas, all EEC Members' vessels have equal rights of access. Subject to this, however, the coastal state continues to enjoy fisheries jurisdiction (including the right to prescribe conservation measures) throughout its national waters and fishery zone, as long as this jurisdiction is not exercised in a discriminatory fashion.

58. Article 102 goes on to provide that, from the sixth year after Accession at the latest, the Council, acting on a proposal from the Commission, shall determine conditions for fishing with a view to ensuring protection of fishing grounds and conservation of the biological resources of the sea.[112] Article 103 provides that, before 31 December 1982, the Commission shall report to the Council on the economic and social development of the coastal areas of the Member States and on the state of stocks. On the basis of that report, and of the objectives of the Common Fisheries Policy, the Council, acting on a proposal from the Commission, "shall examine the provisions which could follow the derogations in force until 31 December 1982". In other words, before the authorized derogations from the equality of access established by the Structure Regulation expire the whole question will be reviewed, and it is not inconceivable that these derogations will be continued and perhaps even extended.

59. The overall pattern of allocation in the North Sea which emerges from all of these agreements is extremely complicated.

(i) As far as the mutual relations of EEC members are concerned, until 1983 they will, in the absence of contrary agreement, be entitled to maintain an exclusive fishery zone in the "inner six", but outside this belt (apart from the "outer six" areas specified in the Act of Accession) they must accept equality of access. Unless these (or similar) arrangements are continued after 1982, freedom of access up to the shoreline will then become the rule for the Community.

(ii) The right of the five North Sea states which are Members of the EEC to protect their coastal fisheries against non-Members will not, as things stand at present, be governed by Community law.

(iii) Four of these states (the United Kingdom, Belgium, Denmark and the Netherlands) are parties to the European Fisheries Convention, and, *vis-à-vis* other parties to the Convention who are not members of the EEC, will be able to claim an exclusive fisheries zone within the "inner six", and in the "outer six" will be obliged to respect only the limited "acquired rights" recognized by the Convention. Once again,

[112] So far as the relations of member states *inter se* are concerned, the measures in question could extend beyond territorial and fishery limits to the high seas. See Vignes, "The EEC and the Law of the Sea", in Churchill, Simmonds and Welch (eds.), *New Directions in the Law of the Sea*, III, p. 335 at pp. 342–343. The Commission of the Communities participates, in the name of the EEC, in the work of various international organizations concerned with fisheries, such as the NEAFC.

this regime is subject to derogation and supplementation by further agreement.

(iv) The right of these four states to protect their coastal fisheries against states which are parties to neither the EEC Treaty nor the European Fisheries Convention depends principally on specific agreement.[113] In the absence of agreement, it would seem that they have the right unilaterally to proclaim an exclusive fisheries zone of up to 12 miles, possibly subject to "acquired rights".[114]

(v) The right of Federal Germany (which is not a party to the European Fisheries Convention) to protect coastal fisheries against non-Members of the EEC is governed by the same principles as in (iv) above. At present, however, Federal Germany does not claim an exclusive fishing zone.

(vi) Although Norway obtained special concessions for her fishermen in the Treaty of Accession to the European Communities, she did not ratify it. Nor has she become a party to the European Fisheries Convention. Consequently, her right to enforce her claim to a 12-mile exclusive fishery zone is governed by the principles referred to in (iv) above.[115] Norway has recently threatened to extend her fishery limit, perhaps to 50 miles in emulation of Iceland's example, but, in view of the precariousness of her economic position following her failure to accede to the EEC and her consequent need to obtain trading concessions from that body, it is perhaps unlikely that she will seek to enforce any such limit against Community Members.

(d) Policing

60. Before leaving the subject of fisheries, one final topic deserves to be mentioned, namely policing. Policing is necessary principally in order to enforce conservation measures and exclusive (or semi-exclusive) fishing rights, and in order to reduce conflicts between fishermen (particularly those arising out of interference with each other's operations). Policing in

---

[113] Cf. e.g. United Kingdom–U.S.S.R., Exchange of Notes Constituting an Agreement on Matters arising from the Establishment by the U.K. of the Fishery Regime provided for by the Fishery Limits Act, 1964, Moscow, 30 September 1964 (entered into force on the same day); 539 UNTS 160; UKTS No. 63 of 1964 (Cmnd. 2506); and United Kingdom-Norway, Agreement (with Exchange of Notes) for the Continuance of Fishing by Norwegian Vessels within the Fishery Limits of the U.K., London, 28 September 1964 (entered into force 11 March 1965); 548 UNTS 63; UKTS No. 43 of 1965 (Cmnd. 2654). These treaties are reproduced in UN Leg. Ser. *National Legislation and Treaties* at pp. 910 and 909 respectively.
[114] Cf. *supra*, note 95.
[115] This claim was recognized by the United Kingdom (subject to a now expired "phase-out" period) in the Fishery Agreement signed at Oslo on 17 November 1960 (entered into force 3 March 1961); 398 UNTS 190; UKTS No. 25 of 1961 (Cmnd. 1352); UN Leg. Ser. *National Legislation and Treaties*, p. 895.

national waters or fishery zones is primarily a matter for the coastal state, but outside these areas, and in the absence of agreement, only the flag state has jurisdiction to enforce conservation regulations and the like. Governments have a common interest in preventing the escalation of conflicts and in helping one another to exercise their supervisory powers, and consequently have proved willing to enter into agreements to facilitate the policing of fisheries.

61. An important early example was the North Sea Fishery Convention of 1882,[116] but this was too closely tied to the three-mile territorial sea and was denounced by the United Kingdom Government shortly before it called the European Fisheries Conference which drew up the London Fisheries Convention of 1964. Arising out of a recommendation of the Conference, a new policing Convention, covering substantially the whole of the North Atlantic, was concluded in 1967.[117] So far the Convention has received only five out of the ten ratifications needed to bring it into force, but the others will probably be forthcoming in due course. The Convention makes provision for the marking of fishing vessels, nets, lines and gear, lighting and sound signals, the avoidance of interference, and the settlement of disputes regarding damage to gear or vessels. It also grants limited powers to "authorized officers" of Contracting States to stop and board foreign fishing vessels, principally in order to ascertain whether there has been a breach of the Convention, with a view to reporting the matter for action by the flag state. Reference should also be made here to the Scheme of Joint Enforcement recommended in 1969 by the NEAFC, which adopts a similar scheme for the purpose of conservation on the high seas outside national waters and fishery zones.[118] A number of bilateral treaties also deal with police matters.[119]

C. Navigation

[*Note:* Pollution by ships will be dealt with in sub-Section D (paras. 70–114 below), and navigation by military vessels, in so far as it raises special problems, in sub-Section E (paras. 119–127)].

62. The freedom to pass over the surface of (and through) the waters of the sea is one of the interests protected by international law. As we have

---

[116] 75 BFSP 39; UN Leg. Ser. *Law and Regulations on the Regime of the High Seas*, p. 179.

[117] Convention on Conduct of Fishing Operations in the North Atlantic (London, 1 June 1967); U.K. Misc. No. 11 of 1968 (Cmnd. 3645).

[118] Lay, Churchill and Nordquist (eds.), *New Directions in the Law of the Sea: Documents*, I, p. 484.

[119] E.g. the Anglo–Norwegian Fishery Agreement of 17 November 1960, cited *supra*, note 115; Norway–U.S.S.R., Agreement Concerning the Handling of Claims in Connection with Damage to Fishing Gear, Moscow, 9 December 1959 (entered into force 1 January 1960), 361 UNTS 93.

seen, it is subject to certain derogations in favour of coastal states, who generally, and in the absence of contrary agreement, have the right to exclude foreign vessels from their internal waters, and may require compliance with national regulations when innocent passage through the territorial sea is being effected. But on the high seas, freedom of navigation – subject to a few very limited exceptions[120] – prevails. This principle is complemented by the further principle that the flag state has exclusive jurisdiction over a ship on the high seas.[121]

63. However, these rules are not in themselves enough to cope with the multifarious problems which arise in connection with navigation. For one thing, since ships of different nationalities can collide anywhere at sea, there is a clear need for internationally accepted codes of conduct designed to avert at least some catastrophes. Again, since a ship of any given nationality may find itself subject to the territorial jurisdiction of any number of coastal states, it is important, in the interests of free communications, that there should be as much standardization as possible of national laws relating to shipping (including private international law). This has necessitated the conclusion of a number of conventions (many of them under the auspices of the Inter-Governmental Maritime Consultative Organization – IMCO) aimed at promoting the safety and convenience of navigation.

64. The principal maritime safety convention is the 1960 International Convention for the Safety of Life at Sea ("the SOLAS Convention").[122] Attached to the Convention, and constituting an integral part of it, are a series of Regulations which are applicable to ships registered in Contracting States and which the latter undertake to implement and enforce, by national legislation if necessary.[123] Article 9 of the Convention makes provision for the amendment of the Convention either by the Assembly of IMCO or by a diplomatic conference, but such amendments do not enter into force unless they are accepted by a two-thirds majority of Contracting Governments, and there is also provision for opting out before the amendment comes into force. Amendments to the Regulations were, in fact, adopted in 1966, 1967, 1968, 1969 and 1971, but have not yet come into

[120] The principal limitations relate to the rights of the coastal state in the contiguous zone (*supra*, paras 26–27), and the right of hot pursuit, whereby a ship can be arrested on the high seas in respect of an offence committed in the coastal state's national waters or contiguous zone (cf. High Seas Convention, Art. 23). The Convention also deals with the repression of privacy and the slave trade on the high seas, but happily these activities are not sufficiently common in the North Sea to warrant discussion here.

[121] Cf. *supra*, paras. 7–8.

[122] London, 17 June 1960 (entered into force 26 May 1965), 536 UNTS 271; 16 UST 185; TIAS 5780; UKTS No. 65 of 1965 (Cmnd. 2812); reproduced (without annexes) in UN Leg. Ser. *National Legislation and Treaties*, p. 807. Virtually all maritime states of any importance, including all six North Sea states, are parties to the Convention.

[123] Cf. Geneva Convention on the High Seas, Art. 10.

force. The Regulations in force at the present time deal with construction, life-saving appliances, radiotelegraphy and radiotelephony, safety of navigation, and the carriage of grain and dangerous goods, as well as making special provision for nuclear-powered ships.[124]

65. Another important convention on maritime safety promoted by IMCO is the International Convention on Load Lines, 1966,[125] which provides for the painting of Plimsoll lines on ships and the issue of International Load Line Certificates and International Load Line Exemption Certificates. Contracting Governments are obliged to prevent ships flying their flag from putting to sea without the appropriate Certificate; they are also required to accept each other's Certificates, though when the ship is in port the coastal state has certain limited powers of control even over ships with the proper documentation.[126]

66. The IMCO Regulations for Preventing Collisions at Sea form a sort of Highway Code of the Sea. They differ from the Highway Code in important respects, however. Breach of the Regulations, even without damage, gives rise to criminal liability under the law of the flag (although prosecutions are rare because substantial discretion rests with the master, especially where manoeuvring is concerned).[127] On the other hand, breach does not give rise to any presumption of civil liability; the standard of maritime law is actual negligence. The Regulations at present in force are attached to the 1960 SOLAS Convention, but do not form part of the SOLAS Regulations; a juridical anomaly, they have a quasi-independent existence.[128] The Regulations apply to all vessels on the high seas or in navigable waters connected therewith, other than harbours and certain other (mainly inland) bodies of water. Their purpose is to establish common standards respecting lights and signals, and to achieve some degree of

[124] Chap. I (General Provisions) deals with application and definititions, etc.; surveys and certificates; and the investigation of casualties.

[125] London, 5 April 1966 (entered into force 21 July 1968); 640 UNTS 133; 18 UST 1857; TIAS 6331; UKTS No. 58 of 1968 (Cmnd. 3708). All of the most important maritime states, including the North Sea states, are parties. The 1971 amendments to the Convention are not yet in force – U.K. Misc. No. 37 of 1972 (Cmnd. 5093).

[126] On another aspect of maritime safety, cf. the Agreement between Denmark, Finland, Norway and Sweden Concerning Uniform Rules for the Marking of Navigable Waters, Helsinki, 18 September 1962 (entered into force 18 October 1962); 442 UNTS 228; reproduced in UN Leg. Ser. *National Legislation and Treaties*, p. 814. And cf. Article 15(2) of the Territorial Sea Convention, which requires the coastal state to give appropriate publicity of dangers to navigation in its territorial waters of which it has knowledge.

[127] Cf. Warbrick, "The Regulation of Navigation", in Churchill, Simmonds and Welch (eds.), *New Directions in the Law of the Sea*, III, p. 137.

[128] UKTS No. 23 of 1966 (Cmnd. 2956); 16 UST 794; TIAS 5813; entered into force 1 September 1965. About three-quarters of the parties to the SOLAS Convention are parties to the Collision Regulations, including all the principal maritime powers and all the North Sea states.

predictability of manoeuvring in collision situations, though they can never prescribe in advance for all situations, other than by falling back on such general concepts as the requirements of "good seamanship".

67. The 1960 Collision Regulations were perhaps not entirely satisfactory even when they were adopted, and have since come under heavy criticism on a number of technical grounds. Probably the most important defect, in the present context, was their failure to require compliance with traffic separation schemes.[129] Since 1967 IMCO has recommended some 50 such schemes, and the 1971 session of the Assembly adopted a revised Regulation of the SOLAS Convention whereby states were urged to "use their influence" to have their ships follow the recommended routes; but although states had the power to make it a criminal offence to diverge from IMCO-approved routes, they did not have the duty to do so. In the light of these criticisms, IMCO convened a diplomatic conference at the end of 1972, the outcome of which was the Convention on the International Regulations for Preventing Collisions at Sea, 1972.[130] This Convention will not enter into force before 1 January 1976 at the earliest[131] but, when it does, it will bring revised Collision Regulations into effect. For present purposes, the most significant change is the new Rule 10, which will make observance of traffic separation schemes compulsory. However, it should be noted that only the flag state will have jurisdiction to punish those who violate such schemes on the high seas; the most that coastal states will be able to do is report the master to the flag state. The latest IMCO edition of "Ships' Routeing" establishes traffic separation schemes in several North Sea areas, including the approaches to the River Elbe and to the Hook of Holland, and a deep-water route leading to Europoort.[132] Reference should also be made to a routeing system not under the aegis of IMCO: the NEMEDRI routes.[133] This is a voluntary system of mineswept and buoyed channels introduced especially in the eastern North Sea and Skagerrak/Kattegat immediately after World War II.

68. Three Conventions, signed at Brussels on 10 May 1952, deal with some of the jurisdictional problems which arise out of collisions or other incidents. The International Convention for the Unification of Certain Rules relating to Penal Jurisdiction in Matters of Collision or other Incidents of Navigation[134] reverses the rule laid down by the Permanent

[129] Cf. Warbrick, *op. cit.*
[130] London, 20 October 1972; U.K. Misc. No. 28 of 1973 (Cmnd. 5471).
[131] Art. 4.
[132] IMCO, "Ship's Routeing", 3rd ed. (1974).
[133] North European & Mediterranean Routeing Instructions; cf. Admiralty Notice to Mariners No. 6 of 1972.
[134] 439 UNTS 233; UKTS No. 47 of 1960 (Cmnd. 1128); entered into force 20 November 1955. Parties include Belgium, Federal Germany, the Netherlands and the United Kingdom. Cf. also Art. 11 of the High Seas Convention, to similar effect.

Court of International Justice in *The Lotus*.[135] It provides that, in the event of any collision or other incident of navigation concerning a sea-going ship and involving the penal or disciplinary responsibility of the master or any other person in the ship's service, only the flag state may institute criminal or disciplinary proceedings or arrest the ship. The Convention does not apply in ports or inland waters, and territorial waters may be excluded by declaration. The International Convention relating to the Arrest of Sea-going Ships[136] established the principle that a ship flying the flag of one of the Contracting States may be arrested within the jurisdiction of another such state "in respect of any maritime claim, but in respect of no other claim". The International Convention on Certain Rules concerning Civil Jurisdiction in Matters of Collision[137] seeks to unify the rules of private international law by giving plaintiffs the right to commence proceedings before a court in the country where the defendant has his habitual residence or a place of business, or where arrest of the ship (or another of the defendant's ships) has been effected (or bail granted), or, if the collision took place within a port or inland waters, in the court of the place of collision.

69. Limitations of space prohibit more than an outline of the ground covered by the other treaties relating to navigation. One group is intended to facilitate access to, arrival at and departure from ports;[138] another with the welfare, etc. of seamen;[139] and a third with the unification of private law with respect to matters connected with the carriage of passengers and cargo.[140] Other treaties relate to such diverse matters as a uniform system of tonnage measurement, damage to submarine cables, and the establish-

---

[135] PCIJ Ser. A, No. 10 (1927).

[136] 439 UNTS 193; UKTS No. 47 of 1960 (Cmnd. 1128); reproduced in part in UN Leg. Ser. *Laws and Regulations on the Regime of the Territorial Sea*, p. 733; entered into force 24 February 1956. Parties include Belgium, Federal Germany and the United Kingdom.

[137] 439 UNTS 217; UKTS No. 47 of 1960 (Cmnd. 1128), reproduced in part in UN Leg. Ser. *Laws and Regulations on the Regime of the Territorial Sea*, p. 721; entered into force 14 September 1955. Parties include Belgium, Federal Germany and the United Kingdom.

[138] E.g. the Convention on the International Regime of Maritime Ports, Geneva, 9 December 1923 (entered into force 26 July 1926); 58 LNTS 285; UKTS No. 24 of 1925 (Cmnd. 2419); reproduced in part in UN Leg. Ser. *Laws and Regulations on the Regime of the Territorial Sea*, p. 706; and the IMCO Convention on the Facilitation of Maritime Traffic, London, 9 April 1965 (entered into force 5 March 1967); 591 UNTS 265; UKTS No. 46 of 1967 (Cmnd. 3299); as amended, UKTS No. 63 of 1972 (Cmnd. 5006).

[139] E.g. International Labour Organisation Convention No. 22 on Seamen's Articles of Agreement, 24 June 1926 (entered into force 4 April 1928); (Cmnd. 2745).

[140] E.g. International Convention relating to the Limitation of Liability of Owners of Sea-going Ships, Brussels, 10 October 1957 (entered into force 31 May 1968); UKTS No. 52 of 1968 (Cmnd. 3678).

ment of the International Hydrographic Organization. It should also be mentioned that several states, including the United Kingdom, lay seamarks, dredge channels and disperse wrecks in areas adjacent to their coasts, whether or not they are within national waters. Such activities on the high seas have not been objected to by other states, understandably, because, as well as being a reasonable exercise of the freedom of the high seas, the activities are beneficial to the entire maritime community.

D. Pollution[141]

70. Preventing, and dealing with the consequences of, marine pollution cannot be allowed to depend wholly on unilateral action by the states affected. If a state unilaterally attempted to exercise jurisdiction over a foreign vessel on the high seas, serious conflict could ensue;[142] on the other hand, if the state relies entirely on its "zonal" jurisdiction, it may find itself without protection against pollution by substances which are initially dumped or escape on the high seas. Accordingly, further rules are needed whereby, *inter alia*, flag states agree to co-ordinate their actions and to take steps to prevent pollution by their nationals on the high seas, and whereby coastal states undertake to act in accordance with agreed rules.

71. By analogy with the decision in the *Trail Smelter Arbitration*,[143] in which Canada was held liable to the U.S.A. in respect of noxious fumes emanating from a smelter operating in her territory, it is possible to conclude that, even in customary law, no state has the right to use or permit the use of its territory or the waters under its jurisdiction or control in such a manner as to cause significant injury by marine pollution in or to the waters or territory of another state or to property or persons therein,[144] but this does not take us very far. For example, it does not necessarily follow that this principle would render a state liable merely because a ship flying its flag dumped on the high seas a pollutant which ultimately caused harm to the property of an individual living on the coast of another state, let alone to a fishery which was the property of no-one. In general, the rules of customary law are neither comprehensive enough, nor stringent enough, to cope with the growing problem of pollution.

---

[141] On this subject, cf. e.g. Brown, *The Legal Regime of Hydrospace*, Part 3; UN, *Report on the Conference on the Human Environment* (Stockholm, 1972), Action Plan, Recommendations 86–94 (U.N. Doc. A/CONF. 48/14 and Corr. 1.).

[142] For example, controversy has arisen regarding Canada's right to pass the Arctic Waters Act, 1970.

[143] (1938:1941), 3 UN Rep. of Int. Arbitral Awards, p. 1905.

[144] Cf. also the *Corfu Channel* case, Int. Court of Justice Rep. 1949, p. 4. But note that the Court held only that the coastal state has a duty to warn of dangers to navigation in its territorial sea, not that it has a duty to prevent the creation of the dangers (in this case, a minefield). Moreover, the obligation seems to be limited to cases where the state has actual or imputed knowledge.

72. Matters are taken a stage further by the Geneva Convention on the High Seas. Article 2 provides that the freedom of the high seas "shall be exercised by all states with reasonable regard to the interests of other states in their exercise of the freedom of the high seas", while Articles 24 and 25 make specific reference to pollution. Article 24 requires parties to draw up regulations to prevent pollution of the seas by the discharge of oil from ships or pipelines or resulting from the exploitation and exploration of the seabed and subsoil. Article 25 requires states to take measures to prevent pollution of the seas from the dumping of radioactive waste, taking into account standards and regulations formulated by the competent international organizations, and to co-operate with the competent international organizations in taking measures to prevent pollution resulting from any activities with radioactive materials or other harmful agents. In addition, Article 5 of the Continental Shelf Convention seeks to prevent the exploration or exploitation of the shelf from interfering unduly with navigation or fisheries,[145] and, in particular, requires the coastal state to undertake, in the safety zones, all appropriate measures for the protection of the living resources of the sea from harmful agents.[146]

73. These provisions are not, however, sufficient in themselves. They need to be filled out and supplemented by treaties establishing precise standards, resolving jurisdictional issues, and providing for all necessary measures to be taken against those responsible for pollution. In examining the present state of the law, we shall first consider oil pollution, then nuclear pollution, and finally pollution by other harmful agents.[147]

1. Oil Pollution from Ships

(a) *Prevention*

74. One of the most serious dangers of oil pollution comes from the intentional discharge of oil from ships at sea. The International Convention for the Prevention of Pollution of the Sea by Oil, 1954,[148] as amended in 1962,[149] is designed to meet this problem. The Convention prohibits the

---

[145] Cf. *supra*, para. 21.

[146] Para. (7).

[147] As will be seen, there is a tendency in the most recent treaty practice to treat pollution by different types of substance in the same convention. However, the framework adopted here probably remains the most convenient for the purposes of exposition.

[148] London, 12 May 1954 (entered into force 26 July 1958); 327 UNTS 3; 12 UST 2989; TIAS 4900; UKTS No. 56 of 1958 (Cmnd. 595).

[149] London, 11 April 1962 (entered into force 18 May 1967, except for the amendment to Art. 14, which entered into force 28 June 1967); 600 UNTS 332; 17 UST 1523; TIAS 6109; UKTS No. 59 of 1967 (Cmnd. 3354); amended text reproduced in UN Leg. Ser. *National Legislation and Treaties*, p. 787. Among the 44 parties to this amended version of the Convention are all the North Sea states.

discharge of "oil" (defined as crude oil, fuel oil, heavy diesel oil and lubrication oil) and "oily mixture" (i.e. a mixture with an oil content of 100 parts or more per million parts of the mixture) in the "prohibited zones" defined in Annex A. The whole of the North Sea is one of these prohibited zones. Ships with a displacement of more than 20,000 gross tons for which the building contract has been placed after 18 May 1967 are prohibited from discharging oil in any part of the sea whatsoever, unless in the opinion of the master it is neither reasonable nor practicable to retain it, in which case it is to be deposited outside the prohibited zones. The Convention applies to ships registered in the territories of a contracting government or having the nationality of a contracting party, subject to certain exceptions, including tankers of under 150 gross tons or other ships of below 500 gross tons. Naval ships and ships being used for the time being as naval auxiliaries are also exempted, but by Article 2(2) the parties undertake to ensure that requirements equivalent to those in the Convention are, as far as is reasonable and practicable, applied to such vessels. In certain exceptional circumstances the discharge of oil or oily mixture *is* permitted, such as when this is necessary to secure the safety of the ship, its crew or cargo. The prohibition makes sense only if facilities are provided at ports and oil loading terminals for the disposal of oil residues, and Article 8 accordingly requires parties "to take all appropriate steps to promote the provision of such facilities". If a ship to which the Convention applies, other than a tanker, is proceeding to a port or terminal which does not have adequate facilities of this kind, discharge is permitted, though it should be made as far as possible from land. To facilitate enforcement of the Convention, a ship must carry Oil Record Books in which all discharges or escapes, as well as certain specified operations, are recorded. The Book may be inspected on board by officials of any Contracting State, but only while the ship is within that state's port. Article 6 requires Contracting States to make violations of the Convention punishable under their national law. However, only the flag state can impose penalties; other states can do no more than report the alleged violation to the flag state, unless, of course, the offence took place in an area subject to their jurisdiction.

75. Quite early on, this regime was found to be not entirely satisfactory. Subsequent to the adoption of the 1962 amendments, the oil industry developed the "load on top" system, whereby tanker washings are collected in a slop tank and, after settling, the water beneath the oil is discharged, leaving behind only the oil slops, which are subsequently either removed or incorporated into the next fresh cargo of crude oil. This system is preferable to the former practice of discharging almost all cargo tank washings into the sea, but the water discharged from the slop tank will often be technically an "oily mixture" of the type prohibited by the Convention. Accordingly, a further amendment of the Convention was

called for. Such an amendment was also necessitated by scientific advances in the determination of what constituted harmful pollution,[150] and by the realization that it was not sufficient to prohibit oil pollution only near important land masses – i.e. in the prohibited zones.

76. The Convention will be considerably altered if and when the amendments adopted in 1969[151] enter into force, which will occur twelve months after acceptance by two-thirds of the Contracting States.[152] "Oily mixture" is redefined to mean a mixture with *any* oily content, and the list of "prohibited zones" in Annex A is deleted. Instead, all tankers are prohibited from discharging oil or oily mixture *anywhere* unless all of the following conditions are satisfied:

(i) the tanker is proceeding *en route*;
(ii) the instantaneous rate of discharge of oil content does not exceed 60 litres per mile;
(iii) the total quantity of oil discharged on a ballast voyage does not exceed 1/15,000th of the total cargo-carrying capacity;
(iv) the tanker is more than 50 miles from the nearest land.

This amendment enables tankers to operate the "load on top" system without violating the Convention. For other ships to which the Convention applies, there are substituted for conditions (iii) and (iv) above the following conditions:

(iii) that the oil content of discharge is less than 100 parts per million of the mixture; and
(iv) that the discharge is made as far as practicable from land.

Discharge of oil or oily mixture from a tanker's machinery space bilges is governed by the same rules as those applying to ships other than tankers. In addition, tankers are permitted to discharge ballast from a tank which has been effectively cleaned since cargo was last carried in it. There are also consequential amendments and improvements to the rules regarding the keeping of Oil Record Books, and related matters. There has not, however, been any substantial improvement in policing arrangements.

77. Under the 1969 amendments, the North Sea will no longer be a prohibited zone, and ships will be able to discharge oil or oily mixture into it provided that they do so at a rate at which (in the opinion of the drafters of the amendments) no harmful pollution would result. This might be regarded as a retrograde step, particularly since scientists are by no means agreed that permissible discharges can never cause environmental damage. As against this, however, must be weighed the gain that, as part of the

---

[150] But cf. *infra*, para. 77.
[151] London, 21 October 1969; UK Misc. No. 7 of 1970 (Cmnd. 4347); 9 *Int. Legal Materials* (1970), p. 1.
[152] So far, 21 of the 32 acceptances needed have been received.

package, excessive discharges will be prohibited everywhere and the operation of the "load on top" system will be facilitated.

78. In addition to the problem of *intentional* pollution, with which the London Convention is primarily concerned, there is also a danger of serious *accidental* pollution if a tanker is involved in a collision or grounded, as the *Torrey Canyon* was in 1967. To some extent this danger can be reduced by improvements in navigational aids, traffic separation schemes, collision regulations, and so on, but the possibility of a serious escape of oil from a tanker remains. One way of reducing the danger is to make structural modifications to tankers so as to reduce the likelihood that large amounts of oil will escape if there is an accident, and to this end the IMCO Assembly, in 1971, passed a resolution[153] further amending the 1954 Convention by adding a new Article 6*bis*.[154] When it comes into force, this will require new tankers (broadly, those for which the building contract is placed after 1971) to comply with specified standards of construction designed to reduce the size of oil cargo tanks and the rate of escape of oil in the event of an accident. A certificate of compliance must be carried, without which the ship is to be prohibited from trading by the flag state; furthermore, if a coastal state, after consulting the state of registry, is satisfied that the tanker does not comply with the constructional requirements, it can forbid it access to its ports or off-shore terminals. The importance which the IMCO Assembly attached to this amendment can be seen from its decision that parties to the London Convention are to lose that status if they do not accept the 1971 amendment within a year of its entry into force. By a further resolution of the same date, the Assembly invited governments to put the amendment into effect as soon as possible, without waiting for its entry into force.[155]

79. By 1973 the 1954 Convention, even with its amendments, was felt to be unsatisfactory, for a variety of reasons. In the first place, further updating of the Convention was thought to be necessary in the light of scientific and technological developments. Secondly, there was increasing concern about the pollution of the sea by *all* noxious substances emanating from ships, not only oil. Dumping had already been dealt with in the 1972 London Convention,[156] but it was thought desirable to regulate the accidental or operational release of these substances from ships which might occur in other ways. Thirdly, experience had shown that the procedure for bringing amendments to the 1954 Convention into effect was unduly cumbersome. Despite their importance, the 1969 amendments –

---
[153] Res. A. 246 (VII) of 15 October 1971.
[154] London, 15 October 1971; UK Misc. No. 36 of 1972 (Cmnd. 5071); 11 *Int. Legal Materials* (1972), p. 267. The amendment has so far received 8 of the 32 acceptances needed to bring it into force.
[155] A. 247 (VII).
[156] *Infra*, para. 108.

let alone those of 1971 – had still not come into force. In an age of very rapid scientific and technological advance, new machinery had to be devised to ensure that the technical rules could be speedily and conveniently brought up to date.

80. Accordingly, in 1973 the International Marine Pollution Conference adopted a new International Convention for the Prevention of Pollution from Ships.[157] It will enter into force 12 months after the date on which not less than 15 states, the combined merchant fleets of which constitute not less than 50 per cent of the gross tonnage of the world's merchant shipping, have become parties to it.[158] Upon its entry into force the new Convention will supersede the 1954 Convention as amended.[159] However, since it was anticipated that some time might elapse before the entry into force of the new Convention, the Conference passed resolutions urging governments which had not yet adopted the 1969 and 1971 amendments to the earlier Convention to do so as soon as possible.[160]

81. The new instrument contains provisions aimed at eliminating pollution of the sea both by oil and by other noxious substances which may be discharged operationally (either intentionally or accidentally), and at minimizing the amount of oil which would be accidentally released in such mishaps as collisions or strandings. The Convention applies to all types of ship, including hydrofoils, air-cushion vehicles, submersibles, floating craft and fixed or floating platforms operating in the marine environment.[161] It covers all types of discharge but not dumping (which is covered by the Dumping Convention), the release of harmful substances directly arising from the exploration, exploitation and associated off-shore processing of seabed mineral resources, or the release of harmful substances for purposes of legitimate scientific research into pollution abatement or control.[162]

82. The Administration of the ship[163] must set up the necessary legal machinery for the punishment of violations and must bring proceedings

---

[157] IMCO, International Conference on Marine Pollution, 1973, Final Act of the Conference. Convention opened for signature 15 January 1974.
[158] Article 15(1).
[159] Article 9(1).
[160] Final Act, Resolutions 1 and 11.
[161] Article 2(4).
  It does not, however, apply to warships, naval auxiliaries or other ships owned or operated by a state and used, for the time being, only on non-commercial service. Nevertheless, each party undertakes to ensure, by the adoption of appropriate measures not impairing the operations or operational capabilities of such ships, that they act in a manner consistent with the Convention so far as is reasonable and practicable (Art. 3(2)).
[162] Article 2(3).
[163] Defined as a state whose flag the ship flies or is entitled to fly or, in the case of a fixed or floating platform engaged in exploration or exploitation of the seabed and subsoil over which a coastal state has jurisdiction, that coastal state.

against those guilty of violations if it considers that there is sufficient evidence to justify bringing them. Where a violation occurs within the jurisdiction of a party to the Convention, that party must either institute proceedings itself or pass the information on to the ship's Administration for it to take proceedings. The penalties specified under a party's national law must be adequate in severity to discourage violations of the Convention and equally severe irrespective of where the violation occurs.[164] Provision is made in Article 5 for the mutual recognition of certificates issued under the Regulations contained in the Annexes. Ships in port or at off-shore terminals may be boarded by local inspectors, but generally only for the purpose of verifying that a valid certificate is on board. Ships which do not comply with the requirements of the Convention may in certain circumstances be refused permission to leave ports or off-shore terminals, or access to them. Provision is also made in the Convention for co-operation in the detection of violations and enforcement, as well as for making reports on incidents involving harmful substances. Protocol I to the Convention contains detailed provision concerning such reports and Protocol II deals with the special procedure for the arbitration of disputes between parties to the Convention regarding its interpretation or application.

83. The substantive Regulations of the Convention on the Prevention of Pollution are contained in five Annexes and these, together with their Appendices and the Protocols, can be amended relatively easily under a new amendment procedure laid down in Article 16. Although provision is made for amendment by a specially convened conference, the normal procedure will be for proposed amendments to be considered by a committee of IMCO in whose proceedings all parties to the Convention, whether or not members of IMCO, will be entitled to participate. (By Resolution A.297(VIII) of 23 November 1973, the IMCO Assembly established the Marine Environment Protection Committee to perform this function, amongst others.) If a proposal for amendment is adopted by a two-thirds majority of the parties to the Convention present and voting in the Committee, it will be transmitted by the IMCO Secretary-General to all the parties to the Convention for acceptance. Different types of procedure for acceptance are prescribed for different types of amendments.

(i) An amendment to an Article of the Convention itself will be deemed to have been accepted on the date by which it is accepted by two-thirds of the parties, the combined merchant fleets of which constitute not less than 50 per cent of the gross tonnage of the world's merchant fleet;
(ii) an amendment to an Appendix to an Annex to the Convention will be deemed to have been accepted at the end of a period (not less than ten months) to be determined by the Committee, unless within that

[164] Art. 4.

period not less than one-third of the parties, *or* parties whose combined merchant fleet constitute not less than 50 per cent of the world's gross tonnage, object;

(iii) an amendment to an Annex is deemed to have been accepted in accordance with the procedure specified in (ii) above unless the Committee, at the time of its adoption, determines that the requirements in (i) above must be met instead;

(iv) an amendment to Protocol I will be subject to the same procedures as for amendments to Annexes;

(v) an amendment to Protocol II will be subject to the same procedures as for amendments to an Article of the Convention itself.

Amendments will enter into force six months after the date of their acceptance. For what may be described as the more technical amendments, a "tacit approval" procedure will apply. Where the amendment is to Protocol I, to an Appendix to an Annex or to an Annex to the Convention dealt with under the procedure described in (ii) above, it will enter into force for all parties six months after the date of acceptance except for those which, before that date, have made a declaration that they do not accept it or, in the case of Annexes, have made a declaration that their express approval will be necessary before an amendment enters into force for them. This is a considerable advance on traditional amendment procedures, for it means that all parties will be bound by the amendment unless they specifically opt out. Accordingly, mere procrastination on the part of a state will not prevent an amendment from coming into force, either for parties in general or for that state in particular. This simplified procedure was not, however, considered appropriate where more substantial amendments were concerned: in the case of an amendment to an Article of the Convention itself or to Protocol II, or in the case of an amendment to Protocol I or to an Annex to the Convention in respect of which the procedure specified in (i) above has been selected, the amendment will come into force six months after the date of acceptance only with respect to the parties which have expressly declared their acceptance. Provision is also made for the adoption and entry into force of new Annexes subject to the same procedures as for the adoption and entry into force of amendments to Articles of the Convention itself.

84. Annexes II, III, IV and V contain regulations for the prevention of pollution from ships by substances other than oil, and will accordingly be dealt with in the appropriate paragraphs below.[165] Annex I contains the regulations for the prevention of pollution by oil. Chapter I deals with general matters such as definitions, surveys and certification. Chapter II sets out the requirements for control of operational pollution. The oil discharge criteria prescribed in the 1969 amendments to the 1954 Con-

[165] Paras. 110–112.

vention will remain without substantial changes except that the maximum permissible quantity of oil which may be discharged in a ballast voyage will be reduced from 1/15,000th to 1/30,000th of the cargo-carrying capacity for new oil tankers. These criteria will apply equally to both persistent (black) and non-persistent (white) oils. The Mediterranean, the Black Sea, the Balkan Sea, the Red Sea and the Gulf Area, but not the North Sea, are designated as special areas in which oil discharge will be completely prohibited, except where very small ships are concerned. All oil-carrying ships will be required to be capable of operating with the method of retention on board and "load on top" system of discharge to reception facilities. To this end, all new and existing oil tankers and other ships will, with certain exceptions, be required to be fitted with appropriate equipment, which includes an oil discharge monitoring and control system, oily water separating equipment or filtering system, slop tanks, sludge tanks, piping and pumping arrangements, etc. New oil tankers, i.e. those for which the building contract is placed after 31 December 1975, will, if over 70,000 tons deadweight, have to be fitted with segregated ballast tanks sufficient in capacity to provide adequate operating draught without the need to carry ballast water in cargo oil tanks. However, this requirement does not call for the fitting of double-bottomed tanks. Chapter III of Annex I, like the 1971 amendment to the 1954 Convention,[166] lays down technical constructional requirements for minimizing oil pollution from oil tankers due to side and bottom damage.

(b) Protective Action

85. Although it is to be hoped that the amendments to the 1954 Convention and, ultimately, the 1973 Convention itself will considerably reduce the danger and extent of oil pollution damage, the possibility of its occurring, particularly as the result of a collision or grounding, cannot be completely discounted. If such an accident occurs, steps have to be taken to eliminate or reduce the damage and, in the absence of an international organization equipped and authorized to perform the task, the responsibility will in practice lie with the coastal states most affected. Since this may involve destroying a foreign ship on the high seas (cf. the *Torrey Canyon*), it was thought best to regularize the matter by treaty, and accordingly the International Convention relating to Intervention on the High Seas in Cases of Oil Pollution Casualties ("the Public Law Convention") was concluded in Brussels in 1969.[167] The Convention is not yet in force.

86. The principal provision of the Convention is Article 1(1), which reads: "Parties to the present Convention may take such measures on the

---

[166] Cf. para. 78 *supra*.
[167] 29 November 1969; UK Misc. No. 8 of 1970 (Cmnd. 4403); 9 *International Legal Materials* (1970), p. 25.

high seas as may be necessary to prevent, mitigate or eliminate grave and imminent danger to their coastline or related interests from pollution or threat of pollution of the sea by oil, following upon a maritime casualty or acts related to such a casualty, which may reasonably be expected to result in major harmful consequences." The following points should be noted:

(i) The right to take action exists only in serious cases: there must be a "grave and imminent danger" and a reasonable expectation of "major harmful consequences".

(ii) On the other hand, it is enough if the threat is not to the coastline itself, but to related interests, defined in Article 2(4) as:
". . . the interests of a coastal State directly affected or threatened by the maritime casualty, such as:
(a) maritime coastal, port or estuarine activities, including fisheries activities, constituting an essential means of livelihood of the persons concerned;
(b) tourist attractions of the area concerned;
(c) the health of the coastal population and the well-being of the area concerned, including conservation of living marine resources and of wildlife."

(iii) Like the 1954 London Convention, but unlike the Brussels Civil Liability Convention,[168] the definition of "oil" adopted here includes non-persistent oils (Art. 2(3)).

(iv) Article 2(1) defines "maritime casualty" as "a collision of ships, stranding or other incident of navigation, or other occurrence on board a ship or external to it resulting in material damage or imminent threat of material damage to a ship or cargo". Although "ship" is given a broad definition in paragraph (2) of the same Article, installations or devices which do not float, and floating installations or devices engaged in seabed exploration or exploitation, are excluded. However, as far as the North Sea is concerned, the latter would at any rate presumably be covered by the coastal state's continental shelf jurisdiction.[169] Warships and other ships owned or operated by governments for non-commercial purposes are also expressly placed outside the Convention by Article 1(2).

87. In cases of extreme urgency, the coastal state may take the necessary measures without prior notification or consultations or without continuing consultations already begun (Art. 3(d)). Otherwise it must first consult other affected states, particularly the flag state or states, and notify the proposed measures to any persons, physical or corporate, of which it has

---

[168] *Infra*, para. 91.
[169] Cf. Brown, *The Legal Regime of Hydrospace*, pp. 151–152.

or acquires knowledge and which have interests which can reasonably be expected to be affected by the measures. It must "take into account any views they may submit" (Art. 3(b)). In addition, it *may* consult members of an IMCO panel of experts. After intervention, the measures taken must be notified without delay to the state and persons concerned, and to the Secretary-General of IMCO. The coastal state is, of course, obliged to use its best endeavours to avoid any risk to human life, to afford persons in distress the assistance they need and in appropriate cases to facilitate the repatriation of ships' crews. The measures which may be employed (towing away, bombing, etc.) are not specified, but Article 5 lays down the principle that the measures taken must be proportionate to the damage threatened, account being taken of the extent and probability of imminent damage if the measures are not taken, the likelihood of their being effective, and the extent of the damage which may be caused by them. The measures must also be "reasonably necessary". A coastal state which takes measures in contravention of the Convention is liable to pay compensation (Art. 6). Machinery is provided for the settlement of disputes arising out of the Convention.

88. Article 7 declares: "Except as specifically provided, nothing in the present Convention shall prejudice any otherwise applicable right, duty, privilege or immunity or deprive any of the Parties or any interested physical or corporate person of any remedy otherwise applicable." As Brown[170] observes, the following situations would seem to be envisaged:

(i) action taken by a coastal state in its territorial sea to prevent pollution by oil or other harmful substances;
(ii) action taken by a coastal state on the high seas to prevent, mitigate or eliminate danger to its coastline or related interests from pollution or threat of pollution by harmful substances other than oil;[171]
(iii) action taken by the coastal state on the high seas to prevent, mitigate or eliminate danger to its interests *on the high seas* from pollution or threat of pollution by oil or other harmful substances;
(iv) action taken by the coastal state to prevent, mitigate or eliminate danger to its coastline or related interests from pollution or threat of pollution as a result of exploration or exploitation of the resources of the seabed or subsoil.

In these circumstances, and in the absence of other relevant provision, the rights of the coastal state will depend on the principles of customary law. Of particular relevance will be the rules of zonal jurisdiction and the principle of proportionality established in the case of the *I'm Alone*, in which the United States was held responsible for using excessive measures

---

[170] *Ibid.*, p. 157. The case of pollution arising out of exploitation on the continental shelf is dealt with below, paras. 95–96.
[171] Now dealt with in the 1973 Protocol – cf. *infra*, para. 113.

in sinking a foreign vessel engaged in smuggling, even on the assumption that she was entitled to invoke the right of hot pursuit.[172]

89. Although the Public Law Convention gives the coastal state the right to intervene in certain circumstances to protect itself from oil pollution, experience has shown that even a highly developed state may be unable to cope with a serious escape by itself. Accordingly, in 1967 the Council of IMCO included in its list of matters requiring urgent study the question of regional co-operation,[173] and in 1969 Belgium, Denmark, France, Federal Germany, the Netherlands, Norway, Sweden and the United Kingdom concluded the Bonn Agreement for Co-operation in Dealing with Pollution of the North Sea by Oil.[174] Since effective action will often depend on proper advance preparation, Article 4 of the Agreement provides for the exchange of information on national organizations for dealing with oil pollution, on competent authorities to receive reports of pollution and deal with mutual assistance questions, and on new ways of avoiding and dealing with oil pollution. In addition, for the sake of more efficient co-operation, the "North Sea area" (which, in the Convention, includes the Skagerrak and the English Channel) is divided into eight zones of responsibility. Six of these are "national zones" and are the respective responsibility of each of the parties except Belgium and France. The remaining two are "zones of joint responsibility", one of which is allocated to those two states plus the United Kingdom, and the other (in the Channel) to France and the United Kingdom. Whenever a party is aware of a casualty or the presence of oil slicks in the North Sea area likely to constitute a serious threat to the coast or related interest of any other contracting party, it must inform that other party without delay. Furthermore, parties undertake to request the masters of all ships flying their flags and pilots of aircraft registered in their countries to report without delay, through the channels which may be most practicable and adequate in the circumstances, all casualties causing or likely to cause oil pollution of the sea, and the presence, nature and extent of oil slicks on the sea likely to constitute a serious threat to the coast or related interests of one or more parties. In addition, the zonal authority has the duty to make the necessary assessment of the nature and extent of any casualty or, as the case may be, of the type and approximate quantity of oil floating on the sea, and the direction and speed of the movement of the

[172] 3 UN Rep. of Int. Arbitral Awards, p. 1609. Cf. also Res. III B of the 1969 (Edinburgh) Session of the Institute of International Law, *Annuaire de l'Institut de Droit International*, 1969–II, p. 382. And, for further discussion of the applicable principles, cf. e.g. Brown, *op. cit.*, pp. 139–146; Fleischer, "Pollution from Sea-borne Sources" in Churchill, Simmonds and Welch (eds.), *New Directions in the Law of the Sea*, III, p. 78.
[173] IMCO Doc. C/E.S. III/5 (8 May 1967), para. 11.
[174] 9 June 1969 (entered into force 9 August 1969); UKTS No. 78 of 1969 (Cmnd. 4205); 9 *Int. Legal Materials* p. 359. All of the signatories are now parties.

oil; and it must immediately inform all other contracting parties of its assessments and of any action which it has taken to deal with the floating oil, and keep it under observation as long as it is drifting in its zone.

90. The parties are not actually obliged to take steps to deal with the oil, but normally the coastal state will wish to do so, in which case it may call on the help of the other parties, starting with those which also seem likely to be affected. States must use their "best endeavours" to provide the requested assistance. A further agreement was concluded between Norway, Denmark, Finland and Sweden in 1971.[175] This refers to the Bonn Agreement and repeats many of its provisions, but also provides for the preparation of the equipment necessary for dealing with oil slicks, and for mutual assistance in the investigation and notification of offences by ships against oil pollution regulations.[176]

(c) Liability

91. Despite all of these precautions, oil pollution is still liable to occur and cause damage, and some legal machinery is required for allocating the responsibility to compensate those states, corporations or individuals which suffer thereby. To this end, there was concluded – at the same time as the Public Law Convention – the International Convention on Civil Liability for Oil Pollution Damage ("the Private Law Convention"),[177] whose purpose, as the preamble states, is to establish uniform international rules and procedures for determining questions of liability and providing adequate compensation to persons suffering damage resulting from the escape or discharge of oil from ships. Following a resolution passed by the conference which adopted this Convention, there was also concluded, in 1971, the International Convention on the Establishment of an International Fund for Compensation for Oil Pollution Damage.[178]

92. The Private Law Convention provides that the owner of a tanker is, subject to a number of exceptions, absolutely liable for any damage caused by oil pollution. On the other hand, he may limit the extent of his liability (unless he has been guilty of "actual fault or privity") to 2,000 gold (Poincaré) francs per ton of ship's tonnage, subject to a ceiling of 210

---

[175] Copenhagen, 16 September 1971 (entered into force 16 October 1971); text in Lay, Churchill and Nordquist (eds.), *New Directions in the Law of the Sea: Documents*, II, p. 637.
[176] Cf. also North Atlantic Fishing Convention, 1967, Annex V, Rule 4 – *infra*, para. 105.
[177] Brussels, 29 November 1969 (not yet in force); UK Misc. No. 8 of 1970 (Cmnd. 4403); 9 *Int. Legal Materials* (1970), p. 45.
[178] Brussels, 18 December 1971 (not yet in force); UK Misc. No. 26 of 1972 (Cmnd. 5061); 11 *Int. Legal Materials* (1972), p. 284. Cf. Note in 21 *Int. & Comp. Law Quarterly* (1972), p. 572.

million francs (in the region of US $15 million). There are thus two situations in which the victim of oil pollution will not receive full compensation. The first is where the incident arises in circumstances in which the Convention exonerates the owner from liability, such as *force majeure*, the act of a third party, the failure of a government to maintain lights, etc. The second is where the amount of damage suffered exceeds the tanker owner's liability. It is here that the 1971 Convention will come to the victim's aid, for if the owner is able to avoid paying full compensation for either of the two reasons just mentioned, or if he is unable to meet his financial obligations under the 1969 Convention,[179] the victim can claim compensation from the Fund. Even here the compensation is limited to a maximum of 450 million gold francs (though this limit can be raised up to a maximum of 900 million gold francs by the Assembly of the Fund), and is further reduced if the victim has been guilty of contributory negligence. If the damage results from acts of war or is caused by a state-owned ship engaged in government non-commercial activities (two of the exceptions under the 1969 Convention), or if it cannot be shown that the damage resulted from an incident involving one or more tankers, there is no duty on the Fund to pay. As with the 1969 Convention, the 1971 Convention is applicable only to damage caused in the territory or territorial sea of a contracting state, and to preventive measures (including measures on the high seas) taken to avoid such damage.[180] The other main function of the Fund is to relieve shipowners of some of the burden imposed upon them by the 1969 Convention; under the 1971 Convention, the Fund is to pay that part of the owner's obligation which exceeds 1,500 francs per ton or 125 million francs altogether, up to the 1969 Convention limits (2,000 and 210 million francs respectively). This entitlement may in certain circumstances be enjoyed by the guarantor or insurer of the vessel. On the other hand, the Fund is not obliged to compensate the owner where he has been guilty of wilful misconduct, or where the damage is the result of a failure to observe the provisions of the Convention for the Prevention of Oil Pollution, the SOLAS Convention, the Load Lines Convention, the Collision Regulations, or approved amendments thereto. An ancillary function of the Fund is to assist states in taking measures to combat oil pollution, and, if requested, the Fund is to use its good offices to procure technical assistance and to provide credit facilities to enable the necessary measures to be taken. There are also similar provisions in both Conventions regarding the bringing of claims, the reciprocal enforcements of judgments, subrogation, etc.

---

[179] Though it should be noted in this connection that under Art. 7 of the 1969 Convention the owner of a ship carrying more than 2,000 tons of oil in bulk as cargo will be obliged to maintain insurance or other financial security.

[180] For the complicated questions which can arise in this connection, cf. Brown, *op. cit.*, pp. 168–171.

93. The 1971 Convention also contains organizational provisions, dealing with the legal personality of the Fund, its organs (Assembly, Executive Council and Secretariat) and such matters. One very significant feature is that, whereas the Fund itself is an inter-governmental body, the contributions necessary to run it will come from *companies* importing oil by sea into a contracting state, the amount of each contribution being fixed by the Assembly. It is one of the premises of the Fund Convention, therefore, that the cost of dealing with oil pollution damage shall be borne by the oil industry as well as the shipping industry.

94. The Liability Convention will enter into force 90 days after eight states, including five each with not less than 1 million gross tons of tanker displacement, have accepted it. The Fund Convention may be ratified only by states which are parties to the Liability Convention, and will not come into force until (a) it has been accepted by at least eight such states whose total imports of oil in the preceding year were not less than 750 million metric tons, and (b) the Liability Convention has entered into force. To date the Liability Convention has been ratified by only seven states altogether, and the tanker tonnage requirements have not yet been fulfilled. Only one state has so far accepted the Fund Convention. It is not anticipated that either Convention will come into operation before mid-1975 at the earliest. In the meantime, the victims of oil pollution will have to look to the tanker industry's voluntary compensation schemes. The Tanker Owners' Voluntary Agreement Concerning Liability for Oil Pollution (TOVALOP)[181] provides that, in the event of a negligent discharge of oil – negligence being presumed unless the contrary is shown – which pollutes or causes grave and imminent danger of pollution to coastlines, the tanker owner involved will reimburse the government (not individual) concerned for oil removal costs reasonably incurred by it up to a maximum of US $100 per gross registered ton or $10 million, whichever is the lesser. In addition, an interim plan – the Contract Regarding an Interim Supplement to Tanker Liability for Oil Pollution ("CRISTAL") – was adopted on 14 January 1971[182] and came into force on 1 April 1971. The Contract makes provision for compensation (to individuals as well as to governments) in circumstances where the tanker owner would be liable if the 1969 Liability Convention were in force, beyond the level of liability envisaged in that Convention or in TOVALOP, pending the entry into force of the International Fund Convention. The liability of the Institute which is to administer the compensation fund is limited to $30 million per incident (i.e., somewhat lower than the limit provided for in the 1971 Fund Convention).

[181] 7 January 1969 (came into force 18 September 1969); 8 *Int. Legal Materials* (1969), p. 497.
[182] 10 *ibid.* (1971), p. 137.

2. Oil Pollution from Drilling and Related Operations[183]

95. The exploration and exploitation of the oil resources of the seabed can also lead to pollution in a number of ways: "Blow-outs may occur in drill pipes or pipelines; escapes may occur from submarine or floating storage tanks, from well-to-shore pipelines or during tanker loading operations; pollution may result from collisions with shipping caused by inadequate lighting of installations."[184] In the North Sea, drilling operations will always be in an area subject to the jurisdiction of a particular state (internal waters, territorial sea or continental shelf), and that state will accordingly be able to make the appropriate arrangements for the protection of its territory from, and the compensation of its nationals for, oil pollution damage resulting from such operations. There is, however, a further problem: oil which originally escapes in an area subject to the jurisdiction of state A may drift away and cause pollution damage in the territory (or national waters) of state B, or harm B's other interests (e.g. fishing).

96. Under customary law, the state under whose jurisdiction the operations are conducted may, on *Trail Smelter* principles,[185] be obliged to take reasonable steps to ensure that such operations do not cause serious harm to another state's territory. As we have seen,[186] the Geneva Conventions on the High Seas and on the Continental Shelf also require states to take steps to ensure there are no escapes from pipelines and that the exploration and exploitation of the shelf does not result in unjustifiable interference with such other maritime activities as fishing and conservation. But neither the customary law nor these treaties appear to impose an absolute liability on the state in question; and, more important, they do not make the polluter himself liable, let alone provide machinery for enforcing the liability. This is in marked contrast to the varied and sophisticated arrangements which have been made to prevent, or compensate for, oil pollution damage emanating from ships,[187] and there is clearly a need for comparable arrangements to be made in this field.[188]

[183] Cf. Lay, "Pollution from Off-Shore Oil Wells", in Churchill, Simmonds and Welch (eds.), *New Directions in the Law of the Sea*, III, p. 103.
[184] Brown, *op. cit.*, p. 181.
[185] Cf. *supra*, para. 71.
[186] *Supra*, para. 72.
[187] Though it should be noted that the Bonn Agreement (*supra*, paras. 89-90) is wide enough to cover oil escaping from oil extraction and storage installations; *aliter* the Brussels Public Law Convention (*supra*, paras. 86 and 88). The 1973 International Convention for the Prevention of Pollution from Ships (*supra*, para. 80) includes fixed and floating platforms in its definition of "ships", but expressly excludes from the definition of "discharge" release of harmful substances directly arising from the exploration, exploitation and associated off-shore processing of seabed mineral resources – cf. Art. 2 (3) and (4).
[188] The North-West European states have this matter under consideration – cf. *The Times*, 20 March 1973.

3. Nuclear Pollution[189]

97. Another possible source of marine pollution is radioactive material. Pollution from testing nuclear weapons will be dealt with below in the sub-section on Military Uses of the Sea.[190] Nor is it proposed to dwell on the subject of harmful contamination of the sea through the explosion of nuclear devices for peaceful purposes. The duty not to cause such contamination can be found in *Trail Smelter* principles and, possibly, in Article 25(2) of the Geneva Convention on the High Seas: "All states shall co-operate with the competent international organizations in taking measures for the prevention of pollution of the seas or air space above, resulting from any activities with radioactive materials or other harmful agents." But such explosions are probably a long way off, at least so far as the North Sea is concerned. Accordingly, attention will be concentrated on pollution arising out of the transport of radioactive substances, out of accidents involving nuclear-powered ships, and out of the disposal of radioactive wastes.

(a) Pollution from the Transport of Radioactive Substances

98. In 1961 the International Atomic Energy Agency (IAEA) drew up Regulations for the Safe Transport of Radioactive Materials (subsequently revised in 1964 and 1967),[191] the purpose of which is to control and limit the risks of irradiation and radioactive contamination, mainly by making provision for packaging and labelling. Meanwhile, IMCO adopted the 1960 SOLAS Convention,[192] Chapter VII of whose Regulations includes provisions for the classification, packaging and labelling of dangerous goods, among them radioactive materials. In addition, the International Maritime Dangerous Goods Code, which again makes provision for radioactive materials, was adopted by IMCO in 1966, with the recommendation that members adopt the Code as the basis for national regulation.

99. Special provision regarding liability is made in various Conventions.[193] The Vienna Convention on Civil Liability for Nuclear Damage, adopted by an IAEA Conference on 19 May 1963,[194] is not yet in force, but similar provision was made in the Paris Convention on Third Party Liability in the Field of Nuclear Energy, 1960,[195] which, with its Additional Protocol,[196] was concluded by all the members of the Organisation for

[189] Cf. esp. Brown, *op. cit.*, Chap. 6; Bowett, *The Law of the Sea*, pp. 46–50.
[190] Para. 125.
[191] Safety Series No. 6; cf. also the "Notes on Certain Aspects of the Regulations", Safety Series No. 7. The regulations cover transportation by land and air, as well as by sea.
[192] *Supra*, para. 64.
[193] Cf. Cigoj, "International Regulation of Civil Liability for Nuclear Risk", 14 *Int. & Comp. Law Quarterly* (1965), p. 809.
[194] UK Misc. No. 9 of 1964 (Cmnd. 2333); 2 *Int. Legal Materials* (1963), p. 727.
[195] 29 July 1960; UKTS No. 69 of 1968 (Cmnd. 3755).
[196] Paris, 28 January 1964; *ibid.*

European Economic Co-operation (succeeded by the OECD in 1961) except Ireland and Iceland, and entered into force on 1 April 1968. Both Conventions seek to make operators of nuclear installations strictly liable for damage caused by nuclear incidents of all types and provide for insurance and limitation of liability. However, although the terms of both Conventions are wide enough to cover the maritime carriage of nuclear materials, they do in fact specifically provide that treaties on maritime carriage and related subjects shall not be affected. This created the possibility that the shipowner, rather than the operator of the nuclear installation, would be held liable, and accordingly, in 1971, a further Convention was concluded at Brussels under the auspices of IMCO, with a view to ensuring that liability is exclusively channelled through the operator – a more convenient solution.[197] The Convention is not yet in force.

(b) Pollution from Nuclear-powered Ships[198]

100. A further hazard is presented by ships which do not merely carry nuclear materials, but are powered by them. Chapter VIII of the SOLAS Convention Regulations deals with nuclear ships, other than warships, in somewhat general terms. It requires flag states to approve the reactor installation; to take measures to ensure that there are no unreasonable nuclear hazards to the crew, passengers or public, or to waterways, water resources or food; to provide safety certificates; and to make safety assessments available to any state whose port the ship wishes to use.

101. The Brussels Convention on the Liability of Operators of Nuclear Ships, 1962,[199] seeks to impose strict liability on the operator of a nuclear-powered ship for all nuclear damage caused by it. However, the very strict nature of the liability and the relatively high limitation figure have made it unpopular with many states, and it has also incurred the hostility of the U.S.A. and the U.S.S.R. because it does not exclude warships. Accordingly it has not come into force, and is unlikely to do so. It has therefore been found necessary for flag states to enter into special bilateral agreements enabling their nuclear ships to visit foreign ports and providing for an indemnity in the event of nuclear damage.[200]

[197] Convention relating to Civil Liability in the Field of Maritime Carriage of Nuclear Material, 17 December 1971; UK Misc. No. 39 of 1972 (Cmnd. 5094).
[198] Cf. Cigoj, *op. cit.*
[199] 25 May 1962; text reproduced in British Inst. of Int. & Comp. Law, *Developments in the Law of the Sea, 1958–1964*, p. 196.
[200] E.g. U.S.A.–United Kingdom, Exchange of Notes (with annexes) constituting an Agreement relating to the Use of the U.K. Ports and Territorial Waters by the Nuclear Ship "Savannah", London, 19 June 1964 (entered into force on same day), 530 UNTS 99; UKTS No. 37 of 1964 (Cmnd. 2411); Exchange of Notes constituting an Agreement modifying the Agreement, 12 June 1967 (entered into force on same day), 610 UNTS 350; UKTS No. 68 of 1967 (Cmnd. 3372).

(c) Pollution from the Disposal of Nuclear Waste

102. As has already been mentioned, Article 25 of the High Seas Convention, as well as imposing a duty on states to co-operate with international organizations in taking measures to prevent nuclear pollution of the sea, also imposes, in paragraph (1), a specific obligation to "take measures to prevent pollution from the dumping of radioactive waste, taking into account any standards and regulations which may be formulated by the competent international organizations". In addition, the Geneva Conference passed a Resolution recommending the IAEA to formulate standards. Shortly afterwards, the Agency set up a Panel on Radioactive Waste Disposal into the Sea. The Panel reported in 1961,[201] and made 13 recommendations, three of which were specifically concerned with nuclear-powered ships. The others provide that there should be no release into the sea of high-level radioactive waste; that wastes of low and intermediate level might be disposed of into the sea, but only under controlled and specified conditions; that the recommendations of the International Commission on Radiological Protection should be used as a guide to the assessment of the safety of the proposed disposal; that only disposal methods which do not involve an unacceptable risk to the individual and to the population as a whole should be used (with the figure of 1/25th of the genetic dose to the population as a whole, arising from peaceful uses of nuclear energy, suggested as the maximum which should result from marine waste disposal); that exclusive disposal sites should be designated and regulated by responsible national or international authorities; that the IAEA should keep an International Register of Disposal, which would receive information on licensing requirements for the various sites, monitoring arrangements, etc.; that the IAEA should provide for the necessary standardization of monitoring techniques; and that it should at appropriate intervals review, in collaboration with other international organizations, the problems connected with radioactive waste disposal at sea.

103. Although it was originally intended that the Report should form the basis of a treaty, none has been concluded. Some dumping does go on, although it appears that the states concerned do in practice conform to the recommendations of the IAEA Panel. When the London Convention on Dumping[202] comes into force, it will prohibit the dumping of high-level radioactive material, and will make the issue of a specific permit a precondition of dumping radioactive material of lower levels. Nuclear material is not, on the other hand, specifically included in the Annexes to the Oslo Convention on Dumping.[203] Finally, it should be noted that, under Chapter III of the EURATOM Treaty,[204] Member States are

[201] IAEA, "Radioactive Waste Disposal into the Sea", Safety Series No. 5, 1961.
[202] *Infra*, para. 108.
[203] *Infra*, paras. 105–107.
[204] 298 UNTS 169.

obliged to notify the Commission of the European Communities of their plans for the disposal of radioactive waste in whatever form will make it possible to determine whether this is liable to result in the radioactive contamination of the water, soil or airspace of another Member State; the Commission may make recommendations on this subject, and, in cases of urgency, can issue binding directives requiring the Member State in question to take all necessary measures to prevent infringement of the appropriate "basic standards" and regulations. The intentional dumping of radioactive material into the North Sea itself is unlikely to occur. However, the possibility of contamination from, say, the Western Atlantic sites cannot be completely ruled out, and there may well be a need for a treaty prohibiting the dumping of these dangerous substances or regulating it more strictly than do existing agreements. The discharge into the sea of radioactive effluent from nuclear power stations will be governed by the Paris Convention for the Prevention of Pollution from Land-based Sources[205] when it comes into force.

4. Pollution by Other Hazardous Substances

104. Probably the most common, and certainly the most evident, form of marine pollution is that caused by oil, and for this reason a considerable amount of international law has been generated on the subject, as we have seen. In the field of nuclear pollution, too, attempts at international regulation have not been entirely lacking. In addition to these two sources, however, there is also a danger of pollution from domestic sewage, pesticides, inorganic wastes (including heavy metals, petrochemicals and organic chemicals), organic wastes (including pulp and pulp wastes) and heat. However, it is only very recently that states have taken these dangers seriously enough to take steps to deal with them on the international plane.[206] At the moment, more attention is being given to the marine pollution which results from ships and aircraft than to that emanating from the land. There is also more concentration on prevention than on attributing liability – understandably, because in this field the identification of pollution sources and the establishment of causal links is by no means easy, and the harm that can be done cannot always be compensated for by money payments.

---

[205] *Infra*, para. 118.
[206] A passing reference to the problem is to be found in Art. 25(2) of the Geneva High Seas Convention: "All states shall co-operate with the competent international organizations in taking measures for the prevention of pollution of the seas or air space above, resulting from any activities with radioactive materials or *other harmful agents.*"
Cf. also Art. 5(7) of the Continental Shelf Convention: "The coastal state is obliged to undertake, in the safety zones, all appropriate measures for the protection of the living resources of the sea from harmful agents."

(a) Pollution from Ships and Aircraft

(i) Dumping

105. The subject of the dumping of noxious substances is first mentioned in the Convention on the Conduct of Fishing Operations in the North Atlantic, 1967,[207] Annex V, Rule 4 of which prohibits any *fishing* vessel from "dumping in the sea any article or substance which may interfere with fishing or obstruct or cause damage to fish, fishing gear or fishing vessels except in cases of *force majeure*". More detailed provision is made in the Oslo Convention for the Prevention of Marine Pollution by Dumping from Ships and Aircraft, concluded under the auspices of the North-East Atlantic Fisheries Commission on 15 February 1972.[208] The Convention applies to the high seas and territorial seas of the North-East Atlantic and North Sea, though the parties undertake to apply the measures adopted in such a way as to prevent the diversion of dumping to seas outside the Convention area (Art. 3). The main part of the Convention applies to ships and aircraft (including, for these purposes, hovercraft and fixed or floating platforms) which are:

(a) registered in the territory of a Contracting Party;
(b) loading the substances to be dumped in the territory of a Contracting Party; or
(c) believed to be engaged in dumping within the territorial sea of a Contracting Party.

Dumping is defined as "any deliberate disposal of substances and materials into the sea ... other than

(a) disposal incidental to, or derived from, the normal operation of ships and aircraft and their equipment;
(b) the placing of substances and materials for a purpose other than the mere disposal thereof, if not contrary to the aim of the Convention" (Art. 19(i)).

Under the Convention, dumping is divided into three categories: that which is completely prohibited; that which is subject to permit; and that which is subject to approval. Article 5 prohibits absolutely the dumping of substances listed in Annex I – the "black list", which includes organohalogen and organosilicon compounds, substances likely to be carcinogenic, mercury, cadmium and their compounds, persistent plastics and other persistent synthetic materials. Article 6 provides that "significant" quan-

---

[207] *Supra*, para. 61. The Convention is not yet in force.
[208] UK Misc. No. 21 of 1972 (Cmnd. 4984); 11 *Int. Legal Materials* (1972), p. 262; entered into force 7 April 1974. So far, the only North Sea states to have become parties are Denmark and Norway, but the United Kingdom is on the point of ratifying.

tities of substances on the "grey list" (Annex II) may only be dumped subject to a permit from the appropriate national authorities. The list contains such substances as arsenic, lead, copper, zinc, cyanides and fluorides, and pesticides and their by-products not covered by Annex I; it also mentions bulky substances which may present a serious obstacle to fishing or navigation and "substances which, though of a non-toxic nature, may become harmful due to the quantities in which they are dumped, or which are liable to seriously reduce amenities". These substances must be dumped not less than 150 miles from land in water not less than 2,000 metres deep, which excludes virtually the whole of the North Sea. Under Article 7, other substances may be dumped only with the approval of the national authorities; Annex III sets out the considerations to be taken into account by these authorities when considering whether to allow such dumping.

106. The machinery for implementation is twofold. National authorities are to be responsible for dealing with applications for the permits and approvals mentioned in Articles 6 and 7. They are to keep records of such permits and approvals, and transmit them to a Commission comprising representatives of each of the Contracting Parties; instruct their maritime inspection vessels to report on any incident which gives rise to the suspicion that dumping contrary to the provisions of the Convention has occurred, and, if appropriate, report this to other Contracting Parties; and take in their territory "appropriate measures to prevent and punish conduct in contravention of the provisions of this Convention". The Commission is to meet regularly and exercise overall supervision over the implementation of the Convention. In particular, it is to receive and consider the reports of permits and approvals granted by national authorities and review generally the condition of the seas to which the Convention applies, the efficacy of the control measures being adopted, and the need for any additional or different measures. It is also to recommend, where necessary, amendments to the Annexes, but these recommendations must be adopted unanimously, and will enter into force only after they have been approved by all of the Contracting Parties. Provision is also made for the revision or amendment of the Convention itself.

107. The parties are also obliged to co-operate in scientific research concerning pollution, in monitoring, and in promoting in the relevant international bodies measures to deal with pollution by oil, radioactive material and other noxious substances (Arts. 12–14). Article 1 also contains a general undertaking – not confined to dumping – "to take all possible steps to prevent the pollution of the sea by substances that are liable to create hazards to human health, to harm living resources and marine life, to damage amenities or to interfere with other legitimate uses of the sea".

108. Shortly after the Oslo Convention was concluded, it was decided to extend a similar regime to the seas (other than internal waters) of the entire world in the London Convention on the Prevention of Marine Pollution by Dumping of Wastes and other Matter.[209] Apart from the question of geographical scope, the main differences between the London and the Oslo Conventions are as follows:

(a) The definition of "dumping" here is in some respects wider than in the Oslo text: *inter alia*: it also covers the deliberate disposal of vessels, aircraft, etc.
(b) Instead of establishing a special Commission, it is provided in the London Convention that, within three months after its entry into force, the parties will meet to designate a competent (existing) organization to perform the duties of a secretariat. In the meantime, these duties are entrusted to the United Kingdom Government.
(c) Amendments to the London Convention will be easier to effect than under the Oslo system. The Convention itself can be amended by a two-thirds majority of the Contracting Parties present at the meeting, and such amendment will come into force for each state accepting it, while amendments to the Annexes will come into force for *all* Contracting Parties either on acceptance by them, or automatically 100 days after the adoption of the amendment by the meeting, unless within that 100-day period the state in question opts out (Art. 15).
(d) Three notable additions to the "black list" are oil, materials produced for biological and chemical warfare, and high-level radioactive matter; other radioactive matter is included in the "grey list".
(e) Article 10 contains an undertaking by Contracting Parties to develop procedures for the assessment of liability and the settlement of disputes concerning dumping. The wording of the Article also appears to indicate that states can be responsible for environmental damage even to areas outside the sovereignty of other states, including most especially the high seas.
(f) After the Third United Nations Conference on the Law of the Sea, and in any event before 1977, the Contracting Parties will meet "with a view to defining the nature and extent of the right and responsibility of a coastal state to apply the Convention in a zone adjacent to its coast"; this envisages the possibility of creating pollution protection zones contiguous to the territorial sea. Article 13 also contains the general proviso that the Dumping Convention is not to prejudice the codification and development of the Law of the Sea by the UN Conference on the Law of the Sea, nor is it to prejudice "the present or future claims and legal views of any state concerning the Law of the Sea and the nature and extent of coastal and flag state jurisdiction".

[209] Opened for signature on 29 December 1972; 11 *Int. Legal Materials* (1972), p. 1291. The Convention is not yet in force.

(ii) *Other forms of accidental or intentional pollution*

109. Until the adoption of the Dumping Convention, relatively little attention was given to the question of the pollution of the sea by substances other than oil or radioactive material.[210] The passing of that Convention did not, however, solve the problem completely, for it does not deal with other forms of intentional pollution, or with accidental pollution, by such noxious substances. The purpose of Annexes II–V of the 1973 International Convention for the Prevention of Pollution from Ships, of which nos. III, IV and V are optional, is to fill this gap. The general structure of the Convention has already been described above,[211] and it will suffice now to outline the provisions of these four Annexes.

110. Annex II contains the Regulations for the Control of Pollution by Noxious Liquid Substances in Bulk. These apply to all ships carrying such substances, which are divided into four categories depending on the degree of hazard which they represent to marine resources, human health, amenities or other legitimate uses of the sea. More than 400 substances have been evaluated and included in Appendices to this Annex. The list will be kept up to date by modifications and additions. The most dangerous substances may be discharged only through a reception facility – at any rate until the remaining residue reaches the prescribed level of dilution. Other substances may be discharged into the sea but only in accordance with detailed conditions laid down in the Regulations.

111. Annex III contains Regulations for the Prevention of Pollution by Harmful Substances carried by Sea in Packaged Forms, or in Freight Containers, Portable Tanks or Road and Rail Tank Wagons. The government of each party will be obliged to issue detailed requirements on packaging, marking and labelling, documentation, stowage, quantity limitations and other aspects aimed at preventing or minimizing pollution of the marine environment by such substances.

112. Annexes IV and V contain Regulations for the Prevention of Pollution from Ships by Sewage and Garbage respectively. Annex IV will apply to new ships with a displacement of at least 200 gross tons or certified to carry more than ten persons, while existing ships covered by this description will not be affected until ten years after the entry into force of the Annex. Under the Annex, ships will not be permitted to discharge sewage within four miles of land unless they have in operation an approved treatment plant. Between 4 and 12 miles from land, sewage will have to be comminuted and disinfected before discharge. Annex V will apply to all ships. Here, specific minimum distances from land have been set for the

---

[210] The prevention of accidental pollution by such substances was, however, one of the objects of the Collision Regulations and of Ch. VII of the SOLAS Convention (*supra*, paras. 66–67 and 64 respectively).

[211] *Supra*, paras. 80–83.

disposal of all the principal types of garbage. The disposal of all plastics is prohibited.

113. The other major decision of the 1973 Conference was the adoption of the Protocol relating to Intervention on the High Seas in case of Marine Pollution by Substances other than Oil.[212] This Protocol is designed to extend the provisions of the 1969 Brussels Convention relating to Intervention on the High Seas in Cases of Oil Pollution Casualties[213] to "substances other than oil which may reasonably be expected to result in major harmful consequences". These substances are to be enumerated in a list to be established by an appropriate body designated by IMCO, together with "those other substances which are liable to create hazards to human health, to harm living resources and marine life, to damage amenities or to interfere with other legitimate uses of the sea". Where an intervening state takes action with regard to an unlisted substance which, it claims, falls within the definition just quoted, that state will have the burden of establishing that the substance, under the circumstances present at the time of the intervention, could reasonably pose a grave and imminent danger analogous to that posed by any of the listed substances.[214] The Protocol is intended to come into force 90 days after the fifteenth state becomes a party to it, provided, however, that it will not, of course, come into force before the 1969 Convention itself.

(b) Pollution from Drilling Operations

114. Except in the case of dumping, pollution of the sea by noxious substances emitted by, or as a result of, the operation of drilling rigs is largely unregulated by treaty, though, in the case of drilling on the continental shelf, Article 5(7) of the Geneva Convention on the Continental Shelf does provide that "The coastal State is obliged to undertake, in the safety zones, all appropriate measures for the protection of the living resources of the sea from harmful agents".

(c) Pollution from the Land[215]

115. Far more pollution of the sea – by substances of all types – emanates from the land (*via* sewers, rivers, etc.) than from ships, aircraft or drilling rigs. It is therefore surprising at first to discover that, until recently, there has been hardly any treaty law on the subject.[216] The explanation is not

---

[212] IMCO, International Conference on Marine Pollution, 1973, Final Act of the Conference, p. 125.
[213] *Supra*, paras. 85–88.
[214] Article 1(2).
[215] Cf. Schachter & Serwer, "Marine Pollution Problems & Remedies", 65 *American Jl. of Int. Law* (1971), p. 84 at pp. 99–105.
[216] There is already, of course, a substantial body of law on the pollution of international drainage basins as such; cf. e.g. Lester, "Pollution", in Garretson, Hayton and Olmstead (eds.), *The Law of International Drainage Basins* (1967), p. 89.

far to seek, however. The main effect of land-based pollution is likely to be felt in the internal waters or territorial sea of the very state from whose land territory the pollution emanates. Such a state is thus in a position to take steps to reduce this pollution, and has an incentive to do so without having to rely on, or be encouraged by, international conventions.

116. It would, however, be incorrect to assume that land-based pollution of the sea is never a subject suitable for regulation by international agreement. In the first place, pollution can spread to the national waters of neighbouring states. Secondly, the high seas themselves may become polluted, to the detriment of those who use them. Thirdly, the cost of abating pollution may necessitate an increase in the price of the goods produced by the polluting industries; in order to prevent producers being undercut by other producers in less public-spirited countries, it may be desirable to ensure by agreement that pollution abatement action is concerted internationally. Accordingly, increasing attention is being paid to the possibility of international action for the abatement of land-based marine pollution.

117. Regional action is particularly appropriate here, and there have been a number of initiatives. The Rhine is the largest single cause of the pollution of the Netherlands' coastal waters, and in 1959 the International Commission for the Protection of the Rhine, which had been constituted in 1949–50,[217] was authorized to organize investigations and propose measures for the protection of the river against pollution.[218] Recently the Rhine has also attracted the particular attention of the European Communities in the context of their Programme of Action on the Environment.[219] Another European organization which has manifested great interest in water pollution is the Council of Europe. An illustration of this interest was the conclusion in 1968, under its auspices, of the European Agreement on the Restriction on the Use of Certain Detergents in Washing and Cleaning Products.[220] Yet another example of a regional initiative designed to improve the standard and quality of both freshwater and seawater is the Brussels Agreement on the Implementation of a European Project on Pollution on the Topic of "Sewage Sludge Processing".[221]

[217] By an exchange of Notes between Switzerland, France, Luxembourg, the Netherlands and the Occypying Powers of West Germany.
[218] Whiteman, *Digest of International Law*, Vol. III, p. 1045.
[219] Cf. the Declaration of the Council of Ministers of the European Communities and of the Representatives of the Governments of the Member States meeting in the Council on 22 November 1973 on the "Programme of Action of the European Communities on the Environment", 16 OJ C112 (20 December 1973); 13 *Int. Legal Materials* (1974), p. 164ff at pp. 189–191.
[220] Strasbourg, 16 September 1968 (entered into force 16 February 1971); UKTS 23 of 1971 (Cmnd. 4646). Of the North Sea states, Belgium, Federal Germany, the Netherlands and the United Kingdom are parties.
[221] 23 November 1971 (entered into force 1 August 1972); UKTS 114 of 1972 (Cmnd. 5122); 12 *Int. Legal Materials* (1973), p. 9.

118. However, the most recent initiative has come from neither the Council of Europe nor the European Communities but from the states which drew up the Oslo Dumping Convention of 1972.[222] Early in 1974 they convened a Conference[223] on the Prevention of Marine Pollution from Land-based Sources, the result of which was the adoption on 21 February 1974 of the Paris Convention for the Prevention of Pollution from Land-based Sources.[224] Like the Oslo Convention, the Paris Convention applies to the high seas and territorial seas of the North-East Atlantic and the North Sea, though the parties undertake in Article 7 not to apply the measures they adopt in such a way as to increase pollution originating from other sources, or land-based pollution in the seas outside the Convention area. Annex A to the Convention is divided into three parts, taking into account the persistence, the toxicity or other noxious properties, and the tendency to bio-accumulation, of the various substances. Part I, the "black list", includes organohalogen compounds and substances which may form these compounds; mercury and mercury compounds; cadmium and cadmium compounds; persistent synthetic materials which may float, remain in suspension or sink, and which may seriously interfere with any legitimate uses of the sea; and persistent oils and hydrocarbons of petroleum origin. Part II, the "grey list", includes substances which, although exhibiting similar characteristics to Part I substances and requiring strict control, seem less noxious or are more readily rendered harmless by natural processes; this group includes non-persistent oils and hydrocarbons of petroleum origin. Radioactive substances, including wastes, are separately dealt with in Part III. In Article 4 the parties undertake to eliminate, if necessary by stages, pollution of the maritime area from land-based sources by substances listed in Part I, and to "limit strictly" such pollution by substances listed in Part II by means of a licensing system. Under Article 5 they undertake to adopt measures to forestall and, as appropriate, eliminate pollution of the maritime area from land-based sources by radioactive substances referred to in Part III, taking full account of the recommendations of the appropriate international organizations and agencies. In Article 12 contracting parties undertake to ensure compliance with the provisions of the Convention and to take in their territory appropriate measures to prevent and punish contraventions, and they are also to report on the legislative and administrative measures taken by them. Provision is also made for co-operation, consultation, the settlement of disputes, and so on. In Article 13 the parties "undertake to

---

[222] *Supra*, para. 105. The Oslo Convention was itself concluded under the auspices of the North-East Atlantic Fisheries Commission.
[223] Attended by Austria, Belgium, Denmark, France, Federal Germany, Iceland, Luxembourg, the Netherlands, Norway, Portugal, Spain, Sweden, Switzerland and the United Kingdom, with Finland and Italy as observers.
[224] Opened for signature 4 June 1974; 13 *Int. Legal Materials* (1974), p. 352.

assist one another as appropriate to prevent incidents which may result in pollution from land-based sources, to minimize and eliminate the consequences of such incidents, and to exchange information to that end". The Convention establishes a Commission made up of representatives of each of the parties, but in order to avoid unnecessary duplication, the Conference which adopted the Convention recommended that the Commissions established under the Paris and Oslo Conventions should, as far as possible, be composed of the same representatives and meet at the same time, and that a joint secretariat should be established. The EEC will be entitled to a number of votes equivalent to the number of its members which are parties to the Convention, but it will not be entitled to vote when its member states exercise their right to do so, and vice versa. The duties of the Commission will include overall supervision of the implementation of the Convention, drawing up programmes and measures for the elimination or reduction of pollution from land-based sources, and making recommendations regarding amendments to the lists of substances included in Annex A. If a recommendation for such an amendment is approved by a three-quarters majority vote of the members of the Commission, it will enter into force 230 days later for all parties other than those who have opted out. Provision is made for accession to the Convention by states other than those present at the Paris Conference. The Convention will come into force 30 days after the deposit of the seventh acceptance.

E. Military Uses

119. This study is concerned with the normal peacetime uses of the North Sea. Accordingly, an examination of the law relating to the use of force in connection with maritime claims is beyond its scope. Nor is it proposed to deal in this sub-Section with the use of naval forces for regulatory purposes (e.g. to enforce fishery conservation regimes or to ensure that ships observe navigational prescriptions). Although there are problems here, it will be more convenient to consider them in the Chapter dealing with the deficiencies of the present system and making proposals for improvement.[225]

120. The naval forces of states are, however, important users of the sea in their own right, and some account must be taken of this fact when examining the interaction between the various users. It will, of course, be appreciated that we are here dealing only with the North Sea, so that certain questions do not arise. For example, its shallow depth makes the construction of underwater nuclear missile silos improbable, for they would be too easy to locate; similarly, its small area and the fact that it is surrounded by relatively important, powerful and densely populated states

---

[225] *Infra*, Chap. VI.

makes it – happily – most improbable that either littoral or outside states will use it for testing nuclear weapons.

121. The military aspect must be taken into account when considering the demarcation of jurisdictional zones. States with substantial naval forces are naturally anxious that these forces should enjoy the maximum freedom of movement. Since there is some dispute whether, and in what circumstances, the right of innocent passage through the territorial sea extends to warships,[226] and since, in any event, the right of innocent passage is a more restricted right than that of freedom of navigation on the high seas,[227] such states have traditionally tended to favour the narrowest possible breadth of territorial sea and to oppose the erosion of the freedom of the high seas, for instance by the creation of special zones adjacent to the territorial sea. States which are nervous of the presence of foreign naval vessels near their coasts may well be expected to take a different stance. This is not the context in which to speculate on how these interests will be reconciled at the UN Conference on the Law of the Sea; suffice it to say here that the naval aspect cannot be ignored in any account of what states do or are likely to do in relation to zonal jurisdiction.

122. Another important consideration is sovereign immunity. Warships are generally immune from the jurisdiction of states other than the flag state, not only on the high seas but also in the national waters of those other states. This restricts the ability of coastal states to prevent interference with their interests by foreign warships, whether such interests relate to security, fisheries, environmental protection, or whatever. Moreover, whereas states have been, at least to some extent, prepared to enter into treaties limiting the freedom of action of their own merchant ships – sometimes even to the extent of allowing foreign states to exercise some degree of control over them on the high seas – they have been most reluctant to agree to any restriction where their warships are concerned.

123. The traditional immunity of warships, together with practical problems connected with the functions which they have to perform, makes it difficult to apply directly to naval forces the same international legal rules as apply to other vessels. For example, it would seriously impair the efficiency of warships if they were obliged invariably to obey traffic separation schemes. In the field of maritime safety in general, however, the divergence is not very marked, since the hazards of navigation are similar for all types of vessel. There is no exception for warships in the Collision Regulations, for example, and where naval vessels are technically outside the scope of a particular treaty, its principles may well be extended to them *de facto* by their flag states. With regard to pollution, on the other hand, matters are not as simple.

[226] Cf. *supra*, para. 34.
[227] Cf. Franklin, "The Law of the Sea: some Recent Developments", 53 *International Law Studies* (U.S. Naval War College) (1959–60), pp. 121–123.

124. More than half of the total world shipping tonnage is government-owned, much of it naval, and although navies do not carry oil in bulk for gain, they do carry it for the purposes of replenishment at sea – an exercise which is quite common, even in the North Sea. A tanker used for these purposes could be involved in a serious accident, but no action could be taken under the Brussels Intervention Convention,[228] because it does not apply to warships or to government-owned ships used for non-commercial purposes, such as the British Royal Fleet Auxiliary. Nor do the provisions of other treaties concerning oil pollution apply to them directly. The danger may not be as serious as it appears at first sight, for the naval regulations of several states (e.g. the United Kingdom) require compliance with the same or similar rules "so far as is practicable"; indeed, the 1954 International Convention for the Prevention of Pollution of the Sea by Oil expressly requires states to apply to naval ships and naval auxiliaries rules equivalent to those laid down in the Convention itself – though again with the proviso "so far as is reasonable and practicable".[229] Whether this voluntary system is a sufficient protection against oil pollution cannot be determined without more information; it is doubtful, however, whether states would agree to closer control.

125. Radioactive pollution of the sea is another possible problem. In the first place, although by far the greater part of the nuclear-powered ships at present in operation are warships (and, in particular, submarines), these are not covered in Chapter VIII of the SOLAS Convention Regulations, nor in the Brussels Nuclear Liability Convention.[230] Here again, the secrecy which surrounds the construction and operation of these vessels makes it unlikely that any effective system of international control can be applied to them.[231] Another possible source of radioactive pollution of the sea arises from nuclear explosions. A major drawback of the Test Ban Treaty[232] is that it does not bind non-parties, but fortunately the likelihood of nuclear weapons' being tested in the North Sea is negligible.[233] There may, on the other hand, be greater practical relevance in the Seabed

---

[228] *Supra*, para. 86.
[229] Art. 2(2).
[230] Cf. *supra*, paras. 100–101.
[231] It is fair to point out, however, that under normal conditions the amount of radioactive effluent discharged by nuclear submarines is so small as to be undetectable, and that few states are likely to tolerate standards of design or operation which might constitute a danger to their own ports and nationals.
[232] Treaty Banning Nuclear Weapon Tests in the Atmosphere, in Outer Space and Under Water, Moscow, 5 August 1963 (in force 10 October 1963); 48 UNTS 43; 14 UST 1313; TIAS 5433; UKTS No. 3 of 1964 (Cmnd. 2245).
[233] Though the possibility of an *accidental* release of a nuclear weapon cannot be discounted, as was demonstrated in 1966 when a nuclear weapon was accidentally released into the waters off the coast of Spain after the crash of a U.S. military aircraft: *Annual Register of World Events*, Vol. 208 (1966), p. 537.

Weapons Treaty of 1971.[234] Within a 12-mile "seabed zone" measured from its baseline, only the coastal state may emplace nuclear or other weapons of mass destruction in or on the seabed; outside this zone, the prohibition is total. There are provisions for verifying compliance, and the parties agree to continue negotiations for further measures of seabed demilitarization. With regard to pollution by other types of material, it should be noted that the London Dumping Convention includes in its "black list" materials produced for biological and chemical warfare.[235]

126. Military exercises, including firing practice, could at first sight appear to constitute a hazard to navigation on the high seas, or even amount to an attempt to exclude others from a particular area. In practice, however, this would seem not to be the case as far as the North Sea is concerned. Several North Sea states, including the United Kingdom, have established "permanent practice areas" as well as temporary practice or testing areas. However, the notices which are issued in connection with these activities are purely warning and advisory;[236] they do not purport to take powers over foreign vessels on the high seas, nor to exclude them from any part of these seas. Moreover, the rules under which the firing is permitted are designed to ensure that there is no danger to navigation, with the onus of avoidance on those doing the firing rather than on those who might be endangered thereby. So long as these principles are firmly adhered to, the activity would seem to be a lawful exercise of the freedom of the high seas.

127. Apart from the emplacement of weapons, there are several other possible military uses of the seabed, including bottom-based submarine detection systems, which are already in operation. In national waters, the sovereign state has an exclusive and almost unlimited[237] right of emplacement. On the continental shelf, however, the position is more complex. It will be recalled that the Continental Shelf Convention gives the coastal state "sovereign rights" only "for the purpose of exploring [the shelf] and exploiting its natural resources"; it says nothing about other activities. So far as the right to lay cables for military purposes on the continental shelf of other states is concerned, Article 4 of the Continental Shelf Convention and Article 26 of the High Seas Convention give *all* states

---

[234] Treaty on the Prohibition of the Emplacement of Nuclear Weapons and Other Weapons of Mass Destruction on the Seabed and the Ocean Floor and in the Subsoil thereof, London, Moscow and Washington, 11 February 1971 (entered into force 18 May 1972), UKTS No. 13 of 1973 (Cmnd. 5266); 10 *Int. Legal Materials* (1971), p. 145.

[235] Cf. *supra*, para. 108.

[236] Cf. Admiralty Charts, "PEXA" Series; Admiralty Notice to Mariners No. 5 of 1972.

[237] It may be limited to some extent by the principle *sic utere tuo ut alienum non laedas* ("use your own property in such a way as not to injure that of another person").

the right to do so, subject to the coastal state's right to take "reasonable measures for the exploration of the continental shelf and the exploitation of its natural resources".[238] As regards other military uses of the bed and subsoil of the shelf, the position is more obscure.[239] As far as non-coastal states are concerned, strictly speaking there seems to be nothing to prevent them from establishing military installations on the part of the shelf which "belongs" to the coastal state; however, if the latter can make out a claim that this might constitute an impediment to its exploration and exploitation of the shelf, it can presumably exclude them, as long as it knows of their existence. A further question is whether the coastal state is entitled to appropriate areas of its shelf for its own exclusive military use. Some writers consider that effective control over a seabed area can in some circumstances give rise to sovereign rights. The present writer is doubtful whether such a derogation from the freedom of the high seas can occur without the clearest evidence of consent by the international community, but in practice little may turn on whether *sovereign* rights can be acquired by occupation, for it would seem that no outside state would be entitled to interfere with the installation or object to its being set up – unless, of course, it conflicted unreasonably with other legitimate uses of the high seas. Strictly speaking, the fact that the superjacent waters are high seas may mean that there is no right to establish safety zones above the installations in order to protect them and protect others from them.[240] If such installations do, in fact, constitute a serious hazard to other users of the sea, the state responsible for them may be under an obligation not to emplace them, on the ground that this is inconsistent with the duty to show "reasonable regard to the interests of other states in the exercise of the freedom of the high seas".[241] At the very least, by analogy with the *Corfu Channel* case,[242] there would seem to be a legal obligation to warn others of the hazard, even though this may not be consistent with the need to maintain secrecy.[243]

F. Miscellaneous

128. Two further, and to some extent connected, matters are worthy of mention: artificial islands and pirate broadcasting. Both raise very complicated questions of law which can be only outlined within the confines of this paper.

---

[238] Cf. Convention for the Protection of Submarine Cables, 1884, *supra*, note 30.
[239] Cf. Brown, "The Legal Regime of Inner Space: Military Aspects", 1969 *Current Legal Problems*, p. 181 at pp. 186–188.
[240] Cf. Brown, *ibid.*; *contra*, Franklin, *op. cit.*, pp. 65–67.
[241] Geneva High Seas Convention, Art. 2.
[242] *Supra*, note 144.
[243] On the question of seabed installations, cf. also *infra*, paras. 129–131.

1. Artificial Islands[244]

129. "Artificial island" is not a term of art, but is used to denote man-made structures, entirely surrounded by sea (thereby differentiating them from jetties, etc.), used for operations in a fixed place. One type of artificial island is a man-made piece of land, such as has been created off the Californian coast by sinking blocks of concrete, rocks and sand. Another type is the million-gallon oil-storage tank shortly to be towed to the Ekofisk oil field. Different types of fixed or semi-mobile platform have also been developed, some of which are implanted into the seabed by means of piles or submersible feet, others simply floating in the same place. Ships are also sometimes confined to a particular spot, for example lightships. Much of the development in this field has been connected with the exploration and exploitation of the mineral resources of the seabed, but not exclusively; artificial islands may be used for purposes of defence (e.g. "Martello" or "Texas" towers), broadcasting (by "pirate" stations), oceanographic research, navigation (lightships), and have other potential uses (e.g. "Sea Cities" and landing strips). The location of such installations varies: they may be established in national waters, implanted in or on the continental shelf, or float on the high seas (within or beyond the contiguous zone).

130. After some initial hesitation, international lawyers are generally agreed that these structures cannot be assimilated to true islands, and an island properly so-called has been defined in the Geneva Territorial Sea Convention as "a *naturally-formed* area of land, surrounded by water, which is above water at high tide" (Art. 10(1)). One consequence of this is that artificial islands do not possess their own territorial sea or continental shelf.[245] As far as devices and installations used for the exploration and exploitation of the natural resources of the continental shelf are concerned, this is expressly stated in the Continental Shelf Convention, which provides:

"Such installations and devices, though under the jurisdiction of the coastal State, do not possess the status of islands. They have no territorial sea of their own, and their presence does not affect the delimitation of the territorial sea of the coastal State" (Art. 5(4)).

On the other hand, artificial islands (except, perhaps, fully or almost fully mobile ones) cannot simply be regarded as ships. To the extent that any

---

[224] On this subject, cf. esp. Charles, "Les iles artificielles", 71 *Revue générale du droit international public* (1967), p. 342; Papadakis, "Legal Aspects of Artificial Islands", published in mimeographed form by the David Davies Memorial Institute of International Studies, 1974; Council of Europe, Consultative Assembly; Report by Mr. Margue on the Legal Status of Artificial Islands Built on the High Seas, Doc. 3054 (9 December 1971).

[245] Papadakis, *op. cit.*, p. 30, suggests that an exception should be made enabling any "Sea Cities" which may be established to claim their own territorial sea, though not continental shelf rights.

such structures encounter or present similar problems to those of ships, it may be justifiable to apply the same rules to them, for example in the field of navigational aids[246] or pollution control.[247] But there remain important differences, among which are the fact that these structures are not used for the purpose of transporting people or goods, and that while ships use the sea as a means or place of passage, artificial islands generally stay in the same place and are engaged in what has been called "une utilisation privative" of the sea.[248] They cannot, then, be subsumed under any existing classification and, in the absence of special arrangement, the principles which apply to them must be gleaned from the general rules of the international law of the sea and, in particular, from the rules governing zonal and flag jurisdiction.

131. As far as the national waters of states are concerned, the position is relatively simple. Subject to the possible limitation that it ought not to authorize anything which might interfere with the right of innocent passage through its territorial sea, the coastal state, in the exercise of its territorial sovereignty, has the exclusive right to determine whether, where and by whom an artificial island may be erected, and to extend its laws to it. As far as the high seas are concerned, the question is more complicated. It would seem fairly clear that the jurisdiction of the coastal state over its contiguous zone (if such a zone is claimed) is limited to the rights referred to in Article 24 of the Geneva Convention on the Territorial Sea and Contiguous Zone, *viz.*, to prevent and punish infringements of its customs, fiscal, immigration or sanitary regulations within its territory or territorial sea; outside these spheres, the coastal state cannot invoke contiguous zone jurisdiction as such over artificial islands or those upon them. The next question to consider is whether the coastal state has jurisdiction over them by virtue of its "sovereign rights" over the continental shelf, which, it will be recalled, lies under virtually the whole of the high seas portion of the North Sea.[249] As far as artificial islands not in contact with the seabed or subsoil are concerned, it seems clear that the coastal state has no special rights; shelf rights do not extend to the superjacent waters, which retain their character of "high seas proper", with all the freedoms that this entails. As far as structures which *are* in contact with the shelf are concerned, the answer may depend on their character. Artificial islands used for the purpose of the exploration or exploitation of the natural resources of the shelf are specifically dealt with in the Continental Shelf Convention which, as we have seen, gives the coastal state extensive, though not unlimited, rights.[250] Whether these rights extend to other types

---

[246] Cf. e.g. the IMCO Assembly Resolution of 18 October 1963 (AIII/RES.50).
[247] Cf. e.g. The Oslo Dumping Convention, *supra*, para. 105.
[248] Charles, *op. cit.*, p. 351.
[249] Cf. *supra*, para. 20.
[250] *Supra*, para. 21.

of structure is more debatable. As has already been indicated,[251] the present writer, in common with many others, takes the view that the exclusive rights given to coastal states by the Continental Shelf Convention, representing as they do a derogation from the principle of the freedom of the high seas, must be strictly construed, and that consequently the coastal state cannot, under existing law, claim to regulate or exclude other activities merely because they take place on "its" shelf. It is noteworthy that when the Netherlands Government took action against Radio and TV "Noordzee", which was operating from an artificial structure erected on the seabed outside Dutch territorial waters, it was careful not to claim that its right to do so was based on its "ownership" of the shelf. Instead, it based its action on the alleged existence of a legal vacuum which it was entitled to fill, on the principle of contiguity, and on the right to protect its legitimate interests.[252] The Netherlands approach raises questions of international law which are at once complex and fundamental, but which cannot be fully explored here for reasons of space. Suffice it to say that the Dutch view is by no means universally accepted. There need be no complete legal vacuum, because the state which sets up such an installation itself will be responsible for it, while the individual or company which sets up an installation will be subject to the jurisdiction of his (or its) national state. It is only in those rare cases where the owner or operator is stateless, and the device is not a ship flying the flag of a state, that there is a vacuum to be filled.[253] However, this is not to say that the coastal state will never have jurisdiction. The general jurisdictional rules of international law permit a state to exercise jurisdiction, not only over its territory, but over its nationals wherever they may be, and in certain circumstances over aliens whose acts, though performed outside the territory of the state in question, have harmful consequences within its territory. Although the exact scope of these permissive rules is controversial, it would seem that the coastal state has at least some jurisdiction over those who use artificial islands in a manner harmful to its legitimate interests.[254] Moreover, it should be noted that the freedom to use the high seas is subject to the duty not to interfere unreasonably with the exercise of that freedom by others. If the above analysis is correct, it means that a state has no automatic jurisdiction over artificial islands merely because they are established on "its" shelf: devices for exploring and exploiting the shelf's natural resources apart, it will have jurisdiction only if the facts of the particular case justify the application of an "extended jurisdiction". On the other

---

[251] *Supra*, para. 127.
[252] Cf. Van Panhuys and Boas, "Legal Aspects of Pirate Broadcasting: a Dutch Approach", 60 *American Journal of International Law* (1966), p. 303.
[253] It is, of course, conceded that the state or states entitled to exercise jurisdiction on these grounds may fail to do so.
[254] Cf. *Supra*, para. 127.

hand, it must be recognized that there is an increasing tendency to consider that rights over the continental shelf should be both inclusive and comprehensive, and it may be that the Third Conference on the Law of the Sea will sanction such claims, either by extending shelf rights to superjacent waters, or in the context of an Exclusive Economic Zone or the like. Be that as it may, it is certainly true to say that many of the legal problems raised by the proliferation of artificial islands await authoritative resolution.[255]

2. Pirate Broadcasting[256]

132. From about 1958 there was a rapid proliferation of unauthorized radio (and, in one case, television) stations broadcasting to the territory of North Sea states from ships or artificial islands in the North Sea, usually just outside territorial waters. These have come to be called "pirate" radio stations. Although it is quite clear that it is not piracy in the technical sense, *inter alia* because it involves no "illegal acts or violence, detention or ... depredation" on the high seas,[257] governments have been anxious to suppress the stations, on three main grounds:

(i) Radio frequencies are a scarce resource, apportioned under the auspices of the International Telecommunications Union, so stations which pick their own wavelengths can interfere with this system, as well as with emergency broadcasts at sea. For this reason the Radio Regulations attached to the International Telecommunications Convention prohibit the operation of a broadcasting service by mobile stations at sea and over the sea, and the establishment and use of broadcasting stations on board ships, aircraft or any other floating or airborne objects outside national territories.[258]
(ii) Unregulated broadcasting interferes with national monopolies or public control over this type of activity.
(iii) The broadcasts may contravene national law on such matters as advertising, sedition, obscenity, defamation, etc.

133. For the state which wishes to suppress these stations, however, the jurisdictional difficulties are formidable. The complex legal position with regard to artificial islands has already been touched upon. No less complex

---

[255] Cf. Council of Europe Consultative Assembly, Recommendation 653 (1972), which *inter alia* notes that artificial islands do not come under the legal order of any particular state and recommends the Council of Ministers to ask member states to define a common attitude for the Third United Nations Conference on the Law of the Sea.
[256] On this subject, cf. esp. March Hunnings, "Pirate Broadcasting in European Waters", 14 *Int. & Comp. Law Quarterly* (1965), p. 410; Van Panhuys and Boas, *op. cit.*
[257] High Seas Convention, Art. 15.
[258] ITU Radio Regulations 1968, Rules 28(6) and 7(1), respectively.

are the problems relating to stations established on ships outside territorial waters. The coastal state's contiguous zone and continental shelf jurisdiction does not cover broadcasts from such vessels. Ships on the high seas are subject to the exclusive jurisdiction of the flag state, and for any other state to interfere with them entitles the flag state to bring an international claim. But the flag state may be unwilling or unable to exercise sufficient control over the ship to suppress the undesirable activity. This is particularly likely to be the case if the ship is operating under a "flag of convenience"; nevertheless, as has been seen,[259] it is by no means clear that international law permits the coastal state to treat the ship as "stateless" when it is flying a flag of convenience. Moreover, even when the ship is unregistered, it or those operating it may be subject, on the ground of nationality, to the jurisdiction of some state other than the one on whose territory the broadcasts are received. On the other hand it may well be, of course, that a state with only a tenuous connection with the ship will in practice be unlikely to protest at interference with the ship.

134. Since the law of maritime jurisdiction as such is thus of little help to states wishing to suppress pirate stations, the solution lies in recourse to the rules of general international law relating to extended jurisdiction. This subject is too complex and controversial to be dealt with in anything more than outline here,[260] but in brief the position is as follows: (a) A state has jurisdiction to make laws relating to the acts of its nationals wherever they may be. (b) By customary law a state has a measure of jurisdiction to apply its laws to acts committed by foreigners outside its territory. Different states adopt different positions about the extent of this jurisdiction, but it is certainly arguable that it extends to acts committed abroad or on the high seas which have their effect on the territory of the state in question, particularly if there is a quasi-physical effect, as from broadcasting. (c) This does not necessarily mean that the state in question has a right to *enforce* its laws outside its territory but, if it has jurisdiction to prescribe, it can exercise its jurisdiction over anyone (national or alien) who enters its territory, as well as over anyone who aids or assists the wrongdoer in any way within its territory. (d) The state having national, flag or territorial jurisdiction over the person, ship or installation in question can agree to waive its rights in favour of some other state, and thereby extend the latter's customary rights under (b) and (c) above.

135. The European Agreement for the Prevention of Broadcasts Transmitted from Stations outside National Territories[261] is not an agreement of

---

[259] *Supra*, note 12.

[260] For a more detailed examination, cf. e.g. O'Connell, *International Law*, Vol. II, Pt. 7. Cf. also the analysis by March Hunnings, *op. cit.*, at pp. 430–431.

[261] Strasbourg, 22 January 1965 (entered into force 19 October 1967); Council of Europe Treaty No. 53; 634 UNTS 239; UKTS No. 1 of 1968 (Cmnd. 3497). Among the parties are all of the North Sea states except the Netherlands, and the latter is taking steps to become a party.

type (d); essentially its purpose is to bind the parties to exercise their existing powers against pirate stations for the common benefit. The Agreement covers "broadcasting stations installed or maintained on board ships, aircraft, or any other floating or airborne objects and which, outside national territories, transmit broadcasts intended for reception or capable of being received, wholly or in part, within the territory of any Contracting Party, or which cause harmful interference to any radio-communication service operating under the authority of a Contracting Party in accordance with the Radio Regulations" (Art. 1). The parties agree to take appropriate steps to make punishable as offences under their domestic law the establishment or operation of such stations, as well as specified acts of collaboration, such as the provision of supplies, transport, equipment and so on, and the ordering of material of any kind, including advertising. Each party is to apply these provisions to (a) its nationals and (b) non-nationals who have committed the offences on the territory, ships or aircraft of the state, or on board any floating or airborne object under its jurisdiction (Art. 3). Article 4 provides that nothing in the Agreement is to prevent offences other than those specified being treated as punishable, or prevent its provisions being applied to persons other than those specified in Article 3. However, the Agreement does not in itself permit action to be taken by the state against aliens outside its jurisdiction, or against the station itself (unless the latter is within the state's jurisdiction by virtue of its position, its registration or the nationality of its owners); here one is thrown back on to customary law. Article 4 also states that nothing in the Agreement is to prevent parties from applying its provisions to broadcasting stations installed or maintained on objects affixed to or supported by the bed of the sea, and on 29 January 1965 the Consultative Assembly of the Council of Europe recommended an examination of the possibility of extending the obligations contained in the Agreement to such fixed installations. So far, no such extension has been made.

136. Although the Agreement is not a great innovation from a jurisdictional point of view, cutting stations off from the closest and most convenient sources of supplies, equipment and, above all, revenue, has been remarkably successful. In the few cases in which it has failed, police action of debatable international legal validity has normally succeeded, for the simple reason that no other state was prepared to object. As a result, pirate broadcasting stations have almost – but not entirely – disappeared from the North Sea.

CONCLUSIONS

137. To summarize this vast, diverse and complex body of laws in a few paragraphs is clearly impossible. One impression which does emerge fairly clearly, however, is the difficulty that international law appears to have in keeping up with rapid technological change, let alone in making provision for the solution of new problems before they actually arise in practice. In an era of gradual change, the law can afford to be conservative; but in an era of rapid flux, and when the issues at stake are as great as they are in the North Sea, this relative inflexibility can be very unfortunate. The rather unsatisfactory response of international law to the changes of technology is not, however, due to any inherent unadaptability, or to lack of imagination on the part of international lawyers. Treaties are almost infinitely adaptable to the will of states, and it is probably safe to say that there are virtually no insurmountable legal difficulties of a technical kind in establishing whatever regime states agree on.

138. Responsibility for the inadequate response of international law must, therefore, be laid more at the door of the diplomat and the statesman than at that of the lawyer. States have been excessively cautious in agreeing to the innovations necessitated by a changing environment. In particular, they have perhaps been unduly awed by the emphasis traditionally placed on the exclusiveness of flag-state jurisdiction. The freedom of the seas does, it is true, depend on protecting ships on the high seas from unjustifiable and unreasonable interference on the part of states other than the one whose flag they fly. At the same time, it must be borne in mind that, very often, the activity complained of causes significant harm to the interests of states which are geographically very remote from the flag-state; accordingly the latter's interest in punishing violations of the rules will tend to be relatively small. If a Ruritanian citizen committed a murder in London, no sane man would suggest that this offence should be left to be dealt with by the Ruritanian authorities on his return home; but this is not unlike what happens when, for example, a tanker commits a violation of pollution laws on the high seas. That this violation has not occurred within the national waters of the aggrieved states should not be permitted to obscure the fact that important local interests have nevertheless been jeopardized.

139. This is not to advocate unilateral action on the part of coastal states. What would be greatly preferable would be the consensual modification of the sacrosanctity of flag-state jurisdiction in agreements which take into account the legitimate interests of all concerned and seek to achieve a reasonable balance between them. Some faltering steps have already been taken in this direction, but the approach of governments has, on the whole, been characterized by an excessive timidity. It is worth emphasizing once again that it is not international law which is the obstruction; international law can provide virtually any form of regulatory machinery, but it is for governments to decide what form of regulation they wish to establish. The Study Group's own suggestions will be found in Chapter VI below.

V
The Present Legal Regime of the North Sea: National Law*

1. Conflicts arising from the common use of limited world resources cannot be solved solely on an international plane while international law and organization remain in their present undeveloped state. It rests with every sovereign state to fill the gaps left by international law and to implement and enforce, by means of its own municipal legislation, such treaty and customary law as does exist.

2. The relationship between international law and English[1] municipal law is intricate, having been approached by the courts from a practical viewpoint rather than on any theoretical basis. That part of international law which is customary (arising from the practice of states rather than from any formal agreement) is generally considered to be included in the Common Law of England and can be enforced as such in so far as it does not conflict with any other principle of municipal law.[2] On the other hand, treaties, in which the law of the sea is increasingly to be found, have to be specifically implemented by legislation passed by, or under the authority of, Parliament, in order to have any effect in English law. The conclusion and ratification of treaties are within the prerogative of the Crown but, with one or two exceptions,[3] the international obligations which are

---

* This chapter has been written by Elizabeth Wilmshurst, formerly lecturer in law at Bristol University, and Dr. Maurice Mendelson. Unless otherwise indicated, it is based on information available up to 1 June 1974.

[1] Scotland and England have separate legal systems although the increasing use of statutes – which apply to both countries unless Scotland is expressly excluded – means that in many spheres their laws do not diverge significantly. This study will focus on English law but will point out material differences with Scotland when they occur.

[2] For differing views on the extent to which international customary law needs to be incorporated into municipal law, cf. Brownlie, *Principles of Public International Law* (2nd ed., 1973), p. 45; *Halsbury's Laws of England* (3rd ed., 1954), Vol. VII, p. 264; Oppenheim, *International Law* (8th ed. 1955) Vol. I., p. 39 *et seq.*

[3] E.g. the acquisition of territory by virtue of the Crown's prerogative powers. It seems that the 1958 Geneva Convention on the Territorial Sea and Contigu-

thereby created have no internal effect in themselves but must be "transformed" by Act of Parliament.

3. To the courts of the United Kingdom the legal competence of Parliament to legislate in any way and in respect of any matter in which it sees fit is undoubted; furthermore, any statute it passes is of superior authority to any other form of law.[4] In assessing the British contribution to the solution of the problems of the North Sea it is therefore not sufficient to assert that the country has ratified almost every major multilateral convention having effect in this area: it is also necessary to show, first, that the United Kingdom has enacted the legislation required by the relevant conventions; and, secondly, that other British legislation does not conflict with international law.

4. The jurisdiction of any state to prescribe rules and to enforce them is limited by international law. Before examining the legal regime relating to specific marine activities this study will therefore consider the extent of application of English law to occurrences in the seas.

I JURISDICTIONAL ZONES

A. Internal Waters[5]

5. These waters lie on the landward side of the baselines, from which the territorial sea is measured. Baselines are defined by the 1964 Territorial Waters Order in Council,[6] promulgated 14 days after the Geneva Convention on the Territorial Sea and Contiguous Zone[7] came into force. In general, they follow the low-water line along the shore but one exception is provided for on the deeply indented coast of West Scotland, where a series of straight baselines is formed by joining specified points defined by co-ordinates of latitude and longitude between Cape Wrath and the Mull of Kintyre. The Order in Council also established rules for defining bays

---

ous Zone, in so far as it extended national sovereignty (for instance, by relaxing the rules for straight baselines), had its effect in English law from the moment when it came into force, having been ratified by the Crown; cf. Diplock L.J. in *Post Office v. Estuary Radio Ltd.* [1968], 2 QB 740 at 756.

[4] There is a presumption in court proceedings involving the interpretation of a statute that the latter does not conflict with international law (*Salomon v. Commissioners of Customs and Excise* [1967], 2 QB 116); but where there is a manifest divergence the statute must prevail.

[5] See Chapter IV, paras. 37 ff.

[6] Not issued in the official Statutory Instrument series, but it may be found in 23 *Halsbury's Statutory Instruments*, p. 165; *National Legislation*, UN Legislative Series ST/LEG/SER/B.15 (1970), p. 129.

[7] See Chapter IV, para. 30. The source reference of this and all other treaties herein mentioned can be found in the appropriate footnote in Chapter IV.

and low-tide elevations which follow the Geneva Convention more or less exactly;[8] for example, the permitted length of bay-closing lines is extended from 10 to 24 miles. As a result of the Order, internal waters were significantly increased in area, and this had the effect of enclosing rich fishing grounds in such places as the Moray Firth, which had until then been the subject of considerable controversy.[9]

6. Although the Order in Council thus largely reproduces the rules laid down by the Convention, except in the above-mentioned stretch of the west coast of Scotland, it does not set out the baselines as such, but simply indicates the principles on which they are to be drawn.[10] There is in use a small-scale chart which has been prepared by the Hydrographic Department of the Admiralty and which purports to show "the three-mile limit of the Territorial Sea measured from baselines in accordance with the 1958 Geneva Convention" but it displays the warning "this chart is illustrative, not definitive".[11] The chart has not, apparently, been challenged by any foreign country with fishing interests[12] although baselines are used to measure both territorial sea and fishery limits and are consequently of considerable interest to foreigners wishing to use these waters. However, the lack of a definitive map, and the resulting uncertainty as to the extent of internal waters, has led to litigation. It is open to parties to a dispute to refer to a representative of the Crown for a conclusive answer as to the status of any portion of water, since the determination of British territory still lies within the Crown's prerogative,[13] but this course of action has not recently been followed. The two related cases of *R. v. Kent Justices ex p. Lye*[14] and *Post Office v. Estuary Radio Ltd.*[15] make it clear that different courts can differ markedly in their judgment on whether a particular spot is within internal waters or the territorial sea, or outside the jurisdiction

---

[8] But cf. *Post Office v. Estuary Radio Ltd* [1968], 2 QB 740, where some suggestion was made that the definition of low-tide elevation contained in the Order in Council might diverge from that in the Convention; the point was not decided.

[9] The Scottish case of *Mortensen v. Peters* (1906) 8F (J.C.) 93 decided that the Herring Fishery (Scotland) Act, 1889, applied to foreigners in the Moray Firth even while outside the three-mile limit. However, the Act was not subsequently invoked against them in practice and, as a result, conservation measures in the Firth were binding upon Scottish but not foreign fishermen, a situation which gave rise to considerable ill-feeling. (See Lauterpacht (ed.), *The Contemporary Practice of the United Kingdom in the field of International Law* (1962), i, 48).

[10] The explanation may lie in the difficulties involved in defining with exactitude a low-water line which is constantly changing due to geographical factors.

[11] Ref. HW 316/64(2).

[12] O'Connor J. at first instance in *Post Office v. Estuary Radio Ltd.* [1967] 3 All ER 663 at 672.

[13] *The Fagernes* [1927] p. 311.

[14] [1967] 2 QB 153.

[15] [1968] 2 QB 740.

altogether.[16] Nor are they willing to treat such a determination as a binding rule of law for the future so that, presumably, it will always be open to an individual to re-open the question of the status of a particular area at a later date.[17] Although the Crown has sovereignty over internal waters, there may and do exist private rights of ownership extending from, and inclusive of, the foreshore[18] to varying distances from the coast. These rights are relevant to the consideration of fisheries and pollution and will be discussed in the appropriate sections.[19]

B. Territorial Sea[20]

7. The jurisdictional competence of the Crown extends to the outermost limit of the territorial sea measured from the baselines along the coast. The United Kingdom has traditionally been one of the foremost proponents of a three-mile territorial sea; this limit has never been laid down as such in statute[21] but its validity in Engish law is no longer questioned. (Possibly a new limit will be adopted following the Third UN Conference on the Law of the Sea).

The Legal Regime of Internal Waters and the Territorial Sea

(*Note:* The term "national waters" is used as a matter of convenience throughout this paper to refer to internal waters and territorial sea together. It is not, however, a term of art in English law.[22])

8. Internal waters are as much a part of United Kingdom territory as the land, and consequently both statute and case law apply to them unless a contrary intent is expressed. Probably the only substantial difference between their juridical nature and that of the territorial sea is that foreign ships enjoy no right of innocent passage through internal waters (except in those areas provided for by Art. 5(2) of the Geneva Convention on the

---

[16] In each of the two cases the guilt of the accused depended on whether the Red Sands Tower was within English jurisdiction. In the first it was held that the Tower stood in the territorial sea; in the second that it was within a bay and therefore in internal waters.

[17] See, in particular, Diplock L.J. in *Post Office v. Estuary Radio* [1968], 2 QB 740.

[18] The foreshore is that part of the shore between high- and low-water mark.

[19] Sections B and D *infra*.

[20] See Chapter IV, paras. 30–36.

[21] The Territorial Waters Jurisdiction Act, 1878, is sometimes quoted as statutory authority for the three-mile limit, but s.7 of the Act specifies this width for the purpose of criminal jurisdiction only. In fact, the Preamble states that the territorial sea extends "to such a distance as is necessary for the defence and security" of the realm, but a Preamble does not, of course, have legislative effect. Other statutes make use of the three-mile limit for certain specified purposes, e.g. North Sea Fisheries Act, 1893, s.9; Customs and Excise Act, 1952, ss. 52, 75, 76 & *passim*.

[22] It has, however, occasionally been used in statutes with the meaning of internal waters; cf. Sea Fishing Regulation Act, 1966, s.1(1) (a).

Territorial Sea),[23] and the United Kingdom has the right to close her ports to them.[24] There is, however, some controversy as to whether the territorial sea is just such an extension of the land domain as internal waters, or whether jurisdiction over it is more restricted.[25] The problem relates chiefly to foreign vessels, for British ships are governed by the law of their port of registration whether they are within or without national waters.[26]

9. There are a number of matters upon which the United Kingdom has applied its legislation specifically to foreign vessels within the country's national waters: such matters as the control of navigation[27] (collision regulations, compulsory pilotage, harbour charges and light dues); the safety of ships[28] (construction regulations); the enforcement of customs laws;[29] oil pollution control;[30] claims to, and the regulation of, fisheries and seabed resources.[31] The question arises as to whether foreign ships are subject only to such laws as these or whether they are "invaded"[32] by English law in its entirety as soon as they enter territorial limits. In spite of the majority decision of the Court for Crown Cases Reserved in *R. v. Keyn*,[33] which laid down in 1876 that the realm of England did not extend beyond low-water mark and that jurisdiction was to be exercised only for the very limited purposes of defence and security,[34] the law today appears to be that the rights over the territorial sea are those of sovereignty and

---

[23] Art.5(2) provides that the right of innocent passage shall exist in those areas of internal waters which have been enclosed by the establishment of straight baselines but which were previously considered as part of the territorial sea or of the High Seas. Consequently, in the case of the United Kingdom, the Minch is "open" for innocent passage.

[24] Her right to do so has been restricted in respect of the ships of the Contracting States of the 1923 Convention and Statute on the International Regime of Maritime Ports (Chapter IV, para. 38).

[25] For a useful discussion of the juridical nature of the territorial sea, see O'Connell, "The Juridical Nature of the Territorial Sea", *British Y.B. of Int. Law*, 1971, p. 303.

[26] For British ships see para. 18(i) *infra*.

[27] Section C *infra*.

[28] Section C *infra*.

[29] Para. 13(i) *infra*.

[30] Section D *infra*.

[31] Sections A and B *infra*.

[32] See O'Connell, *International Law* (2nd ed., 1970), Vol. II, p. 612.

[33] (1876) 2 Ex. D. 63.

[34] An alternative reading of the case is that the court's decision related only to the narrow question of the extent of jurisdiction of the English courts which, for historical reasons, did not reach further than the low-water mark of the counties; this was a separate issue from that of the outer boundaries of U.K. territory. See O'Connell, *British Yearbook of Int. Law*, 1971, p. 303 at pp. 372-377. Nevertheless, both the majority and the minority judges thought that their decision did turn directly on the definition of United Kingdom territory. Even if the *ratio* of the case is not limited to the more restricted ground, it is possible that the Crown's ratification of the Geneva Convention on the Territorial Sea

plenary jurisdiction, subject always to rights of innocent passage. This may seem to be in conflict with the international legal rules on the territorial sea, but the practical exercise of the United Kingdom's jurisdiction does conform in most respects to international law; there is a policy of non-interference in occurrences on board foreign ships except in the areas of specific enactment mentioned above or, generally, where the peace of the port or of the territorial sea is affected.[35] In this respect the two zones of national waters are treated alike.

10. Criminal Law: It follows that all offences under English criminal law which are committed in any part of the national waters may be prosecuted in English courts,[36] and for this purpose the alleged offender may be arrested on board ship.[37] Compliance with the policy that foreigners are not prosecuted except for offences involving the peace of the port, or the good order of the territorial sea, is aided by the fact that proceedings for most offences in national waters can be instituted only with the consent of the Attorney-General, a Secretary of State or the Director of Public Prosecutions.[38] Certain states[39] have concluded agreements with the United Kingdom to ensure that personnel on their ships are immune from prosecution except for offences such as those involving the peace of the

---

in 1964 (Art. 1 of which declares the sovereignty of a State to extend to the territorial sea, its bed and subsoil), may have had the effect of extending British territory by the act of ratification alone, at any rate if the remarks of Diplock L.J. in *Post Office v. Estuary Radio Ltd.* [1968] 2 QB 740 at 756 are accepted.

[35] See the United Kingdom reply to Experts' Questionnaire, Hague Codification Conference, Replies XII and XV; League of Nations Docs. C74 M39 1929 V. Compare the more restricted view of jurisdiction expressed in the United Kingdom protest against the United States' liquor laws in U.S. For. Rel. 1923, Vol. 1, p. 133.

[36] Indictable offences by virtue of the Territorial Waters Jurisdiction Act, 1878; for summary offences, see *R. v. Kent Justices ex p. Lye* [1967], 2 QB 153. There is no restriction on prosecutions resulting from collisions since the United Kingdom entered a reservation on ratifying the Brussels Convention for the Unification of Certain Rules relating to Penal Jurisdiction in Matters of Collision (Chapter IV, para. 68) withdrawing the territorial sea from the ambit of the Convention, in accordance with Art. 4. The Convention does not in any event extend to internal waters.

[37] Arrest may also be effected in respect of extraditable offences committed in the country requesting the extradition.

[38] E.g. Territorial Waters Jurisdiction Act, 1878, s.3, in respect of indictable offences; Prevention of Oil Pollution Act, 1971, s.19, in respect of most oil pollution offences; Mineral Workings (Offshore Installations) Act, 1971, s.10, in respect of offences under the Act committed within any part of the territorial sea, and in respect of any offence committed in or under offshore installations or within a 500-metre surrounding zone – as to which see paras. 15–17 *infra*.

[39] Orders in Council have been made in respect of Austria, Belgium, Denmark, the Federal Republic of Germany, Hungary, Italy, Japan, Spain, the U.S.S.R. and Yugoslavia.

port; in their case the policy of non-interference has been given the force of law. Accordingly, s.5 of the Consular Relations Act, 1968, provides that no criminal proceedings may be instituted without the consent of the consul of the country concerned in connection with an incident alleged to have occurred on board a ship belonging to such a country, unless the offence (a) has been committed by or against a United Kingdom citizen, or (b) is one "involving the tranquillity or safety of a port, or the law relating to safety of life at sea, public health, oil pollution, wireless telegraphy, immigration or customs", or (c) is an arrestable offence. The jurisdiction of English courts in national waters includes the power to entertain habeas corpus proceedings in respect of those detained on board any ship; the Act accordingly provides that crew members held in custody on board the ships of certain[40] states for disciplinary offences shall not be deemed by British courts to be unlawfully detained unless (a) the detention is unlawful under the laws of the state concerned or the conditions of detention are inhumane or unjustifiably severe, or (b) there is reason to believe that the life or liberty of the detainee will be endangered in any country where the ship is likely to go because of race, nationality, political opinion or religion.[41]

11. Civil Law: English courts have almost unlimited jurisdiction to decide any civil cause brought before them if the defendant submits to their jurisdiction, or if process can be served on the defendant whether within the country (which includes internal and territorial waters)[42] or, by the court's leave, outside.[43] This jurisdiction is restricted in certain ways:

(a) By virtue of s.4 of the Consular Relations Act, 1968, no proceedings may be brought relating to the remuneration or contract of service of the master, commander or crew member of a ships belonging to a state specified by Order in Council,[44] except where the state's consular officer has been notified of the intention to invoke the jurisdiction of the English courts and has not objected within a specified time.[45]

(b) S.4 of the Administration of Justice Act, 1956 (which substantially reproduces Art. 1 of the 1952 Brussels Civil Jurisdiction Convention),[46]

---

[40] States specified under this section are all those referred to in note 39 above, together with France, the U.S.A., Greece, Mexico, Norway and Sweden.

[41] S.6.

[42] *Rules of the Supreme Court*, Order 11/1/2. Another consequence of the fact that territorial waters are treated as English territory is that English law is applied as the *lex loci delicti* (law of the place of commission) in cases of torts committed in such waters; *Carr v. Fracis Times* [1902] AC 176.

[43] Under *Rules of the Supreme Court*, Order 11.

[44] States specified under this section are all those referred to in note 39 above together with Greece, Mexico, Norway, Sweden, Bulgaria, Poland and Romania.

[45] The time specified in each Order so far is two weeks.

[46] International Convention on Certain Rules concerning Civil Jurisdiction in Matters of Collision (Chapter IV, para. 68).

provides that no personal action may be brought in respect of damage, loss of life or personal injury resulting from a collision between ships unless the defendant has his habitual residence or place of business in England or Wales, or the cause of action arose within internal waters, or an action arising from the same incident or series of incidents is proceeding before the court.

(c) Proceedings *in rem* (i.e. brought "against" a ship or goods rather than against a person, and authorizing the arrest of the ship or goods in question) may be taken only in respect of certain specified claims;[47] a rule which is substantially in conformity with the 1952 Brussels Convention relating to the Arrest of Sea-going Ships.[48] The Rules of the Supreme Court[49] require that notice of intended action be sent to the relevant consul before a warrant of arrest is issued against a foreign ship in an action *in rem*.

(d) There is no rule of English law which prohibits the judicial arrest of a foreign ship while it is merely passing through the territorial sea but, in practice, conformity with Article 20(1) of the Geneva Convention on the Territorial Sea[50] is achieved.

12. The subject of jurisdiction cannot be left without a brief reference to the immunity from suits *in rem* of state-owned ships by virtue of the principle of sovereign immunity. As the law stands at present, this immunity can be claimed in English courts even where the foreign vessel is engaged in commercial activities.[51] With the proliferation of public commercial undertakings, this principle of English law may pose a threat to the regulation of navigation.

C. High Seas[52]

13. The outer limit of the territorial sea forms the boundary between the territory of the United Kingdom and the high seas. Britain has not availed

---

[47] I.e. all cases involving the ownership and possession of a ship, or where a maritime lien or other charge attaches to the ship or property. Generally maritime liens attach in respect of service done to the ship, damage caused by it, salvage and seamen's wages: Administration of Justice Act, 1956, ss.3(2) and (3).

[48] Chapter IV, para. 68.

[49] Order 75 r.5(5).

[50] "The coastal State should not stop or divert a foreign ship passing through the territorial sea for the purpose of exercising civil jurisdiction in relation to a person on board the ship". See Chapter IV, para. 35. Cf., however, *The Rhenamia* (*Shipping Gazette*, 12 November 1909).

[51] *The Parlement Belge* [1880] 5 PD 197; *The Porto Alexandre* [1920] P30. The rule has been subject to a certain amount of criticism, not least from the judges themselves; cf. especially the remarks of Lord Denning in *Rahimtoola v. Nizam of Hyderabad* [1958] AC 379 at p. 418; and in *Mellenger v. New Brunswick Development Corporation* [1971] 1 WLR 604.

[52] See Chapter IV, paras. 12ff.

itself of the possibility offered by Article 24 of the Geneva Convention on the Territorial Sea of claiming a contiguous zone, but the country does exercise certain rights outside its national waters, some of which are analogous to contiguous zone jurisdiction.

(a) *Enforcement of Customs Laws.* Under the so-called "Hovering Acts", the United Kingdom long exercised jurisdiction over foreign vessels outside her territorial waters. The Acts have now been repealed[53] but a relic of them seems to remain, for s.75 of the Customs and Excise Act, 1952, provides that a ship which is or *has been* "within the limits of any port or within three ... nautical miles of the coast of the United Kingdom ... while constructed, adapted, altered or fitted in any manner for the purpose of concealing goods ... shall be liable to forfeiture", and s.78 provides that "where any ship liable to forfeiture as aforesaid has failed to bring to when required to do so and chase has been given thereto by any vessel in the service of Her Majesty, and after the commander of that vessel has hoisted the proper ensign and caused a gun to be fired as a signal, the ship fails to bring to, the ship may be fired upon." This provision has a resemblance to the Common Law (and international) right of hot pursuit, but lacks the necessity, which is insisted upon by international law, for the pursuit to be "hot".

(b) *Intervention Following Oil Pollution Casualties.* Following a shipping accident, the Secretary of State has power to take direct action against the ship involved – whether British or foreign – if pollution by oil of British coasts or waters is threatened. Only "grave and imminent danger" of pollution will justify such action against foreign ships; the subject will be discussed below in more detail.[54]

(c) *Coastwise Shipping.* The right to regulate coastwise trading or to reserve it for a state's own nationals has long been established in international law. The United Kingdom no longer reserves it exclusively for her nationals; for certain purposes, however, she treats foreign ships navigating between ports in her territory in the same way as British ships.[55]

---

[53] The first of these was passed in 1736 (9 Geo. II c. 35); see Colombos, *International Law of the Sea* (6th ed., 1967), pp. 136–138. The Acts were repealed by the Customs Consolidation Act, 1876, which, however, left extant provision for the jurisdiction over ships within three leagues of the coast if they were "British" – a definition which included ships which, though foreign, had British subjects on board up to a half of their complement. This was repealed as late as 1952.

[54] Section D, *infra.*

[55] The governing statutes are the Customs Consolidation Act, 1876, s.141; Customs and Excise Act, 1952, ss.57–62; and the Merchant Shipping Act, 1970, s.49. Some of the provisions apply only if the ship carries passengers between ports.

(d) *Submarine Cables*. Article 27 of the Geneva Convention on the High Seas requires states to take legislative measures to prevent interference with submarine cables by persons or ships under their jurisdiction, but the United Kingdom has made it an offence for any person whatsoever to break or injure cables in the high seas.[56] Jurisdiction to try such cases has been given to all courts in the United Kingdom.[57]

14. In addition to the above, the United Kingdom exercises jurisdiction for specific purposes in respect of two further zones, while continuing to recognize the status of the waters as high seas. They are the 12-mile fishery zone and the Continental Shelf; since jurisdiction within the fishery limits is exercised solely for the one purpose it will be dealt with in the section relating to Fisheries.[58]

The Continental Shelf[59]

(*Note:* this section deals with the extent and nature of jurisdiction claimed by the United Kingdom over the Continental Shelf; the regulation of mineral workings on the Shelf is discussed in Section II A below.)

15. The Geneva Convention on the Continental Shelf[60] was implemented in English law by the Continental Shelf Act, 1964, s.1 of which vests in the Crown rights "outside territorial waters with respect to the seabed and subsoil and their natural resources...". There is no reference in the Act to any of the criteria given in Articles 1 and 6 of the Convention for determining the outer limit of the Shelf, but rights are stated to be exercisable only over those areas which have been "designated" by the Crown in pursuance of the power conferred by s.1(7) of the Act. A number of Orders in Council have been promulgated which thus designate large blocks of Shelf area in an almost continuous, though irregular, belt around the United Kingdom.[61] The bed of the North Sea has been apportioned between the United Kingdom and each of the states opposite, with the exception of Belgium, by a number of bilateral agreements;[62] the outer

---

[56] By the Submarine Telegraph Act, 1885, as supplemented by the Continental Shelf Act, 1964.
[57] Continental Shelf Act, 1964, s.11(1).
[58] Section B, *infra*.
[59] See Chapter IV, paras. 17ff.
[60] See Chapter IV, para. 18.
[61] Continental Shelf Act (Designation of Areas) Order, 1964, S.I. 1964:697; Continental Shelf Act (Designation of Additional Areas) Order, 1965, S.I. 1965:1531; Continental Shelf Act (Designation of Additional Areas) Order, 1968, S.I. 1968:891; Continental Shelf Act (Designation of Additional Areas) Order, 1971, S.I. 1971:594; Continental Shelf Act (Designation of Additional Areas) Order, 1974; S.I. 1974:1489. See the map between pages 4 and 5 of *Continental Shelf Act, 1964: Report for the Year* (H.M.S.O., 1972).
[62] Listed in Chapter IV, note 28.

limits of the designated areas correspond substantially with these internationally agreed boundaries. The United Kingdom is therefore exercising upon her eastward coast national jurisdiction to the full extent of her international competence. This jurisdiction is for limited purposes only, which are not identified with any precision by the Act. It refers only to "rights exercisable ... outside territorial waters with respect to the seabed and subsoil and their natural resources"[63] without specifying what these rights are. Since the Act itself does not purport to create the rights, but is merely vesting in the Crown such rights as already exist, it must be inferred that their source lies in public international law.[64] Reference to the Geneva Convention shows that the rights are "for the purpose of exploring ... and exploiting [the] natural resources" of the Continental Shelf.[65]

16. The entire[66] criminal law of England, Scotland and Northern Ireland[67] has been extended by s.3(1) of the 1964 Act to the offshore installations of the Continental Shelf and to a 500-metre zone surrounding each one. As far as the civil law is concerned, the Continental Shelf

---

[63] S.1(1).

[64] With regard to the Parties to the Geneva Convention, the source of law will be the Convention, particularly since it is referred to in the long title to the Act. (The reference is in fact to "the Convention on the High Seas" but it is presumed that this means the Continental Shelf Convention.) Rights opposable against non-parties will be based on international customary law, but it is probable that this differs little, if at all, from the Convention in this respect.

[65] Art. 2.

[66] Of course the section does not achieve a blanket transfer of English criminal law: See Samuels, "The Continental Shelf Act 1964", in British Institute of International and Comparative Law, *"Developments in the Law of the Sea 1958–1964"* (International Law Series No. 3, 1965), p. 166: "... it remains to be seen how far, if at all, the drinking and betting and gaming laws will be applied to installations as having comparable conditions and constituting a 'microcosm of the United Kingdom'." Cf. also *Cox v. Army Council* [1963] AC 48 on the interpretation of s.70 of the Army Act, 1955, which extended the English criminal law to the armed forces wherever located. It was held that not all English laws could be thus translated: they had to have the "character of universality". There had to be a degree of similarity between the act or omission committed abroad and any act or omission which could be committed in England, the requisite degree of similarity depending upon the nature of the offence. This test seems appropriate to the question of Continental Shelf jurisdiction.

[67] The effect of s.3(1) appears to be that the criminality of any act on an installation or within its safety zone may be tested by reference to any of the legal systems in the United Kingdom. See Lauterpacht (ed.), *British Practice in International Law*, 1964, pp. 55–56: "In theory it would be possible to prosecute in Scotland for any offence against Scots law a person committing on an installation off the coast of Cornwall an act which was not an offence under English law". *Contra* Samuels, *op. cit.* The guarantee against this actually happening rests in the provision by s.10 of the Mineral Workings (Offshore Installations) Act, 1971, that prosecutions for offences committed on an offshore installation can be instituted only with the consent of the Director of Public Prosecutions.

(Jurisdiction) Order, 1968,[68] extends to the installations and their surrounding zones that part of the law which relates to acts or omissions "in connection with the exploration of the seabed or subsoil or the exploitation of their natural resources":[69] whether it is Scottish, English or Northern Irish law which is applicable depends on the position of the installation concerned. In addition, a number of statutes are extended to the designated areas specifically, including the Radioactive Substances Act, 1960.[70] As regards the machinery of law enforcement, any criminal court in the United Kingdom is given competence to try an alleged criminal offence if it could have done so had the offence been committed in its part of the country;[71] for civil disputes jurisdiction is conferred on the English High Court when the cause of action arose in the "English part" of the designated areas, or on the Scottish Court of Session, or the Northern Irish High Court, according again to the location of the cause of action.[72] A British constable is to have on any offshore installation (though apparently not within the 500-metre zone) all the powers, protection and privileges which he has in the area for which he acts as constable.[73] Acting under powers conferred by s.2 of the 1964 Act, the Secretary of State has made regulations prohibiting the entry of unauthorized ships into specified 500-metre zones.[74]

17. A few points may be made about the extent to which U.K. Continental Shelf legislation complies with the provisions of the 1958 Convention.

(a) The Convention provides that installations are "under the jurisdiction of" the coastal state:[75] a form of words that does not appear to impose any limitation on the subject-matter of the law which the coastal state

---

[68] S.I. 1968:892 as amended by the Continental Shelf (Jurisdiction) (Amendment) Order, 1971, S.I. 1971:721 and the Continental Shelf (Jurisdiction) (Amendment) Order, 1974, S.I. 1974:1490. These must be read in conjunction with s.3(2) of the Act.

[69] This leaves open the question of what is the civil law to be applied if an act does not come within the wording of the section. What, for example, is the *lex loci delicti* (law of the place of commission) of an alleged slander spoken on an installation?

[70] Also Part II of the Coast Protection Act, 1949 (by s.4 of the Continental Shelf Act, 1964); a part of the Submarine Telegraph Act, 1885 (by s.8 of the Continental Shelf Act, 1964); the Wireless Telegraphy Act, 1949, and the Radioactive Substances Act, 1960, by the Continental Shelf (Jurisdiction) Order, 1968, *supra*.

[71] S.3(1).

[72] Continental Shelf (Jurisdiction) Order, 1968, *supra*.

[73] S.11(3) of the 1964 Act and s.9(5) of the Mineral Workings (Offshore Installations) Act, 1971.

[74] The Continental Shelf (Protection of Installations) (No. 6) Order, 1973, S.I. 1973:284, and the Continental Shelf (Protection of Installations) (No. 7) Order, 1975, S.I. 1975:511.

[75] Art. 5(4).

may apply. Hence the United Kingdom's extension of her entire criminal law to the installations does not appear to go beyond what the Convention allows; nor, *a fortiori*, does the application of that part of her civil law which concerns the exploration and exploitation of natural resources.

(b) Within the "safety zones" extending 500 metres around each installation, the Convention provides that the coastal state may take "measures necessary for [the] protection of the installation" and that all ships must "respect" the zones.[76] The 1964 Act, on the other hand, has applied to these zones the national criminal and civil law to the extent mentioned above and has prohibited all ships from entering them without consent. It may be that to forbid access to ships does not go beyond what is required for the safety and protection of the installations, for which purposes alone the Convention permits the exercise of coastal state jurisdiction, but the "blanket" extension of the law does not seem necessary; a murder committed on board a foreign ship within a safety zone, but nevertheless still upon the high seas, would not appear to affect the safety of an installation but, by virtue of the Act, could be punished in accordance with English law.

(c) S.10 of the Mineral Workings (Offshore Installations) Act, 1971 (a statute which, as its name implies, deals with the regulation of certain matters on installations), permits the prosecution of offences under the Act which have been committed in a designated area, without restricting itself, as does the 1964 Act, to installations and safety zones only. It appears that there is only one class of offence under the Act which it would be possible to commit in a part of the designated area other than an installation, namely offences under possible regulations (not yet promulgated) concerning the transport of persons and things to and from an installation.[77] The Act expressly provides that it applies to all individuals, whether or not they are British subjects.[78] There is nothing in the Convention which authorizes such wide coastal state jurisdiction. There is, however, a possibility that the prosecution of offences will be carried out only in conformity with international law, for before prosecution the consent of the Secretary of State or the Director of Public Prosecutions is required.[79]

18. Elsewhere on the high seas the United Kingdom exercises jurisdictional control over her own ships alone, recognizing the exclusive competence of the flag state in respect of other ships.

British ships: The term "British ship" is not defined by statute. The Merchant Shipping Act, 1894, contains some circuitous provisions requir-

[76] Art. 5(2) and (3).
[77] S.6(2).
[78] S.12(4).
[79] S.10(3).

ing on the one hand every "British ship" to be registered unless exempted, but stating that no ship is deemed to be British unless it is so registered.[80] The term as applied to a non-registered ship must be taken to mean a ship which is owned by British subjects (or by a corporation registered in, and with its principal place of business in, Great Britain), but which does not, until it is registered, enjoy the benefits of British ships such as protection; it is, however, subject to all their liabilities, including taxation and criminal jurisdiction. The other category of British ships comprises those properly so called, having been registered in accordance with the Merchant Shipping Act. Every occurrence on board either category of British ship is governed by the law of England, Scotland or Ireland as the case may be.[81] A dramatic illustration of the consequences of this was seen in the 1824 case of *Forbes v. Cochrane*.[82] It was held that slaves who had escaped from a plantation to a British warship lying off Florida were free "the moment they put their feet on board a British Man-of-War, not lying within the waters of East Florida". Best J. gave a clear statement of the law which remains true today: "These men, when on board an English ship, had all the rights belonging to an Englishman and were subject to all their liabilities. If they had committed any offence they must have been tried according to English laws. If any injury had been done to them they would have had a remedy by applying to the laws of this country for redress."[83] The jurisdiction of the courts to try criminal offences in accordance with English law remains the same wherever the ship may be – whether upon the high seas or in territorial waters.[84] In civil proceedings jurisdiction depends, as we have seen, on the defendant's submission to jurisdiction or his presence in the country, unless the court grants leave for service of the process elsewhere.[85] If one of these conditions is satisfied the case can be heard and English law will apply.[86]

---

[80] See ss.1, 2 and 72.
[81] It does not follow that every law applied on the territory of the United Kingdom will necessarily be applied on a British ship; see *Cox v. Army Council* [1963] AC 48, *supra*, n. 66.
[82] (1824) 2 B. & C. 448.
[83] *Ibid.* at p. 467.
[84] MSA 1894, sc.684–686. See, e.g., *R. v. Anderson* (1868) 11 Cox's CC 198, where the offence by a foreign sailor took place in French waters. His conviction before the Central Criminal Court was confirmed by the Court for Crown Cases Reserved, although it was agreed that the French authorities had concurrent jurisdiction and might have enforced it had they wished.
[85] See para. 11, *supra*.
[86] Including English rules for choice of law, which may mean that foreign law will eventually govern the case. If it is an action in tort the presence of the ship in foreign territorial waters at the time of the alleged tortious act may result in both foreign and English law being referred to, according to the rule in *Phillips v. Eyre* (1870) LR 6 QB, as interpreted by *Chaplin v. Boys* [1902] 2 All ER 1085. See also *Carr v. Fracis Times* [1902] AC 176; British goods on board a British

19. Foreign Ships: The general rule is that a foreign ship is subject only to the law of the state whose flag it flies. English courts will not exercise jurisdiction in respect of any occurrence on board.[87] However, if an alleged offender is a British subject, it seems that jurisdiction concurrent with that of the flag state may be exercised in respect of the offence.[88] The procedural rules for jurisdiction over civil disputes[89] give rise to the possibility of English courts hearing a case involving an incident on the high seas between foreigners on board a foreign ship;[90] the courts have a discretion, however, to stay proceedings where injustice would be caused to the foreign defendant if the case were to be heard in England.[91]

II REGULATION OF PARTICULAR ACTIVITIES

A. Mineral Workings[92]

20. The United Kingdom was one of the first states to produce a detailed system of licensing and control in respect of the exploitation of mineral resources on the Continental Shelf, the Continental Shelf Act, 1964, coming into force as it did two months before the Geneva Convention.[93] Mineral working is carried out on the bed and subsoil of both national

---

ship within the territorial waters of Muscat were seized by an officer of the British Navy under the authority of a proclamation of the Sultan. It was held by the House of Lords that since the act was justifiable by the *lex loci delicti* no action could be maintained in England. The *locus delicti* was Muscat, territorial waters being for this purpose "as much a part of the Sultan's dominions as the land over which he exercises absolute and unquestioned sway" (*per* Lord Macnaghten at p. 183).

[87] There are certain exceptions to this principle which will not be discussed since they have little or no relevance to the North Sea, e.g. rights exercisable in respect of pirate ships, slave traders, etc.

[88] See the statement of H.M. Government to the U.S.A. following the case of *Anderson (The Whitmore)* (1879), Moore's Digest, Vol. I, pp. 932-935.

[89] See para. 11, *supra*.

[90] For the purpose of the law to be applied it appears that where the act complained of had its effect solely within the ship, the *lex loci delicti* will be that of the foreign "flag State". Where it has an effect outside the ship – for instance, in cases involving collision damage – it appears that the "general maritime law" will apply, i.e. that part of the Common Law which relates to maritime disputes. See Cheshire, *Private International Law* (8th ed., 1970), p. 282ff.

[91] It will not be easy for the defendant to discharge the burden of proving that injustice will be so caused; *Maharanee of Baroda v. Wildenstein* [1972] 2 All ER 689 and *The Atlanta Star* [1973] 2 All ER 175.

[92] See Chapter IV, para. 40. The extent of jurisdiction claimed by the United Kingdom over the Continental Shelf is dealt with in paras. 15–17 *supra*.

[93] Royal Assent to the Act was given on 15 April 1964. The Geneva Convention on the Continental Shelf came into force on 10 June 1964.

waters and the Continental Shelf,[94] and the law regulating it is, in general, the same for either area. The 1964 Act had the effect of extending to the Continental Shelf law which already applied to territorial waters, and it was supplemented by the Mineral Workings (Offshore Installations) Act, 1971, which related chiefly to the safety and welfare of persons in and on installations and applies to both national waters and the Continental Shelf. The mineral substances with which we are chiefly concerned in the North Sea are petroleum and natural gas, coal, sand and gravel.[95] Of these, all rights with regard to coal vest in the National Coal Board;[96] operations by the Board on the Continental Shelf may not, however, be undertaken without the consent of the Secretary of State for Energy, which consent may be made subject to specified conditions.[97] Rights in all other minerals on or under the seabed vest in the Crown.[98] The Crown Estate Commissioners are responsible for the regulation of sand and gravel dredging and issue licences to prospectors and operators, having consulted the Department of the Environment on the effects on coastal erosion, and the Ministry of Agriculture, Fisheries and Food on the danger to fisheries.[99] A further control exists by virtue of Part II of the Coastal Protection Act, 1949, which requires the consent of the Secretary of State for Trade to the carrying out of any works if obstruction or danger to navigation is likely to result.[100]

21. Oil and Natural Gas: Provision for the grant of licences for searching and boring for petroleum and natural gas[101] in national waters was made by the Petroleum (Production) Act, 1934.[102] The Act was extended to the Continental Shelf by s.1(3) of the 1964 Act. The licences may be made subject to any conditions relating to the manner of exploitation, fees payable, model clauses, etc. which the Secretary of State may by regulation prescribe.[103] Regulations at present in force under this Act are the

[94] In the legal sense of the term the Continental Shelf lies outside national waters: s.1(1) of the Act. For the limits of the United Kingdom Shelf see paras. 15–17 *supra*.
[95] See Chapter I, part A, section 2.
[96] Beneath both national waters and the Continental Shelf. The governing statute is the Coal Industry Nationalisation Act, 1946, which was extended to the Shelf by s.1(2) of the 1964 Act.
[97] S.1(2) of the 1964 Act. The Secretary of State for Energy now exercises the functions of the Minister of Power.
[98] S.1(1) of the 1964 Act with regard to the Continental Shelf. No legislation is necessary in respect of national waters. In a few places private rights may exist in internal waters (e.g. the Duchy of Cornwall) but these are rare.
[99] Crown Estate Act, 1961, s.1. The Commissioners are responsible for the regulation of all minerals except oil, gas and coal.
[100] Ss.34–36.
[101] The Petroleum (Production) Act, 1934, defines petroleum as including any mineral oil or relative hydrocarbon and natural gas, but not coal.
[102] Ss.1(8), 2 and 6.
[103] Exercising the functions of the Board of Trade by virtue of the 1970 Secretary of State (New Departments) Order, S.I. 1974:692.

Petroleum (Production) Regulations, 1966, as amended;[104] these set out conditions for granting exploration and production licences and provide detailed sets of model clauses to be incorporated in the five different kinds of licences.[105] They consequently form a code covering most aspects of exploration, drilling, production and transportation. Licences will be issued only to citizens of the United Kingdom and Colonies resident in this country or to companies incorporated here;[106] more than one licence may be held by the same person.[107] The regulations divide the seabed into "landward" and "seaward" areas, the landward areas being almost coincidental with internal waters.[108] In view of the environmental problems raised by installations in the landward area, slightly more stringent conditions are stipulated in their licences.

22. A production licence[109] is granted in the first instance for six years but may be continued at the option of the licensee for a further term of 40 years in respect of part of the licensed area; the remainder must be surrendered at the expiry of the first six years.[110] Revenue from the licences is drawn from three sources: initial payment, royalties, and taxation. Originally a uniform rate of initial payment was charged, but in 1971 fifteen blocks were offered for tender; a total sum of £37 million was received. Royalties of $12\frac{1}{2}$ per cent of the wellhead value are charged on oil and gas; at present these are drawn mainly from natural gas since no oil

[104] S.I. 1966:898 as amended by S.I. 1971:814 and by S.I. 1972:1522.
[105] I.e. production licences in landward areas, production licences in seaward areas, exploration licences for seaward areas or landward areas below the low-water line, exploration licences for landward areas above the low-water line, methane drainage licences. The last mentioned authorize the licensee "to get natural gas in the course of operations for making and keeping safe mines whether or not disused" (Schedule 6 of the 1966 Regulations, Model Clause 2). Certain changes in the licensing conditions are proposed in the Petroleum and Submarine Pipelines Bill, 1975.
[106] Reg. 4. This does not, of course, mean that the shareholders or holding companies must be British. Any such limitation is, in any case, required to be removed by virtue of Annex I to the Treaty of Accession to the European Communities; see the Petroleum and Submarine Pipelines Bill, 1975.
[107] Reg. 12.
[108] See Schedule 1. The account which follows relates to a production licence in a seaward area. The material differences for one in a landward area are as follows: the term is for an initial four years but may be continued for a further 30 years if at least half of the licensed area is first surrendered; the licensee must give at least 21 days' written notice of any proposed seismic survey of an area which is not wholly on the seaward side of the low-water line; the planning authorities must be consulted about such surveys and planning permission must be obtained for the drilling of a well above the low-water line; since the field cannot straddle an international boundary, no provision is necessary for unit development; nor is there any requirement that oil be delivered first in the United Kingdom.
[109] An exploration licence is for three years; many of the other conditions attached to production licences are inappropriate and do not apply.
[110] Regs. 3, 5 and 7.

is likely to be brought ashore in any quantity before 1976. Taxation is at the normal rate, though a change in the law has been proposed to improve the effective tax yield from Continental Shelf operations and to cover the probable set-off of losses which will be claimed by many operating companies in respect of their trading in other parts of the world.[111] For the purpose of calculating the royalties to be paid, a half-yearly statement is to be delivered to the Secretary of State giving the values of all quantities of oil and gas won during the period (Reg. 11); methods of weighing and measuring petroleum are to be approved and are anyway to be in accordance with "good oilfield practice" (Reg. 9); accounts are to be kept and submitted half-yearly showing the quantity of petroleum won and saved and such other particulars as the Secretary of State may direct (Reg. 10). If any payment is not made on time the Minister may authorize the boarding of the licensee's installation and the seizure and sale of his stock and equipment (Reg. 29). Certain working obligations are imposed on the licensee: he is to carry out with "due diligence" the programme of prospecting and development, if any, that is laid down in his licence (Reg. 12); to discourage the temptation to trespass on his neighbour's plot, no well is to be drilled less than 125 metres from his boundaries without the Minister's consent (Reg. 14); in fact no well-drilling at all is to be commenced without consent (Reg. 13); the licensee is to co-operate with other specified persons in the working and development of an oilfield if it seems to the Secretary of State that it would be in the national interest to carry out unit development in order to avoid unnecessary competitive drilling (Reg. 19); if the oilfield straddles an international boundary he is to comply with any directions whatsoever that the Secretary of State may think fit to give with regard to the manner in which his production rights are to be exercised (Reg. 20). The model clauses recognize the possibility of conflict with other uses of the seas and provide that operations are not to be carried out in such a manner as to "interfere unjustifiably with navigation or fishing in the waters of the licensed area or with the conservation of the living resources of the sea" (Reg. 17). Pollution is to be avoided by confining the petroleum in tanks and other receptacles by methods customarily used "in good oilfield practice" and by plugging and sealing wells in accordance with the Minister's directions (Regs. 15, 13); notice is to be given of any escape of petroleum within three days of the occurrence (Reg. 16(3)).[112] All apparatus is to be kept in good repair and the licensee is to comply with any instructions given him for securing the safety, health and welfare of his employees (Regs. 16, 18) – this general provision being supplemented by the more detailed regulations which the

---

[111] See the Oil Taxation Bill, 1975.
[112] The creation of a criminal offence in respect of oil pollution from offshore installations will be discussed in Section II D, *infra*.

Secretary of State is empowered to make under the Mineral Workings (Offshore Regulations) Act, 1971. The licensee is to keep samples of substances encountered in any well and to permit authorized persons to inspect these and all other documents which he is required to keep – accounts, records, returns, plans and maps (Regs. 24, 26). Confidentiality is assured but the Secretary of State is authorized to publish such matter as is necessary for the purpose of his report under the 1964 Act or for similar purposes (Reg. 25). In addition to these detailed provisions, the Regulations impose an all-embracing obligation: all operations are to be undertaken "in a proper and workmanlike manner in accordance with methods and practice customarily used in good oilfield practice" (Reg. 16). The phrase "good oilfield practice" occurs several times in the model clauses: no guiding principles are given to aid in its interpretation.

23. These licences relate to both oil and natural gas and the regulations are in general the same for either substance. One important distinction is, however, made: whereas oil may be sold where and to whom the licensee wishes (though it must first be delivered on shore in the United Kingdom unless the Minister consents to delivery elsewhere),[113] natural gas is subject to certain restrictions on its disposal. The licensee must not use the gas in Great Britain or supply it to premises in Great Britain without the consent of the Secretary of State; such consent shall not be given unless the supply is for certain industrial purposes (which do not involve the use of the gas as a fuel) and the Area Gas Board has been given an opportunity of purchasing the gas at a reasonable price.[114] This avoids any competition with the nationalized gas industry.

24. The safety and good order of offshore installations is provided for by the Mineral Workings (Offshore Installations) Act, 1971.[115] The Act requires the appointment of a manager on each installation who "to the best of the knowledge and belief of the owner, has the skills and competence suitable for the appointment" and who is not to be absent in normal circumstances from the installation at any time when it is manned.[116] The manager is given wide powers. He is to exercise authority over persons "in or about" the installation in all matters affecting safety, health and welfare, including the maintenance of order and discipline for these purposes. If anything is done which endangers the safety of the installation or of any person, he is entitled to place in custody the individual at fault;

---

[113] Reg. 21. An export licence must, of course, be obtained if it is wished to take the oil out of the United Kingdom.

[114] S.19 of the Continental Shelf Act, 1964, relates to natural gas on the Continental Shelf; s.4 of the Petroleum (Production) Act, 1934 (in similar though not identical terms), as amended, relates to that in the territorial sea.

[115] The Act does not apply to internal waters unless specified by Order in Council.

[116] Ss.4 and 5.

in cases of emergency he may take "any such measures as are necessary or expedient to meet or avoid the emergency".[117] In addition, the Act empowers the Secretary of State to make regulations for the registration of installations;[118] for their construction, testing and inspection;[119] for requirements to be fulfilled in the appointment of the installation manager;[120] for the safety, health and welfare of persons on the installations[121] and the prevention of accidents on or near them. The Secretary of State for Social Services may make regulations extending the National Insurance Acts (which are already applicable to the territorial sea) to installations on the Continental Shelf.[122]

B. Fishing[123]

Fishery Limits

25. In 1964 the United Kingdom convened the European Fisheries Conference, following claims by a number of states to exclusive fishing limits extending beyond their territorial sea. These claims were adversely affecting British distant-water fishermen while no corresponding benefit was being derived for those fishing nearer home, for it was only in her three-mile territorial sea that the United Kingdom claimed exclusive fishery rights for her nationals. The Convention[124] which resulted from the

---

[117] These powers are all contained in s.5 of the Act.
[118] S.2. The power has been exercised by the Offshore Installations (Registration) Regulations, 1972, S.I. 1972:702. On or after 30 June 1972 all mobile and fixed installations in the "relevant waters" (i.e. waters up to the seaward limits of the territorial sea and waters in designated areas) must be registered with the Register of Offshore Installations at the Department of Energy. Applications for registration must give particulars, including the name and address of the person(s) seeking to register, the name of the installation and its function, its location and the period for which it is intended to be stationed there. Registration is ordinarily effective for 25 years (10 years for mobile installations).
[119] S.3. The power has been exercised by the Offshore Installations (Construction and Survey) Regulations, 1974, S.I. 1974:289.
[120] S.4(2). The power has been exercised by the Offshore Installations (Managers) Regulations, 1972, S.I. 1972:703, which lay down a form of notice of appointment to be given to the Secretary of State and a form of notice of termination of appointment. There must be listed, *inter alia*, the "qualifications, skills and experience which are considered to make (the manager) a suitable person for the appointment".
[121] S.6. This power has been exercised by the Offshore Installations (Logbooks and Registration of Death) Regulations, 1972, S.I. 1972:1542, the O.I. (Inspectors and Casualties) Regulations, 1973, S.I. 1973:1842, and the O.I. (Diving Operations) Regulations, 1974, S.I. 1974:1229.
[122] The power has been exercised by the National Insurance (Continental Shelf) Regulations, 1964, S.I. 1964:1855.
[123] See Chapter IV, paras. 41–61.
[124] European Fisheries Convention; Chapter IV, paras. 50 and 51.

Conference was swiftly implemented by the Fishery Limits Act, 1964. The Act established an "exclusive fishery limit" extending six miles from the baselines and an outer belt beyond this of a further six miles.[125] Following a brief transitional period when existing rights were continued, the inner zone was – and is – reserved for national fishing vessels alone. In respect of the outer belt it was provided that Ministerial Orders might designate countries granted fishing rights; many of the states parties to the Convention were thus designated. At about the same time as the Act was passed, British baselines were re-defined by the Territorial Waters Order in Council[126] and this meant that both internal and territorial waters were enlarged, adding – in some places substantially – to national fishing grounds.

26. The next development came with the United Kingdom's accession to the European Economic Community. The Community had adopted a policy of equal access to national fishing grounds which would have necessitated opening the United Kingdom's fishery limits to fishing boats from the other Community States. However, following protracted negotiations, the Treaty of Accession finally incorporated substantial exceptions to this policy.[127] A Ministerial Order[128] was promulgated to give effect in the United Kingdom to this part of the Treaty, and it has amended or repealed most of the previous Orders in force.[129] The present position with regard to United Kingdom fishery limits on its *North Sea* coast can be stated as follows:

(a) "Exclusive fishery limits" to a distance of six miles from baselines: reserved for British vessels only (the position after 31 December 1982 with regard to Community States will be reviewed before that date by the Community).[130]

(b) "Outer belt" – six to twelve miles zone:
   (i) Community States[131] may fish between Berwick Breakwater Head Lighthouse and Coquet Island Lighthouse and between Flamborough Head and the Strait of Dover. The remainder of the outer belt is reserved for British vessels *except for* specified areas in which boats of certain of the Community States may fish for named species of fish only:

---

[125] S.I.
[126] Para. 5 *supra*.
[127] Arts. 100 and 101; see Chapter IV, para. 57.
[128] The Fishing Boats (European Economic Community) Designation Order, 1972, S.I. 1972:2026.
[129] The Orders at present in force other than 1972:2026 above are: 1965:1241; 1965:1569; 1965:1448; 1964:1600. Apart from the last numbered they do not relate to the North Sea coast.
[130] See Art. 100 of the Treaty of Accession.
[131] S.I. 1972:2026 *supra*.

State	Area	Fish
Belgium	Between Noss Head and Troup Head (East Scotland)	Demersal fish
Federal Republic of Germany	(a) Between the southernmost point of the Shetland Islands and Fair Isle (b) Between Coquet Island Lighthouse and Whitby High Lighthouse	Herring
Netherlands	(a) Between the southernmost point of the Shetland Islands and Fair Isle (b) Between Coquet Island Lighthouse and Flamborough Head	Herring

(ii) Norway[132] may fish for basking sharks and dogfish in certain areas of water off the Orkney and Shetland Islands.

(iii) States other than the above are excluded altogether from the outer belt.

27. The Sea Fisheries Act, 1968, provides that any foreign fishing boat which is not designated under the Fishery Limits Act, 1964, as having rights within the British limits "shall not enter the fishery limits of the British Islands except for a purpose recognized by International Law, or by any Convention for the time being in force between ... the United Kingdom and ... the country to which the boat belongs".[133] While within the fishery limits for any such lawful purpose, a foreign boat must not fish or attempt to fish and must have its fishing gear stowed; it is liable to be boarded and searched by any British sea fishery officer in order to ensure that it is complying with these requirements.[134] Foreign boats which have the right to fish within the "outer belt" by virtue of an Order so designating them must obey the law of the United Kingdom with regard to their fishing operations while they are within the fishery limits.

28. At Common Law British vessels are entitled to fish freely anywhere within the national fishing limits or elsewhere. However, whether they are within or outside the national fishing limits, they are subject to a multiplicity of legislative provisions regulating the conduct, method, time and place of their fishing operations. In the main these laws are directed at conservation, but some relate to safety of fishing and to means of enforcement.

---

[132] By virtue of S.I. 1964:1600, in consequence of the Agreement between Norway and the United Kingdom (1965 UKTS No. 43); these rights will last until 1984.
[133] S.6(1).
[134] S.8.

Conservation[135]

29. The method adopted by the United Kingdom to introduce measures of conservation has been to provide a general legislative framework by which more detailed regulations are left to Ministers to make, as and when they see fit. These regulations can implement recommendations of international fishery commissions[136] with the minimum of delay and can easily be adapted to swiftly changing environmental conditions. Under the Sea Fisheries Regulation Act, 1966, consolidating earlier statutes, sea fisheries districts have been created which comprise areas of the sea within territorial limits[137] along the whole length of the English and Welsh coast.[138] The local fisheries committee for each district is empowered to make byelaws to be applied within its own area which, among other things, may prescribe methods of fishing and descriptions of fishing gear, restrict or prohibit fishing for any period or within any area, regulate the deposit of any substance detrimental to fishing, and prescribe means of protecting or developing any kind of shellfish.[139] All byelaws must be confirmed by the Minister and may be revoked by him.[140]

30. These byelaws apply only to the individual sea fishery districts within territorial limits, but the principal conservation statute, the Sea Fish (Conservation) Act, 1967, relates to British vessels in any waters and to foreign vessels within national fishing limits. The Act authorizes the making of Orders prescribing minimum sizes of fish which may be landed or sold in Great Britain, or carried in fishing vessels; regulating the construction, mesh size, design, etc. of nets and other fishing gear; prescribing closed seasons and closed areas, and prohibiting the landing of fish caught in certain areas.[141] Another method of conservation is by the imposition of quotas on fishermen's catches. By s.4 of the Act Ministerial Orders may be made prohibiting fishing in certain areas and for specified periods

---

[135] See R. R. Churchill, "The United Kingdom and the Law of the Sea", in Churchill, Simmonds and Welch (eds.), *New Directions in the Law of the Sea*, Vol. III.

[136] In the North Sea the Commission concerned is the North-East Atlantic Fisheries Commission, established by the 1959 North-East Atlantic Fisheries Convention, to which the United Kingdom is a party.

[137] But cf. XIII Halsbury's Statutes, p. 972, with reference to this Act: "It may be ... that for the purposes of the law relating to sea fishing ... the territorial waters of the United Kingdom extend at least to the exclusive fishery limits laid down in the 1964 Fishery Limits Act".

[138] Apart from a small strip of coastline opposite the fishery laboratory of the Ministry of Agriculture, Fisheries and Food at Lowestoft. For the Scottish coast see para. 31 *infra*.

[139] S.5.

[140] Ss.7 and 8.

[141] Ss.1, 3, 5 and 6. Various Orders having effect in the North Sea have been made under these sections but they are continually being varied or replaced by further Orders, and consequently none is listed.

PRESENT LEGAL REGIME: NATIONAL LAW

without the authority of a licence. The licensing powers are to be exercised "for the purpose of preventing overfishing" and licences may be granted subject to such conditions as appear expedient for this purpose. Quotas are not specifically mentioned in either the section or the Orders which have been made under it, but the Minister is able to include them as one of the conditions on which he grants licences. If the Orders relate to sea fish (not including salmon or migratory trout) outside the fishery limits, they may be put into effect only if "measures substantially equivalent ... are being taken by the Governments of other countries interested in fishing in that area". Another potential control of overfishing is provided by s.9 of the Sea Fish Industry Act, 1970, which requires all vessels used in the White Fish Industry[142] to be licensed if over 40 feet in length. Conditions may be imposed, including those with the aim of preventing overfishing.

31. The Acts mentioned above apply to Scotland[143] as well as England, with the exception of the Sea Fisheries Regulation Act, 1966, which established sea-fishery districts and committees. However, equivalent provisions empower the Department of Agriculture and Fisheries for Scotland to make byelaws for coastal waters similar to those which may be made by the English sea-fishery committees for English waters. Several statutes have been passed which apply to Scotland alone. The main regulatory provisions[144] in force are s.6 of the Herring Fishery (Scotland) Act, 1889, which imposes a prohibition on beam and otter trawling within the three-mile limit and other specified areas scheduled by the Act; Byelaw No. 10 made under s.7 of the 1889 Act, which prohibits otter and beam trawling in the whole of the Moray Firth within certain limits;[145] and Byelaw No. 17 made under the Sea Fisheries (Scotland) (Amendment) Act, 1885, which prohibits the use of nets "by trailing or dragging along the bottom of the sea" for the capture of certain fish. There are a number of concessions and exceptions to these regulations in force in certain areas. Salmon fisheries[146] are subject to their own system of control framed to meet their particular needs.

Other Measures of Regulation and Enforcement

32. To ensure the safety and good order of fishing activities, the Sea Fisheries Act, 1968, empowers Ministers to make Orders regulating the

---

[142] "White Fish" is defined by s.59 of the Sea Fish Industry Act, 1970, to mean any fish found in the sea except for herring, salmon and migratory trout. It includes shellfish.
[143] For further details of the regulation of Scottish fisheries see *Report of the Scottish Inshore Fisheries Committee* ("the Cameron Report"): *"Regulation of Scottish Inshore Fisheries"* (1970, H.M.S.O., Cmnd. 4453).
[144] For a fuller list of Acts and Byelaws in force see Appendix II, *Cameron Report*.
[145] For a history of fishery regulation within the Moray Firth see Appendix IV, *Cameron Report*.
[146] See Section XI, *Cameron Report*.

conduct of fishing operations for the purpose of giving effect to any international convention.[147] The Act was passed partly as a result of the 1967 Convention on the Conduct of Fishing Operations in the North Atlantic,[148] which is not yet in force. Orders under the Act may relate to such matters as the identification and marking of fishing boats and fishing gear. The Fishing Vessels (Safety Provisions) Act, 1970, which is not yet in force, will authorize the making of "fishing construction rules" with requirements for the hull, equipment and machinery of United Kingdom registered fishing boats.[149] "Fishing vessel survey rules" may be made with respect to their surveying and periodic inspection.[150] If, after survey, a vessel complies with the requirements of the construction rules and of the applicable provisions of the Merchant Shipping Acts, a certificate to that effect will be granted; the vessel will not be permitted to go to sea without one.[151] It must be remembered that large parts of the Merchant Shipping Acts relate to fishing vessels, and regulations made under them are in force which govern the ascertainment of the tonnage, registry, lettering and numbering of British fishing boats.[152]

33. The Sea Fisheries Act, 1968, also provides policing measures for enforcing fishery limits and conservation rules. Enforcement is to be carried out by sea-fishery officers. British officers include such persons as sea-fishery inspectorate officials, commissioned officers of H.M. ships, Coastguard inspectors and other persons specially appointed.[153] They may order vessels to stop and may board and search them, inspect any net or gear and make any inquiry that seems to them necessary.[154] These powers may be exercised with respect to British vessels wherever they may be and to foreign vessels within the fishery limits. Foreign sea-fishery officers are recognized if they come within a class specified by Ministerial Order,[155] and their powers with regard to British vessels are the same as those of British officers if they are exercised within a Convention area for the

---

[147] S.5.
[148] See Chapter IV, para. 61.
[149] S.1.
[150] S.2.
[151] Ss.3 and 4.
[152] S.I. 1927:642, Merchant Shipping (Fishing Boats Registry) Order, made under s.373 of the Merchant Shipping Act, 1894.
[153] S.7.
[154] S.8 of the 1968 Act and s.15 of the Sea Fish (Conservation) Act, 1967, as amended by the 1968 Act.
[155] S.7(4). The Order made under this section is the Foreign Sea-Fishery Officers (North-East Atlantic Fisheries Commission Scheme) Order, 1969, S.I. 1969: 1822, as amended by S.I. 1972:758, 1973:127; 1973:789; 1973:1701 and 1973: 1998. It specifies the class of persons to be foreign sea-fishery officers within the Convention area outside British fishery limits, and sets out in the Schedule the recommendation of the North-East Atlantic Fisheries Commission for the Scheme of Joint Enforcement.

purpose of enforcing that Convention. The enforcement of the byelaws of fisheries committees within territorial limits is carried out by fishery officers appointed by the committees and their powers are similar to those given by the 1968 Act.[156]

Structure and Regulation of the United Kingdom Fishing Industry[157]

34. This subject will not be discussed here in detail. The White Fish Authority and the Herring Industry Board exercise functions of general supervision and control of the industry; they are also responsible for administering the system of grants, loans and subsidies provided by the Government. The United Kingdom's accession to the European Economic Community could result in sweeping changes in the industry.

Marine Fish Farming[158]

35. It seems likely that marine fish farming will play an important part in the future of the fishing industry; but in the United Kingdom it is still in the experimental stage with the exception of some commercial exploitation of shellfish. Even if all biological, technological and economic hurdles were surmounted, it is clear that at present a large number of legal obstacles stand in the way of the prospective fish farmer.

(a) *Ownership:* In general the public has free fishing rights within national waters and the fishery limits. In a few stretches of coastal waters, however, there exist private fisheries which originate in a grant from the Crown before the time of Magna Carta.[159] New private fisheries can now be created only by or under the authority of Act of Parliament. The Sea Fisheries (Shellfish) Act, 1967, consolidating earlier legislation, provides that the Minister may by Order create a fishery for shellfish on any part of the shore or seabed, or of an estuary or tidal river, and may confer upon individuals exclusive fishing rights or rights of fishery regulation.[160] Such an Order may not be made without the consent of the owner of the foreshore; if the foreshore[161] belongs (as most of it does) to the Crown, the consent of the Crown Estate Commissioners must be obtained. The owner's consent must also be

---

[156] Ss.10 and 17 of the Sea Fisheries Regulation Act, 1966.
[157] See Sea Fishery Industry Act, 1970, as amended by a 1973 Act of the same name, for further details.
[158] On this subject, see Newton and Richardson, "Marine Fish Farming – Some Legal Problems", *New Directions in the Law of the Sea*, Vol. III; *Cameron Report* at paras. 227–246 and Conclusions 30–32; White Paper, "Marine Science and Technology" (1969, H.M.S.O., Cmnd. 3992).
[159] See *Halsbury's Laws of England* (3rd ed., 1954), Vol. 8, p. 453ff. and Vol. 17 (1956), p. 303ff. Scottish private law rights differ slightly from those at English Common Law – see Cameron Report, *passim*.
[160] S.1(1) and (3).
[161] See note 18 *supra*.

obtained if existing exclusive fishing rights would be interfered with.[162] Rights granted are not to last for longer than 60 years.[163] The general rule at Common Law is that fish which have not been reduced into possession "belong" to no-one, but the Act provides that where a Ministerial Order has established a shellfishery – or where a private oyster fishery exists independently of the Act – the shellfish belong absolutely to the person owning the fishing rights and are deemed to be within his possession.[164] The present position is therefore that, in respect of shellfish, a legal framework exists for the promotion and development of commercial fish farming; for free-swimming fish, however, there are no corresponding powers which will make it economically attractive to the cultivator to spend time and money on fish to which he will ultimately have no better right than any other member of the public has. Sweeping legislative provisions will be necessary to allow the fish farmer to enclose areas of the sea for nurseries, hatcheries and "ponds" for rearing; to exclude members of the public from exercising their former undoubted right of fishing in those areas; to remove or restrict the public right of navigation which at present exist over all waters; and to provide that the cultivator will have the absolute rights of ownership over all fish within his farm sufficient to enable him to sue in respect of pollution and other damage to his property and to found a prosecution for theft if any fish are removed by unauthorized persons. Clearly, in exercising any powers given him by such legislation, a Minister would have to consider the opposing interests competing with fish farming for the use of any particular stretch of water: different claimants might wish to use the required area as a nature reserve, or a recreational area, for navigation or public fishing.

(b) *Ancillary Rights:* Fish farms must be stocked and, although ultimately this may be done from enclosed hatcheries, it seems likely that initially fish fry will have to be caught in the open sea. A cultivator may here find himself in contravention of conservation regulations relating to the catching of immature fish and the usage of nets of illegal mesh size and design. S.9 of the Sea Fish (Conservation) Act, 1967, does, however, provide that exceptions may be made by Ministerial Order to the regulations for minimum sizes of fish and nets if the operations concerned are for the purpose of scientific investigation or of "transplanting fish from one fishing ground to another". Potential protection is therefore already available. The fish farmer will require a number of other legal powers for the functioning of his farm; there will have to be rights of access over the foreshore adjoining his artificial lagoons (at present the public has no right to walk over the foreshore except when it is necessary for the enjoyment of the *public* rights of fishing

[162] S.1(4) and (5).   [163] S.1(3).   [164] S.7.

and navigation)[165] and the cultivator must be able to use the land both above and below high-water mark for jetties and other necessary structures and be able to prohibit unauthorized persons from access by land. Grants, loans and taxation concessions for the cultivator will also need to be considered. Finally, means of enforcement of the above provisions will be necessary, since it is unlikely that the existing fishery protection service will be adequate – or indeed suited – to deal with the protection of the essentially private rights of the fish farm. If, as promised, marine cultivation of this kind will shortly be a commercial possibility, a legal framework dealing with the matters mentioned above must swiftly be provided.

C. Navigation[166]

(*Note:* Pollution caused by ships will be dealt with in Section II D and the particular rules of navigation relating to warships in Section II E.)

36. We are told that over one-tenth of the world's shipping accidents occur in the North Sea.[167] Their causes may stem from such factors as insufficient or incompetent manning, the construction of unseaworthy or unsafe ships, the lack of internationally agreed "traffic rules" or the use of inadequate navigational aids. We shall examine briefly the ways in which the law of the United Kingdom attempts to deal with each of these problems within the limits of the international legal rules relating to jurisdiction. The corpus of British shipping law does, of course, cover many topics besides those relating to maritime safety[168] but it is the latter which will most directly affect the other users of the North Sea.

37. Manning and Certification: Part II of the Merchant Shipping Act, 1894, requires British ships to be provided with a number of duly certificated officers, including in each case a certified master; the requirement applies also to foreign ships carrying passengers between places in the United Kingdom. This part of the Act is shortly to be replaced by sections of the Merchant Shipping Act, 1970, which are not yet in force.[169]

---

[165] See *Beckett v. Lyons* [1967] I All ER 833 at p. 842; *Blundell v. Catterall* (1821) 5 B & Ald. 268.
[166] See Chapter IV, paras. 62–69.
[167] Chapter II, Section 1.
[168] E.g. carriage of goods by sea: see Payne and Ivamy, *Carriage of Goods by Sea* (9th ed., 1972); salvage: see Kennedy, *Civil Salvage* (4th ed., 1958); generally: see Chorley and Gibbs, *Shipping Laws* (6th ed., 1970).
[169] Ss.43–54. The 1970 Act largely implements the recommendations of the Final Report of the Court of Inquiry into certain matters concerning the Shipping Industry and replaces a large part of the 1894 Act. The Act is also to repeal the Merchant Shipping (Certificates) Act, 1914, which provides for examinations for certificates of competency, and s.5 of the Merchant Shipping Act, 1948, which provides for the certification of able seamen. Regulations at present in force under the 1948 Act, which will be continued under the 1970 Act, are the Merchant Shipping (Certificates of Competency as A.B.) Regulations.

Requirements for manning and certification will then be contained in regulations to be made by the Secretary of State for Trade. They will specify the number and description of qualified officers and seamen who are to be carried by ships of various types, and the standards of competence and other conditions to be attained by such persons. Masters attempting to put to sea with a smaller or less qualified crew, and owners who permit such action, will be liable on conviction to a fine, and the ship itself may be detained in port. The grant of certificates is not irrevocable: the Act provides for an inquiry to be held if it appears that an officer is unfit to discharge his duties by reason of incompetence, misconduct or any other reason; if he has been seriously negligent in the discharge of his duties or has failed to give assistance or information following a collision. The inquiry is to be carried out in accordance with rules made for that purpose, and the outcome may be that the officer's certificate is suspended or cancelled. Similar provision is made for the withdrawal of a seaman's certificate.

38. Safety of Ships: It is an offence to send or attempt to send to sea a ship which is in an unseaworthy state such "that the life of any person is likely to be thereby endangered".[170] Further, where either a British or foreign ship is unsafe by reason of a defective hull, or equipment, undermanning or loading and is thereby unfit to proceed to sea without endangering human life, it may be provisionally detained in port pending survey and thereafter either released or detained until the defect is remedied.[171] These rather general provisions of the 1894 Act are supplemented by more recent safety standards to be observed by ships before they can put to sea. Ministers are empowered to make rules for the construction, equipment and survey of different types of ship: "construction rules" for passenger ships, "cargo ships construction and survey rules", load line rules and rules for lifesaving appliances, radio equipment and direction-finders.[172] By means of these rules the safety provisions of various international conventions are incorporated into the municipal law of the United Kingdom. The application of the different rules varies slightly but the general principle is that neither British nor foreign ships

---

[170] The Merchant Shipping Act ("MSA"), 1894, s.457.

[171] MSA, 1894, ss.459, 462.

[172] Regulations at present in force are as follows: Merchant Shipping (Passenger Ship Construction) Rules, 1965, S.I. 1965:1103, made under the Merchant Shipping (Safety Convention) Act, 1949; Merchant Shipping (Cargo Ship Construction and Survey) Rules, S.I. 1965:1104, made under MSA, 1964; Merchant Shipping (Load Line) Rules, 1968, S.I. 1968:1053, and various other regulations made under the Merchant Shipping (Load Lines) Act, 1967; and the Merchant Shipping (Life-Saving Appliances) Rules, 1965, S.I. 1965: 1105, the Merchant Shipping (Radio) Rules, 1965, S.I. 1965:1107, Merchant Shipping (Direction-finders) Rules, 1965, S.I. 1965:1112, all made under the Merchant Shipping (Safety Convention) Act, 1949.

may leave United Kingdom ports unless they have been certified as complying with the regulations. Where the rules are based on a convention, provision is made for the recognition of international certificates granted by convention countries. The incentive to attain a certain standard of seaworthiness is provided in practice by the insurance companies, whose classifications for insurance purposes are based on a ship's standard of construction and state of maintenance.

39. *Collision Regulations and Traffic Routeing*
(a) *Collision Regulations:* Customary rules of navigation have existed in Britain from very early times; then, in 1840, the first general set of rules for the avoidance of collisions was published by Trinity House and enforced by the Admiralty Court.[173] Collision regulations are now made under the authority of the Merchant Shipping Act, 1894,[174] and those at present in force incorporate the rules of the 1960 SOLAS Convention.[175] They apply to the ships of certain of the Contracting States[176] and to British ships wherever they may be; they apply to other foreign vessels only while within British national waters.[177] Although wilful infringement of the rules is a criminal offence,[178] the sanction for non-compliance will generally be applied more in civil proceedings than by a criminal prosecution. In proceedings resulting from a collision the fact that a rule has been broken does not give rise *per se* to a presumption of fault;[179] the party alleging negligence must prove that the breach of the rule was the cause or partial cause of the collision or damage. However, the courts have stressed that, generally speaking, non-compliance will be evidence of negligence, since the rules give the standard of navigation which it is the duty of the vessel to observe.[180] Nevertheless, each case must be considered individually, and Rule 27 of the Regulations provides that "due regard shall be had to all dangers of navigation and collision, and to any special circumstances, including the limitation of the craft involved, which may render a departure from the ... rules necessary in order to avoid immediate danger". Damages will be payable by the negligent party,

[173] Colombos, *op. cit.*, p. 353.
[174] S.418.
[175] International Convention for the Safety of Life at Sea; see Chapter IV, para. 64. The Regulations are the Collision Regulations (Ships and Seaplanes on the Water) and Signals of Distress (Ships) Order, 1965, S.I. 1965:1525; and the Merchant Shipping (Signals of Distress) Rules, 1965, S.I. 1965:1550.
[176] Listed in Schedule 2 to the Order.
[177] Foreign ships are not to be prosecuted for any offence committed outside national waters: Rules 3 and 5.
[178] MSA, 1894, s.419.
[179] Since the passing of the Maritime Conventions Act, 1911.
[180] *The Raithwaite Hall* (1874), 2 Asp. MC. 210. See generally IV British Shipping Laws: Marsden, *Collisions at Sea* (ed. McGuffie), Part III.

and if a breach of the rules was due to the owner's "actual fault or privity" he will not even be able to limit his liability.[181]

(b) *Traffic Routeing:* The first British-recommended traffic routes for shipping were introduced in the Dover Strait; these have now been made compulsory, together with a large number of other traffic separation schemes in various parts of the world, including the North Sea.[182] Each scheme comprises a traffic separation zone or traffic separation line with a traffic lane for shipping on either side. The regulations establishing them contain directions for their use by vessels and are to be treated as forming part of the Collision Regulations. Hence infringement of them by British vessels will be a criminal offence and they will have evidential relevance in civil proceedings.

(c) *Ports and Harbours:* Control of the movement of ships in port may be exercised by the appropriate harbour authority in pursuance of a Ministerial Order establishing a scheme for safe and uninterrupted navigation.[183] Local byelaws which must be confirmed by the Minister are promulgated in each case to put the scheme into effect and these often provide that the Collision Regulations are to apply within the harbour subject to specified exceptions, for example, channels for entry into the harbour may be prescribed and particular lights required for vessels such as dredgers and pilot ships.[184] In addition, the harbour authority may from time to time designate routes or channels which ships are to use or refrain from using, or prohibit ships from entering the harbour in times of low visibility, unless fitted with radio, navigational aids, etc.[185] Similar Orders may be made in respect of dockyard ports.[186] It seems that, where local rules conflict with the general

---

[181] MSA, 1894, ss.502, 503, as amended by the Merchant Shipping (Liability of Shipowners and Others) Act, 1958.

[182] Collision Regulations (Traffic Separation Schemes) Order, 1972, S.I. 1972:809, and Collision Regulations (Traffic Separation Schemes) (Amendment) Order, 1974, S.I. 1974:1890. Schemes in the North Sea are in areas off the Oslo Fjord, off Oksoy, off Lindesnes, off Lister, off Felstein, in the German Bight, in the approaches to the River Elbe, north of the entrance to the Nieuwe Waterweg Rotterdam, off Texel Light Vessel, in the Strait of Dover and its approaches, off Newarp/Cross Sand, West Hinder and North Hinder, off the Goeree.

[183] Harbour Act, 1964, s.20.

[184] E.g. Humber and Lower Trent Navigation Byelaws, 1956. For a full list of the waters and areas where local rules are in force, cf. IV British Shipping Laws (*supra*), Chapter 28. The rules derive their authority either from local Acts or from MSA, 1894, s.421(2), the Harbour, Docks and Piers Clauses Act, 1847, the Harbour Act, 1964, or the Port of London Act, 1968, as the case may be.

[185] Harbour Act, 1964, s.20(3).

[186] Dockyard Ports Regulation Act, 1865, ss.5 and 7. A "dockyard port" is a port in or near which Her Majesty has a dockyard, arsenal, wharf or mooring, etc. For a full list of byelaws in force for dockyard ports see IV British Shipping Laws (*supra*), Chapter 28.

Collision Regulations, the former will prevail provided that they deal with the "whole scope of the subject".[187] Under the Pilotage Act, 1913, Orders have been made establishing compulsory pilotage districts within which use of a pilot is obligatory for every ship entering, leaving or navigating in any port. Pilotage authorities, which have statutory origin, may make byelaws regulating the pilotage system generally.

40. Navigational Aids: Responsibility for the provision and maintenance of lighthouses, beacons and buoys in England has long rested with Trinity House, an independent non-statutory corporation which received its charter in 1514.[188] Its powers and duties have been confirmed by legislation and are expressed to extend to England, Wales and "the adjacent seas and islands".[189] This definition of its geographical scope is not unambiguous, but in practice it exercises its functions within national waters and, where necessary, beyond. Trinity House acts in a considerable number of advisory capacities and provides pilots for the English Channel and the approaches to the Thames. In Scotland it is the Commissioners of Northern Lighthouses who have the responsibility for the provision and maintenance of lights, but they have a statutory duty to submit their schemes to Trinity House for approval and advice.[190] Local lights throughout the country are the responsibility of the appropriate harbour authority. In many countries the cost of installing and maintaining these navigational aids is a charge on the national revenue, but in the United Kingdom it is borne by the persons making use of British ports. Light dues are payable by all vessels other than H.M. ships, with certain other minor exceptions. They are paid in respect not of the number of lights from which the ships derive benefit, but of the number and type of voyages they make. In the event of non-payment, goods or anything belonging to the ship may be distrained upon. Another invaluable navigational aid is provided by Admiralty Charts, which are supplemented by Admiralty Notices to Mariners.[191] These are issued by the Ministry of Defence Hydrographic Department and give ships warning of, for example, manoeuvres to be made in appropriate situations and of signals, or lights, carried by naval ships which differ from those set out in the Collision Regulations. They are of considerable importance though they have no statutory authority. Local notices to mariners may be issued by such bodies as harbour authorities and relate to matters within their jurisdiction.[192]

---

[187] MSA, 1894, s.421 provides that local rules are to have effect notwithstanding anything in the Act with regard to Collision Regulations.
[188] Colombos, *op. cit.*, p. 336.
[189] MSA, 1894, s.634. For lighthouses and light dues generally see Part XI of the Act and the Merchant Shipping (Mercantile Marine Fund) Act, 1898.
[190] MSA, 1894, s.640.
[191] Cf. IV British Shipping Laws (*supra*), p. 653.
[192] For the effect of local notices, cf. *The Humbergate* (1952), Ll. L.R. 168.

41. Enforcement of Shipping Laws: Where a shipping casualty has occurred, the Department of Trade has power to institute a preliminary inquiry into the matter; and, whether or not this has been done, a formal investigation may be ordered.[193] As a result of the findings, a British officer's certificate may be cancelled or suspended. The enforcement of regulations relating to the safety standards and manning of ships is relatively easy; the vessel – whether British or foreign – may simply be detained in port until it meets the specified requirements. Compliance with collision regulations can be attempted in a more limited way by criminal prosecution if the breach of the regulation was occasioned by wilful default; but the vessels of certain foreign states may be prosecuted only if the offence was committed within British national waters.[194] More effective is the civil liability for damages for any injury caused through negligence; as we have seen, the breach of a collision regulation is of evidential value in proving fault. Arising from the early rise to prominence of English maritime law, the Admiralty Court has for long been the forum for maritime disputes, even between foreign litigants who have no connection with the United Kingdom.[195]

D. Pollution[196]

42. There are many sources of marine pollution and they have a multiplicity of harmful effects. Of those which are detrimental to the United Kingdom – whether to her inhabitants directly or to her shores – not all are susceptible to the control of her laws for, as we have seen, international law restricts the jurisdictional competence of each individual state. The United Kingdom is entitled to – and does – exercise legal control over: (i) the quality of water flowing from her territory into the sea, including direct discharges from land into coastal waters ("land-based pollution"); (ii) discharges from ships of whatever nationality within national waters, from British ships wherever they may be, and from offshore installations within national waters and on the British portion of the Continental Shelf ("pollution from ships and installations").

Land-based Pollution[197]

43. Common Law: At Common Law control of water pollution is based upon the property rights of owners of land abutting a river or a part of the sea. (The owner of the sea shore is presumed to be the Crown unless a

[193] MSA, 1894, ss.465–470, to be replaced by MSA, 1970, ss.55–58.
[194] See para. 39 (a), *supra*.
[195] For the law to be applied in such cases see note 86, *supra*.
[196] See Chapter IV, paras. 70–118.
[197] See McLoughlin, *The Law Relating to Pollution* (1972); Wisdom, *The Law on the Pollution of Waters* (2nd ed., 1966). They do not, of course, cover the Control of Pollution Act, 1974.

claimant can prove a grant to him or to his predecessors.) The owner has the right to have the water of the river or sea come to him in its natural state in flow, quantity and quality, and he has a Common Law action in nuisance against anyone who interferes with this right, whether or not the interference has caused him actual damage.[198] The Court may grant an injunction to prevent further acts of pollution and damages in respect of any harm already caused. In addition to riparian owners, the law protects persons with certain interests derived from the owner, such as purchasers of fishing rights. Interference by pollution with public rights in the sea, such as navigation and fishing, is actionable only at the suit of the Attorney-General. That pollution control by private litigants exercising their Common Law rights can still be effective was manifested in the case of *Pride of Derby and Derbyshire Angling Association v. British Celanese and others*,[199] where the Association, as the owner of fishing rights, was awarded damages and a suspended injunction against the defendant companies, one of which had discharged insufficiently treated sewage into the River Trent. However, the complexity and expense involved in proving by a private action that one or more large industrial concerns have caused pollution damage render the Common Law system of control totally inadequate. Proposals to remove riparian owners' Common Law rights by statute have not yet succeeded, but the main emphasis is now on statutory control.

44. *Statute:* The Water Act, 1973, set up nine regional water authorities to take over functions previously carried out by other statutory undertakings with regard to public water supply, sewerage and sewage disposal, control of inland water pollution, land drainage and freshwater fisheries. It was originally intended that the Act should include comprehensive anti-pollution measures for the new authorities to apply, but in the event these were left to be dealt with by a subsequent measure, the Control of Pollution Act, 1974.[200] Part II of this Act, which is not yet in force, replaces the Rivers (Prevention of Pollution) Acts, 1951–1961, by re-enacting with amendments their basic provisions relating to water pollution and extending the system of control to virtually all inland coastal waters.

---

[198] *John Young & Co. v. Bankier Distillery Co.* [1893] A.C. 691 : "Every riparian proprietor is ... entitled to the water of his stream, in its natural flow, without sensible diminution or increase and without sensible alteration in its character or quality. Any invasion of this right causing actual damage or calculated to found a claim which may ripen into an adverse right entitles the party injured to the intervention of the court" (*per* Lord Macnaghten at p. 698). The latter part of the second sentence refers to the possibility of acquiring after 20 years a prescriptive right to discharge polluting matter into water.

[199] [1953] Ch. 149.

[200] The Conservative Government's Protection of the Environment Bill lapsed on the 1974 dissolution of Parliament but Labour's Control of Pollution Act incorporates substantially similar provisions with regard to water pollution. The Act is to come into force on a day appointed by the Secretary of State.

By s.31 it is an offence to cause or knowingly permit "any poisonous, noxious or polluting matter to enter any . . . 'relevant waters' " or to cause any matter to enter a stream so as to impede the proper flow of the water and lead to a substantial aggravation of pollution due to other causes. "Relevant waters" include rivers and watercourses, whether above or below ground; all tidal waters; the sea within three miles of low-water mark and any other part of the territorial sea which may be prescribed. A recent House of Lords decision on the meaning of the phrase "cause or knowingly permit" held that the offence could be committed by a person who had no knowledge that polluting matter was entering the stream; neither negligence nor intention to pollute need be proved.[201] This case has, of course, made it much easier to place the responsibility for pollution on the person causing it, since liability for the offence is strict and open only to the defence that the polluting act was not the act of the defendant but that of some other person for whom he was not responsible. However, s.31(2)(d) provides that no offence is committed when the discharge occurred in an emergency and was made in order to avoid danger to the public; particulars must be furnished to the relevant water authority as soon as is reasonably practicable after the occurrence.

45. The Act gives new powers to the Secretary of State to make regulations requiring precautions to be taken for the avoidance of water pollution and to specify areas where certain activities likely to cause pollution must be restricted or discontinued (s.31(4) and (5)).

46. S.32 makes it an offence to cause or knowingly permit trade or sewage effluent to be discharged (a) into any "relevant waters"; or (b) from land through a pipe into any part of the sea; or (c) from a building or plant into a pond or lake or on to land. The offence is also committed by water authorities or local authorities which permit any matter other than trade or sewage effluent to be discharged into "relevant waters" from a sewer or drain under their control. The maximum penalty for an offence under ss.31 or 32 is in each case imprisonment for up to three months and/or a fine not exceeding £400 on summary conviction; on indictment, imprisonment for up to two years and/or a fine.

47. The prohibitions against discharging effluent or other polluting matter are relaxed in favour of persons who have obtained consent to the discharge from the water authority (s.34). Applications for consent must state the place of the proposed discharge, the nature, composition and maximum temperature and quantity of the matter, and the rate at which it will be discharged. On any consents that it grants the water authority may impose such reasonable conditions as it thinks fit, for example with regard to the nature of the matter discharged or as to facilities for taking samples. If a discharge is made in accordance with a consent and with any

---

[201] *Alphacell v. Woodward* [1972] 2 All E.R. 475.

conditions that may have been imposed, no criminal offence is committed; the Act, however, leaves unchanged Common Law remedies which are available to riparian owners. The water authority has a duty to review from time to time the consents and conditions which it has made; it has powers to revoke the consent or vary the conditions (ss.37 and 38). S.46 requires the authority to exercise these powers where it appears "that pollution injurious to the fauna or flora of a stream in its area has been caused in consequence of discharges made by virtue of a consent given by the authority". The authority is also required to carry out, as soon as is practicable, appropriate operations for remedying or mitigating the pollution in question and for restoring the fauna and flora to their previous state as far as is practicable. Criticism has frequently been directed towards the rule requiring authorities to maintain secrecy on applications for consents submitted to them; the rule was defended on the ground that industry was entitled to protect trade secrets from competitors, but it made informed protest against the granting of a proposed consent very difficult. The new Act requires water authorities to keep registers giving particulars of consents given and applied for and samples taken, and to provide access to these registers by the public (s.41). If an applicant for a consent can satisfy the Secretary of State that such publicity would prejudice some private interest "to an unreasonable degree" by disclosing a trade secret, or would be contrary to the public interest, exemption from disclosure may be granted (s.42). Exemption may similarly be granted from the requirement that the water authority publish any application for consent in the local newspapers and the *London Gazette*. Subject to the exercise of the Minister's discretion in awarding exemptions, these provisions for publicity should ensure that the public is informed in advance of any consent being granted and is kept informed of the nature of effluent being discharged. A written representation by any person relating to an application for a consent must be duly considered by the water authority (s.36(1)).

48. Now that a single body, the water authority, is responsible both for providing sewers – and consequently discharging effluent – and for protecting water from pollution – and consequently having to judge the level of permissible pollution – it may find itself in the position of policeman, judge and accused at one and the same time. Accordingly, s.55 provides that consents necessary for the discharge of any matter by a water authority may be required by regulation to be granted by the Secretary of State rather than by the authority itself. The Act also contains various miscellaneous provisions for the control of pollution, for example with regard to the keeping of sanitary appliances on small boats (s.33).

49. Statutory control of pollution is directed not only to the direct entry of effluent into watercourses, but also to discharge into sewers and drains. S.1 of the Public Health (Drainage of Trade Premises) Act, 1937, provides that occupiers of trade premises may discharge into the public sewers any trade effluent passing from those premises – but only with the consent of the water authority. The Act left certain discharges unregulated but the Control of Pollution Act brings these under full control. S.43 provides that previous authorizations for premises to discharge effluent into sewers may be reviewed, and conditions attached to them.

Pollution from Ships and Installations

50. The United Kingdom has no general anti-pollution law. Legislation tends to follow the international conventions (though, as we shall see, the statute often comes into force before the convention upon which it is based) and, like the conventions themselves, it was originally concerned more with pollution by oil than with any other kind. We shall consider first oil pollution, then pollution by radioactive substances, and finally pollution by other harmful agents.

(a) Oil Pollution

(i) Prevention

51. Ships: The Prevention of Oil Pollution Act, 1971, consolidating earlier legislation,[202] provides that it is an offence for British ships to discharge oil (crude, lubricating, fuel and heavy diesel oil) in any part of the sea outside the United Kingdom.[203] With this "blanket" prohibition, the Act replaces the old system whereby the discharge of oil in specified "prohibited zones" was a criminal offence but discharging oil anywhere else in the sea was permitted. Clearly the Act's provisions draw their inspiration from the 1969 Amendments to the London Convention,[204] but the Act is far more stringent than the Amendments, which permit ships to discharge oil anywhere beyond 50 miles from land if certain conditions – such as a maximum rate of oil discharge – are fulfilled. The Amendments are in any case, not yet in force. As regards British national waters, British and foreign ships are prohibited by the Act from discharging oil therein;[205] such a prohibition on foreign ships would seem to be justified by general international law and is certainly not ruled out by the London Convention. Criminal liability for a forbidden discharge of oil rests with the owner or

---

[202] Consolidating the Oil in Navigable Waters Acts, 1955–71, and s.5 of the Continental Shelf Act, 1964. The Act came into operation on 1 March 1973.
[203] S.1. "Heavy diesel oil" is defined by the Oil in Navigable Waters (Heavy Diesel Oil) Regulations, 1967, S.I. 1967:710. Certain ships are exempted f om the operation of the section by virtue of the Oil in Navigable Waters (Exceptions) Regulations, 1972, S.I. 1972:1928. These and other regulations made under the 1955–71 Acts remain in force by virtue of s.33(2) of the Prevention of Oil Pollution Act, 1971.
[204] International Convention for the Prevention of Pollution of the Sea by Oil, 1954–62: for 1969 Amendments, see Chapter IV, para. 76.
[205] S.2.

master of the vessel and the penalty on conviction is a fine not exceeding £50,000.[206] This figure represents the maximum payable and, in practice, courts tend to impose a much lower sum.[207] Defences which may be advanced under the Act are almost identical with those in the Convention:[208] that the discharge of oil was effected to secure the safety of human life or of a vessel, or to prevent damage to ships or cargo, or that it resulted from damage to the vessel or unavoidable leakage – with the additional requirement in the Act, in the case of the first two defences, that the discharge was a reasonable step to take in the circumstances. The Act, like the Convention, requires that vessels carry Oil Record Books containing particulars of specified operations.[209] This applies to British ships and to those of any "Convention country" specified by Order in Council,[210] though with regard to the latter, of course, enforcement of this requirement is possible only when the foreign ship is within British national waters. The Oil Record Book must be produced when requested and copies may be made of it; criminal penalties are imposed on those in default. Ships which are neither British nor flying the flag of a "Convention country" are nevertheless required to keep records of all transfers of oil taking place within United Kingdom national waters.[211] Powers are conferred on a harbourmaster to board such ships while they are within his harbour, to require production of the transfer records, and to inspect any part of the ship or its equipment in the course of an inquiry relating to an alleged discharge of oil into harbour waters.[212]

52. To aid compliance with the Act there is a policy of providing adequate facilities for the reception of oil residues in accordance with the requirements of the Convention. Some of these facilities are privately run by commercial undertakings, but by s.9 of the Act the harbour authorities are empowered to provide such facilities themselves, whether or not in

---

[206] On summary conviction; on indictment no maximum is set to the fine which may be imposed. Almost invariably summary trial is chosen. Both master and owner may be prosecuted in respect of the same discharge (*Federal Steam Navigation Co. Ltd. v. D.T.I.* [1974] 1 WLR 505).

[207] Cf. report of the Advisory Committee on Oil Pollution of the Sea (*The Times*, 2 July 1973). The average fine in 1971 was £200. In spite of the raising of the maximum penalty to £50,000 in June 1971, initially there does not appear to have been much improvement in the fines actually imposed by the courts, and Lord Kennet, Chairman of the Committee, comments that "the level of fines was clearly quite nugatory" and "more of a sick joke than a deterrent".

[208] S.5 of the Act; Art. IV of the Convention.

[209] S.17. See Oil in Navigable Waters (Records) Regulations, 1972, S.I. 1972:1929.

[210] S.21. See Oil in Navigable Waters (Enforcement of Convention) Order, 1958, S.I. 1958:1526. Various Orders in Council have been made under the equivalent sections of the earlier statutes specifying "Convention countries".

[211] S.17(2). See Oil in Navigable Waters (Transfer Records) Regulations, 1957, S.I. 1957:358.

[212] S.18(6).

conjunction with any other person. If it appears to the Secretary of State that these facilities are inadequate, he may arrange that they be improved. The Convention contains a requirement that ships are to be so fitted as to prevent the escape of oil into the ship's bilges or otherwise to ensure that the oil in the bilges is not discharged; the Act incorporates this provision by empowering the Secretary of State to make regulations requiring British ships to be fitted with equipment to prevent or reduce the discharge of oil and to comply with any other specified requirements.[213]

53. The construction of oil tankers ever larger in size gives rise to the possibility of very serious pollution from even a single accident. In recognition of this, amendments to the 1954 London Convention were agreed upon in 1971, prescribing requirements for tank arrangements and the limitation of tank sizes to be complied with by tankers to which the Convention applies.[214] In the United Kingdom, Part II of the Merchant Shipping Act, 1974, provides for the implementation of the 1971 amendments by empowering the Secretary of State to make rules for the design and construction of United Kingdom oil tankers. The Act differs from the amendments in that the rules may be applied to tankers whenever constructed, where the international provisions cover only tankers constructed after a certain date.[215] The rules may be applied whether or not the amendments or any other Convention on this subject is at the time in force and binding on the United Kingdom Government. One of the sanctions for failing to meet these standards is to be found in the prohibition of any tanker from leaving a United Kingdom port unless it qualifies for a certificate confirming its compliance with the rules or exempting it from their application. Tankers not registered in the United Kingdom may be issued with leave to sail by the Secretary of State if he considers it appropriate and if the tanker complies with any conditions which he sees fit to impose with a view to preventing or limiting the danger of oil pollution. Certificates issued by other Convention countries will be recognized. Moreover, tankers without certificates may be refused entry to all United Kingdom ports or to one or more specified ports, or conditions may be imposed upon their entry. Non-compliance with the prohibitions on entry or exit from a port will be met by fines.[216]

[213] S.4. See Oil in Navigable Waters (Ships' Equipment) (No. 1) Regulations, 1956, S.I. 1956:1423; Oil in Navigable Waters (Ships' Equipment) Regulations, 1957, S.I. 1957:1424.
[214] 1971 Amendments to the International Convention for the Prevention of Pollution of the Sea by Oil, 1954, concerning Tank Arrangements and limitation of Tank Size (Adopted by the IMCO Assembly, Resolution A.246 (VII)); cf. Chapter IV, note 154.
[215] Article VI bis (1).
[216] Up tp £10,000 on summary conviction for illegal exit, up to £15,000 on summary conviction for illegal entry; no maximum limit for a fine on conviction or indictment.

54. Offshore Installations: Ss.2(1)(e) and 3 of the Prevention of Oil Pollution Act, 1971, which replace s.5 of the Continental Shelf Act, 1964, make it an offence to discharge oil into the sea from a pipeline or from an offshore installation as a result of operations of exploration or exploitation of the seabed; this applies both to national waters and to the designated areas of the Continental Shelf. The penalty on conviction is a fine not exceeding £50,000; the person criminally responsible is the owner of the pipeline or the operator of the installation. It is a defence to prove that neither the escape of oil "nor any delay in discovering it was due to any want of reasonable care and that as soon as practicable after it was discovered all reasonable steps were taken for stopping or reducing it". The defence is therefore wider than that allowed to masters of ships prosecuted under ss.1 or 2 of the Act. As we have seen, licences granted under the Petroleum (Production) Act contain clauses designed to prevent pollution.[217]

(ii) Protective Measures

55. In March 1967 the *Torrey Canyon*, a Liberian-registered vessel, ran aground on the Seven Stones rocks and lost some 10,000 tons of oil.[218] The ship was outside British territorial waters but grave pollution damage to the coast was threatened, and the Attorney-General was asked to consider the legality of certain measures which the Government contemplated taking in order to prevent this.[219] His reply may have been uncertain, since the ship was not bombed until 10 days after it struck the rocks, a delay which subjected the Government to a certain amount of criticism.[220] Subsequent attempts at justification of the bombing were drawn from the concept of necessity in international customary law,[221] but a more fruitful result of the incident was the convening of the 1969 Conference at Brussels at which the Public Law Convention was drawn up.[222] The Convention was duly signed and ratified by the United Kingdom Government and implementing legislation was swiftly passed. The relevant provisions are contained in the Prevention of Oil Pollution Act, 1971, which entered into force before the Convention itself did. Following the occurrence of a shipping accident resulting in the likelihood of oil pollution on a large scale in the United Kingdom or its national

---

[217] Para. 22, *supra*.
[218] See, with regard to the incident generally, *"The Torrey Canyon"*: *Cabinet Office Report of the Committee of Scientists* (H.M.S.O., 1967); Petrov, *The Black Tide*; Smith (ed.), *Torrey Canyon, Pollution and Marine Life* (1968).
[219] *The Times*, 28 March 1967.
[220] The reasons for the delay may have been of a purely scientific nature: see Cabinet Office Report, *supra*.
[221] By, e.g., Brown, *The Legal Regime of Hydrospace* (1971), pp.141–145.
[222] International Convention relating to Intervention on the High Seas in cases of Oil Pollution Casualties; see Chapter IV, paras. 85–88.

waters, the Secretary of State is authorized to give directions, if he feels they are "urgently needed", relating to the removal or salvage of the ship. If the power to give such directions is inadequate to the situation, the Minister may take any action with regard to the ship or its cargo, including its sinking or destruction, by which the pollution may be prevented or restricted.[223] The Minister's power to give directions under the Act is exercisable only in relation to United Kingdom citizens or corporations, but his power to undertake operations with respect to the ship itself is applicable also to foreign ships, if he is satisfied that there is "grave and imminent danger of oil pollution".[224] It is therefore in the last instance only that extra-territorial jurisdiction is exercisable over foreigners.

56. The provisions of the Act are similar to, but by no means identical with, those of the Convention. Under the Act the powers of intervention may be exercised following an "accident" to a ship – defined as "the loss, stranding, abandonment of or damage to a ship" (s.12(9)); the Convention is more specific and lists the different kinds of "marine casualty" which bring the powers into operation.[225] There seems to be little significance in this distinction unless it be that the Convention provides that damage (or the threat of damage) to a ship's *cargo* is sufficient to allow the use of the powers of intervention, whereas the Act refers only to damage (or the threat of damage) to the *ship*. Before any protective action may be taken, a fairly elaborate procedure of consultation and notification of interested parties is required by the Convention;[226] the Act, on the other hand, imposes no duty on the Minister to consult the state against whose ship it is proposed to take action, or to notify anybody at all. Perhaps the most important difference between the two instruments is that the Convention specifies the "interests" which are to be protected from oil pollution by the exceptional measures of intervention permitted.[227] The Act, on the other hand, does not name any particular kind of damage that it aims at preventing and there is no scale of values to assist the Minister in deciding on the degree of forcible action to be taken where the threatened damage is, say, to a recreation area, on the one hand, or to a commercially valuable oyster bed, on the other. S.13, however, provides that compensation is recoverable from the Minister when action under the Act has been taken which was disproportionate to the damage or expense caused; in considering a claim account is to be taken of the extent of the threatened pollution, the likelihood of the action's being effective and the damage

---

[223] These powers are all contained in s.12 of the Act.
[224] This is provided by the Oil in Navigable Waters (Shipping Casualties) Order, 1971, S.I. 1971:1736, made under the 1971 Oil in Navigable Waters Act, s.8(10), and saved from repeal by s.33(2) of the Prevention of Oil Pollution Act, 1971.
[225] Art. II; see Chapter IV, para. 86.
[226] Art. III; see Chapter IV, para. 87.
[227] Art. II (4).

which the action has caused. This corresponds to the requirement for compensation in appropriate circumstances provided by Article VI of the Convention.

(iii) Civil Liability

57. At Common Law the owner of property damaged by pollution may have the right to sue the person who has caused the damage in nuisance, negligence or trespass. The plaintiff in an action resulting from oil pollution will generally be the owner of the foreshore or of coastal fisheries. The Common Law remedies have proved inadequate in modern conditions, largely because the success of an action depends on proving some degree of fault by the defendant[228] – for example, in navigating the ship or in transferring the oil – and this may be a difficult, if not impossible, task.[229] The Merchant Shipping (Oil Pollution) Act, 1971,[230] has now created a statutory tort which places near-absolute liability on a shipowner for any damage in the United Kingdom caused by an escape or discharge of oil from his ship. His liability covers the cost of preventive measures and of any damage such measures may have caused.[231] The only defences are that the discharge of oil resulted from an act of war or from an "exceptional, inevitable and irresistible natural phenomenon",[232] or was due wholly to the act of another individual (who was not the owner's servant or agent) done with intent to cause damage, or to the negligent or wrongful act of an authority charged with the function of maintaining navigational aids.[233] The Act excludes any Common Law action the plaintiff might otherwise have brought; the liability of the shipowner (and his agent) is to stem from the Act alone.[234] Common law remedies are, however, still available against persons other than the shipowner and his agent and the Act here strengthens the plaintiff's rights by providing that, just as with the statutory tort, where preventive measures are taken the defendant is to be liable for their cost as well as for any actual damage caused by the oil.[235]

58. The Act is clearly modelled on the Brussels Private Law Conven-

---

[228] The necessity for proving fault in order to found an action in trespass or nuisance differs from situation to situation but, as a general rule, the statement in the text is accurate: see Winfield and Jolowicz on Tort (9th ed., 1971), pp. 306, 328–333; Salmond, *Torts* (15th ed., 1969), pp. 49–50, 78–79.

[229] See *Esso Petroleum v. Southport Corporation* [1956] AC 218.

[230] For a comment on the Act, see Forster, "Civil Liability of Shipowners for Oil Pollution", 1973 *Journal of Business Law* 23.

[231] S.1(1).

[232] The wording of this phrase is taken from the Brussels Private Law Convention (*infra*), Art. III; it is similar (*pace* Forster, *op. cit.*) to the Common Law defence of Act of God: "circumstances which no human foresight can provide against and of which human prudence is not bound to recognise the possibility" (*Tennant v. Earl of Glasgow* (1864) 2 M (H.L.) 22, 26, approved by the House of Lords in *Greenock Corporation v. Caledonian Railway* [1917] AC 556).

[233] S.2.   [234] S.3.   [235] S.15.

tion[236] which has recently been ratified by the U.K. Some of the Act's provisions are not yet in force and are presumably awaiting the entry into force of the Convention. They will extend the shipowner's liability to damage caused in any "Convention country" specified by Order in Council as being a party to the Convention.[237] Proceedings will not, however, be maintainable in this country in respect of such damage unless damage has also been caused in the United Kingdom by the same incident.[238] Further provisions not yet in force relate to the limitation of liability, which is permitted if the discharge of oil occurred without the fault of the defendant.[239] His liability is not to exceed 2,000 gold francs for each ton of the ship's displacement or 210 million gold francs, whichever is the less (the Secretary of State being given power to specify the sterling equivalent of these sums).[240] So that one plaintiff does not exhaust the total sum due from the defendant up to the limit imposed by the Act to the detriment of other plaintiffs, it is provided that a limitation fund may be set up in court and distribution made on a pro rata basis;[241] following the establishment of the fund no property belonging to the defendant may be seized in purported satisfaction of any claim.[242] In spite of these limitation provisions, damages awarded against a defendant shipowner may be very large. In order to ensure that the plaintiff receives what is due to him, s.10 of the Act – when it comes into force – will require compulsory insurance, or other security, for all tankers, British or foreign, carrying a bulk cargo of more than 2,000 tons of oil. The section provides that the ship shall neither enter nor leave a port in the United Kingdom, or a terminal in the territorial sea, unless there is a certificate in force showing that the insurance requirements have been met. The certificate is to be issued by the Secretary of State or by the Government of a Convention country, as the case may be.

59. The Act therefore provides a measure of financial protection to many victims of oil pollution damage, but there will still be persons who suffer loss in spite of, or even because of, the terms of the Act. These include persons suffering damage which comes within one of the exceptions to the Act, and for which the victim cannot therefore recover any compensation, and persons who cannot obtain *full* compensation because the owner of the ship is either unable to meet all his obligations or has limited his liability under the Act and the damage suffered exceeds that amount. To provide compensation for persons such as these in all convention countries an international fund will be set up when the 1971 International Convention on the Establishment of an International Fund for Compensation

---

[236] International Convention on Civil Liability for Oil Pollution Damage; see Chapter IV, paras. 91 and 92.
[237] S.1(2).   [238] S.13(2).   [239] S.4.
[240] He has not yet done so since the section is not in force.
[241] S.5.   [242] S.6.

for Oil Pollution Damage[243] has come into force. Part I of the Merchant Shipping Act of 1974 provides for its implementation in the United Kingdom. Contributions are to be made to the Fund "in respect of oil carried by sea to ports or terminal installations in the United Kingdom"; they are payable by importers of oil or persons by whom it is received if the total amount imported or received by them annually is in excess of 150,000 metric tons. The amount of the contribution is to be fixed by the Assembly of the International Fund in accordance with the Convention.

60. The Fund will be available to those previously mentioned who cannot obtain full compensation from the shipowner responsible for the damage; it is not, however, available where the pollution was caused by act of war or hostilities or where the ship involved was a non-commercial Government ship or cannot be identified by the victim. The Fund will also be of assistance to the shipowners themselves. If they incur liability by virtue of the Merchant Shipping (Oil Pollution) Act, 1971, they may recover from the Fund that part of their total liability which exceeds an amount of 1,500 gold francs for each ton of their displacement (or 125 million gold francs in all, if less) but which is not in excess of 2,000 francs per ton (or 210 million gold francs in all, if less). The latter figure is the amount by which the shipowner may limit his liability under the 1971 Act. The policy behind this provision is to take a part of the responsibility for the economic consequences of oil pollution damage from the shoulders of the shipowners and place it with oil cargo interests.

61. The Merchant Shipping (Oil Pollution) Act, 1971, does not deal with liability for the escape of oil resulting from operations on the seabed. The Common Law rules are still applicable here and in most cases it will therefore be essential to prove fault before an action in respect of pollution damage can succeed.[244] This seems an unsatisfactory situation and there is

---

[243] See Chapter IV, paras. 91 and 92.
[244] The defendant could be held liable without proof of fault if the Prevention of Oil Pollution Act, 1971, were interpreted as creating not merely criminal responsibility but a civil statutory duty for breach of which compensation could be recovered by any individual suffering damage; it would be possible but most unlikely that a court would give such an interpretation to the Act. Strict liability would also exist if the rule in *Rylands v. Fletcher* ((1866) L.R. 1 Ex. 265) were held to apply. The rule imposes liability without fault for damage caused by the escape of dangerous things collected by the defendant on his property. Difficulties in applying the rule in *Rylands v. Fletcher* to a situation involving an escape of oil include doubts as to whether the dangerous material must be collected on the defendant's *premises* (see *Charing Cross Electricity Supply Co. v. Hydraulic Power Co.* [1914] 3 KB 772 and remarks made thereon by Lord Simonds in *Read v. Lyons* [1947] AC 146 at 183), the illogicality of thus creating a distinction between an escape of oil from a pipe or tank and an escape from the ground caused by the defendant's drilling – the latter escape could not conceivably come within the scope of the rule – and finally dispute as to whether the collection of oil is a "non-natural" user of land within the terms of the rule.

need for further legislative intervention to extend the statutory tort of strict liability to pollution from such operations.

(b) Nuclear Pollution[245]

(i) From the Transport of Radioactive Materials

62. There are in force in the United Kingdom a number of different kinds of regulations covering the carriage of dangerous – including radioactive – materials; those relating to carriage by sea are the Merchant Shipping (Dangerous Goods) Rules, 1965, as amended,[246] which provide for the packaging, labelling, stowage, etc. of certain classes of dangerous goods, thus implementing Chapter VII of the Regulations to the 1960 SOLAS Convention.[247] The Rules apply to British ships registered in the United Kingdom and to other ships while loading cargo within a port in the United Kingdom or its territorial sea.[248] Criminal penalties may be imposed in the event of non-compliance with the Rules.

63. If damage nevertheless results from the carriage of radioactive materials civil liability is apportioned by the Nuclear Installations Act, 1965 (as slightly amended by a 1969 Act of the same name). The Act provides that no premises in the United Kingdom may be used for operating a nuclear reactor or other installation without a licence from the Minister[249] – and it is on the operator of such a licensed site that liability is placed for all damage caused by radioactive materials which are in transit "on his behalf".[250] The Act thus creates another tort of strict liability, but fewer defences are allowed than for oil pollution – not even the classic "Act of God" may be pleaded. It is a defence, however, to prove that the occurrence causing the damage was due to hostilities or to the reckless conduct of the plaintiff himself.[251] Damages awarded against any one defendant in respect of any one occurrence are not to exceed £5 million,

---

[245] On the subject generally, see Street and Frame, *Law relating to Nuclear Energy* (1966).

[246] S.I. 1965:1067, as amended by S.I. 1968:332 and S.I. 1972:666. The Rules refer to the "Blue Book", i.e. the 1971 *Report of the Department of Trade and Industry's Standing Advisory Committee on the Carriage of Dangerous Goods in Ships.*

[247] 1960 International Convention for the Safety of Life at Sea (see Chapter IV, para. 98), incorporated into the Merchant Shipping (Safety Convention) Act, 1949, by the Merchant Shipping Act, 1964.

[248] A single Rule also relates to all ships while within a port or while embarking or disembarking passengers within the territorial sea or loading fuel or discharging cargo or fuel within these waters.

[249] S.1. The Minister is the Secretary of State for Energy.

[250] S.7. The United Kingdom Atomic Energy Authority is exempt from the requirements of licensing but s.7 liability is applied to it by s.8.

[251] This may be only a partial defence if the plaintiff's conduct was only contributory (s.13(4)).

and the licensee must have financial cover – by insurance or otherwise – sufficient to meet any claims against him.[252]

(ii) From Nuclear Ships

64. There are no laws relating specifically to nuclear-powered vessels; they are subject to the same controls as shipping generally. Civil liability for damage caused by, e.g., a collision involving one or more nuclear ships will be subject to the rules of general law.[253]

(iii) From Radioactive Waste

65. The Radioactive Substances Act, 1960, which, as we have seen,[254] has been extended to the Continental Shelf, provides that, except in accordance with an authorization under the Act, no person may dispose of any radioactive waste from any premises used by him for an undertaking involving dealing with radioactive materials;[255] nor may any person who receives waste to be disposed of by him do so without authorization. "Disposal" includes discharge and dumping into water.[256] There are criminal penalties for non-compliance. Further control is exercised by means of the Nuclear Installations Act, 1965, which, as we have seen, requires operators of nuclear installations to obtain a site licence from the Secretary of State. When the Minister receives a request for a licence, he may direct that the applicant serve a notice on the local authority, the water authority and the appropriate sea fishery committees. They may make representations to the Minister within three months, and conditions may be attached to the licence, including requirements for a monitoring system, specified waste disposal methods, etc. We have seen that under the 1965 Act there exists a tort of strict liability for damage caused by radioactive

---

[252] Ss.16(1) and 19.
[253] Including the "general maritime law". There must be proof of fault for an action to succeed, unless the *Rylands v. Fletcher* principle of strict liability is held to apply. In *Howard v. Furness Houlder Ltd.* [1936] 2 All ER 78 there was an escape of steam on a ship which injured a crew member of that ship. The judge at first instance held that "premises" for the purposes of the rule in *Rylands v. Fletcher* included a ship but that there was not an escape *from* the ship which was necessary before the rule could be invoked. It may be, therefore, that if persons on another ship are injured then the rule may be invoked, but not if the injuries are to passengers on the nuclear ship itself. This supposes, however, that a nuclear reactor is a "non-natural" use of a ship – a hypothesis which is uncertain. Ruling on such questions as these must be left to the courts; it is likely that their policy would be to ensure financial compensation as far as possible to defendants injured as a result of such hazardous activities; see further Street and Frame, *Law relating to Nuclear Energy* (1966), pp. 190, 191.
[254] See para. 16, *supra*.
[255] S.6. The authorization is granted by the Minister of Agriculture, Fisheries and Food (s.8). There are exceptions to the provision by virtue of the Act itself and Ministerial Regulations.
[256] S.19.

materials while in transit on behalf of the site operator; the same applies to damage or injury caused by emissions from radioactive waste disposed of by the operator,[257] and the same limited defences are available. A watchful eye is kept on the possibility of any kind of radioactive danger by the National Radiological Protection Board, an independent advisory body established by the 1970 Radiological Protection Act.

(c) Pollution by Other Harmful Agents[258]

66. As we have seen, the dumping of any substance harmful to sea fish within the territorial limits is controlled by the sea fisheries committees through their statutory byelaws.[259] For pollution purposes it would seem sensible to extend the jurisdiction of such committees to incorporate also the exclusive fishery limits. Outside the three-mile limit there has been, until recently, no system of statutory pollution control, but merely a voluntary scheme whereby the firm or individual intending to dump waste informed the Minister of Agriculture, Fisheries and Food of the nature, source and quantity of the substance and his proposed site of disposal.[260] The position has now been changed by the Dumping at Sea Act, 1974. The Act, which is already in force, implements the Oslo and London Conventions on Dumping[261] and makes compulsory the previously voluntary system of control. Persons without a licence from the Minister[262] are prohibited from dumping "substances or articles" in (i) territorial and internal waters; and (ii) the high seas, if the dumping is from a British ship, aircraft, hovercraft or marine structure (s.1). Dumping includes deposit from a structure on land whose purpose is to deposit solids in the sea. The penalty on summary conviction is a fine of not more than £400 and/or imprisonment for a term of up to six months; on indictment, imprisonment for not more than five years and/or a fine. S.2 requires the Minister, in determining whether to grant a licence, to have regard "to the need to protect the marine environment and the living resources which it supports from any adverse consequences of dumping the substances or articles" in question. Conditions may be attached to the licence, and the licence

---

[257] S.12.

[258] See McLoughlin, *The Law Relating to Pollution* (1972).

[259] Para. 29, *supra*. In Scotland, the Department of Agriculture and Fisheries for Scotland is consulted about major proposals for the dumping of materials in coastal waters.

[260] Most dumping is carried out by commercial waste firms. For details of the voluntary scheme see *Third Report of the Royal Commission on Environmental Pollution* (H.M.S.O., 1972), Cmnd. 5054, para. 135.

[261] See Chapter IV, paras. 105–108.

[262] I.e. the Minister of Agriculture, Fisheries and Food in relation to substances loaded in England or Wales or in United Kingdom waters adjacent to England or Wales; the Secretary of State in relation to Scotland or waters adjacent thereto.

revoked if the holder is in breach of a condition or if there has been a change of circumstances relating to the marine environment, "including a change in scientific knowledge". The appointment of officers to enforce these provisions is provided for by s.5; the officers are empowered to inspect land, buildings and vehicles in the United Kingdom, ships in United Kingdom ports, and British ships and marine structures wherever they may be. They may take samples, examine equipment and require production of licences, records or documents; regulations may be made to provide for these powers to be exercised in relation also to the ships of a specified contracting state and for the powers to be exercised by a foreign enforcement officer in relation to British ships outside territorial waters.

67. The transport by sea of dangerous materials is regulated, as we have seen, by the Merchant Shipping (Dangerous Goods) Rules, 1965.[263] They provide for criminal sanctions but leave the Common Law unaltered on civil liability for damage caused in transit.

E. The Legal Regime of Warships[264]

(*Note:* This section deals with British ships only. Foreign warships are protected from the effect of most of English law by their immunity from suit in the English courts.[265] Nor, when they are within British territorial waters, will jurisdiction generally be claimed in respect of crimes committed on board.[266])

68. In time of peace the Royal Navy uses the North Sea for military exercises and, where necessary, for operations of rescue and law enforcement. In the carrying out of their duties H.M. ships[267] are governed by the Queen's Regulations for the Royal Navy, made under the Queen's prerogative; very few of the statutes which we have been considering in relation to the various uses of the seas apply to them.[268]

---

[263] Para. 52, *supra*.
[264] See Chapter IV, paras. 119–127.
[265] See para. 12, *supra*.
[266] In the case of *Chung Chi Cheung v. R*, [1939] AC 160, it was stated that jurisdiction would not be exercised by local courts over offences committed on board a warship by one member of the crew against another unless the flag State had waived its own jurisdiction – as had occurred in this case.
[267] The term is used here to include all British warships. The Naval Discipline Act, 1957, distinguishes between "H.M. ships" (commissioned ships flying the white ensign), "H.M. vessels" (ships and vessels other than H.M. ships engaged in the naval service of H.M. whether belonging to Her Majesty or not) and "H.M. naval forces" (the Royal Navy, the Naval Reserve Forces and certain Commonwealth forces). To these must be added the Royal Fleet Auxiliaries.
[268] The Crown Proceedings Act, 1947, extends certain sections of the shipping statutes to H.M. ships; see, e.g., ss.5 and 6.

Jurisdiction of the Courts

69. No sovereign immunity equivalent to that enjoyed by foreign public ships attaches to British warships before the British courts. Since the Crown Proceedings Act, 1947, the Crown has been placed, in general, in the same position before the courts as a private individual. Accordingly, for *jurisdictional* purposes the fact that the vessel is a British warship can be virtually ignored; in the action itself, however, the rules of law to be applied may differ from those relating to a private merchant ship.[269]

Navigation

70. H.M. ships are exempted from the application of the Collision Regulations by s.741 of the Merchant Shipping Act, 1894. Nevertheless, the courts have held that, although the Regulations are not laid upon warships as a statutory duty, they do constitute a general standard of care to which the ships should conform in the absence of special circumstances.[270] This standard is indeed insisted upon by the Queen's Regulations themselves. Article 3433 provides that when manoeuvring with other warships, or in the proximity of merchant ships, the Collision Regulations are to be strictly adhered to except as specifically laid down in Naval Tactical Publications. Article 3449 holds out the Admiralty Manual of Navigation as the standard work on navigational questions in the Fleet and provides that the information it contains is to be studied "most carefully"; in particular, the Collision Regulations, set out therein, are to be "very carefully observed". The Queen's Regulations contain a number of other navigational directions, and more detailed instructions are provided by the Manual of Seamanship. H.M. ships are not bound by the byelaws of harbour authorities in commercial ports, but captains are to comply with them as far as possible, and with the requests and directions of the harbour authorities.

71. A question sometimes arises in civil proceedings as to the status of the Queen's Regulations as against other users of the seas. In the case of H.M.S. *Truculent*[271] it was contended for the Admiralty that the Regulations applied to H.M. ships only as a matter of departmental discipline and imposed on them no duty towards other vessels. It was held, however, that the breach of the Regulations which had been proved in that case was a breach of a duty owed by H.M. ships to other mariners; by publishing the Regulations it had been proclaimed to the world at large that H.M. ships were taking upon themselves the same duty to obey the

---

[269] E.g. the captain of a naval ship may be able to put forward the defence of Act of State in an action for tort brought against him by an alien (*Buron v. Denman* [1848] 2 Ex. 167). Today this defence is rarely claimed.

[270] *Thomas Stone Shipping Company Ltd. v. The Admiralty*: "*The Albion*" [1953] P. 117.

[271] *The Admiralty v. Owners of the Steamship "Divina" and others* [1952] P. 1.

Collision Regulations as was imposed on other vessels. The case concerned the lighting of a submarine, and it was accepted in evidence that the positioning of lights on such vessels in accordance with the Collision Regulations was a difficult if not insuperable task; nevertheless the Admiralty was held to be at fault in not conforming to the rules.[272]

Pollution

72. It is stated in the Queen's Regulations that the Ministry of Defence has decided that H.M. ships will comply with the pollution legislation although the statutes expressly exempt warships from their provisions. Accordingly – although, as with the Collision Regulations, there is no statutory duty laid upon H.M. ships – they will be subject to the same requirements as those relating to merchant shipping. Article 2991 provides, however, that compliance with the legislation is subject to overriding operational requirements.

F. Marine Broadcasting[273]

73. For the United Kingdom the problem posed by unlicensed transmitting stations arose in a particularly acute form in 1964, when – one after another – Radios Caroline, Atlanta, Sutch, Invicta and London began broadcasting from ships or disused forts in waters off the British coast.[274] To counter this threat to the international regulation of telecommunications and the allocation of radio frequencies, the United Kingdom joined with other European states in signing and ratifying the 1965 Strasbourg Agreement.[275] Subsequently Britain passed the Marine, &c., Broadcasting (Offences) Act, 1967. The Act's coverage is wider than that of the

---

[272] Since the case was decided a new Rule of the Collision Regulations, Rule 13(6), has come into operation: "Whenever the Government concerned shall have determined that a naval or other military vessel or waterborne seaplane of special construction or purpose cannot comply fully with the provisions of any of these Rules with respect to the number, position, range or arc of visibility of lights or shapes, without interfering with the military function of the vessel or eaplane, such vessel or seaplane shall comply with such other provisions in regard to the number, position, range or arc of visibility of lights or shapes as her Government shall have determined to be the closest possible compliance with these Rules in respect of that vessel or seaplane."
[273] See Chapter IV, paras. 132–136. Preceding the section on marine broadcasting, Chapter IV has a section on the international law concerning artificial islands; in so far as English law bears on this subject at all, it is covered here in the section on the Continental Shelf (paras. 15–17) and in the present Section F on Marine Broadcasting.
[274] See Hunnings, "Pirate Broadcasting in European Waters", 14 *Int. & Comp. Law Quarterly* (1965), p. 410.
[275] European Agreement for the Prevention of Broadcasts Transmitted from Stations outside National Territories; see Chapter IV, para. 135.

Agreement in that it relates to broadcasts from marine structures and other objects in the water, as well as from ships, but in the main its provisions comply faithfully with the Agreement's requirement that each Contracting Party prohibit certain acts relating to marine broadcasting if committed by its own nationals, wherever they may be, and by non-nationals who are for the time being under its jurisdiction. Thus the Act makes it an offence to transmit an unlicensed broadcast from a ship or marine structure within national waters, or from a British ship located anywhere else.[276] United Kingdom citizens (and certain others of analogous status) are prohibited from making such transmissions whether from a ship or other object, and whether or not in the high seas.[277]

74. As well as prohibiting direct involvement in, or responsibility for, such transmissions, the Act creates the offence of supporting unlawful broadcasts by such means as advertising, or otherwise participating in their programmes, writing for them, supplying the ship or structure with goods, apparatus or artistic works, and transporting persons or materials to or from them.[278] This prohibition applies to acts done in national waters or on a British ship, and to acts done by United Kingdom nationals on the high seas. It is clear that the Act has carefully restricted itself to national and territorial jurisdiction and achieves its purpose without interfering with the freedom of the seas. It does not, therefore, catch within its jurisdictional net foreigners who are transmitting from foreign ships just outside territorial waters, but since it cuts them off from their most convenient source of supply and revenue the Act, together with similar legislation in neighbouring states, has almost succeeded in eliminating the problem of "pirate" radio ships from our North Sea coasts.

CONCLUSIONS

75. This summary of the law of the United Kingdom makes it apparent that in many areas of law the national rules are simply the response to the international agreements to which they give effect. To a certain extent, therefore, they share the same merits or defects as the conventions themselves; in some respects, however, the national situation has the advantage over the international. Some of the British Acts of Parliament, for example, have come into force long before there is any prospect that the conventions which they implement will obtain the required number of ratifications, and in some cases the British Act has improved on the substantive provisions of the convention (compare the more stringent anti-pollution measures of the Prevention of Oil Pollution Act, 1971, with the 1969 Amendments to the London Convention).

[276] Ss.1 and 2.
[277] S.3.
[278] Ss.4 and 5.

76. However good the law may be, it will fail to achieve its purposes if it is not enforced. Recent anti-pollution statutes have placed very high upper limits to the fines which may be imposed on offenders; but, unless the courts use this maximum in guiding them as to the fine to be imposed in a particular case, the intention of the legislators may still be frustrated. A final point on the enforcement aspect must be stressed: a state's national law cannot trespass beyond the bounds of its jurisdictional limits; it may hope to control its own nationals, its own ships and occurrences on its own territory, but it must rely on international agreements if it wishes to control events outside these limits.

VI
Summary and Recommendations

In this concluding chapter, an attempt is made to sum up briefly the various issues raised in the preceding chapters; to survey, equally briefly, the existing legal situation; and to suggest possible courses of action to deal with the problems of the uses of the North Sea. It is, of course, obvious that it is not possible to consider the North Sea as an entirely closed area for which a specific regime suitable only for that area can be established. Some of the problems and the remedies discussed are necessarily of wider application, but to attempt to narrow the study to purely North Sea problems would be largely to negate its real usefulness.

The survey will first consider the general question of resource management, linked with some specific problems; it will then set out the existing legal regime and the need for further controls, and will end with a series of recommendations for dealing with the area.

1. RESOURCE MANAGEMENT

It is clear, at the outset, that different activities in the North Sea are regulated at different levels and with varying degrees of thoroughness. The only common factor in the arrangements is that they have all emerged over the years as an often slow response to change and evolution, both now rapidly accelerating, and, on the whole, it is only where a problem or situation has been seen as critical that measures have been taken to try to meet it. Otherwise, inertia and the usual short-term view that characterizes most politics prevails. Machinery is thus lacking for considering, evaluating and regulating for the long term the complex of interrelated activities which the present study, in the specific context of the North Sea, has tried to set out; and this lack must be attributed to the absence of a general awareness of the need for such an integrated approach. Moreover, present international machinery is largely limited to controlling fisheries, pollution, oil extraction and maritime traffic.

There is, however, some evidence that this situation is changing. The growing concern about the environment in the industrialized parts of the world has gradually led to a widespread, if rather unfocused, realization

SUMMARY AND RECOMMENDATIONS

that there is a need for overall environmental planning. Interestingly enough, this development originated at a non-governmental, even popular, level and was forced on the attention of governments because one particular country (Sweden) made it an international issue through the United Nations Environment Conference – renamed the Environment Programme. In consequence, there is now in most countries, at least on paper, some degree of government recognition that environmental considerations must be given due weight when national policy is being decided. The danger, as always, is that lip-service to an idea may become a substitute for hard thinking and eventual action; and this can postpone the recognition of the immediacy and gravity of the problem.

It must be assumed that, for the foreseeable future, the primary responsibility for action will remain at the national or local level and that therefore the fundamental political, economic and social choices will be made by national governments. This is the level at which, in the first place, an integrated approach must be evolved; the existence of international or regional groupings can provide an additional incentive or support for such an approach, but no more. Management responsibility may be vested at a number of different levels, from international down to local. It must, however, be recognized that in some cases no action can be taken without prior international agreement.

Here it might be useful to emphasize yet again that, in order to reach a better understanding of the environmental and management problems implicit in any attempt to achieve a measure of agreement on the priorities in the conflicting uses of the North Sea, it is necessary in the first place to attempt to assess the extent of our knowledge, or ignorance, of the prevailing physical, chemical and biological conditions. There is a considerable area in which reliable information is not yet available and this emerged clearly from a symposium on the science of the North Sea held at Aviemore in November 1971.[1]

In the first instance, there is a lack of adequate knowledge of the water budget of the North Sea, the inflow and outflow rates, the residual currents and diffusion processes, the long-term variations of residual currents, the long-term changes in wind direction and wave climatology, i.e. the pattern of wave movement in a given area. The interrelation between these factors is still obscure but their bearing on increased exploitation of the seabed is obvious.

The distribution of sediment characteristics, the paths of sediment transport and deposition sites are insufficiently mapped. The history of sedimentation may reflect physical, chemical and biological changes in the North Sea. Without a fuller understanding of these processes it is difficult to assess the contribution made by the activities of man to any such

[1] Edward D. Goldberg (ed.), *North Sea Science*, M.I.T. Press, June 1974.

changes. The methods available for ascertaining atmospheric deposition rates are still crude. Nor is it yet possible to chart with accuracy sea–air interaction or estimate the effects of possible long-term changes of climate.

Changes in fish stocks may be due to alterations in the pattern and intensity of fishing, to increasing use of the area for waste disposal, or to natural changes in the physical or ecological environment itself. While it is certain that the first factor plays a very important, if not preponderant, role, other factors are not as well understood. There are still large gaps in our knowledge of primary production, of the role of micro-organisms in the food web, of the life of bottom communities and the place of commercial fish stocks in the food web. There are equally large gaps in our study of the relationships between benthic organisms and sediment movements and the physical, chemical, inorganic and organic characteristics of both water and sediments.

As to the situation in the estuaries, it seems that this is equally unsatisfactory as far as basic chemical information is concerned. Not enough is known of the interaction which takes place between dissolved and solid phases in the transition from river to saline waters, the extent of residual time in the estuary and the interactions taking place during that period. Nor is there sufficient understandings of the bio-accumulation of trace materials – the building up of toxic material in fish, sea-birds and mammals – particularly as regards the uptake of metal pollutants. The distribution and nature of nutrients and the rate of the mixing process are largely unknown and, apart from radio-active materials, knowledge of the toxicological significance of many of the substances added in wastes is almost totally lacking.

So far, apart from damage to shellfish and fish in near-shore areas, there is no definite evidence of an adverse influence of pollution on major fish resources, but over the last decade there has been: (1) a drastic reduction of pelagic stocks which has been interpreted as the effect of increased exploitation; and (2) an increase in demersal stock, interpreted as due to a higher level of recruitment. Further research is required, particularly into the distribution of pollution danger areas and coastal ecology. At present the apparent inversion of the relationship between pelagic and demersal stocks cannot be explained by any factors which are known. Here reliable distribution maps are badly needed.

Equally important is the necessity for a better appraisal of the impact of man's activities on the marine ecology. Research should be undertaken on the probable effects of hydrocarbon exploitation in the North Sea, which has one of the most savage and unpredictable marine weather patterns to be found, and linked with this is the necessity for reliable meteorological forecasts to enable work to be undertaken in the most propitious conditions. It is also essential to establish the stability of the seabed as far as possible where oil rigs and pipelines are sited.

SUMMARY AND RECOMMENDATIONS

Where waste disposal is concerned, further information is still needed on the movement of the wastes, their dispersion, mixing and distribution; the rate of the mobilization of metals from sediments, the interaction between constituents of wastes, and the pathway of persistent chemicals through the food chains. We lack understanding of the acute and chronic effects of certain wastes on marine organisms, the process of biodegradability of organic wastes in the marine environment, and of the ecological effects of discharged and dumped wastes.

The early recognition of man-made marine ecological changes is a prerequisite of any attempt to prevent avoidable environmental damage and at the same time to enable the maximum sustainable utilization of the living resources of the North Sea, and here what is required is the precise definition of the distribution and the habitat requirements of certain inshore species of commercial importance, including the early stages of their development.

It remains to establish to what extent, and over what period of time, the extraction of sand and gravel may affect marine life, fishing exploitation – here the effect upon the herring spawning grounds should be borne in mind – and coastal erosion. Research on these topics is, however, proceeding.

From this short and very condensed account, it emerges clearly that much more research remains to be done before a completely adequate and viable regime for the international control of the uses of the North Sea can be set up. This must not be made an excuse for postponing the establishment of initial machinery to control certain agreed areas – machinery which is sufficiently flexible to enable its adaptation to deal with the changing situation as it emerges.

It is not, however, only in the field of the physical sciences that a serious information gap exists. The preparation of this Report has revealed the enormous extent to which the relevant legal information is inaccessible for all practical purposes. Of course, the relevant legislative instruments and treaties have been published, but the fact that the information exists somewhere does not, in practice, mean that it is accessible in any systematic form. The flow of the necessary information is impeded at innumerable points. In the first place, the division of responsibility within various departments of individual governments means that there is no one person or department within the administrative machine who has a complete picture of the total legal position. This is particularly true if "the total legal position" is taken as involving the treaty law as well as national legislation. Foreign Offices tend to be primarily responsible for the former, but other departments for the latter. Furthermore, even Foreign Offices do not seem to have a complete and integrated picture of the entire international legal regime – a regime which is, of course, constantly changing as new treaties are entered into and as participation in treaties fluctuates. This failure of communication, found within single governments, is often more marked between different governments. Governments of the North Sea area States seem to know very little about the legislation of their neighbours. This is unfortunate for two reasons: (a) such legislation may prove a valuable source of inspiration; and (b) proposals for international action may not have much prospect of success unless they take into account the domestic legal difficulties which particular participants might encounter.

There is, furthermore, a one-way information blockage between international organizations and the governments which they are intended to serve. The governments of the North Sea States are generally reasonably well-informed as to the activities of the international organizations in which they participate, but the reverse is not always true. For example, one would search in vain in the library of one well-known inter-governmental organization prominent in maritime matters for copies of the legislation of even the principal maritime states on matters of vital concern to that organization.

Nor are these failures of communication within and between administrations (governmental or inter-governmental) remedied by scholarly research. A certain kind of legal research has, of course, been done on certain specific topics, but there have been few attempts to provide an exhaustive survey – or even a broad overall perspective – of the international or national legal regime of a particular region and, so far as we are aware, none at all of the North Sea. It is not with the purpose of self-congratulation, but rather to point out the seriousness of the problem, that mention is made of the fact that, as far as the authors of this Report are aware, no studies comparable to those contained in Chapters IV and V above have previously been made. The difficulties are, of course, considerable. Even in the case of the law of one specific country, although the legislative instruments are readily accessible (at any rate in that country), a great deal of effort has to be put into systematizing legislation which is listed on a chronological rather than on a systematic basis. When it comes to obtaining detailed information about the legislation of foreign countries, the task is well-nigh impossible. Even if the language barrier can be overcome it is not at all easy for a scholar in one country to find a complete collection of the legislation (including subordinate legislation) of another country. Moreover, even if this information is available, to utilize it may require familiarity with the whole system and legal philosophy of the country concerned. Nor can this problem be solved simply by asking other scholars in the relevant countries for the appropriate information; for the most part they do not have the information themselves and could produce it only after extensive research. It was, indeed, obstacles of this kind which prevented the authors of the present study from carrying out their original intention of including reports on the national legislation of each of the North Sea States.

At first sight, it might appear that the communication and information failures referred to above are not serious. After all, it might be said, appropriate governmental or inter-governmental authorities, even if they do not have the necessary information at their fingertips, know where it can be found and can always call it up. However, it is submitted that this is not a complete answer. In the first place, it is the principal thesis of this Report that the problems of the North Sea require an integrated approach which takes into account all the different aspects of the use of these waters; this clearly requires an integrated and up-to-date knowledge of the total legal regime. Secondly, there are grounds for suspecting that those who do not have the necessary information about activities somewhat peripheral, though important, to their own concerns, do not always seek it out. It would seem that, at least in some cases, the effort of digging out the information is too much and that officials or scholars prefer to carry on in ignorance of it. Established patterns of departmental or academic compartmentalization tend to encourage this somewhat ostrich-like attitude.

If legal scholars are not sufficiently interested to do the necessary research, it must be done by someone. Governments should either do it themselves, or pay for others to do it for them. The results of this research should be published; it is in the common interest that such information should be readily accessible to all who may be interested, and there is nothing confidential about the contents.

2. SOME SPECIFIC PROBLEMS

(a) Fisheries Conservation

This is a field where international action is, in some respects, well developed. The North-East Atlantic Fisheries Commission is an inter-governmental regulatory body with the benefit of a constant flow of scientific information from another intergovernmental body, the International Council for the Exploration of the Sea. It has promulgated a number of agreed regulations on fishing, covering, *inter alia*, close seasons, mesh size and the minimum size of fish in markets. In this connection, it should be noted that, with modern methods of herding fish into the nets and trawlers which sweep the sea floor, mesh sizes alone are not the controlling factor regulating the size of fish caught.

Moreover, the effectiveness of NEAFC has been, and still is, limited by the following facts:

(i) The original Convention did not allow regulation by means of catch and/or fishing effort quotas without its reference back to the governments of the member countries, in order that they could activate a particular article. This proved to be a lengthy procedure because of (a) Parliamentary difficulties, especially in Belgium; and (b) the

Icelandic 50-mile limit claim. The Article has now been activated and quota regulations are, in fact, now possible.
(ii) In certain member countries the fishing industry has built up large, highly efficient modern fleets. To seek to regulate a fishery and to obtain the maximum sustainable yield (MSY) by means of catch or fishery effort quotas is to call for an immediate cut in the takings of these fleets in which large amounts of capital have recently been invested; the difficulty for the representative of such a country to support an objective which gives long-term gains – including the continued survival of the fishery industry – but which causes short-term hardship in his own country is obvious. The difficulty is compounded when representatives of the fishing industry concerned are present during meetings.
(iii) Overfishing of a particular stock has, in most cases, stemmed from the creation of these modern fishing fleets in one or two countries. If regulations of the fishery by the quota system is sought, then the problem is to get agreement in NEAFC on a formula on which to base the quota. The country with the modern fleet (Country A) argues that the formula should give the greater weight to the most recent years' performance (i.e. those when its own catches were highest); the other countries argue that the formula should give most weight to historic performance (i.e. the catch rates in the years before the modern fleet of Country A made its impact on the stock).

It is true that any member of NEAFC can object to a particular recommendation, but by doing so, if all the remaining members observe it, the objector puts itself openly in a very awkward moral position, which it may find extremely uncomfortable.

While members of NEAFC do have national enforcement procedures with regard to minimum sizes of catches, and those in the United Kingdom are very effective, there are still a few countries in which enforcement of these regulations is, to say the least, somewhat haphazard. A possible means of enforcing agreements relating to the size of catch would be control of the fish when it reached the markets. If infringements of the regulations were penalized by withdrawing the resulting catch from sale as a result of market inspection, the economic factor would immediately come into play. On the other hand, this would mean a loss of the catch and it might be better to levy a sufficiently heavy fine on the offender.

An additional weapon, as far as possible quotas are concerned, could be the use of subsidies up to the amount of the quota on the same lines as agricultural subsidies. But such subsidies would have to be payable as a result of a separate, inter-governmental agreement since the constitution of NEAFC precludes it from entering into any such financial arrangements designed to offset the immediate losses caused by the introduction of regulatory measures like quota systems.

Another factor which adds to the pressures on fisheries is the very heavy cost of the sophisticated technical equipment installed in most modern trawlers and the scale of the profits expected from a single voyage.

(b) Fish Farming

If fish farming ever becomes a significant commercial undertaking in the North Sea it may involve the enclosure of certain areas of inshore coastal waters, or, in the case of mollusc farming, the erection of structures in coastal waters. At the present time, however, it would seem unlikely that such a development will take place to any great extent. A more serious problem is the possibility of the creation of enclosures for other purposes. For example, there are serious Dutch proposals to reclaim the Waddenzee by building dams between the Frisian Islands. The Waddenzee is the nursery area of a number of important North Sea fish stocks. Similar problems, affecting local geophysical features and the immediate environment, would arise from the erection of artificial islands, already planned for sites in the North Sea, to be used as industrial centres, oil terminals or as amenity and recreational areas, or a combination of all three. Such islands, based solidly on the seabed, would also create problems of effluent and sewage disposal. Should such schemes materialize, they will necessitate important changes in national and international law. Also, if there is to be any question of stocking fish farms from the sea, there will have to be modifications in national and international regulations on mesh sizes, which at present prohibit the taking of young fish. In the United Kingdom, however, national regulations already allow the taking of immature fish with small mesh nets for the stocking of fish farms.

(c) Oil Rigs

There are no international standards on safety margins for construction of oil rigs in the North Sea, largely because the conditions there have not been encountered elsewhere. An association of United Kingdom professional bodies recently submitted proposals to the Government on codes of practice and standards which, they hope, may gain general acceptance; and work is being carried out on standards and directives within the EEC as well as in inter-governmental meetings in the Hague. There is need for a concentration of these efforts.

There is no international system of liability for damage resulting from an accident.[2] Such liability could be created either by international convention or, as suggested below, by making provision for litigation between the parties concerned: in the latter case this would still have to be established

[2] It is, however, generally admitted that the occurrence of a major accident is merely a question of time.

on an international basis. There would seem to be a weakness in the present system where the responsibility for safety rests largely with the oil industry, but, at the same time, it is both protected by the Government and dependent on the Government to take action on its behalf.

In the meantime, a North Sea oil pollution compensation fund amounting to £6.7 million, to be known as OPAL, has been set up by most of the major oil exploration companies operating off-shore from Britain. This provides for the creation of an association whose members will accept strict, as opposed to fault, liability to pay for pollution damage and/or remedial measures arising from an oil spillage incident attributable to their off-shore operations, as at 18 August 1974. Some 20 companies have agreed to join this association and, while it refers only to operations on the United Kingdom continental shelf, it has been drawn up in a way that readily enables it to be extended to waters of other countries in the European zone. It is hoped that it may become world-wide in its scope.

There are accepted principles or "guide lines" on construction and safety margins in the United Kingdom. The United Kingdom legislation covering offshore activities is the Mineral Workings (Offshore Installations) Act, 1971. This is very general and was supplemented by the Offshore Installations (Construction and Survey) Regulations, which came into effect only on 1 May 1974 and which set out the Department of Energy's methods of control over design and construction of installations used in United Kingdom offshore areas. There is, in fact, only one regulation – that every offshore installation shall have a certificate of fitness by 31 August 1975. The rest consists of instructions on how to get the certificate, by submitting the design to an independent certifying authority whose supervisory inspector shall be satisfied as to correct construction, materials and workmanship and with its installation and platform equipment.

On 24 June 1974 the major ship classification societies – Lloyd's of London, Det Norske Veritas of Norway, Bureau Veritas of Paris, Germanischer Lloyd's of Germany and the American Bureau of Shipping – were authorized by the Department of Energy to carry out this work. The American Bureau of Shipping has no statutory or otherwise mandatory rules recognized in the United States over oil installation design or operation, but would apply United Kingdom regulations in British waters.[3]

Because of the rapid developments in offshore technology, the regulations prescribe only in broad terms the minimum standards of design and construction. More detailed technical standards required can be found in "Guidance on the Design and Construction of Offshore Installations" (H.M.S.O., 4 April 1974). This standard will be amended from time to time in the light of further developments. Norway accepts only the certificate of the Petroleum Directorate acting through Det Norske

---

[3] Military and coastal control vessels in the United States are not subject to pollution restrictions, nor are they bound by oil pollution measures.

Veritas. In July 1974 Det Norske Veritas published its own "Rules for Design Certification and Inspection of Fixed Offshore Structures".

In the case of a serious leakage from a pipeline or oil rig the United Kingdom offshore operators' emergency group, set up jointly by the oil companies, has agreed plans for co-operation with the Marine Division of the Department of Trade and, if the leak is sufficiently serious, they can call upon the backing of the Royal Navy.

With regard to the question of safety and of supply ships and pipeline barges, the standard is still unsatisfactory but is in the process of improvement, and efforts are being made to agree minimum standards with the owners and operators. However, under present circumstances, once these ships are outside territorial waters they are subject only to the jurisdiction of the flag State, even when they are over continental shelf waters, save for the 500-metre safety zone around each oil rig which is under the coastal State's jurisdiction. This situation may change as a final result of the Third United Nations Conference on the Law of the Sea.

While expert opinion is certainly divided, there is a strongly held view that if the cost of the benefits of drilling for oil in the North Sea are examined objectively the oil should be left in place until offshore drilling and control techniques are better developed. As it is, as already pointed out earlier, it seems certain that under prevailing conditions there will be major oil spills.

As regards the safety of oil pipelines, a recent Post Office Report on the fouling of telephone cables by trawler nets states that, on average, one cable is fouled every week, the cost for repairs being some £20,000 per year. Recently an oil pipeline laid on the seabed was found some nine months later to be six feet above the level of the seabed. This is a known hazard owing to fluctuations in the level of the seabed due to sand waves and shifting clay and this applies both to the northern and southern North Sea.

It goes without saying that it will be necessary to take every possible technical precaution in the months to come, but the oil companies claim that, although it is acknowledged that operations in the North Sea are being carried out at the limits of present technology, a balanced view of the risks is taken by the classifying societies in each case.

A related problem, concerning the need for insurance against damage from oil leaks, is likely to become more acute as the number of wells in the North Sea continues to increase. By 1980 there are likely to be between 100 and 300 wells in areas under United Kingdom jurisdiction alone. This development will pose the further hazard of accidents to the rigs, such as capsizing due to gales, as has already occurred, or a shift in the seabed, or a collision. At present there is a difference of opinion between governments and industry on the degree of risk involved, but clearly it is important that, if there is to be a question of marine insurance cover, guidelines should be laid down as soon as possible.

(d) Navigation

It must be further recognized that with the estimated 100 drilling rigs and some 50 production platforms to be erected in the North Sea over the next five years, together with a number of refinery reception points on the coasts, a new pattern of traffic will develop, including the use of deep-draught heavily-laden tankers, much of which will run counter to normal routes of coastal and ocean-going shipping, and this will result in creating new navigational hazards. In spite of the international agreements concluded under the auspices of IMCO,[4] there are a number of matters which require further regulation. One of these concerns communication – within ships, between ships and between ship and shore. Signals are often not understandable between the many different nationalities which make up ships' crews. There is a need for international shipping traffic control to be as closely organized as air traffic control is, and it may be that the time has come for the principle of the complete freedom of the high seas, which is basic to the existing arrangements, to be re-examined.

However that may be, a first step could be to draw up a code of regulations analagous to those evolved by ICAO, which would serve to bring some order out of the growing chaos since the code would apply to all ships regardless of owner or registration. The chief stumbling block to the establishment of such a code is, of course, the age-old tradition of the absolute authority of a Master over his ship, but modern conditions of navigation in narrow waters have already tended to erode this, at least to a certain extent.

3. POLICY QUESTIONS

(a) Administrative: Choice of Policy

One of the most difficult policy decisions concerns the relative value of the whole range of North Sea activities, considered in the total environmental context, with the additional complication of a frequent clash between long-term interest and short-term expediency. In fact, some kind of "cost-benefit" evaluation of different activities is usually possible on the purely economic level but the result may omit too many non-quantifiable aspects and therefore may not be acceptable. Also, much depends on the efficiency of the machinery for consultation between the different government departments involved and the public. It seems probable that the better the opportunities for all points of view to be presented, the less likely it is that the pure "cost-benefit" arguments will prevail. As an example, for mineral extraction where, as has been described elsewhere, a very efficient consultation procedure exists before licences are granted, there is almost always a clear economic case for exploration to proceed, but

[4] See Chapter IV, paras 64 to 67.

this does not necessarily carry the day in the overall considerations deciding the government's final conclusion.

It is quite likely that the various interests and objectives involved cannot be finally reconciled, but this does not remove the necessity for choices to be made and priorities assigned; the fact that *deliberate* choices were made would be an advance on the present somewhat *laissez faire* approach to the uses of the North Sea. Again, take the example of North Sea oil: there would seem to be a choice between, on the one hand, making every effort to get as much oil ashore as soon as possible to meet immediate energy needs and, on the other, treating it, as there is evidence to show that other producers are beginning to do, as an asset to be husbanded.[5] In the first case – which appears to be the option chosen so far – there are clear consequences for the future of a number of coastal areas in Scotland which, because of the assumed overriding importance of our energy needs, are: (a) not being fully and openly recognized; and (b) treated, on the whole, as particularly local difficulties rather than as a matter of overall policy.[6] In the second case, there are problems concerning the return of the oil companies on their investment and the durability of the necessary equipment.

What is needed is a comprehensive examination of the whole question of where, in both cases, it would be best to site the oil terminals in the United Kingdom with due regard to their ultimate places of distribution. The question of speed of extraction is one which is relevant also to gas and mineral reserves; in the case of the former there might be an argument from a United Kingdom point of view, either for extracting our reserves quickly, storing them and using them as a bargaining counter *vis-à-vis* oil from other sources, or allowing them to remain *in situ* for the time being. There seems to be evidence that when a government reaches a clear decision on such a choice and makes it known – as has the Norwegian government over the exploitation of their North Sea oil reserves – the resulting removal of uncertainty finds favour with the electorate and is accepted by other governments and vested interest groups.

As against this, it must be recognized that governments are subject to a variety of political and social pressures that may render their choices arbitrary or irrational, or make it seem expedient to conceal the fact that a

[5] The reserves, however, are now thought to be of a magnitude which would not preclude the extraction of sufficient oil to meet the immediate financial crisis while, at the same time, allowing sensible conservation measures of a necessarily wasting asset. Similarly, the resources of gravel and sand are far from inexhaustible and a rapid exploitation of these might well prove to be undesirable.

[6] If accepted, the 1974 Report by a Committee of the Oil Development Council for Scotland, *North Sea Oil and the Environment*, would ensure that oil-related development on land and close to the shore would take place within a rational and imaginative planning context.

particular choice has been made. There are also many areas where the necessary knowledge for decision-making is incomplete; indeed it is rare for governments to have the time to collect or commission all the information they would like before decisions have to be made. Furthermore, it is possible that the nature of the political and social pressures may be misinterpreted: governments and civil servants make a number of assumptions about public opinion which might in themselves need re-examination. Despite all these difficulties there still seems to be a strong argument for governments to show that the need for difficult choices has been squarely faced; and that all aspects of the situation have been taken into consideration even though the answers to all the questions may not be known. The practice in the United States might offer a possible means of improving the situation in this respect. When a new Federal project is proposed, and before planning permission is granted, the Federal Government requires the planners to submit an Environmental Impact Statement to the President's Council on Environmental Quality. This statement must be published and the Council has the power to issue an injunction forbidding any work on the project until a decision has been reached. The work of the Council is backed up by the powerful Environmental Protection Agency and elaborate licensing machinery.

(b) Financial and Industrial: Management Criteria

On the management level, this approach has to be translated into practical terms. Here the kind of question that has to be put is: "Taking into account all identified factors and future needs, how can the best sustainable use of resources be achieved and how is it possible to counteract the tendency to consider problems in relation solely to terms of relative cost?"

In other words, there must be a constant awareness of the need to approach the use and management of any resource in the *whole* environmental context.

Environmental management can be seen as involving a number of distinct, though closely interconnected, "notions". On the broad scale there is *conservation*: the rationally restrained optimal economic use of certain renewable and non-renewable resources; and its opposite, *waste*: or destruction; other important aspects are *preservation*: or the protection of a particular region or landscape for genetic or aesthetic reasons; *pollution*: which is any damage to the environment or its resources; and *economic exclusion*: which is the prevention of the use of certain resources by particular agents (for example, foreign fishermen) for economic reasons. Attempts to answer the questions posed above should try to keep these various notions distinct, though they are, of course, interrelated. One problem is that there is no clear agreement on some of these definitions: in particular the use of the terms "preservation" and "conservation" often causes confusion.[7]

The idea of conservation recognizes that at some point the resources will be needed and used, but seeks to restrain and limit their use. In other words it implies, in "terms of accountancy", that the endeavour should be to limit use to the rate of replacement either of the resource being used or any predictable substitute. Preservation implies a permanent safeguard or protection. In practice, however, organizations and bodies concerned with what is here referred to as preservation, tend to be broadly grouped under the heading of "conservation societies" and, while this may appear to be a minor point of semantics, it is perhaps an additional hindrance to the clear thinking-through of environmental problems which seems so difficult to achieve.

The terminology used by the press and pressure groups tends naturally to differ from that used by governments or industry – or else the same words are used to mean very different things. The hazards of emotional argument are by no means confined to discussions of the environment, but are in this case intensified because there is relatively little underlying bedrock of objective or scholarly study. The scholarship, on the whole, is found in the various scientific and legal aspects of the question; few of the scholars communicate freely with each other or with the lay public and, for the rest, the debate has been conducted in political terms. Probably one of the most valuable single contributions that could be made to our understanding of environmental problems would be a generally comprehensible clarification of the issues involved so that, for example, a term such as "pollution" could be used without emotional heat.[8]

(c) **Military and Strategic**

Roughly speaking, there are two schools of thought on the military aspects of the uses of the seabed. The traditional approach holds that the

[7] In a recent study, *Man's Responsibility for Nature*, John Passmore distinguishes between the *conservation* of resources for future generations and the *preservation* of species and of parts of the world as they now exist.

[8] The seriousness and extent of the problem of pollution should, however, be recognized. A report by Dr. Anatoly Simonov, Head of the Department of Marine Hydrology and Hydrochemistry of the State Oceanographic Institute of the U.S.S.R., following a Soviet survey of the North Atlantic and European seas, shows that the North Sea and Irish Sea are high on the list of oil pollution, far beyond the maximum permissible concentrations. Other seas blacklisted by the Soviet report are the Bay of Biscay and the Tyrrhenian Sea. With growing industrial production and expanding mining on the Continental Shelf, polluted water moves out in currents to contaminate the world's oceans. As a result of the study, the Soviet Oceanographic Committee has drafted an international programme of surveillance over concentrations of harmful substances and has submitted it to an inter-governmental oceanographic commission for consideration. (Extract from *Pravda*, 64 (20303). Report given to the IOC.)

seabed has the same legal status as the superjacent waters; therefore the same freedoms apply to the seabed and subsoil as to the high seas. These freedoms include the right to unilateral weapon-testing and to the disposal of obsolete munitions in the sea, neither of these being so far regulated by international law.

The second approach is that of equating the seabed with outer space; both pose a legal vacuum since no usage or custom has been developed, and laws governing their use must be established by practice and international treaties. On this view the use of the seabed for military or other purposes beyond the limits of national jurisdiction would be unlawful. According to the United Nations General Assembly Resolution 2574D, "States and persons are bound to refrain from all activities of exploitation of the resources of the seabed beyond the limits of national jurisdiction" pending the establishment of an international regime. A number of States, however, are unwilling to be bound by this.

The installation of nuclear weapons and weapons of mass destruction on the seabed is prohibited by the Seabed Weapons Treaty of 11 February 1971 (approved by the Political Committee of the United Nations on 17 November 1970) but whether this will be effective in halting the seabed arms race remains to be seen.

Since the primary concern of the major powers is the maintenance of a credible nuclear deterrent, embodied as far as the Navy is concerned in a submarine fleet composed of submarines carrying nuclear missiles operating undetected on the high seas, the emphasis lies on the need for maximum manoeuvrability outside minimum territorial waters and unhindered passage through international straits. Proposals to extend national jurisdiction to 12 miles and beyond would not necessarily affect freedom of submarine movements although, under the Geneva Convention on the Territorial Sea, and without special provisions for straits and narrows, submarines would be forced to surface and show the flag when passing through the territorial sea. However, it should be remembered that the ULMS (Underwater Launching Missile System) is capable of delivering payloads to targets 6,000 miles from the launch site.

Extending national jurisdiction to 12 or 200 miles would not severely limit the mobility of warships through neutral territorial waters under the "innocent passage" provisions of the Geneva Convention but a large number of States already deny the entry of warships into their territorial sea.

Active and passive sonar listening devices to keep track of missile-carrying submarines are placed both on the deep ocean floor and at the bottom of continental shelves with cables running from the devices to the shore. Here it is obvious that there is the possibility of conflict between the interests of naval security and the exploration and exploitation of mineral resources. But sonar devices are limited in their effectiveness and new "infra-red" techniques used by earth satellites can detect submarines even when lying stationary on the seabed.

However, "the major maritime powers will be unwilling to accept an international regime for regulating ocean uses beyond the shelf unless some means can be devised to accommodate military activities on the sea floor with the other uses of that region".[9]

4. INTERNATIONAL AND NATIONAL CONTROL OF ACTIVITIES

A. Existing Legal Regime

At this point it may be helpful, before considering what conclusions can be drawn about North Sea environmental management, to summarize the existing legal position, in particular with regard to the level at which responsibility for the different activities at present rests.

Fisheries

Fishing is largely controlled internationally through regional agreements.

On allocation, the 1964 European Fisheries Convention accounts for most of the North Sea States, and the gaps are to a large extent filled by bilateral treaties with States which are not parties to it. The EEC arrangements take account of the interests of the new members (the United Kingdom, Denmark and Ireland) but not, of course, of Norway.

On conservation, the North East Atlantic Fisheries Commission controls such matters as mesh, fish sizes, etc., and all North Sea States are parties. Although "conservation" tends to be interpreted by the fishing industry in the light of its own interests, the object of the Commission is to exploit fish stock in such a way as to obtain the maximum sustainable yield.

Policing for these regional arrangements is carried out at the national level. There is also the voice of a strong and well-organized fishing industry. In most North Sea countries this is a non-governmental authority, but one having strong links with the government. Thus in the United Kingdom the White Fish Authority and the Herring Industry Board have general control and supervision and administer government grants and subsidies.

At the local level in the United Kingdom, fishery committees are empowered to make by-laws and have some control over landings.

Mineral Extraction

This is largely controlled nationally since the Continental Shelf Convention recognizes states' sovereign rights over the shelf for the exploration and exploitation of natural resources. These rights are subject to there being no "unjustifiable" interference with navigation, fishing or conservation of

---

[9] Robert A. Shinn, *The International Politics of Marine Pollution Control*, 1974.

living resources, and no interference with research, but these provisos may not be given much weight in practice. The North Sea Continental Shelf has been apportioned in a series of bilateral agreements, with the exception of the Belgian section.

Different minerals - oil, gas, coal, sand and gravel – come under different government authorities. In the case of the United Kingdom these are, respectively, the Department of Energy and the Crown Estate Commissioners. However, apart from coal, the exploitation of minerals is carried out by commercial companies to whom licences for prospecting and operating are issued. There are various controls and limitations: before licences are issued for sand and gravel dredging in the United Kingdom the effects on other users are considered through inter-departmental consultation; for oil and gas exploration, conditions are included in model clauses for licences under the Petroleum (Regulations) Act, 1966. In the latter case the safeguards against conflicts with other users are not very satisfactory, since they are based on the wording of the Continental Shelf Convention.

Also there is still a certain vagueness on the matter of pollution which has had to be avoided until recently by methods customary in "good oilfield practice", a phrase which frequently occurred but which had never been defined, perhaps because it was not definable. However, under the Petroleum (Regulations) Act, 1966, the Mineral Workings (Offshore Installations) Act, 1971, and the Offshore Installations (Construction and Survey) Regulations, 1974, the situation is expected to improve gradually, more especially as the inspectors appointed under the Mineral Workings Act have fairly wide discretionary powers. In general, the responsibility rests with industry but commercial interests, in general, dictate careful practice. Responsibility for the infra-structure support for off-shore mineral exploitation lies largely with the local authorities.

Pollution

(1) Land-Based Pollution

The control of pollution coming into the sea from watercourses and the coast, either directly or through pipes, was, until recently, solely in the hands of the State having sovereignty over the land in question. The United Kingdom's legislation in this field is reasonably comprehensive and is codified for the most part in the Control of Pollution Act, 1974, and the Water Act, 1973. The need for international regulation was recognized by the 1974 Paris Convention for the Prevention of Pollution from Land-based Sources, which sets minimum standards of pollution control for the legislation of contracting States and establishes a Commission to supervise the implementation of the Convention. It is not yet in force. There are also a few international agreements of more limited scope.

(2) Pollution from Ships and Drilling Operations

Since pollution from ships occurs, in general, beyond the limits of national jurisdiction, it is controlled in the first place at the international level, and domestic legislation confines itself largely to the implementation of these conventions on the national plane. The first conventions were concerned solely with pollution by oil but recent developments have extended the system of control to other harmful substances. The legal position is complex, owing to the number of international agreements in this field and to differences in their treatment of the problems according to the nature of the pollutant and its source. So far, pollution from drilling operations falls within the scope of national jurisdiction.

(a) Oil Pollution

Prevention measures are provided by the following Conventions:

(i) *The 1954 Convention for the Prevention of Pollution of the Sea by Oil*, as amended in 1962, prohibits the intentional discharge of oil within certain prohibited zones, one of which is the North Sea. The 1969 Amendments to the Convention, which are not yet in force, institute a new system of pollution prevention by prohibiting the discharge of oil anywhere at sea unless certain conditions are fulfilled.

(ii) *The 1973 Convention for the Prevention of Pollution from Ships* will replace the 1954 Convention ((i) above) with further slight amendments; it has not yet come into force and is not likely to for some years.

(iii) *The 1971 Amendment* to the 1954 Convention ((i) above) foresees the accidental escape of oil resulting from a tanker collision and requires new tankers to comply with specified standards of construction designed to reduce the rate of escape of oil in the event of an accident.

(iv) *The 1969 "Public Law Convention"* (not yet in force) enables protective action to be taken by coastal states to avoid threatened, or already existent, oil pollution in the event of a casualty at sea; this may take the form of towing away or destroying the tanker in distress.

(v) *The Bonn Agreement for Co-operation in Dealing with the Pollution of the North Sea* is a regional arrangement which provides for co-operation and assistance in the event of casualties in the North Sea.

(vi) If pollution does occur in spite of all preventive measures, the victims will need to be able to recover monetary compensation from those in a position to pay. *The 1969 "Private Law Convention"* places absolute liability for the pollution damage on the owner of the tanker which has caused it.

(vii) *A 1971 Convention* establishes an international fund for compensation which both aids victims of oil pollution damage and, to some extent, relieves the financial burden placed on shipowners by the 1969 Convention ((vi) above). Neither (vi) nor (vii) are yet in force.

Oil pollution occurring as a result of Continental Shelf operations is not yet covered in detail by any convention and is largely left to the control of the individual state.

(b) Nuclear Pollution

International regulations seek to prevent pollution arising out of the transport of radioactive materials. The disposal of radioactive waste[10] will be governed by the London Convention on Dumping and the 1973 Convention for the Prevention of Pollution from Ships, when these Conventions come into force. Provision is also made for civil liability if an accident occurs. In addition, the Paris Convention for the Prevention of Marine Pollution from Land-based Sources gives further protection.

(c) Other Hazardous Substances

Detailed provision respecting the intentional dumping of hazardous substances is made in the 1972 Oslo Dumping Convention and, in respect of a wider geographical area, in the 1972 London Dumping Convention. The 1973 Convention for the Prevention of Pollution from Ships deals with other forms of disposal of noxious substances – whether intentional or accidental. The 1969 Public Law Convention on Intervention (see 1(iv) above) has been extended to harmful substances other than oil by a 1973 Protocol, but this is not yet in force.

Transport and Navigation

International law protects two ancient and basic principles: the freedom of the high seas, and the flag State's exclusive jurisdiction over its ships on the high seas. These principles complicate issues of international regulation, but such regulation is clearly necessary and has been directed towards the harmonization of national laws and the elaboration of internationally accepted codes of conduct to ensure maritime safety.

The main conventions, promoted by IMCO, are the 1960 International Convention for the Safety of Life at Sea and the 1966 International Convention on Load Lines. The 1960 Regulations for Preventing Collisions at Sea form a kind of "highway code" of the sea. Their chief omission is that traffic separation schemes are not compulsory, although this will be rectified when the 1972 Convention on the Collision Regulations comes into force. However, this will not be until 1976 at the earliest, and even then only the flag State will have jurisdiction to punish those who violate such schemes on the high seas.

---

[10] It has been estimated that if nuclear power production rises as high as 40 per cent of the total production of energy by the year 2000, this will result in 1,000 to 5,000 tons per year of waste products requiring disposal (Robert A. Shinn, *The International Politics of Marine Pollution Control*, Praeger, 1974).

Other international conventions deal with legal problems arising from collisions and other incidents and with a wide range of issues such as access to ports and the welfare of seamen. One interesting detail is that several States undertake activities to improve navigation in areas adjacent to their coasts but not necessarily restricted to national waters.

Nationally, many traffic separation schemes have been made compulsory, including several in the North Sea area, and in general international conventions have been incorporated into the national law of the North Sea States.

Control of ports and harbours and their approaches is exercised by the particular local authority. In some cases this may involve massive capital expenditure and the power to make far-reaching regulations. Thus, the Rotterdam Regional Authority has responsibility for the development of Europoort, including the development of highly sophisticated technical innovations for dealing with supertankers, and such structures as artificial islands.

B. Necessity for Further Control

It is becoming widely recognized that, in an area like the North Sea, since both water movements and fish are no respecters of man-made boundaries, any attempt to regulate the various marine activities by national governments is inadequate. In order to solve the increasingly complex problems raised by the growth of sophisticated technologies and the intensifying use of the sea and the seabed, action on an international scale is essential. At the same time, there is a need for the quality of the international action to be improved; in other words, for the process of international rule-making to become more efficient. One way which suggests itself is modification of the normal cumbrous process of bringing into force amendments to international treaties: one example of what can be done is to be found in the 1973 IMCO Pollution Convention. Under this Convention a standing committee of the parties can agree new regulations by a given majority; these will come into force within a certain period *unless* States opt out by signifying their dissent.[11] It would be possible to tighten up the opting-out procedures further – e.g., by requiring a detailed written statement of reasons – to the extent that they might well constitute a disincentive. This procedure alters the present situation where adopting any amendment requires a degree of effort from the states involved.

Another possibility that deserves more consideration is that of involving lawyers and scientists at an earlier stage in discussions of the problems which international conventions, regulations, etc. are designed to tackle. Sometimes the resolutions of international bodies which form the basis for subsequent conventions are drafted in such a way that they themselves pose legal difficulties.

[11] See Chapter IV, para. 83.

Apart from the improvement of the processes of public international law there is also the question of whether more problems could be settled by the greater use of private law – e.g., the proposal that claims over damage from pollution should be settled directly between the parties involved rather than by inter-governmental action. This could be applicable, *inter alia*, to pollution from oil rigs and fixed installations, and here it could be made a condition of the granting of a licence that the licensee should be responsible for any damage arising from leaks.

Certain questions of a practical nature would, of course, have to be grappled with. For example, would liability be imposed without proof of negligence? How would causation be established? Would public bodies be able to recover, e.g., for damage to public amenities? Could any injunctive relief be sought, or only compensation? And should there be an established fund from which compensation could be sought without having to resort to litigation? Moreover, it must be admitted that, in certain circumstances, the most efficient way of handling a multiplicity of relatively small claims is to channel them through a government. Nevertheless, there may well be scope for extending the use of private law procedures, which are often more speedy than diplomatic ones, and less dependent on the precise state of diplomatic relations between the governments concerned at the relevant time.

5. THE PROBLEM OF ENFORCEMENT

Any attempt to lay down international standards for any activity raises the problem of checking that these standards are complied with. To some extent, as far as North Sea activities are concerned, inspection can be carried out on shore – e.g. of fishing catches and navigational aids – but this obviously cannot apply to, *inter alia*, prohibited fishery areas, routeing and dumping, although in a case of pollution the co-operation of the port of loading could be invoked. In addition, NEAFC already has in operation an International Enforcement Scheme which allows the Inspectors of one country to board the fishing vessels of the others and to inspect their nets. Naval (Fishery Protection) vessels are used and the Inspectors are usually civil servants. This agreement is also acceptable to the U.S.S.R. and Poland, who are parties to it.

It has become apparent, in general, that the present reliance on flag States to enforce international regulations does not produce satisfactory results. If the flag State will not take action to punish ships involved in infringements of international regulations, the State of the port of destination should be empowered to take action instead. This needs international agreement – at present it would usually be illegal. Action would be taken against a particular ship, not a State, and would have to have regard for the due processes of law. There are difficulties about States' acting on suspicion and then substantiating their case. The principle of port State jurisdiction for purposes of checking on documents, etc. is already present in the 1973 IMCO Pollution Convention, but it depends for effectiveness on co-operation from the port of loading. Also, in view of the cost involved in modern shipping, there should be an effort to cut down delay in the necessary legal processes.

As far as Great Britain is concerned, the direct responsibility of the United Kingdom Navy at the present time lies in the area of fishery protection and mine detection but it has only partial involvement in protection of gas and oil rigs, pollution and traffic control.

Coping with the connected activities round the coasts are, at different times and for different purposes, the Department of Trade, the Department of Energy, the Department of the Environment, the Ministry of Agriculture, Fisheries and Food, the Commissioners of Northern and Irish Lights, local Harbour Boards, the Royal National Lifeboat Institution (RNLI), the Scottish Office, Trinity House, the Royal Air Force and the Royal Navy. Even the Army can be asked for help occasionally.

By the Continental Shelf Convention the United Kingdom gained jurisdiction over seabed resources in an area twice the size of these islands, 100,000 square miles in the North Sea and an equivalent area to the west.

Peacetime protection of oil rigs and platforms against terrorists must be the responsibility primarily of the companies working the deposits by the screening and checking of personnel, safety precautions, inspection rounds and well-understood and practised alarm routines; secondly, a level of military presence in the platform areas by air and surface patrols is required to deter would-be attackers and, thirdly, the facility to call on a force capable of dealing swiftly with any attack must be available.

The increasing density of traffic in focal areas, and the amount at stake if a collision occurs, has led to the introduction of traffic separation schemes, the best-known of which is in the Strait of Dover. The series of incidents in the Channel involving the *Texaco Caribbean*, the *Brandenburg* and the *Niki* in January and February 1971, with grounding, sinking and collision all playing a part, highlighted the need for traffic control – especially when the U.S. aircraft carrier *Enterprise* steered at night right through the middle of the buoys marking the wreck's position shortly afterwards. Since June 1967 a traffic separation scheme has been operating in the Strait of Dover with North-East- and South-West-going corridors and two inshore multi-directional lanes. Use of the scheme has been compulsory on all British ships since 1971.

Some 350 movements take place daily in a South-West or North-East direction and up to 200 cross the Channel. About 35 ships a day do not observe the rules, two particularly difficult areas being the boundary between the South-West-going lane and the English Inshore Zone, and the area north of Sandettie where the North-going deep-draught vessels are permitted to cross over into the South-West-going lane to obtain sufficient water. The Anglo-French Safety of Navigation Group (AFSONG) exists to co-ordinate plans to widen and modernize the surveillance and broadcast facilities but, whatever form this eventually takes, some kind of physical presence will be required in the lanes to deter would-be transgressors or, if deterrence fails, to identify them. Coastal minesweepers, inshore minesweepers, hovercraft, patrol craft, helicopters and fixed-wing aircraft have all been provided for trial purposes to "police" this scheme, and currently two Coastguard ships, a Sea Devon and a coastal minesweeper, are engaged periodically in the task.

Co-ordination between the authorities concerned has improved and representatives of all interested parties in the United Kingdom meet in the AFSONG and SAR (Search and Rescue) Committees, including members from Trinity House and the RNLI.

The need for greater surveillance of a whole range of marine activities is being increasingly recognized; but the only available bodies for carrying out this task – modern navies – do not have the resources for this role either in terms of equipment, small suitable ships in sufficient numbers, or of trained manpower. At present, moreover, there is no existing organizational framework or system of command and control which would enable such surveillance to be carried out completely effectively, either from the military or civil angle. It is, of course, obvious that oil rigs and installations will offer a tempting target for disaffected groups or individuals attempting to exert political or economic pressure, and it would therefore seem desirable that, as far as is possible, security precautions should be built into the operating system of the installations. The possibility of flexible response to contingency demands must also be developed.

Since 1973, more than one British report has been produced recommending that the Navy should play a greater role in maintaining North Sea activities – partly to protect off-shore installations against sabotage or acts of piracy, which at least conforms to its traditional defence role – but also to exercise surveillance over pollution, dumping and fishery regulations which are essentially civil matters. The Navy has indicated that it does not, at present, have the facilities, but there is little likelihood that there will be either an allowance in the defence estimates for new equipment or the setting up of a new civil authority.[12] It is, in any case, doubtful whether

---

[12] In February 1975, after this study was completed, the British Government announced proposals for additional measures aimed at "the protection of the growing number of offshore oil and gas installations from accidental or malicious damage". The proposals included the construction of five new Royal Navy ships, to enter service in 1977, and the provision of up to four aircraft, also in 1977, to carry out surveillance of offshore waters. Meanwhile, the Royal Navy will use an ocean-going tug, to be modified for its new tasks, and will take on loan a fishery protection vessel, similarly modified, from the Department of Agriculture and Fisheries for Scotland. These measures, however, seem grossly inadequate.

such a policing task is best carried out by a military body or by single States. In spite of the difficulties in securing agreement for an international policing body, this would seem to be the most efficient and neutral means of securing compliance with international regulations. It might begin through reciprocal inspection arrangements, based on existing provisions for boarding and inspection (already included in the United Kingdom Dumping at Sea Act, 1974, and the powers given to the Fisheries Protection Service), but if this task is to be carried out comprehensively it will require: (a) administrative machinery: a body with separate divisions for fishing, pollution, traffic routeing; (b) purpose-built "hardware": a number of small ships with sufficient speed and with the necessary scientific equipment for monitoring. In terms of organization and cost it seems most logical to give this authority to an international body. This would result in economies of scale and would considerably increase the chances of detecting offences, compared with a system where only the flag State can carry out the necessary investigations. But there are technical and legal difficulties in actually forcing a ship to stop on the high seas and States need to agree to prosecute ships which *fail to respond* to a challenge to stop.

Co-ordination of Environmental Management

(a) International Co-ordination

Apart from the possibilities of direct international action, a most important influence which could be brought to bear on governments by international bodies might take the form of proposals designed to harmonize their practices of environmental management. This is in many ways implicit in much of the EEC's environmental action plan. At present the North Sea States have very differently divided responsibilities for environmental planning – some, such as Norway, the United Kingdom and France have Ministries of the Environment; Belgium has a Ministerial Co-ordinating Committee on the Environment; in the Federal Republic of Germany the responsibility for environmental affairs rests largely at the level of the Länder.

One can immediately see the difficulties even at the bilateral level, for example, between neighbours like France, with a very centralized government, and Federal Germany, with much greater regional autonomy. Even where Ministries of the Environment exist, their origins and/or composition may be very different – in the United Kingdom the Department of the Environment brought together major departments of Housing, Transport and Public Buildings and Works, and consequently has wide (and sometimes incompatible) responsibilities. In France the Ministry for the Protection of Nature and the Environment was formed from the Ministry of Industrial Development, the Ministry of Agriculture and the Ministry of Cultural Affairs, and its responsibilities are more focused on preventing pollution and protecting natural resources and beauty spots.

At international meetings these different backgrounds are not too apparent, partly because delegations are rarely composed of officials from single ministries, but they undoubtedly have their effect at the national level. It would, of course, be impossible to ensure that all Ministers of the Environment, even in the same country, carried equal weight. One further obstacle to integrated planning is that, as ministerial appointments change, the centres of influence within a cabinet can shift radically.

The various European organizations to which North Sea States belong – the OECD, the Council of Europe, NATO (CCMS), the Nordic Council, the United Nations Economic Commission for Europe and the EEC – have all adopted programmes of study of environmental problems, and in other fields some of these bodies, notably the EEC, have been successful in formulating recommendations for international standards which have been ultimately accepted by governments. As far as the North Sea is concerned, however, only ICES has produced hard facts on an international basis. But now, in order to prevent overlap and to ensure compatibility of results, the OECD, already involved, is collaborating with ICES. The problem lies in converting the mass of information and expertise available into measures which governments agree to implement. One difficulty is undoubtedly the proliferation of organizations and meetings – every international body has felt bound to involve itself in the discussion of the environment, and governments, particularly European governments, in turn feel bound to involve themselves in the discussion in every forum. As long as this pressure persists, the sheer effort of keeping up with information flow and the schedule of meetings must prevent governments from sufficiently considering their own environmental management structures, let alone how they could be harmonized with those of other North Sea or European States, but this would be perhaps *the* most constructive contribution which they could make.

One suggestion might be that the European Economic Community and the Council of Europe should announce their intention of taking active steps to harmonize the practice of environmental management between the North Sea countries, and at the same time promote discussions between governments and the secretariats of the different organizations in the field, with a view to combining programmes of work and reducing the number of inter-governmental bodies involved. This would admittedly call for a rare form of self-denying ordinance from the bodies involved but matters have now reached a stage where the idea has been voiced, not entirely flippantly, that any organization which announced its intention of leaving the environment alone would be much more likely to secure a budget increase and other forms of support than if it proposed an extension to its programme. In any case, to connect these two proposals would give governments a forceful incentive to agree to discussions about their own machinery. Furthermore, a thorough overall examination of all the work at present being done would reveal whether international machinery for co-ordination which might be more fully utilized already exists. The most encouraging development is that, as more and more information comes to light, governments are becoming increasingly aware of the incapacity of any one State to control the sort of problems that arise in an area such as the North Sea.

(b) National Co-ordination[13]

On the national front the problem is rather one of considering whether the various administrative and political responsibilities are exercised at the right level, whether there are gaps and duplications or even conflicts between the different levels, and whether these could be mitigated by greater parliamentary involvement and public participation. Connected with these questions is that of the availability of the necessary information for decision-making, including the organization and commissioning of research. Another cause of difficulties and possible confusion is the constant change of ministerial structure such as has occurred in the United Kingdom over the past few years.

One issue which undoubtedly needs further examination is the relationship between government and industry as far as environmental policy is concerned. The one general principle which has been adopted by many governments, the EEC and the OECD – the so-called "Polluter Pays Principle" – sounds unimpeachable, but has proved far from satisfactory in practice. Pollution is not eliminated but merely penalized and, as the cost to industry is passed on to the consumer in the price of the final product, it is the consumer, not the polluter, who, in fact, does the paying. The point can be made that, should the penalty thus passed on result in pricing the product out of the market, the manufacturer would have the strongest incentive to seek a cheap pollution-free process as an alternative to not being able to produce the goods at all, this could be regarded as a form of licensing by the market. The objection is that there is increasing evidence to show that, in the mixed economy prevailing today, market prices alone seldom achieve their purpose. It is, however, obvious that, if the principle that the polluter must pay is accepted, international bodies must harmonize the law in order to eliminate unfair competition. It is not possible to make a neat economic equation: rate of tax=marginal social cost of economic pollution, and the polluter is not able to insure against the cost of "P.P.P." since he does not know in advance what this will be. Under the circumstances the situation might be improved if the risk were

---

[13] The study addresses itself here chiefly to the situation in the United Kingdom but, on the evidence available, the kind of problem is likely to be common to the other countries under consideration.

to be estimated by experienced "risk assessors" and the cost of insurance included in product cost. What is required is a system of incentives for the invention of processes that are both cheap and clean. The Third Report of the United Kingdom Royal Commission on Environmental Pollution[14] recommends the "licensing" of pollution, with varying charges depending on where and to what extent the pollution occurs, so that competition would force manufacturers to develop pollution-free processes.

This, however, is only one aspect of environmental issues. Government and industry occasionally appear to be united against outside enquiries; on other occasions industry feels under attack from government as much as from the public at large. It should be possible to evolve a more positive joint approach – even perhaps involving some kind of encouraging gesture on the lines of the Queen's Award to Industry – which would show that there was active co-operation between the two in identifying and working out solutions to the range of environmental problems, since in the end it is to industry that we must look for such solutions.

In a number of activities there appears to be a real gap between the central government and local authorities. For example, for North Sea exploration the granting of licences by the government results in large-scale industrial activity in hitherto small communities. While they may welcome the opportunities that such a development brings the local authorities may well find difficulty in meeting the problems of housing and other support services raised by an influx of outside workers, as well as the longer-term consequences of what is probably only a temporary "boom". The problem is complicated by the fact that the companies involved in the oil exploration are anxious to get on with the job as far as possible without restriction, even from central government. There seems here to be a lack of more regional arrangements for planning and consultation, such as exist in the United States where, admittedly, the tradition of regional organization is very much stronger.[15]

It is possible that the recent major re-organization of local authorities into fewer and larger units may help in redressing the balance, although it is inevitable that some anomalies will remain. An important development in the field of pollution control and sewage treatment is the creation of new water authorities, such as the Thames Water Board, which took over powers from the old local bodies at the same time as local government itself was re-organized. Even so, it has not proved possible to put each major estuary under the control of a single authority; so that arrangements for consultation and joint authority will still be necessary. This illustrates the difficulties of rational management.

[14] *Pollution in Some British Estuaries and Coastal Waters*, H.M.S.O. (Cmnd. 5054), September 1972.
[15] See Report by a Committee of the Oil Development Council for Scotland, *North Sea Oil and the Environment* (1974).

In other cases, the gap in authority appears to be more one of simple omission. Thus the provisions of the Town and Country Planning Act, 1971, stop at the low-tide mark. Any question of, for example, extending the National Nature Reserves beyond the low-tide mark would involve changes in legislation. There is no legislation for underwater parks. The best solution would probably be for the Town and Country Planning Act to be extended to the edge of the Continental Shelf. Again, responsibility for berthing, etc., surveys and the preparation of navigational charts rests with the Navy under the Ministry of Defence. There is no civil authority in this field, apart from the hydrographic offices of various port authorities, although the information produced is widely used, especially by other government departments with responsibilities concerning floods, storm surges and estimates of sea levels in the North Sea. Thus, the Ministry of Agriculture, Fisheries and Food (MAFF) is responsible for inland and coastal flooding within the limits of its authority, including the Thames flood warning survey, and the Department of the Environment has responsibility for ports, approaches, harbours and coastal defences. It is possible that a cut in military expenditure may affect the charting work of the Navy with considerable consequences for the civilian users who rely on it. Here there seems to be a case for some kind of joint departmental control. The 1973 Report of the Hydrographer of the Navy indeed claimed that too little money was being spent on defence, "which is the premier traditional role of the hydrographic service", but, at the same time, emphasized that the hydrographic service has a national function beyond the narrower concepts of defence. The Report mentions that "Many of our charts are obsolete. Huge parts of the world's seas remain unsurveyed. Thematic maps of the seabed hardly exist. Approaches to some of our emerging ports are virtually uncharted,"[16] and it goes on to say "We are not meeting the growing needs of either our yachtsmen or our fishermen. We are not providing adequately for future navigational techniques. We are not exploiting the enormous opportunities open to us in expanding markets for new products, our resources in ships and manpower are insufficient." It would seem that a strong case could be made for the creation of a civilian Hydrographic Office since, in the existing situation, the preponderant need for accurate and extensive charts lies with civilian vessels.

Difficulties can also arise over demarcation lines between different authorities, even when the responsibilities seem fairly well defined. The Department of Trade, for example, controls off-shore navigation and passage through the English Channel, while Trinity House, the Port of London Authority and the Thames Water Board control the mouth of the Thames and the approaches. Trinity House has responsibility for all buoys, lighthouses and beacons, the Port of London Authority is answerable for navigation and oil pollution and the Thames Water Board deals with all

[16] This also applies internationally.

other forms of pollution. That the lines of control can become tangled would appear obvious.[17]

In this context it will probably suffice to emphasize that, as things stand, even when dealing with essentially practical and technical matters, there are necessarily failures of communication.

It is at the central government level that demarcation problems are at their most serious and can indeed affect the efficient devolution of authority to a more local level. It is not so much a case of administrative overlap: indeed, on the whole, administrative responsibility is very clearly divided and supervised by a considerable inter-departmental machinery. The problems arise more in subjects in which a number of Ministries have legitimate interests and which require major study – of which environmental matters present probably the finest example. Practically all the major issues require a great deal of research and study which will, in turn, determine the kind of policy decisions that are eventually made. Most of these issues are interconnected and cannot properly be separated, so that there is a clear need for an overall strategic approach to longer planned government research. However, since 1972 (following the Rothschild Report), each Ministry acts completely independently and controls its own funds for research and development. This means that it is very difficult to ascertain exactly what research is taking place, and at what cost. More than one department may easily cover the same ground in its work as areas of research overlap and/or compete due to lack of liaison. In consequence, the understanding of the full range of any problem becomes practically impossible. What is needed is the creation of some body with responsibilities for inter-ministerial co-ordination on research, so that everyone knows who is doing what and, as far as possible, the department best equipped for a particular project finds itself carrying it out. This kind of direction is not possible at the inter-departmental official level, but requires an overriding authority such as the Cabinet Office.

Another important point is that there is a wide range of outside scientific bodies which are in a position to make a major contribution to the information available to the government in the environmental field. The only chance for representations from such bodies to have any impact is for there to be a single focal point where they can be directed. At present, with the exception of Royal Commissions, outside scientific expertise is commissioned by individual departments, in many cases imposing a very great burden in time and commitments on those concerned. As the subject is so amorphous and ill-defined it is most necessary at the same time to organize research as efficiently as possible, and to avoid sharp and artificial divisions of responsibility. A similar situation probably prevails in other North Sea States.

[17] The authority of the Port of London Authority extends from the North Foreland to Falmouth and covers approaches to ports.

SUMMARY AND RECOMMENDATIONS

Apart from the question of the best way to channel outside expert opinion into government planning, the wider issue of communication between government and the public at large is one which needs examination, specifically in terms of whether there might be changes which would improve the efficiency of decision-making. As a starting point the common civil service view is that unsolicited intervention by outside elements can only hinder and slow down this process: indeed this tends to be an article of faith which has a profound effect on the way every department is run. In argument much is occasionally made of the idea that there is a general demand for "wider public participation" in government, with the implication that this would mean some kind of direct involvement: in fact, it seems highly unlikely that any demand of this kind exists, but what *does* exist is a sense of unnecessary exclusion from information. When provision is made for government proposals to be explained and for the interested public to express its views, as in public inquiries, the conduct of the inquiries and the treatment of their findings do not always serve to encourage public confidence.

The civil service bias towards secrecy is reflected in its undoubted overclassification of information, recognized as a fault within the civil service itself, but apparently ineradicable. Clearly there is much which has to be kept confidential, but the tendency is to put a "restricted" distribution on the most neutral, factual reports which automatically prevents their contents from being made available. This may be due partly to the circumstance, discussed above, that research is commissioned entirely by individual departments, so that there is a sense of a particular interest in the findings. Nevertheless, there is a case for freer access by the public, whether technicians or laymen, to information available on the environmental effects of various activities; and much of this information must already be held within the technical divisions of the various Ministries involved.

[On the other hand, all technical information collected by MAFF as a result of research with regard to fisheries and the marine environment can be published and most of it does, in fact, appear in the form of scientific reports.]

A particular problem concerns the confidentiality of information provided by industry: there seems to be some shift of opinion about circumstances where it should be preserved. For example, on water pollution control, the 1961 Act protects the confidentiality of information supplied to River Authorities; but the Prevention of Pollution Act, 1974, removes this protection, following recommendation (from both the Jeger Committee and the Royal Commission on Environmental Pollution) that, in the public interest, there should be a full disclosure of effluents. There are obviously cases where confidentiality must be respected, and these should be clearly spelled out for the benefit of all.

One way in which an unblocking of the flow of information might be achieved could be through a greater measure of parliamentary involvement, for example in the form of a Permanent Committee on the Maritime Environment of the United Kingdom. A possible model would be the President's Council on Environmental Quality in the United States, already mentioned on p. 222, with powers to investigate and report; though transferring this body to the United Kingdom would probably mean that it would have to be a Committee of the Privy Council. For this purpose a Parliamentary Select Committee would not be suitable since it would not enjoy continuity or be appropriate to carry out the functions of a partly executive body. It might be appropriate for such a Permanent Committee to consider ways in which public hearings concerning proposals for, or objections to, particular activities in the waters around the United Kingdom could be improved and extended. This is, in any case, a matter which needs examination by some body with powers to make recommendations that have a chance of being adopted.

There is, in general, also scope for a wider use of Parliamentary Select Committees, with the important proviso that, while they should represent a high degree of knowledge and expertise, they should not be focussed on matters which are, for example, the concern of a single government department. Greater parliamentary involvement of this kind could be one way of forcing the integrated approach which this study advocates. Again, these comments concern conditions in the United Kingdom but a similar situation probably prevails in most, if not all, of the North Sea States concerned.

6. REGIONAL REGIMES

Given a relatively self-contained area, such as the North Sea, and the prior existence of a number of regional organizations in the area, there would seem a clear case for trying to solve the North Sea's problems as far as possible on a regional basis. The bordering States are relatively few in number and have in common the problems arising from an advanced state of industrial development. However, it has been argued that a regional approach which does not come under the aegis of a general international body is really no more than "disguised unilateralism", and that in international terms there is no difference between a group of States' acting contrary to general international law, and a single State's doing so. One solution might be for minimum rules and standards to be agreed by a general body, with provision for more stringent regional action. An alternative approach could take the form of an agreement to withhold support facilities from vessels of other States which did not conform to the region's standards on pollution, safe construction, etc., very much on the lines of the provisions of the Pirate Broadcasting Agreement.[18] This

[18] See Chapter IV, para. 135.

approach would be more likely to command acceptance than would any attempt to manage that area more or less as a closed sea through enforcing the acceptance of a set of rules before allowing outsiders to enter; although, of course, the problem of enforcement cannot be avoided and will be discussed further below.

There remains, however, the problem of what regional organizations should be involved. The closest grouping to "North Sea membership" is that of the EEC, which includes all North Sea States with the exception of Norway, although three EEC members (Ireland, Italy and Luxembourg) are not North Sea States. But even without membership problems, and the additional need to involve States from outside the area with significant interest in particular activities (e.g. the U.S.S.R., Poland and East Germany where fishing is concerned), it is important to take into account the real political barriers which would prevent the EEC from exercising the kind of control in the North Sea that it might appear at least potentially able to carry out. For example, it is highly unlikely that the members with important off-shore mineral resources, notably the United Kingdom and the Netherlands, would be prepared to accept any greater EEC jurisdiction over their area of continental shelf, although this, of course, might depend on the purpose for which the jurisdiction is sought. Since there are already a number of well-established European organizations, many of which have initiated studies and projects on various aspects of the North Sea, the temptation is to concentrate attention upon their structure and how their *modus operandi* could be adapted or enlarged to enable them to carry out the agreed necessary measures of control of activities in the area. But the more fruitful approach is to begin with the need for regional arrangements and to go on to consider what form of grouping or structure would be most likely to be able to deal effectively with the many and varied problems involved.

7. RECOMMENDATIONS

In the light of these considerations and of the other aspects of the subject dealt with more fully in the previous chapters, the Study Group feels that a number of points of substance have emerged. More particularly as set out, there are obviously problems which are not adequately dealt with, either by the existing methods of control or by the generally accepted international rules and regulations. Clearly some of the recent developments, technical and other, in the exploitation of the resources of the North Sea require the creation of new machinery. The Group has therefore embodied its conclusions in the form of a number of Recommendations which it is thought might lead to the establishment of a more generally satisfactory regime for the North Sea, seen as a single unit.

It is proposed that:

A. (1) A Standing Conference of North Sea States should be created by international agreement between them; the EEC and the Council of Europe could also be separate parties, or have corporate participation.

(2) The aims of the Conference should be expressed to be:
   (a) to act as a channel of communication between governments, parliaments, scientists and technicians;
   (b) to collect information and build up a body of knowledge on North Sea activities, and particularly the use of its resources, in the air, waters and seabed, and the resulting problems;
   (c) to further co-operation and harmonization of practice between States in research and development, resource use and management, and legislative policy;
   (d) to provide means of co-ordination of the relevant work of existing organizations, governmental and non-governmental, national and international.

(3) The sphere of operations of the Conference should include fisheries; conservation and management of seabed resources and other marine resources; control and elimination of pollution; sea transport; and air transport in so far as it affects the North Sea.

(4) The Standing Conference might itself meet at Ministerial level every two or three years but it should, in general, function through Committees or working groups, and the greatest possible use should be made of existing organizations, as indicated in paragraph 2(d) above. It must be emphasized that the Conference is *not* to be regarded as a new international body, with executive powers, but a medium of co-ordination, an "umbrella" organization. It would need to be serviced by a bureau or secretariat, which could be administratively incorporated in the EEC or the Council of Europe.

(5) The meetings of the Standing Conference, and those organized through it, should take different forms according to their objects and the matters to be dealt with. The periodic meetings of the Standing Conference itself should deal with broad issues of policy in the light of developments since the last meeting and of future needs. Meetings would also be organized, for example:
   (a) at Ministerial level for such matters as fisheries and seabed resource management;
   (b) at the scientific level for questions involving, e.g., marine biology, pollution standards, climatic change;
   (c) at the technical level for mining techniques and navigation (separation of traffic, etc.).

SUMMARY AND RECOMMENDATIONS

Care should be taken, however, that at the meetings of the Conference and in the activities of all committees, working groups and other bodies, there is representation of all the requisite kinds of expertise, including legal. Further, the participation of parliamentarians should be encouraged as far as practicable.

(6) In the United Kingdom it would be desirable to set up a Permanent Committee and one or more Parliamentary Committees, covering various aspects of uses of the North Sea, with "feedback" from and to the Standing Conference. These should be supported by inter-departmental committees. Parliamentary Committees would ensure exchanges of information, cross-fertilization of ideas and more effective public control of governmental and industrial policies.

(7) The territorial scope of the Standing Conference should be the North Sea basin. The area covered by the North East Atlantic Fisheries Commission and ICES is much wider, but it would be desirable that the Commission and ICES, in pursuing their normal activities, should, as far as the North Sea basin is concerned, collaborate with the Standing Conference.

B. Each North Sea State should enact legislation requiring that, before *any* project involving activity in or under the North Sea is licensed or initiated, an environmental impact statement should be prepared and published. This statement should be subject to full investigation, with free public participation at the scientific level, and the Standing Conference should have an opportunity through a working group to advise the government or governments concerned before a decision on the project is taken.

C. There should be machinery established for checking and co-ordinating the enforcement of existing and future international conventions or other agreements governing uses of the North Sea.

It should be borne in mind that if the 200-mile Exclusive Economic Zone finally receives general acceptance by the Law of the Sea Conference, the effect would be to turn the North Sea into an enclosed area as far as fisheries and its other resources are concerned. The 200-mile limit would also have the effect of extending state jurisdiction and the machinery would therefore exist for enforcing fishery regulations. Rights of navigation could be somewhat affected (particularly in relation to pollution control measures) by the establishment of such a zone, as they might also be by acceptance of a 12-mile breadth for the territorial sea. It would be preferable for any such extension to take place by agreement, if at all possible. The alternative could be a slide into unilateralism and possible anarchy.

The present situation with regard to pollution is highly unsatisfactory. There is no generally agreed procedure for inspection for infringement of pollution regulations by ships outside territorial waters and there are legal and practical difficulties in enforcing these regulations against ships flying the flag of States outside the region. However, nothing would prevent coastal States from exercising jurisdiction to the full in respect of breaches of pollution regulations (including regulations about construction of ships and methods of handling pollutants) committed within their territorial or internal waters. Secondly, since, with certain exceptions already noted, States are free to prohibit access to their ports and internal waters, the coastal State could always refuse to grant access to a ship which could be shown to have violated the relevant regulations on the high seas. These may well be a useful deterrent since, in general, ships do not enter the North Sea unless they intend to put into port there. Prohibiting unloading and/or sale of cargo is a further possibility.

A further and more effective way of coping with these problems would be for the navies of North Sea States to be given the power, by a treaty in which all flag States also participated, to inspect ships for violations on the high seas and possibly to punish them as well. In such a case it might be best for these powers to be exercised by a joint policing unit rather than by individual navies (see below). But, politically, the likelihood of flag States' assenting to such an extension of coastal State jurisdiction seems, at any rate for the moment, somewhat remote.

In the event of such agreement in principle, it would remain to establish means of effective control of ships breaking agreed laws and regulations on fishing, polluting, and dumping prohibited chemicals. In the absence of such agreement, control might be exercised by the application of economic sanctions by:

(a) prohibiting access to ports;
(b) prohibiting unloading of cargoes.

An International Economic Committee to study the economic aspects of the problems could be set up by the Standing Conference.

It is therefore recommended that:

(1) A general level at which enforcement measures become operative should be established.
(2) Serious and deliberate pollution should be held to be analogous to piracy and be subject to similar enforcement measures.
(3) There should be a right of arrest of offenders on the high seas.[19]
(4) It should be possible to recover damages, or apply criminal law, when a ship is caught polluting on the high seas.

[19] It is realized that this might well pose difficulties in carrying out and it also presupposes a fairly extensive surveillance system. It is also clear that, as far as dumping at sea is concerned, there must be agreed inspection of ships.

(5) Where coastal pollution from industrial plants is concerned, in the case of persistent offenders, and in the last resort, there should be power to order the closure of the plant.[20]

(6) Discharge or escape of oil from oil rigs or installations should be subject to the same penalties as those which apply to discharge of oil from ships.

D. The creation of a joint North Sea Policing Service is proposed. There would seem to be two alternative methods open:

(1) to organize an international civil policing force based on existing Coastguard units with adequate vessels equipped with the latest electronic devices. The service would require an air arm, possibly of helicopters; or

(2) to assign the task to a joint naval force, assisted by a joint air force unit. This would probably imply seconding vessels and men to a special naval enforcement unit. The policing force could well operate under the control of the North Sea Standing Conference.

E. *At the United Kingdom national level*, it is further recommended:

(1) That further research into the problems raised by the optimum use of the resources of the North Sea should be urgently undertaken.

(2) That such research should be co-ordinated in order to avoid wasteful overlapping and duplication. This requires the creation of a body with responsibility for inter-departmental collaboration at Cabinet Office level.

(3) That information should be more readily accessible to government departments, interested organizations and the general public, whose welfare is intimately involved. The factor of confidentiality of reports should be reduced to the lowest possible level.

(4) That communication between the government and the public at large should be greatly improved.

---

[20] In the United Kingdom certain powers to do this already exist.

Appendix I

Principal Relevant Treaties in Force

Convention on the High Seas: adopted at Geneva, 29 April 1958; entered into force 30 September 1962.

TERRITORIAL SEA AND THE CONTINENTAL SHELF
Convention on the Territorial Sea and Contiguous Zone: Geneva, 29 April 1958; entered into force 10 September 1964. Norway and the Federal Republic of Germany are non-parties and several other parties have made far-reaching reservations.

Convention on the Continental Shelf: Geneva, 29 April 1958; entered into force 10 June 1964. Of the North Sea states, Belgium and the Federal Republic of Germany are not parties.

Denmark/United Kingdom Agreement relating to the Delimitation of the Continental Shelf between the Two Countries: London, 25 November 1971; entered into force 7 December 1972.

Federal Republic of Germany/United Kingdom Agreement relating to the Delimitation of the Continental Shelf under the North Sea between the Two Countries: London, 25 November 1971; entered into force 7 December 1972.

Netherlands/United Kingdom Agreement relating to the Delimitation of the Continental Shelf under the North Sea between the Two Countries: London, 6 October 1965; entered into force 23 December 1966. Amended 1971.

Netherlands/United Kingdom Agreement relating to the Exploitation of Single Geological Structures Extending across the Dividing Line on the Continental Shelf under the North Sea: London, 6 October 1965; entered into force 23 December 1966.

Norway/United Kingdom Agreement relating to the Delimitation of the North Sea between the Two Countries: London, 10 March 1965; entered into force 29 June 1965.

Denmark/Federal Republic of Germany Treaty relating to the Delimitation of the Continental Shelf under the North Sea: Copenhagen, 28 January 1971; entered into force 7 December 1972.

Denmark/Federal Republic of Germany Agreement and Protocol concerning the Delimitation in Coastal Areas of the Continental Shelf of the North Sea: Bonn, 9 June 1965; entered into force 27 May 1966.

Denmark/Federal Republic of Germany/Netherlands Protocol to the Agreements Delimiting the Continental Shelf in the North Sea: Copenhagen, 28 January 1971.

Denmark/Norway Agreement on the Delimitation of the Continental Shelf between the Two Countries: Oslo, 8 December 1965; entered into force 22 June 1966. Amended 1968.

Federal Republic of Germany/Netherlands Treaty relating to the Delimitation of the Continental Shelf under the North Sea: Copenhagen, 28 January 1971; entered into force 7 December 1972.

Federal Republic of Germany/Netherlands Treaty concerning the Lateral Delimitation of the Continental Shelf in the Vicinity of the Coast: Bonn, 1 December 1964; entered into force 18 September 1965.

Norway/Sweden Agreement on the Delimitation of the Continental Shelf: Stockholm, 24 July 1968; entered into force 18 March 1969.

FISHING AND FISHING LIMITS

Convention on Fishing and Conservation of the Living Resources of the High Seas: Geneva, 29 April 1958; entered into force 20 March 1966. Of the North Sea states, the Federal Republic of Germany and Norway are not parties.

North-East Atlantic Fisheries Convention: London, 24 January 1959; entered into force 15 March 1966.

Convention on the Conduct of Fishing Operations in the North Atlantic: 1 June 1967; not yet in force.

European Fisheries Convention: London, 9 March 1964; entered into force 15 March 1966.

United Kingdom/U.S.S.R. Exchange of Notes Constituting an Agreement on Matters arising from the Establishment by the United Kingdom of a Fishery Regime provided for by the Fishery Limits Act, 1964: Moscow, 30 September 1964; entered into force on the same date.

United Kingdom/Norway Fishery Agreement: Oslo, 17 November 1960; entered into force 3 March 1961.

United Kingdom/Norway Agreement for the Continuance of Fishing by Norwegian Vessels within the Fishery Limits of the United Kingdom: London, 28 September 1964; entered into force 11 March 1965.

United Kingdom/Poland Exchange of Notes regarding the Rights to be accorded to Polish Vessels within the British Fishery Limits to be established on 30 September 1964: Warsaw, 26 September 1964; entered into force on the same date.

Denmark/Norway/Sweden Agreement concerning Measures for the Protection of the Stock of Deep Sea Prawns, European Lobsters, Norway Lobsters and Crabs: Oslo, 7 March 1952; entered into force 26 January 1953. Amended by Protocol, 14 October 1959; in force same date.

Norway/U.S.S.R. Agreement concerning the Handling of Claims in Connection with Damage to Fishing Gear: Moscow, 9 December 1959; entered into force 1 January 1960.

POLLUTION BY OIL
International Convention for the Prevention of Pollution of the Sea by Oil: London, 12 May 1954; entered into force 26 July 1958. Amended in 1962 and 1969. Also amended in 1971, though this amendment is not yet in force.

International Convention relating to Intervention on the High Seas in Cases of Oil Pollution Casualties: Brussels, 29 November 1969; not yet in force.

International Convention on Civil Liability for Oil Pollution Damage (Private Law Convention): Brussels, 29 November 1969; not yet in force.

International Convention for the Prevention of Pollution from Ships: London, 15 January 1974; not yet in force.

International Convention on the Establishment of an International Fund for Compensation for Oil Pollution Damage: Brussels, 18 December 1971; not yet in force.

Agreement for Co-operation in Dealing with Pollution of the North Sea by Oil: Bonn, 9 June 1969; entered into force 9 August 1969.

Tanker Owners' Voluntary Agreement concerning Liability for Oil Pollution: 7 June 1969; entered into force 18 September 1969.

Denmark/Finland/Norway/Sweden Agreement concerning Co-operation in Taking Measures against Pollution of the Sea by Oil: Copenhagen, 16 September 1971; entered into force 16 October 1971.

Norway/United Kingdom Agreement relating to the Transmission of Petroleum from the Ekofisk Field and Neighbouring Areas to the United Kingdom: Oslo, 22 May 1973; entered into force on the same date.

POLLUTION BY NUCLEAR WASTE
Convention on Civil Liability for Nuclear Damage: Vienna, 21 May 1963; not yet in force.

Convention on Third Party Liability in the Field of Nuclear Energy: Paris, 29 July 1960; entered into force 1 April 1968.

Convention relating to Civil Liability in the Field of Maritime Carriage of Nuclear Material: Brussels, 17 December 1971; not yet in force.

United Kingdom/U.S.A. Exchange of Notes constituting an Agreement relating to the Use of United Kingdom Ports and Territorial Waters by the N.S. Savannah: London, 19 June 1964; entered into force on the same date.

Treaty Banning Nuclear Weapon Tests in the Atmosphere, in Outer Space and Under Water: Moscow, 5 August 1963; in force 10 October 1963.

Treaty on the Prohibition of the Emplacement of Nuclear Weapons and Other Weapons of Mass Destruction on the Seabed and the Ocean Floor and in the Subsoil thereof: Moscow, 11 February 1971; entered into force 18 May 1972.

Convention on the Liability of Operators of Nuclear Ships: Brussels, 25 May 1962; not yet in force.

POLLUTION—GENERAL
Convention for the Prevention of Marine Pollution by Dumping from Ships and Aircraft: Oslo, 15 February 1972; entered into force 7 April 1974. Of the North Sea states, Denmark and Norway are the only parties so far.

Convention on the Prevention of Marine Pollution by Dumping of Wastes and other Matter: London, 29 December 1972; not yet in force.

European Agreement on the Restriction on the Use of Certain Detergents in Washing and Cleaning Products: Strasbourg, 16 September 1968; in force 16 February 1971. Of the North Sea states, Belgium, the Federal Republic of Germany, the Netherlands and the United Kingdom are parties.

Agreement on the Implementation of a European Project on Pollution on the Topic of "Sewage Sludge Processing": Brussels, 23 November 1971; entered into force 1 August 1972.

Convention for the Prevention of Marine Pollution from Land-based Sources: Paris, 4 June 1974; not yet in force.

SAFETY, TRAFFIC AND ROUTEING*
International Convention for the Safety of Life at Sea: London, 17 June 1960; entered into force 26 May 1965. All six North Sea states are parties.

International Convention on Certain Rules concerning Civil Jurisdiction in Matters of Collision: Brussels, 10 May 1952; entered into force 14 September 1955.

International Convention for the Unification of Certain Rules relating to Penal Jurisdiction in Matters of Collision or other Incidents of Navigation: Brussels, 10 May 1952; entered into force 20 November 1955.

* Routeing regulations, now part of the national law of both England and France, are in operation in the Strait of Dover, and an International Convention is being formulated.

Convention on the Facilitation of Maritime Traffic: London, 9 April 1965; entered into force 5 March 1967. Amended 1971.

International Regulations for Preventing Collisions at Sea: London, 17 June 1960; entered into force 1 September 1965.

Convention on the International Regulations for Preventing Collisions at Sea: London, 20 October 1972; not yet in force.

Agreement concerning Uniform Rules for the Marking of Navigable Waters: Denmark/Finland/Norway/Sweden. Helsinki, 18 September 1962; entered into force 18 October 1962.

MISCELLANEOUS
International Convention on Load Lines: London, 5 April 1966; entered into force 21 July 1968. Amendments to this Convention, agreed in 1971, are not yet in force.

Convention for the Protection of Submarine Cables: Paris, 14 March 1884; entered into force 1 May 1888.

International Convention relating to the Arrest of Sea-going Ships: Brussels, 10 May 1952; entered into force 24 February 1956.

Convention and Statute on Freedom of Transit: Barcelona, 20 April 1921; entered into force 31 October 1922.

Convention and Statute on the International Regime of Maritime Ports: Geneva, 9 December 1923, entered into force 26 July 1926.

International Convention relating to the Limitation of Liability of Owners of Sea-going Ships: Brussels, 10 October 1957; entered into force 31 May 1968.

Convention on the Protection of the Marine Environment of the Baltic Sea Area: Helsinki, 1974; not yet in force.

Convention on the Protection of the Environment between Denmark, Finland, Norway and Sweden: Stockholm, 1974; not yet in force.

Convention for a Uniform System of Tonnage Measurement of Ships: Oslo, 10 June 1947; in force 30 December 1954.

Optional Protocol of Signature concerning the Compulsory Settlement of Disputes arising from the Law of the Sea Conventions: Geneva, 29 April 1958; entered into force 30 September 1962.

Appendix II

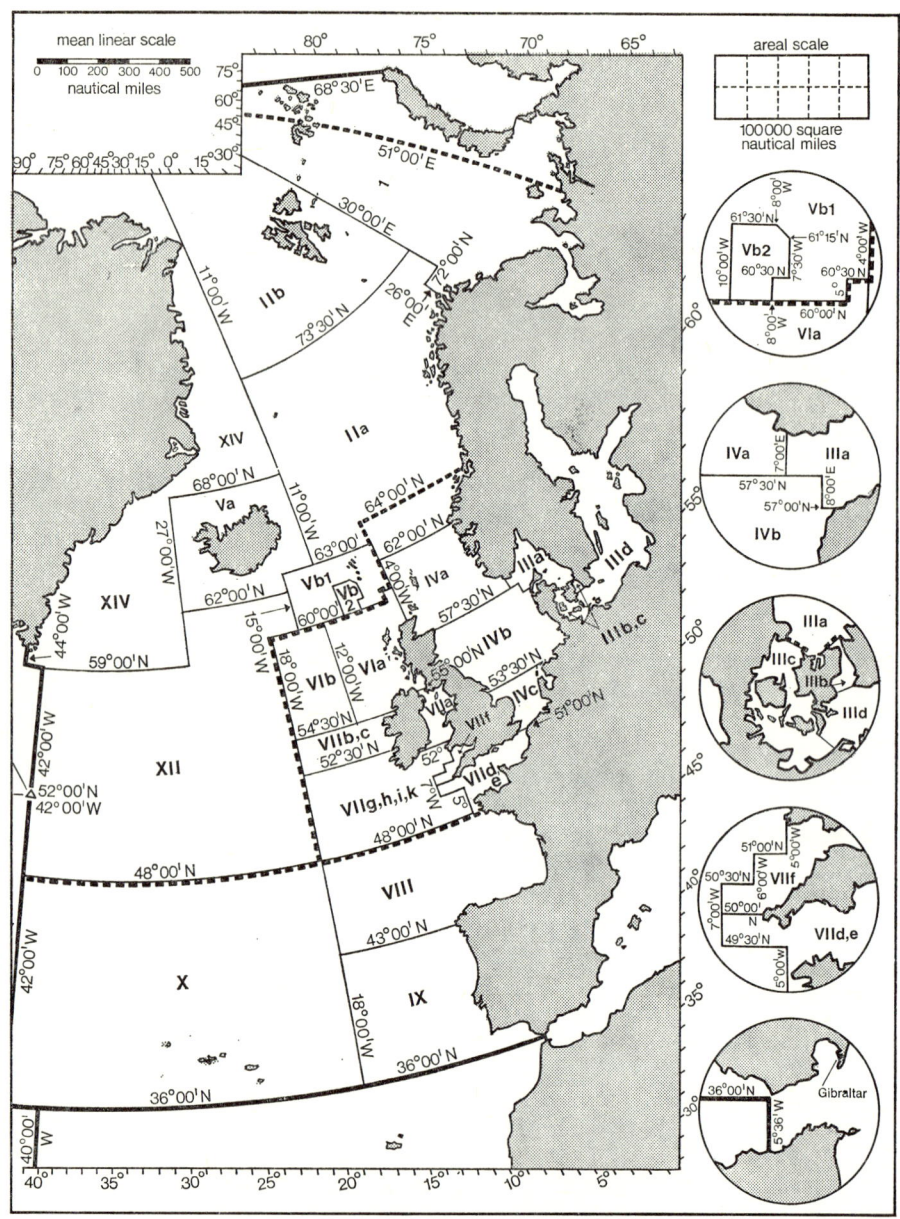

ICES and NEAFC fishing areas (from FAO Fishing Circular C440, October 1972). Areas IVa, IVb and IVc denote the limits of the North Sea. (Reprinted with the permission of the Food and Agricultural Organization of the UN, the copyright holder. This map, prepared by FAO, is based on a base chart drawn by M. J. Pollack and G. G. Pasley, Woods Hole Oceanographic Institution, Woods Hole, Massachusetts, U.S.A.).

Appendix III

Petroleum and Natural Gas: Development of Offshore Oil and Gas Reserves by the United Kingdom, Norway, the Netherlands, Denmark and the Federal Republic of Germany, 1972–74*

The development of North Sea natural gas resources in the 1960s and the first discoveries of large-scale oil reserves in both the U.K. and the Norwegian sectors of the continental shelf towards the end of the decade and in the early 1970s was followed in the period up to July 1974 by further intensive exploration, resulting in additional major discoveries, particularly in the far north-east of the U.K. sector.

Estimates of potential production from the discoveries indicated that by 1980 the United Kingdom would be self-sufficient in oil and Norway a substantial exporter of energy resources, and that the North Sea continental shelf would have become one of the world's major hydrocarbon-producing areas.

In the same period further exploration work in the Dutch, Danish and West German sectors continued to yield disappointing results.

UNITED KINGDOM DEVELOPMENTS

Developments relating to the exploitation of energy resources in the U.K. sector of the continental shelf in the two years up to July 1974 included: (i) a gradual upward revision of estimates of oil resources in the North Sea and their productive potential; (ii) intensive further exploration by oil companies in the North Sea, resulting in a series of important new discoveries; (iii) construction and positioning of the first platforms and pipelines by which the oil would be brought ashore; (iv) further discoveries of natural gas and the signing of major contracts by the British Gas Corporation to ensure adequate supplies from the North Sea in the late 1970s; and (v) the beginning of exploratory operations on the western side of the continental shelf.

In the same period, the British Government became increasingly concerned to promote the rapid development of North Sea reserves and to ensure that British companies were competitive in the large market for goods and services associated with offshore activity.

Following the accession to power of the Labour Government in March 1974, a White Paper was published (in July 1974) containing proposals for more stringent taxation of oil companies operating on the continental shelf, as well as increased State participation in offshore operations and the establishment of a British National Oil Corporation.

---

* Extract (and map) from *Keesing's Contemporary Archives* of July 22-28, 1974 (pages 26625 to 26632). Reproduced by permission of Keesing's Publications, Longman Group Ltd.

THE NORTH SEA

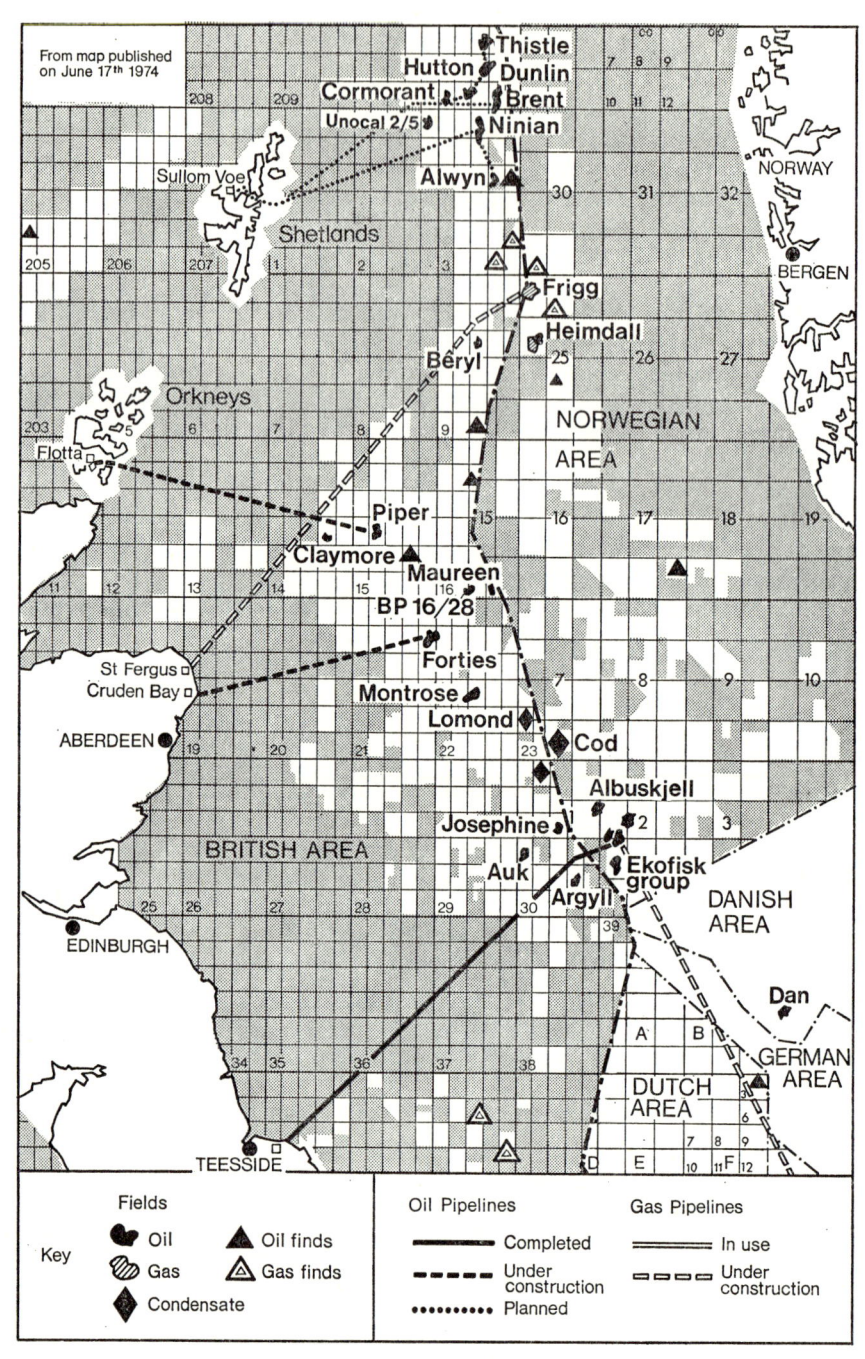

Oil and gas discoveries in the central and northern North Sea (adapted from the *Financial Times*)

Offshore Oil Production Estimates

In the two years after the completion of the fourth round of licensing for the British sector in March 1972, estimates of potential U.K. oil production were steadily revised upwards in the light of further discoveries, from a possible 75,000,000 tons a year by 1980 as mentioned by the then Minister for Industry, Sir John Eden, on 15 March 1972, to between 100,000,000 and 140,000,000 tons a year by 1980, as stated in the annual report on U.K. production and reserves of oil and gas presented to Parliament on 21 May 1974, by the Secretary of State for Energy, Mr. Eric Varley.

The 1974 report confirmed, however, that due to "slippage" in the platform-building and pipe-laying programme, production would reach only 5,000,000 tons in 1975 instead of, as previously forecast, 25,000,000 tons – the latter level being now envisaged as attainable in 1976. The first notice that production would reach only 5,000,000 tons in 1975 had been given by Mr. Varley in the House of Commons on 2 April.

Forecasting that by 1980 Britain would be self-sufficient in oil, the 1974 report said that, allowing for further disoveries, production in 1980 could be in the range of 100,000,000–140,000,000 tons compared with the 1973 estimate of 70,000,000–100,000,000 tons. It continued: "The likelihood of further discoveries, both in areas already licensed and in new areas to be licensed later, opens up the prospect of reserves capable of sustaining production at a rate of 100,000,000–150,000,000 tons a year, or even more, in the 1980s."

The report added that there were 10 proven fields in the North Sea (as against five mentioned in the 1973 report), and that proven recoverable oil reserves were estimated at 895,000,000 tons (500,000,000 tons in 1973). Possible reserves in the known fields could amount to 1,550,000,000 tons, and total reserves in the whole acreage currently under licence could be 2,950,000,000 tons.

The 10 oilfields mentioned in the report as proven were: Forties, Auk, Brent, Argyll, Piper, Beryl, Dunlin, Thistle, Montrose and Ninian.

Discovery of North Sea Oilfields, 1970–74

From late 1970 a series of important oilfields were discovered in the British sector of the North Sea. Some of the finds were of major significance, comparable in productive potential to the large oilfields of the Middle East. Details of these discoveries are given below, together with estimates of the reserves and productive capacity of each field as known at the end of June 1974.

[*Note.* In announcing oil strikes in the North Sea, oil companies tended to be conservative in estimating reserves and productive potential, while in some cases official figures were completely lacking. The figures given below in some cases reflect estimates made by informed press commentators, which in aggregate terms exceeded the estimates issued by the Government, as quoted above.]

Forties. First announced in October 1970 by British Petroleum, the Forties field, situated 110 miles east of Aberdeen, was later discovered to extend into a block licensed to the Shell-Esso partnership. The field's total reserves were estimated at 1,800–2,000 million barrels (260,000,000–300,000,000 tons), of which BP was expected to obtain 90 per cent, and its peak production capacity at 400,000 barrels per day (bpd), or 20,000,000 tons a year. Production was expected to start in late 1975 and peak output to be reached by 1977.

Auk. Shell-Esso's Auk field, first announced in January 1971 and situated about 200 miles east of Edinburgh, was provisionally estimated to contain reserves of 10,000,000–17,500,000 tons and to be capable of a production rate of 2,000,000 tons a year. Production was due to start in mid-1975, with oil being loaded on to tankers over the field.

Brent. First discovered in July 1971 on a block licensed by Shell-Esso and, situated about 100 miles north-east of the Shetland Islands, the Brent oilfield was in October 1973 stated by Shell-Esso to contain estimated reserves of at least 1,500 million barrels (over 200,000,000 tons), making it the second largest to date in the British sector of the North Sea after Forties. At the same time Brent's peak production potential was estimated at 450,000 bpd (22,500,000 tons a year), the first deliveries from the field being expected in the spring of 1976, with peak production being reached at the end of the decade.

After the initial discovery on the Shell-Esso block, the Brent oilfield was found in August 1973 to extend into an adjoining block licensed to Texaco, reserves in that sector being unofficially estimated at 15,000,000–30,000,000 tons, with a potential peak production of 2,500,000 tons a year.

Montrose. The strike announced in November 1971 by a consortium led by Amoco and the British Gas Corporation, situated between the Forties and Auk fields and later designated Montrose, was unofficially estimated to be capable of a peak production level of over 2,000,000 tons a year, although no firm indication was available of the extent of the field's reserves. First production was envisaged for 1976.

Argyll. Announced in June 1972 and situated 200 miles east of the Firth of Forth on a block licensed to Hamilton Brothers and certain other companies (including Rio Tinto-Zinc), the Argyll field was estimated to contain reserves of 15,000,000–20,000,000 tons and to be capable of producing 2,500,000 tons a year. On 29 April 1974 the group announced the discovery of a major new producing zone in the Argyll structure, thereby creating the expectation of a future upward revision of the field's estimated reserves.

The Argyll field was expected to be the first North Sea oilfield to go into actual production in the U.K. sector – the first landings of crude oil from the field being anticipated in the autumn of 1974, from tankers which would be loaded from a mobile rig.

Cormorant. Announced in August 1972, the Cormorant field was situated 25 miles west of Brent, in a block under licence to Shell-Esso, in 500 feet of water. The Cormorant field's reserves were unofficially put at about 30,000,000 tons and its peak production capacity unofficially estimated at 2,250,000–3,000,000 tons a year. Production was scheduled to start by 1977.

Thistle. First discovered in September 1972 under 575 feet of water, the Thistle field was situated in a block licensed to Signal Oil (acting as operator for the Halibut Group). Its reserves were unofficially estimated at about 115,000,000 tons, capable of sustaining peak production at 10,000,000 tons a year. It was envisaged that offtake would begin by 1977.

On 14 June 1974 the Conoco-National Coal Board-Gulf consortium announced that the Thistle field extended south-west from the Signal block into one of their blocks, and that a test well had yielded oil at a rate of 8,300 bpd.

Beryl. A group headed by Mobil Oil, and also including Amerada, Texas

Eastern and the British Gas Corporation, announced on 24 September 1972 that oil had been found on a block about 100 miles north-east of the Orkneys. Confirmed as a major find on 11 July 1973, the Beryl field was subsequently unofficially estimated to contain reserves of some 70,000,000 tons and to have a production potential of 6,000,000 tons a year. Production was due to start in 1975 by tanker loading.

Piper. A group headed by Occidental, and also comprising Getty Oil, Allied Chemical and Thomson Scottish Associates, announced on 17 January 1973 that oil had been discovered in the group's block 100 miles south-east of the Orkneys. Named the Piper field, the discovery was on 8 March 1973 confirmed as a "commercial find with the potential of being a major oil accumulation". Subsequently, the Piper field was estimated to hold over 100,000,000 tons of oil reserves and to be capable of producing over 10,500,000 tons a year. Production was due to begin in 1975.

On 21 May 1974 the Occidental consortium announced that a further strike had been made 20 miles west of the Piper field, oil having flowed at a rate of 2,000 bpd from a test well.

Maureen. A consortium headed by Phillips Petroleum, and including as major shareholders Petrofina of Belgium, the Ente Nazionale Idrocarburi (ENI) of Italy, and Ultramar of the U.K., announced on 20 February 1973 that a "very encouraging" oil strike had been made on the Maureen structure about 30 miles north-east of the Forties field, a test well having yielded a flow of 3,500 bpd of high-grade crude.

On 27 May 1974 the group announced that a second test well had produced 10,000 bpd, and unofficial estimates put the peak capacity of the field at 7,500,000 tons a year, while drilling was continuing to establish the extent of the reserves in the field, which were unofficially estimated at 40,000,000–70,000,000 tons. On 6 June 1974 BP announced that "encouraging oil indications" had been encountered in an adjoining block.

Dunlin. Shell-Esso announced on 4 July 1973 that the test drillings had indicated "an oil accumulation of commercial size" in an area between the Brent and Thistle fields. Named Dunlin, the field was found to extend into an adjoining block under licence to the Conoco-NCB-Gulf partnership; its reserves were unofficially put at between 100,000,000 and 140,000,000 tons (64 per cent being in the Shell-Esso block) and its peak productive capacity at 6,000,000–10,000,000 tons a year.

Hutton. First discovered in September 1973, the Hutton field was confirmed on 5 December 1973 in a statement issued by the Conoco-NCB-Gulf group which said that oil had been tested at "restricted rates" of over 5,000 bpd. Situated immediately to the west of the Brent field, the Hutton field extended into a block under licence to a consortium headed by Amoco and including the British Gas Corporation and Mobil. The field's reserves were unofficially estimated at over 100,000,000 tons (shared equally by the two groups), and potential peak production at 10,000,000 tons a year.

Alwyn. A French consortium led by Total (Compagnie française des pétroles) and including ELF-ERAP and Aquitaine announced on 10 October 1973 that "significant hydrocarbon zones containing both oil and gas" had been encountered in a block under licence to the group, situated about 80 miles east of the Shetlands. The Alwyn field, as it was named, was found to extend into adjoining blocks and drilling continued to determine the extent of the reserves, which were unofficially put at 60,000,000–75,000,000 tons, with a peak productive capacity of 5,000,000–7,500,000 tons a year.

Unocal 2/5. The Unocal-Skelly-Tenneco consortium announced on 15 November 1973 that drillings to the south-west of the Brent field had "encountered oil shows". The following month the group confirmed an "encouraging" flow of over 5,000 bpd from a test well, while on 16 April 1974 a second test well was stated to have produced oil at over 10,000 bpd. While no firm indication was available of the reserves in this field, which became known as "Unocal 2/5" after the number of the block in which it was discovered, they were unofficially estimated at 40,000,000–70,000,000 tons, while potential productive capacity was unofficially put at 5,000,000 tons a year.

Ninian. The BP-Ranger partnership on 25 January 1974 confirmed the discovery of a major new oilfield south-west of the Brent field and about 90 miles east of the northern tip of the Shetlands. Named after the patron saint of the Shetlands, the Ninian field extended to an adjoining block licensed to a consortium led by Burmah Oil and ICI and was believed to be comparable in size to the two largest North Sea oilfields so far discovered, Forties and Brent. Ninian's reserves were provisionally estimated at some 300,000,000 tons (of which about 70 per cent would flow from the Burmah-ICI sector), and peak productive capacity at about 20,000,000 tons a year. Production was due to start in 1977 or 1978, and in June 1974 BP and Burmah reached agreement to develop the field jointly.

Other Finds. Other finds in the British sector of the North Sea up to mid-1974 included the Josephine field by Phillips-Petrofina-ENI and the Claymore field by Hamilton Brothers – the former to the north of the Forties field and the latter to the south; and an oil strike confirmed by the Transworld exploration group on 24 January 1974, on a block north-west of the Forties field. None of these fields had been declared commercial by the end of June 1974, although the Transworld strike was said to be of considerable commercial promise.

British Petroleum announced on 17 July 1974 that a "significant thickness of oil-bearing formation" had been discovered in a block north-west of the Thistle field at a sea depth of over 600 feet. The field, which was named Magnus after the patron saint of the Orkneys, was the most northerly strike yet made in the North Sea.

A further strike of both oil and gas was reported by Hamilton Brothers on 18 July about 13 miles north of the Beryl field.

By the end of March 1974 a total of 278 exploration wells had been drilled in the U.K. offshore sector, of which 102 were in the northern waters of the North Sea, and a further 72 appraisal wells completed. The success rate in the North Sea was sustained at the unusually high rate of one successful strike for every eight wells drilled.

However, a number of major setbacks were recorded, including Shell-Esso's failure to strike oil on the so-called "golden block" north-east of the Shetlands, for the licence to which the partnership had paid the British Government £21,000,000 in June 1971 and on which a further £2,000,000 had been spent in development costs.

Offshore Oil Production Arrangements

It was envisaged that oil from most of the fields discovered in the U.K. sector of the North Sea would be brought ashore by pipelines, which would run from permanent steel or concrete platforms standing on the sea-bed. However, great technological difficulties had to be overcome in positioning the necessary installations in waters of unprecedented depth for such operations, which together with shortages and delays in the construction of equipment onshore constantly threatened the time-table for the start of actual production which the companies had set.

By mid-1974 pipelines from BP's Forties field to Cruden Bay, north of Aberdeen, and from Occidental's Piper field to Flotta in the Orkneys were under construction, while two pipelines to Sullom Voe in the Shetlands from the complex of fields in the far north-east were at the planning stage.

The BP pipeline from the Forties field was being constructed to the company's terminal at Cruden Bay, from where a land pipeline, which was completed in December 1973, would carry the oil down the east side of Scotland to the BP refinery at Grangemouth, on the Forth estuary. It was anticipated that the Montrose field might eventually be linked up with the Forties pipeline. The 135-mile pipeline from the Piper field to the Orkneys was expected to be completed early in 1975.

Of the two proposed pipelines to the Shetlands, one was to be constructed from BP-Burmah's Ninian field, and would also draw production from Total-ELF-ERAP-Aquitaine's Alwyn field. The other was to carry oil from Shell-Esso's Brent field and also serve the Thistle, Dunlin, Hutton and Cormorant fields.

Significant progress in the development of the Forties field – which was expected to be the first major U.K. field to go into production – came at the beginning of July 1974 when the first of four production platforms was towed out from Graythorp, on Teesside, and successfully positioned on the field.

Believed to be the world's biggest fixed-leg oil production platform, the all-steel "Graythorp I" structure weighed over 20,000 tons and was 400 feet high when fully extended. Known as a "jacket", it was intended to support a deck accommodating all the equipment needed to drill 27 oil wells and to process the crude oil before it was pumped by pipeline to the coastal terminal. The total cost of the completed structure was put at £70,000,000.

It was estimated that the cost of developing the North Sea oilfields in the decade up to 1981 would involve the oil companies concerned in investment totalling some £2,500 million.

North Sea Gas – Reserve and Production Estimates – New Discoveries – Supply Agreements

The annual report on U.K. production and reserves of oil and gas presented to Parliament on 21 May 1974 stated that the five established gas-producing fields off East Anglia (i.e. West Sole, Leman Bank, Indefatigable, Hewett and Viking) contained estimated reserves of 27,400,000 million cubic feet, of which 21,900,000 million cubic feet were technically proved (i.e. capable of production). In the northern part of the North Sea, where gas had been found in association with oil, estimated reserves were 14,100,000 million cubic feet, of which 5,800,000 million cubic feet were proved.

These reserves, the report continued, were sufficient to support production of about 5,000 million cubic feet per day (cfd) towards the end of the decade, with production in 1975 reaching some 4,000 million cfd. Moreover, to these estimates should be added anticipated supplies from the Norwegian part of the Frigg field [see below], which were likely to increase U.K. supplies to some 6,000 million cfd by the late 1970s.

New discoveries of gas were made in the North Sea in 1972–74, as follows:

Amethyst. An exploration group led by Burmah Oil and ICI announced on 2 October 1972 that an "encouraging" gas discovery had been made in the North Sea about 23 miles east of Spurn Head at the mouth of the Humber. On 6 June 1973 the group announced that the field had been tested at a rate of 4,400,000 cfd, its reserves being estimated at 500,000 million cubic feet.

Lomond. The Amoco-British Gas Corporation group announced in January 1973 a gas and condensate strike in the northern sector of the North Sea, about 160 miles east of Aberdeen. Gas was tested at a rate of 22,000,000 cfd – comparable to some of the smaller production wells in the southern North Sea – and condensate was obtained at 820 bpd.

Other Strikes. Other discoveries included a strike by the Total-ELF-ERAP-Aquitaine consortium in June 1973 about 40 miles north of the major Anglo-Norwegian Frigg field, in a block adjoining that containing the Alwyn oilfield [see above]; Shell-Esso's Sean field south-east of Indefatigable; Phillips's Ann field north-west of the Viking field; and Conoco-NCB's Boken Bank field a few miles to the south-west. A further gas strike some 20 miles north of the Frigg field was announced by the Total-ELF-ERAP-Aquitaine group on 10 July 1974.

Agreements concerning gas fields in the British sector of the North Sea were made in 1973–74 as follows:

Frigg. The British Gas Corporation announced in July 1973 that it had reached agreement on major contracts for gas supplies from the Frigg field in the northern North Sea with the two operating groups concerned, although difficulties were subsequently encountered in securing Norwegian approval of the contract relating to supplies from the Norwegian sector of the Frigg field.

First discovered in July 1971, the Frigg field straddled the U.K.-Norwegian median line, the blocks in which it was situated being licensed to the Total-ELF-ERAP-Aquitaine group on the U.K. side, and on the Norwegian side to the same group plus Norsk Hydro of Norway (the latter group being known collectively as Petronord). With estimated reserves of about 10,000,000 million cubic feet, Frigg was believed to be the largest gas field yet located in the North Sea and to have a potential production of over 1,500 million cfd.

While the French companies involved were understood to be generally agreed that the U.K. proportion of the field's reserves amounted to some 45–48 per cent, Norsk Hydro claimed that the U.K. share was only a third – the result being that the U.S. consultants were called in to make an independent assessment.

On 13 December 1973 the British Gas Corporation signed a contract with the Total-ELF-ERAP-Aquitaine group, according to which gas was to be supplied for the U.K. network from the British sector of the Frigg field, starting in mid-1976. The price was not officially disclosed, but was reported to be in the region of 2.35p a therm – a considerable increase on the previous highest prices of 1.5p and 1.56p a therm for gas from the Viking and West Sole fields.

Confirmation of the contract for supplies from the Norwegian sector was delayed while Norwegian interests investigated the feasibility of piping gas from the Frigg field to the Norwegian coast across the intervening deep sea bed trench. However, on 10 May 1974 the Norwegian Government published a White Paper containing a recommendation that the U.K. contract should be accepted by the Norwegian Parliament (*Storting*), which was to debate the question later in 1974.

Supplies from the Frigg field were intended by the British Gas Corporation to supplement gas from the operating fields of the North Sea, output from which, at about 4,000 million cfd by 1975, was not expected to meet increased demand in the U.K. The British Gas Corporation had earlier bid for supplies from the Norwegian Ekofisk field, but these had been won by a group of European distributors [see below].

The cost to the British Gas Corporation of gas from the Norwegian sector was reported to have been established at a basic price of 6.2 cents (2.6p) a therm (i.e. slightly higher than the 2.35p a therm applicable to the U.K. sector). However, the agreement was understood to include a considerably more stringent escalation clause linking the price of the gas to the prices of competitive fuel oils and to other market indices – which would effectively make Norwegian gas much dearer than gas from the U.K. sector when deliveries started.

The Norwegian Government's recommendation to the *Storting* was also stated to be subject to gas from the smaller fields around Frigg [see below] being piped to Norway.

Gas from the Frigg field was to be brought ashore by pipeline to St. Fergus on the Aberdeenshire coast, and thence south by pipeline into the Gas Corporation's main distribution network.

Rough. In a written parliamentary answer on 9 July 1973 the then Minister for Industry, Mr. Tom Boardman, announced that the Government's formal consent had been given that day to the assignment of the Gulf concession to the Rough gas field to the British Gas Corporation-Amoco partnership, with the Gas Corporation acquiring a 50 per cent interest. Prior to this agreement, the Gas Corporation had held a 30 per cent interest in a portion of the Rough field which extended into an adjoining block.

Discovered in 1968, the Rough gas field was situated about 16 miles off the Easington terminal in Yorkshire and was thought to contain reserves of about 500,000 million cubic feet, with a producing potential of 75,000,000 cfd. The field has not been brought into production by Gulf, however, on the grounds that the price offered for supplies by the Gas Corporation would render operations uneconomic, and in 1972 Gulf opened talks with the BGC-Amoco group on assigning its licence. The terms under which the assignment was eventually agreed were not disclosed.

It was reported on 21 February 1974 that companies producing gas from the North Sea had, after seven years of negotiations, reached agreement with the Government on the revised calculation of royalty payments for gas output, under which the Government would obtain back royalties of nearly £1,500,000 and an increased income from this source in future.

Western Continental Shelf Developments

Exploratory drilling in the British sector of the Western Approaches – referred to by the oil companies as the "Celtic Sea", being the waters bounded by southern Ireland, Wales, Cornwall and Brittany – began in the summer of 1973, seismic surveys of the area having shown a large area of sedimentary structures likely to contain oil or gas.

The first test well in the British sector was started by Shell in July 1973 off the south-western Welsh coast, and subsequently BP and Atlantic Richfield also commenced exploratory operations in the same area.

From the results of initial surveys, waters further out in the Atlantic were considered to offer the best prospect of oil strikes. However, the allocation of blocks in these areas was delayed by the failure to date of talks between the British and French Governments on the drawing of the median line dividing the continental shelf.

NORWEGIAN DEVELOPMENTS

Major developments concerning the exploitation of oil and gas resources in the Norwegian sector of the North Sea in 1972–74 included: (i) approval by the Norwegian Parliament in April 1973 of plans for piping oil and gas from the Ekofisk field to Britain and Western Germany respectively; (ii) publication by the Norwegian Government of new terms for inclusion in the next round of licences for North Sea exploration; and (iii) further discoveries of oil and gas.

Parliamentary Approval of Ekofisk Pipeline Plans

The Norwegian Parliament (*Storting*) on 26 April 1973 approved plans for (i) a 220-mile, 34-inch diameter pipeline to bring oil from the large Ekofisk oilfield to Teesside in north-east England; and (ii) a second 260-mile, 42-inch diameter pipeline to carry gas from the same field to Emden, on the North Sea coast of Western Germany.

Originally discovered in December 1969 by a consortium led by the American Phillips Petroleum Company, the Ekofisk oilfield was later estimated to contain reserves of about 300,000,000 tons and to be capable of producing 30,000,000 tons of oil a year by the end of the decade. Although the field began limited production in June 1971, with oil being loaded on to tankers moored to buoys anchored over the field, it was envisaged that major exploitation of the Ekofisk reserves would be achieved by means of a pipeline to the British coast (the deep intervening sea bed trench making the construction of a large-diameter pipeline to the Norwegian coast impracticable). At the same time, plans were drawn up for a pipeline to carry the field's large gas reserves to the West German coast. However, long delays were encountered in securing the necessary Norwegian authorization for both pipelines.

The Phillips operating group (which also included Petrofina of Belgium, ENI of Italy and Petronord) on 14 February 1973 accepted a demand by the Norwegian Government for a 50 per cent share in the company which would lay the pipelines.

This participation was to be acquired in return for the Norwegian State oil company (Statoil) subscribing half the company's equity capital (£24,000,000), equal to about 5 per cent of total anticipated expenditure on the project of some £450,000,000, and undertaking to raise its investment in the project to a maximum of 10 per cent. In accordance with Norwegian law, the pipeline company was to have a Norwegian chairman, although he would not have a casting vote in the event of conflict between the two sides, as the Norwegian Government had originally demanded.

On the basis of the *Storting's* authorization, the Norwegian Government on 4 May 1973 granted formal permission for a joint Norwegian-Phillips group company – Norpiepe – to construct the Ekofisk-Teesside oil pipeline and to operate it for 30 years.

Earlier, on 21 December 1972, the Phillips group had signed a 20-year contract to supply 1,000-1,200 million cfd of gas from the Ekofisk field to a consortium of European buyers led by Ruhrgas of Western Germany and including Distrigaz of Belgium, Gasunie of the Netherlands and Gaz de France. Under the terms of the contract, Ruhrgas was to take 50 per cent of the gas, with the other 50 per cent being shared equally among the other partners.

In mid-1973 work began on positioning the Phillips group's large offshore storage tank – "Ekofisk I" – over the Ekofisk field. Built in Stavanger fjord by Norwegian contractors according to a French design, the circular tank cost $28,000,000, measured nearly 300 feet in both height and diameter, weighed about 215,000 tons and had a capacity of 1,000,000 barrels. Resting on the seabed, the concrete tank was to be used as a storage vessel for oil when the tanker-loading programme was interrupted by bad weather, and eventually as an equipment platform when the pipelines came into operation.

New Terms for Norwegian Sector Licences

While the further round of licence allocations for exploration in the Norwegian sector of the North Sea, which had been expected to begin in the autumn of 1972, was delayed by *inter alia* the referendum on EEC entry of October 1972 and the general elections of September 1973, a series of policy statements by the Norwegian Government in 1973–74 disclosed that a relatively small number of blocks would be allocated and that the terms of the licences would considerably strengthen the participation of the Norwegian State in North Sea activities.

The Norwegian Government on 8 December 1972 approved new terms for inclusion in the next round of licences, as follows:

General Conditions. While exploration licences would be allocated, as previously, to Norwegian or foreign companies, the grant of production concessions would, as a general rule, be limited to companies formed in accordance with Norwegian law and having their headquarters in Norway; such production concessions would run for 36 years (compared with 46 years previously), although extensions might be granted.

"Area Levy." The "area levy" payable by oil companies for a production concession was increased to 750 kroner (£58) per square kilometre for the first six years compared with 500 kroner previously, while in order to prevent companies retaining potentially valuable blocks the "area levy" was to be progressively increased after the sixth year until it reached 30,000 kroner (£2,320) per square kilometre from the 17th year onwards.

Royalties. For new oil production concessions, a sliding scale of from 8 to

16 per cent was to be applied for calculating royalties, according to the criterion that higher royalties were payable for the more productive fields, as against the existing universal rate of 10 per cent. For gas production, a flat rate of 12 per cent of value was to be applied. More stringent conditions for calculating the value of oil and gas would be applied, with reference being made to market values rather than to the potentially artificial prices charged by a producing oil company to its distributing subsidiary.

State Participation. All licences were to include a provision giving the State the right to demand participation in commercial finds. The precise proportion of the participation would be the subject of negotiation with the companies concerned, but was stated to be likely to vary from about 30 per cent, in the case of the less promising blocks, to 50 per cent and above in the case of those considered likely to yield oil or gas.

Other Conditions. (i) Licence-holders would be obliged to invite Norwegian firms to tender for all supply contracts and to use Norwegian goods and services when these were competitive; (ii) half of the area covered by a production concession had to be returned to the Norwegian State after six years (compared with one-quarter after six years and a further quarter after nine years hitherto); (iii) licence-holders were to be barred from raising loans against the value of future potential production; (iv) an earlier decision of the *Storting* was reaffirmed that reserves from the Norwegian sector of the North Sea were in principle to be landed in Norway, but that the King could grant exemptions in special cases, such as the Ekofisk field.

The Norwegian Ministry of Industry on 11 July 1973 invited oil companies to apply for licences to 32 previously unallocated blocks or part-blocks, most of them being situated adjacent to the median line with the British sector, thus reflecting Norwegian concern that extensive drillings on the British side could lead to inequitable exploitation of fields which extended into both sectors.

A Ministry statement said that applications were invited under the new terms announced on 8 December 1972, and also specified, as an additional condition, that in the case of certain blocks a cash production bonus would be payable to the Government when production reached a certain level. The statement added that for blocks situated next to the U.K. sector the Government reserved the right to demand the fulfilment of exploration commitments sooner than the usual term of six years.

At the same time, the Ministry announced that nine blocks also situated in the area of the median line had been withheld and that the State oil company, Statoil, had been invited to submit proposals for their development.

The Ministry further stated that two other blocks located immediately opposite the British Brent oilfield were to be allocated as to 50 per cent to Statoil, and it was subsequently announced that the other 50 per cent had been allocated to a consortium led by Mobil and including Conoco, Esso (Exxon), Saga-Amoco and Shell.

A White Paper published by the Norwegian Finance Ministry on 15 February 1974 estimated that State income from oil and tax revenues would reach 8,000-10,000 million kroner (£615-£770 million) by 1978 and 10,000-15,000 million kroner (£770-£1,154 million) by 1981–82, the latter range representing 25 per cent of total State revenue in 1974.

In 1975, the White Paper forecast, oil and gas output would exceed domestic consumption and in 1978 would reach 35,000,000 tons of oil and 30,000 million cubic metres of natural gas, rising to 50,000,000 tons and 45,000-50,000 million cubic metres respectively in 1982.

The White Paper confirmed the Norwegian Government's commitment to close State supervision of exploration, production, safety precautions and the siting of industrial plants, and also proposed the creation of a special agency to secure effective taxation of the oil companies. North Sea reserves would be developed "at a modest speed", and the policy of restricting licences to below the 62nd parallel would be maintained for some years. Norway's new wealth would be used to reduce taxation and to create a "qualitatively better society" (with better education, improved transport, more regional development and shorter working hours), and would also be shared with the developing countries.

A further White Paper was published by the Norwegian Industry Ministry on 15 March 1974.

This White Paper found that the only Norwegian concerns which appeared to satisfy the requirement – for licence eligibility – of active participation in search and exploration activities in the North Sea were the State-controlled Norsk Hydro chemical company and Saga Petroleum; therefore, the many speculative companies which had been established in Norway would not be admitted to North Sea exploration when the next round of licences were allocated.

The White Paper recommended that Statoil should "in principle" have at least a 50 per cent stake in all pending licences and should be allocated its own blocks when it had gained sufficient experience. When the waters north of the 62nd parallel were opened for exploration, Statoil should be given "the main responsibility" for operations in that area.

At a press conference on 15 March to launch the White Paper, the Prime Minister, Mr. Trygve Bratteli, suggested that the Nordic countries should co-operate in supplying the capital needed by Statoil to fulfil its role – the White Paper having estimated that the State company would need to devote 8,000 million kroner (£615 million) to capital investment up to 1978.

An official of the Norwegian Industry Ministry stated on 9 July 1974 that the allocation of licences in the current round would be further delayed, probably until the autumn.

Further Oil and Gas Discoveries

Further exploration in the Norwegian sector of the North Sea was initially concentrated in the area of the major Ekofisk strike, where a series of smaller commercial fields (including Eldfisk, Edda, West Ekofisk, Torfelt, Ergofisk, and Albuskjell) were tested. It was envisaged that most of these fields would eventually be integrated into the Ekofisk production system. Subsequently, exploratory operations were pursued further north, in blocks bordering on the U.K.-Norwegian median line. In the same period a number of new gas strikes were announced.

Oil Exploration. Phillips Petroleum announced on 17 August 1972 that initial testing of the Eldfisk field, situated 11 miles south of Ekofisk, had proved two wells with a production capability of 10,000 bpd each, and on 28 March

1973 an extension well was stated to have produced an aggregate output potential of 13,500 bpd.

The discovery of the Edda field, seven miles south-west of Ekofisk, was announced by Phillips in September 1972, with initial testing indicating a production potential of 10,000 bpd, while in mid-October 1973 the same group announced that a test well on the Albuskjell structure, eight miles north-west of Ekofisk, had shown a 2,900 bpd potential. On 29 November 1973 Phillips confirmed that further oil shows had been encountered north-west of the Torfelt field, also in the Ekofisk area.

Shell made its first strike in the Norwegian sector of the North Sea in November 1972, when oil was found about 10 miles north-west of Ekofisk.

Official Norwegian sources announced on 17 April 1974 that the first well drilled by the group for which Mobil was the operator on one of the two blocks opposite the U.K. Brent field [see above] had been tested at over 10,500 bpd – the highest test result ever achieved on a first well in the Norwegian sector. The find was thought to extend into Conoco-NCB-Gulf acreage in the U.K. sector but to be separate from the Brent field itself.

On 21 May 1974 a strike was announced on the second block about four miles to the north-east, with preliminary tests indicating that both strikes were on the same structure. A third well on the field was stated on 7 June 1974 to have been tested at a rate of over 10,000 bpd.

Gas Discoveries. It was announced on 23 August 1972 that the Petronord group, acting as operators for a broader consortium which also included Pan Ocean, Syracuse and Sunningdale Oils, had struck a major gas field on the Heimdall structure about 22 miles south of the Norwegian-U.K. Frigg field. Heimdall reserves were unofficially estimated at 3,000,000-4,000,000 million cubic feet and productive capacity at up to 1,000 million cfd. On 21 September 1972 Petronord sources stated that oil "impregnations" had also been found in the field.

Further discoveries of gas in the Frigg area were announced by Petronord on 1 October 1973 and 3 May 1974.

Under the terms of the Norwegian Government's approval of the sale of gas from the Norwegian sector of the Frigg field to the British Gas Corporation [see above], gas was to be piped by Petronord and its associated companies from the smaller fields around Frigg to the Norwegian coast in a small-diameter pipeline, the laying of which across the intervening sea-bed trench was thought to be technically feasible.

DEVELOPMENTS IN THE NETHERLANDS, DENMARK AND WESTERN GERMANY

Exploration for oil and gas continued in the Dutch, Danish and West German sectors of the North Sea in the two years up to July 1974, but results were generally disappointing in comparison with the major discoveries made in the U.K. and Norwegian sectors.

Netherlands

At the beginning of December 1972, 16 companies or consortia were awarded licences to explore 26 blocks in the Dutch sector of the North Sea. The first round of Dutch licensing, involving 101 blocks, had taken place in March 1968.

Several of the blocks allocated in December 1972 were situated in the extreme north-west of the Dutch sector – in the area adjoining established British and Norwegian oilfields. The biggest allocation, of six blocks, was made to Shell-Esso's Dutch subsidiary Nederlandse Aardolie Maatschappij (NAM), which had developed the onshore Slochteren (Groningen) gas field – the largest in Western Europe – following its discovery in 1960, and generally the Netherlands Government favoured companies with a previous record of investment in the Dutch sector.

Under Dutch regulations, exploration licences were granted for 15 years for an initial bonus payment of 1,000 guilders (£160) per square kilometre and thereafter at a rental per square kilometre rising from 75 guilders (£12) for five years to 150-225 guilders (£24-36) for the residue. Successful companies could then apply for a production licence, which would be granted at an annual rental of 450 guilders (£72) per square kilometre for a 40-year period.

Royalties on production were payable to the State at a sliding rate of 0 to 16 per cent according to the level of output, while the State also received 50 per cent of net profits made by the companies, minus a 10 per cent deduction for operating costs. In accordance with regulations adopted by Parliament in 1967, the State could also demand a 40 per cent participation in all gas discoveries (in which event its royalty income would be reduced by one-half) – this right having been exercised in the case of the onshore Groningen field.

At the same time, the Government retained the right to withdraw an exploration licence if work commitments – expressed in the form of a minimum investment per square kilometre rising from 6,000 guilders (£960) to 12,000 guilders (£1,920) – were not fulfilled, and also required companies holding reconnaissance and exploration licences to keep the National Geological Service (RGD) informed of all seismic and other data obtained.

In a memorandum presented to the States-General (Parliament) in April 1974, the Minister of Economic Affairs, Mr. Ruud Lubbers, reported that total Dutch onshore and offshore natural gas reserves were estimated at 2,428,500 million cubic metres as at 1 January 1974, of which 1,927,400 million cubic metres were proven.

Of the overall total, the onshore Groningen field accounted for 1,952,200 million cubic metres (1,760,200 million cubic metres proven) and the remaining onshore fields for a further 290,600 million cubic metres (107,600 million cubic metres proven), leaving only 185,700 million cubic metres (59,600 million cubic metres proven) in the Dutch sector of the North Sea.

The memorandum added that there was still considerable uncertainty about the size of reserves in the Dutch sector, and that despite continuing exploration overall gas reserves were expected to fall in 1974.

A survey published by *Het Financieele Dagblad* in mid-1974 showed that a total of 88 wells had so far been drilled in the Dutch sector of the continental shelf, of which 27 had encountered gas and three oil.

Gas Strikes and Exploitation. The offshore gas field announced by Placid International Oil in February 1970 was subsequently estimated to contain reserves of 150,000 million cubic metres, and the first Dutch offshore gas production was scheduled to begin from the field at the beginning of 1975 by way of a pipeline to Eemshaven. Offtake would reach some 6,000 million cubic metres a year, with half the supplies going to Western Germany by arrangement with the State-controlled Dutch monopoly company Gasunie and the other half being fed into the Dutch national grid.

It was reported that after protracted negotiations a price reflecting current market values had been agreed for the gas from the Placid field and that the Dutch Government's initial reluctance to agree to the contract had been overcome by the provision that half the supplies should be taken by the Netherlands. The Government did not exercise its right to take a 40 per cent share of the Placid field.

Other groups with gas strikes in the Dutch sector of the North Sea in the two years up to July 1974 included the U.S. Noordwinning consortium, the French Petroland group, Shell-Esso (NAM) and Mobil. A production licence was granted to Noordwinning in April 1974 in respect of one of its strikes, with the State taking a 40 per cent interest in the field.

Oil Strikes. The three oil strikes made in the Dutch sector by mid-1974 were the two wells sunk by the Tenneco-led group 50 miles north of the island of Vlieland in 1970–71, and a find by Shell-Esso (NAM) in the same area announced in April 1974.

However, the Tenneco find was subsequently reported to be non-commercial, while the Shell-Esso strike, although it was tested at a rate of 4,500 bpd, was believed to be a reservoir of limited size.

Denmark

Having started production from its Dan field in July 1972, the Danish Underground Consortium was reported in August 1973 to have made a "promising" strike 80 miles to the north-west, close to the Norwegian Ekofisk field.

However, on 1 October 1973 the consortium announced that drilling in the area had been suspended because "it could not find sufficient oil to make the operation commercially feasible".

Moreover, due to technical difficulties production from the Dan field, which had originally been forecast at 10,000 bpd (500,000 tons a year), by August 1973 totalled only 175,000 tons, at a rate of 3,500 bpd.

In 1974 Danish hopes of offshore oil and gas production turned to Greenland, on the strength of the major finds in Alaska and northern Canada in the late 1960s and also in the light of limited prospecting of the area in 1969–72. It was anticipated that the first licences for the area would be allocated in 1975.

Western Germany

As the world's fourth largest oil consumer, with a consumption in 1973 of 150,000,000 tons (of which only 7,000,000 tons were produced domestically), Western Germany from 1972 renewed exploration of its sector of the North Sea on a reorganized basis – earlier exploration having been suspended in 1967 after proving largely unfruitful.

Following the settlement in 1971 of a delimitation dispute with Denmark and the Netherlands by which the West German share of the North Sea continental shelf was increased from 23,700 to 35,600 square kilometres, a reallocation of West German licences was effected.

Companies holding blocks in former Danish and Dutch waters retained most of their acreage, while the German North Sea Consortium (including Shell-Esso, Amoco, Texaco and a number of West German companies), which had held a monopoly of exploration in the West German sector, was allocated almost all the remainder of the new territory in an agreement which extended its concession until April 1975. The Consortium was, however, obliged to relinquish much of its acreage within the old boundaries, these areas being subsequently awarded to 16 new groups, including many U.S. companies.

Drilling was started in the former Danish part of the West German sector in April 1974, but no strikes were reported up to July 1974.

Appendix IV

Selected Belgian, Danish, Netherlands and Norwegian legal documents, covering aspects of North Sea exploitation

BELGIUM

Law of 13 June 1969 Concerning the Belgian Continental Shelf

Article 1.

The Kingdom of Belgium exercises sovereign rights on the continental shelf as delimited in Article 2 of this law for purposes of exploration of the shelf and exploitation of its natural resources.

In the context of this law:

(a) the expression "continental shelf" denotes the bed of the sea and the substratum of the submarine regions adjacent to the coasts but situated outside the territorial sea;

(b) the "natural resources" include the mineral resources and other non-living resources on and under the seabed, as well as the living organisms belonging to the sedentary species, that is organisms which, at the stage when they can be fished, are either immobile on the seabed or beneath it, or are incapable of moving without staying in physical contact with the seabed or the subsoil.

Article 2.

The delimitation of the Belgian continental shelf with regard to the continental shelf of the United Kingdom of Great Britain and Northern Ireland is constituted by the median line whose points are all equidistant from the nearest points of the baselines from which the width of the territorial sea of Belgium and the United Kingdom are measured. This delimitation can be arranged by special agreement.

The delimitation of the continental shelf as regards the countries whose coasts are adjacent to the Belgian coasts, that is France and the Netherlands, is determined by applying the principle of the equidistance of the nearest points of the baselines from which the width of the territorial sea of each interested power is measured. This delimitation can be arranged by a special agreement with the interested power.

Article 3.

Exploration and exploitation of the mineral resources and other non-living resources of the seabed and subsoil are subject to the granting of concessions awarded under the conditions and according to the modality determined by the King.

Article 4.

Apart from group or individual exceptions which may be granted by the King, the exploration and exploitation of living organisms which, according to the

definition in Article 1, para. 2 (b), belong to the sedentary species are reserved to Belgian citizens.
Article 5.
Installations and other appliances established on the high seas, necessary for the exploration or the exploitation of the natural resources of the continental shelf, as well as the security zones mentioned in Article 6, must not unjustifiably hinder shipping, fishing or conservation of the biological resources of the sea, nor the utilization of regular maritime routes which are essential for international navigation, nor fundamental oceanographic studies or other scientific studies carried out with the intention of publishing their results.

For this purpose the King decides on measures to be taken as well as methods of execution.

He also lays down any obligation which he considers useful for that purpose, particularly concerning the placing of navigational aids and the methods to be used to avoid pollution of the sea and the deterioration of submarine cables and pipelines.

He decides on the procedure to be followed for the carrying out of the total or partial withdrawal of the authorization or of the concession.
Article 6.
A security zone can be established according to the methods determined by the King for each installation or appliance situated on the continental shelf.

It can extend to a distance of 500 metres measured from each point of the outside edge of these installations or appliances.
Article 7.
The installations or other appliances situated on the high seas fixed permanently on the continental shelf and referred to in this law, as well as the people and possessions on these installations or appliances, are subject to Belgian law.
Article 8.
Any person who has committed an offence punishable under Belgian law on an installation or other appliance mentioned in the preceding Article can be prosecuted in Belgium.

In the absence of other rules attributing competence, the Courts in Brussels will have jurisdiction.
Article 9.
Acts or facts having legal effects other than penal which occur on or affect an installation or other appliance mentioned in Article 7 will be regarded as having happened in Belgium.

In the absence of other rules which attribute competence, these acts or facts will be treated as having happened in the district of the second canton of the Justice of the Peace of the judicial arrondissement of Brussels.

LEGISLATION FOR PROSPECTING FOR AND PRODUCING CRUDE OIL

Under the terms of law-decree No. 83 of 28 November 1939 (*Moniteur belge*, 8 December 1939), confirmed by the law of 16 June 1947, prospecting for and extracting oil and combustible gases can be carried out only in pursuance of an exclusive licence, i.e. valid for a sole beneficiary, within a limited area determined by the beneficiary in his application.

This exclusive licence, which may cover prospecting, extracting, or both, is granted by royal decree following a procedure similar to that for the granting of mining concessions (French law of 1810). The analogy relates in particular to: the publicity given to the application for an exclusive licence; the opportunity given to third parties to present an alternative tender or to raise objections; the proof required of the applicant that he has the necessary technical and financial capacity; the payment of a fixed yearly rent to the owners of the land according to the number of hectares which they possess within the perimeter of the area covered by the licence; the existence of a set of conditions imposed upon the concessionaire.

The methods and terms of procedure in the investigation of applications for exclusive licences are determined by the royal decree of 7 April 1953 (*Moniteur belge*, 10/11 April 1953).

Prospecting and extraction are not at present subsidized directly or indirectly.

A law of 11 July 1960 (*Moniteur belge*, 30 July 1960), however, grants a 50 per cent tax immunity on oil-company profits reinvested in Belgium within a period of five years.

The offshore area is regulated by the basic law of 13 June 1969 (*Moniteur belge*, 8 October 1969) entitled "Law concerning the Belgian continental shelf which subordinates the prospecting for and extraction of mineral resources and other non-living resources on and under the seabed to the granting of a concession".

DENMARK

1. The breadth of the territorial sea of Denmark is 3 nautical miles (from the coastline or from such straight baselines as have been or may be established). The existing rules were promulgated by the Royal Decree on the Delimitation of the Territorial Sea of 21 December 1966.

2. Pursuant to the Customs Act No. 519 of 13 December 1972, the Customs territory covers Danish waters up to a distance of 4 nautical miles (7,408 metres) from the coastline or such straight baselines as have been or may be established in conformity with international law.

3. The fishery limit runs parallel to the baselines in force at any time at the following distances from these lines:

12 nautical miles in the North Sea (Skagerrak, Kattegat, off Greenland and the Faeroe Islands);

3 nautical miles in the Belts and the Baltic Sea.

The provisions governing the fishery limit were laid down in the Salt Water Fishery Act (No. 195 of 26 May 1965, cf. Notice of 8 March 1967).

An English translation of the Law is published in the United Nations Legislative Series (ST/LEG/SER.B/15 and ST/LEG/SER.B/16).

Denmark is a party to a number of treaties relating to exploitation and conservation of the living resources of the North Sea (see Appendix II).

4. The exploitation of the Danish part of the seabed and its subsoil is governed by the provisions of the Royal Decree of 7 June 1963, on the Exercise of Danish Sovereignty over the Continental Shelf, as amended by the Continental Shelf Act of 9 June 1971.

ROYAL DECREE OF 7 JUNE 1963, ON THE EXERCISE OF DANISH SOVEREIGNTY OVER THE CONTINENTAL SHELF*

In accordance with the Convention on the Continental Shelf signed at Geneva on 29 April 1958 at the First United Nations Conference on the Law of the Sea, and with reference to the decision taken by the Folketing on 2 May 1963, the following provisions are laid down:

1. Denmark exercises, for the purposes of exploration and exploitation of natural resources, sovereign rights over that part of the Continental Shelf which according to the Convention on the Continental Shelf signed at Geneva on 29 April 1958 (hereinafter referred to as the Convention) belongs to the Kingdom of Denmark, cf. section 2 below.

2.1 Pursuant to Article 1 of the Convention the term "continental shelf" is used as referring (a) to the seabed and subsoil of the submarine areas adjacent to the coast but outside the area of the territorial sea, to a depth of 200 metres or, beyond that limit, to where the depth of the superjacent waters admits of the exploitation of the natural resources of the said areas; (b) to the seabed and subsoil of similar submarine areas adjacent to the coasts of islands.

2.2 The boundary of the Continental Shelf in relation to foreign States whose coasts are opposite the coasts of the Kingdom of Denmark or which are adjacent to Denmark shall be determined in accordance with Article 6 of the Convention. Accordingly, in the absence of any special agreement the boundary shall be the median line, every point of which is equidistant from the nearest points of the baselines from which the breadth of the territorial sea of each state is measured.

2.3 The Minister of Public Works may, if necessary, order the making of official charts in which the boundary line is shown.

3. For exploration and exploitation of the natural resources of the Continental Shelf referred to in section 1 of this Decree the grant of a licence is required pursuant to Act No. 181 of 8 May 1950 on Prospection and Extraction of Raw Materials in the Subsoil of the Kingdom of Denmark or pursuant to Royal Decree No. 153 of 27 April 1935 on Exploitation of Raw Materials in the Soil of Greenland.

ACT NO. 259 OF 9 JUNE 1971 CONCERNING THE CONTINENTAL SHELF, AS AMENDED IN 1972†

Article 1.

1. The natural resources of the Danish continental shelf shall belong to the Danish State and may only be explored or utilized by other parties under a concession or licence.

---

* This text is an unofficial English translation supplied by the Royal Danish Embassy in London.

† The Act of 1971 entered into force on 1 July 1971, repealing article 3 of Royal Decree of 7 June 1963 concerning the exercise of Danish Sovereignty over the continental shelf, reproduced in ST/LEG/SER.B/15, p. 344. Text of 1971 Act provided by the Foreign Ministry of Denmark in a note verbale of 16 November 1971 and translated by the Secretariat of the United Nations. The amendments were made by Act No. 278 of 7 June 1972. The amendments modified paragraph 3 of article 2 and added paragraphs 4 and 5 thereto as well as a new article 6 (a). English text of these new provisions are based on an unofficial translation done by the Ministry of Justice of Denmark and provided by the Ministry of Foreign Affairs of Denmark in a note verbale of 5 January 1973.

2. For the purposes of this Act the term "natural resources" means:

(1) The mineral and other non-living resources of the seabed and its subsoil, and

(2) Living organisms which, when harvestable, are either immobile on or under the seabed, or are unable to move unless they are in constant physical contact with the seabed or its subsoil.

Article 2.

1. The Minister of Public Works may permit exploration of the natural resources specified in article 1, paragraph 2 (1), where such exploration is not undertaken with a view to utilization. He may also permit the removal of such raw materials as were available for utilization by private interests in Denmark before 23 February 1932. Otherwise exploration and utilization of the resources specified in article 1, paragraph 2 (1), may only take place under a concession granted in accordance with the rules laid down in the Act concerning prospecting for and exploitation of raw materials in the subsoil of the Kingdom of Denmark.

2. The Minister of Fisheries may permit fishing and exploration of the living organism specified in article 1, paragraph 2 (2). If the study of the natural resources specified in article 1, paragraph 2 (1) is required for fisheries or oceanographic research, permission for such study shall similarly be granted by the Minister of Fisheries.

3. A permit under the second sentence of paragraph 1 hereof may be issued as a sole right to recover during the validity of the permit one or more of the said raw materials from the whole of the continental shelf or any particular area thereof.

4. A sole permit shall be issued only to such enterprises as are organized as limited liability companies. Such permits shall be valid for maximum periods of fifteen years at a time and may, *inter alia*, contain the following conditions:

(a) That the Minister for Public Works shall be empowered at any time to impose restrictions with respect to the nature and quantity of the deposits authorized for recovery; restrict or bar all recovery in certain areas, or define general or local limits of depths within or beyond which recovery is authorized;

(b) That the Minister shall be empowered to issue directives for fixing of prices of the deposits recovered and that, with a view thereto, the company shall provide the Minister with detailed information on the annual expenses of the company for administration, repairs, replacements, depreciations, appropriations for reserves, dividends, etc.;

(c) That the company shall not be authorized to increase its share capital or to raise any loan without the consent of the Minister;

(d) That any assignment of shares shall be subject to the consent of the Minister;

(e) That deposits recovered shall be landed in a Danish port or at such other place of discharge as has been approved by the Minister;

(f) That, in accordance with directives issued by the Minister, the Company shall report on their recovery activities, particularly with respect to sites and depths of recovery and also the nature and quantities of the deposits recovered;

(g) That, in accordance with rules issued by the Minister, the company shall accede to supervision of its fulfilment of the directives issued and shall defray the expenses incidental thereto;

(h) That the company shall pay a royalty to the Treasury for its recovery activities; and

(i) That the company shall reimburse the Government for expenditure incurred in respect of payment of compensation under paragraph 2 of article 6 (a) of this Act and for the expenses incidental to the fixing of the compensation.

5. Permits under the second sentence of paragraph 1 hereof for recovery of species of raw materials other than those comprised by a sole permit, or for recovery in areas other than those authorized by sole permit, and also permits under paragraph 2 hereof shall be issued for periods of up to five years at a time and may, *inter alia*, be contingent upon payments of a royalty to the Treasury and upon the raw materials recovered being landed in a Danish port or at such other place of discharge as has been approved by the Minister for Public Works.

Article 3.

1. Danish law shall apply to installations which are to be used for exploration or exploitation of the continental shelf and are situated in the area of the shelf and in safety zones surrounding the installation (cf. however, paragraph 2). In determining the area of jurisdiction of Danish courts and administrative authorities, installations and safety zones shall be deemed to belong to the area nearest to them, save as otherwise provided by the Minister concerned.

2. The following laws shall not apply to installations and safety zones:

(1) The Act on Saltwater Fisheries;
(2) The Act on Hunting;
(3) The Act Concerning the Conduct of Economic Activities in Greenland;
(4) The Act on Hunting and Fresh Water Fisheries in Greenland, and
(5) The Act on Commercial Trapping, Fishing and Hunting in Greenland.

Article 4.

1. The Minister of Public Works may prescribe special regulations concerning safety measures in connexion with the setting-up and operation of the installations specified in article 3, paragraph 1, concerning the laying of pipelines and cables and concerning measures to prevent or remedy pollution. Supervision to ensure compliance with the regulations shall be the responsibility of the authorities entrusted with similar tasks under other laws, and complaints concerning decisions of the supervisory authority shall be made in accordance with the regulations otherwise applicable to complaints concerning such decisions. The Minister may, however, authorize departures from these provisions.

2. The Minister may also prescribe regulations concerning the establishment of safety zones surrounding installations used for such exploration or exploitation. The maximum extent of such zones shall be 500 metres round the installation, measured from any point at its outer edge. The Minister may prescribe rules concerning sailing in safety zones and, in that connexion, may prohibit access to them by unauthorized ships.

3. The Minister of Public Works shall draw up the regulations specified in paragraphs 1 and 2 of this article in consultation with the ministers responsible for dealing with matters of this kind.

Article 5.

1. Violations of the exclusive right of the State under article 1 shall be punishable by a fine or term of detention not exceeding six months save where a higher penalty is applicable under another law.

2. Any failure to comply with the conditions governing a concession or licence granted in pursuance of this Act or in pursuance of the laws specified in article 2, paragraph 1, and article 6, shall be punishable by a fine save where a higher penalty is applicable under another law.

3. Rules issued in pursuance of article 4 may provide for a penalty of a fine for any violation of such rules.

4. In the case of offences committed by joint-stock companies, co-operative societies or the like, the company or society as such may be held liable.

Article 6.

In the case of installations and safety zones (cf. article 3, paragraph 1) situated or established in the part of the continental shelf appertaining to Greenland, the law otherwise applicable to Greenland shall apply. The Minister for Greenland shall exercise the powers specified in articles 2 and 4 in compliance with the regulations laid down in the Act concerning mineral raw materials in Greenland.

Article 6 (a).

1. In the event that a sole permit is issued under article 2, paragraph 3 of this Act the Minister for Public Works shall be empowered to revoke any permits issued prior to January 1972, under the second sentence of article 2, paragraph 1 of this Act in so far as the sole permit is issued for raw materials and areas comprised by previous permits.

2. Any party whose permit for recovery of raw materials is revoked in pursuance of paragraph 1 hereof shall be entitled to compensation from the Treasury for any loss thus incurred. Article 12, paragraphs 2 and 3 of the Utilization of Stone, Gravel and Other Natural Resources in the Soil and Territorial Waters Act are similarly applicable.

3. The Minister for Public Works shall be empowered to decide that such restrictions as may be imposed on a sole permit in pursuance of article 2, paragraph 4, subparagraph a of this Act shall be applicable to any permits issued prior to January 1972, under the second sentence of article 2, paragraph 1 of this Act.

Royal Decree on the Delimitation of the Territorial Sea (21 December 1966)

The delimitation of the territorial waters which consist of the territorial sea and the internal waters shall be governed by the following rules:

1.1 The territorial sea comprises those areas of the sea which, on the inner side, are delimited by the lines referred to in section 4 and which, on the outer side, are delimited by lines drawn in such a manner that the distance from every point on these lines to the nearest point on the inner borderline shall be 3 nautical miles (5,556 metres).

1.2 The outer delimitation of the Danish Customs area and the Danish fishing territory is governed by special rules laid down by law.

1.3 As far as the waters bordering upon Sweden and Germany are concerned, the outer limit of the territorial sea shall not go beyond the lines delimiting the internal waters and the territorial seas established by Declaration of 30 January 1932 between Denmark and Sweden concerning the delimitation in the Sound, cf. Executive Order No. 41 of 22 February 1932, and Executive Order No. 497 of 21 December 1923 concerning the frontier between Denmark and Germany.

2. The internal waters comprise those areas of the sea, such as harbours, harbour entrances, roadsteads, bays, fiords, sounds and belts, which are situated inside the lines referred to in section 4.

3. The provisions of section 2, cf. section 4, shall involve no restrictions in the existing right of passage for foreign vessels through those parts of the internal waters in the Samsø Belt, the Little Belt, the Great Belt, and the Sound, which are normally used for such passage.

4. The lines to be used for delimitation of the territorial sea in pursuance of section 1 shall be those specified below and in the appended map of the coast-line (low-water mark at mean spring-tide) or straight lines between the following points:

(There follows a list of 96 points not given here.)

NETHERLANDS

1. The Netherlands incorporates into its municipal law all treaty law to which it is a party. In the event of a conflict, international law overrides municipal law.

2. The breadth of the territorial sea is 3 nautical miles. The Netherlands has not used the right to draw straight base lines and bay closing lines. The legal regime of internal waters and the territorial sea is similar to that of the United Kingdom.

3. The Netherlands has not claimed a contiguous zone.

4. The Netherlands has not instituted an exclusive fishing zone. The Visserijwet 1963 is the legal basis for the fishing regime in the territorial sea. The Benelux treaty gives the nationals of the three states the right to fish in the territorial waters of the other two. The Netherlands is also a party to the London Fishery Convention of 1964. It has also concluded, with the Federal Republic of Germany the Ems-Dollard treaty (8 April 1960), concerned with delimitation problems and providing for a common fishing area.

Further Points

(a) There is no requirement for foreign ships to carry a number of duly certificated officers.

(b) The 1960 SOLAS Convention has been embodied in Netherlands legislation but the rules apply only to Dutch ships wherever they may be.

(c) There are at present no legal rules concerning traffic routeing.

(d) There is no requirement for compulsory pilotage.

(e) The responsibility for the provision and maintenance of lighthouses, beacons and buoys rests with the Government. The cost of installing and maintaining navigational aids is a charge on the national revenue.

WATER POLLUTION

This is regulated under the Surface Waters Pollution Act which came into force on 1 January 1970. Since the Netherlands is mainly dependent on international rivers (the Rhine and the Maas) for the supply of surface water, improvement in quality is slow and there is no improvement in the Rhine. Dumping at sea is governed by the Law on Surface Waters but a further law is in preparation, incorporating the rules of the Oslo Convention. The first indicative 5-year programme to combat water pollution was completed in 1974. A further programme has been drawn up.

MINING LEGISLATION

I Administrative

A. Public authorities concerned with oil and gas exploration and production.

All government interference with the mining industry is routed through the Minister of Economic Affairs (hereafter called "The Minister"). He is helped by:

Directorate of Mines – part of the Directorate-General for Energy Supply of his Ministry.

Mining Council – a board of non-Government experts advising the Minister on matters of mining policy, e.g. legislation, granting of licences and concessions.

Inspector-General of Mines – who with his service supervises the observance by the mining industry of the mining regulations which are aimed at the promotion of healthy and safe working conditions for those employed, the avoidance of harm to the interests of others and the preservation of the national mineral wealth.

Geological Service – advises the Minister on the geological aspects of the mining policy, e.g. concerning the delimitation of drilling licences and production concessions, and the estimating of reserves. Collects, digests and compiles the data the industry are obliged to submit to it on the basis of secrecy.

In order to protect shipping and military interests certain offshore areas have been excluded from the granting of mining rights. Moreover a licensee, before moving to a drilling location, has to consult with the Minister. In case the location is in an established shipping lane, prior consent from the Ministers of Economic Affairs, Communications and Water Control and of Defence has to be obtained. As to operations in an established military area the prior consent of the Ministers of Economic Affairs and of Defence is necessary for reconnaissance work (e.g.

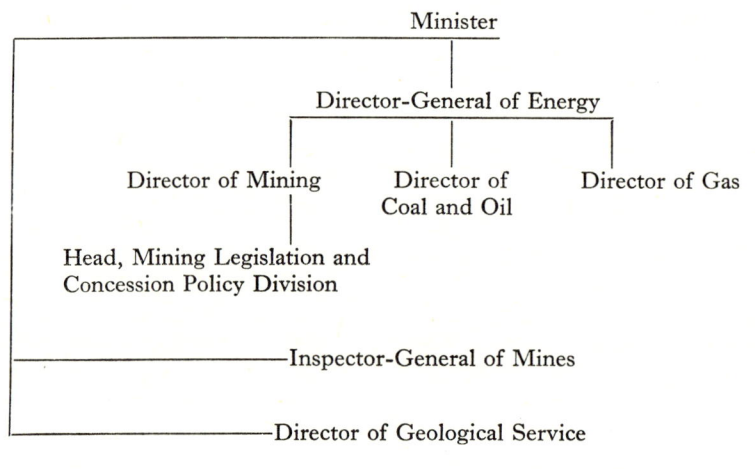

```
                              Minister
                                 |
                    Director-General of Energy
                    ┌────────────┼────────────┐
         Director of Mining  Director of   Director of Gas
                  |         Coal and Oil
         Head, Mining Legislation and
         Concession Policy Division

         ─────────────────────Inspector-General of Mines

         ─────────────────────Director of Geological Service
```

Structure of Responsibility

seismic), as well as for drilling. Moreover, according to the Mining Regulations, for seismic work supervision by a fishery expert is required when explosives are used. The Minister's permission is necessary for conducting scientific research which may lead to proving the presence of minerals as defined by the Continental Shelf Mining Act of 1967, which include oil and gas. To protect public interests on land against any avoidable harm from mining activities (e.g. water pollution) prior consent from a Planological Committee is required for drilling, pipelaying, etc. On this committee the various Ministers concerned are represented. The drilling locations have to be approved only if they are situated in specified areas of interest for recreation and in areas where water is extracted.

B. Research establishments

Research is in private hands. The laboratory for sea mining at the Delft Technical University is concerned mainly with the mining of other minerals.

II Legal

The Netherlands' mining legislation distinguishes between the Territory of the Netherlands, called land hereafter, and that part of the North Sea over which the Netherlands exercises sovereign rights with regard to the mineral resources (called "continental shelf" hereafter). The boundary between the territorial waters and the continental shelf was laid down in a Royal Decree of 7 February 1967.

Shelf Legislation

23 September 1965: Law concerning the exploration for and the exploitations of mineral resources.
27 January 1967: Royal decree concerning the terms on which exploration and exploitation rights for hydrocarbons shall be granted.
7 February 1967: Royal decree establishing the procedures for applying for permits or exemptions required by the Continental Shelf Mining Act of 1967.
13 March 1967: Royal decree establishing Mining Regulations for the continental shelf. Apart from safety aspects, it deals with water pollution, protection of fisheries, etc.
1970: Law concerning the institution of the Mining Council.

Geneva Conventions of 29 April 1958

On 18 February 1966 the Netherlands ratified the conventions concerning: the continental shelf; the territorial seas; the high seas; fishery, etc.; and arbitration. The Netherlands made reservations regarding the first three conventions.

Safety, etc.

The "Mining Regulations, Continental Shelf" cover safety aspects, pollution of the sea, protection of submarine cables and pipelines, as well as radio transmission to and from offshore mining installations. Infringements of these rules are penal offences according to the Continental Shelf Mining Act of 1967.

The "Mining Regulations, Land" cover safety and labour aspects; the other aspects mentioned above are dealt with in the terms of the drilling licences and production concessions for they are not yet covered by other existing general legislation. Moreover, in 1958 a law on the pollution of seawater came into force.

Regime applying to foreign companies and foreign capital

There is no special regime for mining operations by foreign companies.

Conditions governing oil and gas exploration

(a) Introduction

LAND (including territorial waters) – surface exploration, including seismic work (reconnaissance), is free, being subject only to the approval of the landowner. Exploration through borings requires a drilling licence, which is exclusive and restricted to minerals specified in the licence (in this case oil and gas together, being inseparable).

SHELF – surface exploration (reconnaissance) requires a reconnaissance permit, which is non-exclusive. For exploration drilling an exploration licence is required, which is exclusive and restricted to minerals specified in the licence and includes the right to reconnoitre within the licence area. The State holds no preferential rights. Before deciding to participate to a considerable extent in drilling exploration the Government requires prior authorization by law.

(b) Land

1. GRANTING OF DRILLING LICENCES

A licence will be granted by the Minister, after having heard the Mining Council, to an applicant for a geologically reasonably coherent area, provided the applicant can indicate a drilling location. In practice this means that sufficient preliminary seismic work must have been carried out. No bidding is involved. In case of overlap the Minister decides on the basis of the geological information submitted to and judged by the Geological Service. No investigation into the capabilities of the applicant is provided for by the law but, as the Government takes these into account very seriously before granting a production concession, there is protection against the appearance of interlopers.

2. RIGHTS

Though not legally established, the usual terms are:

duration – two years;

extension, automatic – one year, if before the end of the second year one well has been drilled into the prospective formation (total duration three years);

extension, automatic – another year, if before the end of the third year three wells have been drilled into the prospective formation (total duration four years);

extension, automatic – another year, if before the end of the fourth year four wells have been drilled into the prospective formation (total duration five years).

Maximum duration five years, after which the area can be reapplied for. In case of regranting, the terms may be different.

The law sets no limitations to the extension of a licence area but, when introducing the Bill to Parliament, the Minister stated his intention to issue geological units if possible in order to avoid a situation in which two companies were discovering, and later perhaps exploiting, the same accumulation.

The drilling licence is exclusive and hence puts the licensee in a unique position to become the "finder" of oil or gas within the licence area, which is a very important condition of granting a production concession to him.

The licensee has no rights of occupation, let alone expropriation. He is the free owner of the results of his exploration. Transfer of rights needs the prior consent of the Minister, who will seek the advice of the Mining Council.

3. OBLIGATIONS

The licence deed stipulates the obligation to produce copies of the exploration data collected, including part of the samples, to the Geological Service, on the basis of secrecy, and to report periodically to the Inspector-General of Mines.

No financial obligations are imposed and surrender of the acreage may occur at any time.

For failure to comply with his obligations (other than those connected with his working effort), e.g. those concerning water pollution and those stipulated in the Mining Regulations, the licensee can be penalized.

(c) *Continental shelf*

1. RECONNAISSANCE PERMITS

Granted by the Minister of Economic Affairs on a non-exclusive basis. Neither duration nor financial obligations are legally established, but the usual terms imposed are: a maximum duration of six months and a payment of one guilder per square kilometre. The permit holder has to obey the Mining Regulations; in case explosives are used his operation will be supervised by a Government fishery expert. He has also to produce copies of his data to the Geological Service. For indicated military areas a special permit of a more restricted duration is required from the Ministers of Defence and Economic Affairs.

2. GRANTING OF EXPLORATION LICENCES

Granted at the discretion of the Minister, having heard the Mining Council, on conditions described in the Royal Decree of 27 January 1967, which came into force by Act of Parliament. Preparatory work for his decision is in the hands of the Directorate for Mining only.

The information the applicant must supply is laid down in a Royal Decree of 7 February 1967. Apart from indicating the area or areas he is applying for, he has to give information regarding his technical and financial capabilities, as well as about his efforts spent on exploration and production in the Netherlands and its continental shelf, his involvement in the economic life of the country and his possibilities of marketing gas or oil products. No bonuses or working obligations, other than those fixed by law, are being considered by the Government. A licence may be surrendered wholly or partially at any time. Transfer requires prior consent of the Minister, who will seek prior advice of the Mining Council.

3. RIGHTS OF EXPLORATION LICENCE HOLDERS

Licences are granted for 15 years. Licences comprise one or more of the blocks indicated on a map which forms part of the Royal Decree of 27 January 1967. Except near the boundaries of the Netherlands' continental shelf or where for special reasons a part of a block is exempted from granting, the blocks measure 10 minutes in the North-South direction and 20 minutes in the West-East direction. Consequently their sizes vary between 0.2 and 426 sq. km. The law sets no limits to the maximum size of the area one person may be granted.

The right to explore, that is to drill, is exclusive and includes the right to carry out reconnaissance work.

As on land, the licensee has the right to dispose freely of the results of his work.

Proving oil or gas in economic quantities gives the licensee a right to obtain a winning licence for the discovery block on the terms valid at the date the exploration licence was granted and provided his capabilities have not deteriorated to such an extent as to make such granting harmful to the public interest.

4. OBLIGATIONS OF EXPLORATION LICENCE HOLDERS

The licensee is to commence work within eight months of the date of granting and to continue with due diligence.

His working obligation is expressed in money. It amounts to: 6,000 guilders per square kilometre of licence held in the first five years, and double that amount in the subsequent five-year period, to be spent on reconnaissances and exploration drilling.

He has to produce a copy of the information obtained through his works, including samples to the Geological Service, and to supply this service and the Inspector-General of Mines with half-yearly progress reports. Safety aspects of his operations are controlled by the "Mining Regulations, Continental Shelf".

The licensee is to keep financial administration in the Netherlands. Before the placing of a drilling installation the Minister has to be consulted concerning the location. If it concerns a location in one of the indicated military areas prior permission of the Ministers of Economic Affairs and of Defence is necessary. If it concerns a location in one of the established shipping lanes such prior permission is to be granted by both Ministers mentioned and the Minister of Communications and Water Control. Such permission may be given for a restricted period only.

No guarantee deposit is required, but the licensee is to pay once a bonus of 1,000 guilders per square kilometre and yearly surface rentals of about 50 guilders per square kilometre in the first five-year period; of about 100 guilders per square kilometre in the second five-year period; and of about 150 guilders per square kilometre in the last period of five years. The rental rates are revised annually in accordance with the wage index.

Failure to comply with the financial terms of the licence, inclusive of the working obligation and the obligation to keep accounts in the Netherlands, may lead to withdrawal of the licence. Other infringements are penalized in accordance with established law or, in case the Mining Regulations are contravened, in accordance with the Continental Shelf Mining Act.

Conditions governing the exploitation of oil and gas deposits

As stated earlier, mining legislation distinguishes between operations on land and on the continental shelf. The territorial waters are included in the land legislation.

For winning oil or gas on land, a concession is required, granted by the Crown at its discretion.

On the continental shelf a winning licence is required, to be granted by the Minister.

Both for land concessions and for shelf licences the Minister seeks the advice of the Mining Council. Moreover in both cases the State may decide to participate as to 40 per cent in the exploitation of gas from important pure gas accumulations against a refund of 40 per cent of the expenses incurred by the applicant before the date of granting.

(a) Land

1. Granting of concessions

The Crown grants concessions at its discretion to applicants of satisfactory capabilities. In practice the applicant must have proved by a production test, and to the satisfaction of the authorities, that he has discovered oil or gas in economic quantities within the area applied for. Hence after the introduction – in 1967 – of the system of drilling licences a concessionaire will always have been the holder of a drilling licence. There is no bidding system, nor has a limit been set to the size of the concessions one person may hold. To enable the discoverer to utilize production from a well before having been granted a concession, a "permit de vente" may be granted to him by the Minister for the well concerned on terms to be adapted to the circumstances.

A concession cannot be renounced or withdrawn but the Crown may declare the concessionaire negligent in the fulfilment of his obligations, whereupon the concession is sold in public.

Transfer of parts of a concession requires the previous consent of the Crown, who seeks the advice of the Mining Council.

2. Rights of concession holders

The concession is granted for an unlimited period. The right to carry out exploration borings is included. A concession area may cover all or part of a prior drilling licence, depending on whether the area considered is proven with reasonable certainty by previous drilling. A concession is, however, not necessarily limited to the area of the accumulation found, but may include some additional prospects, if considered enhanced by the discovery.

The concessionaire may dispose freely of the substances extracted, but for gas certain limitations are usually laid down in the modern concession deeds including those relating to Groningen. These limitations are: prior approval of the sales price by the Minister; the obligation to deliver gas destined for consumption in the Netherlands to the N.V. Nederlandse Gasunie, which is the sole distributor in the country; the obligation to deliver gas to Gasunie if requested by the Minister, and in quantities defined by him, in order to safeguard consumption in the Netherlands, but only in so far as current delivery contracts of the concessionaire permit.

The concessionaire may exercise his right of occupation of land.

The laying of pipelines is subject to the approval of the landowners and of the authorities concerned with planning, water supply, etc. Through a pipeline concession obtained from the Minister a person may force a landowner to tolerate the use of his land for this purpose.

A concessionaire is the owner of the production facilities, which are sold together with the concession in case the latter is sold in public.

3. OBLIGATIONS OF CONCESSION HOLDERS

Each concessionaire is to win oil and gas with due diligence and in accordance with the principles of rational exploitation.

Drilling programmes of the wells have to be discussed with the Inspector-General of Mines, so as to avoid endangering the water supply, harming the nation's wealth of mineral resources or the interests of others. Drilling sites, too, may need the consent of the authorities concerned with pollution, planning, etc., in case they are situated in specified areas. For the safety of operations the "Mining Regulations, Land" have to be obeyed.

There are no upper or lower limits to production. In case a reservoir straddles a concession boundary concessionaires at either side of it are to conclude an agreement for exploitation by common accord.

Unitization proper will be encouraged, but as the level of the royalties varies with the yearly production rate per concession, *vis-à-vis* the Government, interests cannot be completely merged.

There is no minimum investment obligation, nor is a guarantee deposit required. The accounts have to be kept in the Netherlands and when operations are under way concessionaires must have an office in the Netherlands.

(b) Continental shelf

1. GRANTING OF WINNING LICENCES

The Minister grants winning licences to an applicant either at his discretion or as a consequence of the claim a successful explorer has to winning rights with respect to his discovery block.

In the first case the application follows the pattern set for obtaining exploration licences. The new licensee is to pay the bonus, stipulated for obtaining a new exploration licence.

For a winning licence resulting from an exploration licence no bonus payment is due, the formalities are the same, though reference to information given previously is allowed.

There is no limit to the maximum amount of winning acreage one person may hold. No bids or special offers are taken into consideration by the Minister when granting applications.

Production, i.e. the transportation of the minerals won across the licence boundary, requires a winning licence.

A licensee may withdraw his licence any time upon notification to the Minister. His licence may be withdrawn by the Minister in case of non-fulfilment of the working obligation, and non-compliance with the financial terms of the licence or the obligation to keep accounts or to hold office in the Netherlands.

2. RIGHTS OF WINNING LICENCE HOLDERS

The licence is granted for a period of 40 years. It includes the right to carry out exploration borings and reconnaissance work for oil or gas.

The works and installations are and remain the property of the licensee, even after the licence has lapsed.

The licence comprises all or part of the discovery block, at the choice of the applicant.

In principle two such blocks can be merged. Concerning the freedom of disposing of the substances extracted, the rules set forth for the land concessions apply.

There is no special regime applying to gas and oil pipelines, except the rules laid down in the "Mining Regulations, Continental Shelf".

3. OBLIGATIONS OF WINNING LICENCE HOLDERS

The obligations aiming at avoiding interference with shipping, fishery, communications, military operations and other interests of others, as well as at combating pollution and at promoting safety, are the same as those for exploration licences. They are governed by the "Mining Regulations, Continental Shelf".

In general the other terms of the winning licences are, as far as applicable, similar to those imposed for the concessions on land, the offshore legislation of 1967 having in fact set the pattern for the terms of concessions, in which the Government has a much freer hand.

Provisions applying to both exploration and production

Licensees and concessionaires are responsible for fulfilment of their obligations.

The obligations with regard to the working conditions of the work force are governed by the Mining Regulations and hence supervised by the Inspector-General of Mines. Provisions regarding social welfare, wages and foreigners employed are supervised by the Minister of Social Affairs.

The Minister may withdraw a permit or a licence in case of repeated offence against the Mining Regulations or of non-fulfilment of the five-year working obligations, of non-compliance with the financial obligations, and of those concerning the sales price and delivery of gas, and of the obligations to keep accounts and hold office in the Netherlands, to conclude an agreement regarding a 40 per cent State participation for the exploitation of gas accumulation or to conclude offset-agreements with holders of adjacent licences.

Against such Ministerial decision appeal is possible to the Crown.

Non-observance of the terms of a land concession may lead to a declaration by the Crown of non-compliance followed by public sale.

To simplify appeal routes most of the financial terms are included in a separate agreement between State and concessionaire, stipulating arbitration according to the rules of the "Nederlands Arbitrage Instituut".

To various other provisions, particularly those of the land concessions, the non-mining legislation is applicable, inclusive of appeal possibilities. Infringement of the Mining Regulations is a penal offence, dealt with through Court procedure.

Special provisions applying to offshore operations

After the Netherlands had acceded to the Geneva Convention on the continental shelf the Continental Shelf Mining Act was introduced (1965). In it the mineral resources over which the Netherlands claims sovereign rights have been defined in a manner similar to the definition given by the convention, except that sand and gravel are excluded. They are not considered subjects of mining legislation but their exploration and exploitation will be soon governed by separate law.

Most of the preventive measures have been mentioned in previous chapters on continental shelf legislation (e.g. exploration). In short they are:

To avoid interference with merchant shipping, a licensee, before placing a mining installation, has to consult the Minister concerning the location. If a location in one of the indicated military areas is concerned, prior permission of the Ministers of Economic Affairs and of Defence is necessary. If a location in one of the established shipping lanes is concerned such prior permission is to be granted by both Ministers mentioned and the Minister of Communications and Water Control. These special permissions may be given for a restricted period only.

Seismic operations are supervised by a Government fishery expert when explosives are used which might harm fish.

Scientific research, if officially recognized, may not be hampered.

Oil or a mixture of oil and water should not be drained off into the sea and appropriate measures should be taken to avoid such liquids' reaching the sea by accident.

About the installation and the removal of a mining installation the Minister, the Inspector-General of Mines, the Director-General of Pilotage and, for checking the geographic position, the Hydrographic Service of the Ministry of Defence have to be informed. Such moves will be published in the Official Gazette and in the Guide for Mariners.

A mining installation falls under Netherlands' jurisdiction. A licensee is obliged to give access to the ships engaged in his mining operations, including reconnaissance, to the officials supervising compliance with the Mining Regulations, even when such ships carry foreign flags.

A safety zone of 500 metres around any mining installation may be prescribed in accordance with the Geneva Convention.

With the mainland proper connections are to be maintained, both as regards telecommunication and personnel transport.

The Netherlands exercises jurisdiction over platforms. If infringements of the mining legislation occur, the licence-holder is held responsible. The contractor is responsible only in so far as he has been charged to comply with the Mining Regulations.

The police functions are in the hands of the Inspector-General of Mines and other specialized government agencies.

The Mining Regulations contain rules concerning the laying of pipelines for production purposes in order to safeguard the workers and shipping, to protect the interests of others and to prevent pollution or to restrict it in case of leakage.

For radio communications permission from the Director-General of Posts, Telegraphs and Telephones is required.

There are no special rules for the joint use of installations.

Mining Regulations deal with the safety measures of the mining aspects, inclusive of diving activities.

For non-compliance with the Mining Regulations the Continental Shelf Mining Act provides for a maximum of six months' imprisonment and a fine not exceeding 10,000 guilders. Repeated violation may lead to withdrawal of the licence.

NORWAY*

ROYAL DECREE OF 31 MAY 1963
The seabed and its subsoil in the submarine areas outside the coast of the Kingdom of Norway are subject to Norwegian sovereignty in respect of the exploitation and exploration of natural deposits, to such extent as the depth of the sea permits the utilization of natural deposits, irrespective of any other territorial limits at sea, but not beyond the median line in relation to other states.

ACT NO. 12 OF 21 JUNE 1963 RELATING TO EXPLORATION FOR AND EXPLOITATION OF SUBMARINE NATURAL RESOURCES

Section 1
This Act applies to exploration for and exploitation of natural resources in the seabed or in its subsoil, as far as the depth of the superjacent waters admits exploitation of natural resources, within as well as outside the maritime boundaries otherwise applicable, but not beyond the median line in relation to other states.

Section 2
The right to submarine natural resources is vested in the State.

The King may give Norwegian or foreign persons, including institutions, companies and other associations, the right to explore for or exploit natural resources. Specific conditions for such permission may be stipulated.

Section 3
The King may issue regulations concerning the exploration for and exploitation of submarine natural resources.

Section 4
Existing legislation shall not preclude the issue of regulations pursuant to Sections 2 and 3 of this Act.

Section 5
The rights of navigation and fishing are not affected by this Act.

Section 6
This Act shall enter into force immediately.

ROYAL DECREE OF 25 AUGUST 1967 RELATING TO SAFE PRACTICE, ETC. IN EXPLORATION AND DRILLING FOR SUBMARINE PETROLEUM RESOURCES

Chapter I

Introductory provisions

Section 1
These regulations shall apply to exploration and drilling for petroleum in the seabed or its subsoil in Norwegian internal waters, in Norwegian territorial waters and in that part of the Continental Shelf which is under Norwegian sovereignty.

* Selected from *Legislation concerning the Norwegian Continental Shelf* (unofficial English translation published by the Royal Ministry of Industry and Handicrafts, Oslo, January 1973).

Section 2
The Royal Norwegian Ministry of Industry (hereinafter called the Ministry) or anyone authorized by it may issue further regulations and orders as deemed necessary for the implementation of these regulations.

The Ministry or anyone authorized by it may, under special circumstances, grant dispensations from provisions laid down in or established by virtue of these regulations.

Section 3
Anyone carrying out such activities as mentioned in Section 1, is obliged, in addition to the provisions contained in Royal Decree of 9 April 1965 [see Royal Decree of 8 December 1972] and in Reconnaissance and Production licences, to comply with the provisions of these regulations and of regulations issued pursuant hereto, and to see to it that these provisions are complied with in regard to their activities. This applies to the licensee, as well as to anyone carrying out such activities for him, either personally or through employees or through independent contractors or subcontractors.

Orders shall be directed to the licensee. In cases where delays may create danger, such orders may be directed to the responsible person on a platform, vessel or aircraft or other installation to which these regulations apply. Copies of such orders shall be forwarded to the licensee without delay.

Section 4
Exploration for and exploitation of petroleum must be carried out in a safe manner in accordance with good oilfield practice and with the regulations in force at all times. The activity must not interfere to an unreasonable degree with other activities. Particular care must be taken to avoid any unreasonable impediment or nuisance to shipping, fishing or aviation, and to avoid damage or risk of damage to underwater cables or other underwater installations. Special care must be taken to avoid damage to marine life and to avoid pollution of the seabed and its subsoil, the sea and the air.

Section 5
The licensee shall currently, and in writing, keep the Ministry informed of the names, address and nationality of contractors or subcontractors employed by him in areas mentioned in Section 1, when such contractors are carrying out activities of some importance.

Section 6
Before provisional or permanent installations, including all types of drilling platforms, are placed on or above the seabed or in its subsoil, the Ministry's written consent to the location or relocation must be obtained. Likewise, the Ministry shall be informed, a sufficient time in advance, about removals and movements of the said installations.

A notice concerning an approved location of said installations shall, a sufficient time in advance, be inserted by the licensee in "Etterretninger for Sjøfarende" (Norwegian Notice to Mariners), "Kunngjøring fra Luftfartsdirektoratet" (Notice from the Norwegian Directorate of Aviation) and likewise be announced in the Norwegian Broadcasting Corporation's "Fiskerimeldinger" and in any other manner which the Ministry may decide. It shall contain information as to the type and position of the installation, light and sound signals, etc. The licensee shall, in the same manner prescribed above, also inform about the removal and movements of such installations.

Section 7
In these regulations a drilling platform is defined as any installation, including vessels, which has been equipped for drilling for petroleum.

Chapter II
Exploration

Section 8
Survey vessels and aircraft carrying out exploration must comply with international and Norwegian regulations and rules in force at the time for the particular location, in connection with navigation and aviation respectively.

Vessels and aircraft must – to the extent deemed necessary – be acquainted with the Norwegian rules for marking of floating and stationary fishing gear and with the rules relating to light signals to be carried by vessels engaged in trawling and other fishing.

They must keep at a safe distance from vessels engaged in fishing and from floating and stationary fishing gear. Particular care must be taken when larger gatherings of fishing vessels are observed.

Section 9
Vessels to be used for seismic surveys must be equipped with radar, echo sounder and sonar (asdic).

Section 10
Aircraft are not allowed to be used for seismic surveys without special permission from the Ministry.

Section 11
Seismic surveys are subject to the following rules:

(*a*) Prior to the commencement of seismic detonations the sonar and radar shall be turned on and shall be kept continuously sweeping round a full circle. Echo sounder and sonar shall thereafter be kept in use continuously until the termination of the survey.

(*b*) As long as seismic surveys are undertaken, the survey vessel shall fly the international flag signal in force.

(*c*) Special care must be shown in the use of explosives. They must not be detonated in the vicinity of vessels engaged in fishing or in the vicinity of floating and stationary fishing gear. Nor must they be detonated if schools of fish are discovered under or near the shot point.

Furthermore, detonations must be carried out in such a manner as not to cause damage or risk of damage to underwater cables or other underwater installations.

(*d*) The explosives employed must be of such types as to cause the least possible damage to marine life.

(*e*) Charges must not be larger than necessary and shall be detonated as near to the surface of the sea as possible. The Ministry reserves the right to decide the types of explosives, detonators, etc. to be used in the survey, as well as to fix the maximum charges to be detonated.

(f) The charges shall be equipped with a safety device which render the charges harmless in case they remain in water for more than 2 hours. Such safety devices shall be approved beforehand by the Ministry or anyone authorized by it.

The charges shall furthermore be marked with the name of the licensee or other identification approved by the Ministry.

Section 12
In ample time prior to the commencement of seismic surveys, Fiskeridirektoratet (The Directorate of Fisheries) in Bergen shall be notified. Furthermore, the said Directorate shall be kept informed of the movements of the vessels and their calls at Norwegian ports.

Section 13
A daily log shall be kept of the surveys. In the case of seismic surveys, the log shall include information on the size of the charges and the number of explosions, with a precise indication of the shot points. Charges which fail to fire, or which misfire, shall also be entered into the log. The log shall, as far as possible, contain information of importance regarding the effects of the surveys on marine life. The Ministry may require the log to be produced.

Chapter III

Drilling platforms

Section 14
The licensee shall – in ample time prior to the commencement of drilling operations – transmit to the Ministry or anyone authorized by it a description of the platform, together with the necessary drawings and specifications.

Prior to the commencement of drilling operations, the consent of the Ministry or anyone authorized by it must be obtained for the use of the drilling platform with installations and equipment.

The cost involved shall be covered by the licensee.

Section 15
The drilling platform shall at all times be seaworthy and be provided with such equipment as required for the safe operation of the platform such as the necessary nautical equipment, telecommunication systems for radio communications on both assigned and emergency frequencies with land stations, helicopters, ships and other platforms in the area, position marking equipment, light and sound signals, life saving equipment, firefighting equipment, first aid equipment, etc.

The Ministry or anyone authorized by it may at any time inspect the platform with installations and equipment. The cost involved by this shall be borne by the licensee.

Section 16
The drilling platform must be constructed in such a manner as to be strong enough to withstand the weather and wind conditions which may be anticipated in the areas mentioned in Section 1. The anchoring systems and jack-up legs, etc.

must be so constructed that the platform is kept in place under the weather conditions that may reasonably be anticipated.

The licensee is obliged to ensure that the platform and equipment is in proper working condition at all times.

Substantial damage caused to the platform or its equipment or installations shall be reported immediately to the Ministry or anyone authorized by it. Repair of such damage or substantial changes in construction shall immediately be reported to the Ministry or anyone authorized by it.

Section 17
The drilling platform with equipment and installations shall be equipped with all necessary safety devices in accordance with good oilfield practice in order to prevent accidents.

The derrick with engines and crane equipment such as blocks, winches, wire ropes, etc. shall be of an approved type and be inspected at short intervals. These inspections shall be recorded in the log mentioned in Section 19.

Wire ropes shall be replaced or cut as soon as they show signs of wear and tear or whenever this is rendered necessary by the amount of work in ton-kilometres performed by the wire.

Moving parts, such as chains, travelling blocks, driving belts, gears, shafts, couplings, clutches, etc. shall be properly shielded. The crown block shall be equipped with a safety device in order to prevent the wire from leaving the sheave.

All hooks shall be equipped with safety latches.

When practical, the derrick shall be equipped with escape ropes or similar devices installed in such a manner as to lead away from the derrick. The derrick floor shall have a sufficient number of emergency exits.

Section 18
Walk-ways, stairways and working surfaces shall be equipped with non-slip surface and, when necessary, be equipped with toeboard and railing.

The companionways, stairways, etc. between the various parts of the platform shall be so constructed as to permit safe passage.

Railings shall likewise be installed on platforms leading over or around open tanks, shafts, gutters and other installations presenting hazards to the safety of personnel.

The deck of the drilling platform shall be constructed in such a manner that water washing the decks drains off easily.

The working areas and living quarters shall be equipped with a sufficient number of emergency exits giving easy access to the life saving equipment such as escape ropes, climbing nets, etc.

The drilling platform shall as far as possible be equipped with a sick bay (hospital room) with necessary facilities to care for sick and injured persons. The platform shall have resuscitating equipment and complete first aid equipment in accordance with the regulations and rules in force at all times. The first aid equipment shall be sufficient to give at all times satisfactory aid onboard and during transport to hospital ashore in connection with any foreseeable accident or disease.

The platform shall be constructed in such a manner that living quarters and working areas are adequately separated.

The living quarters shall be sufficiently sound insulated, ventilated and heated. The quarters shall have sufficient equipment and light to ensure the health and comfort of personnel. The ventilation system shall be so constructed as to prevent penetration of poisonous or obnoxious gases, dust, etc. through the system into the quarters. The ventilation system shall be equipped with main switches for immediate shut-down of the system in cases of danger of gases, etc.

Section 19
On the drilling platform the licensee shall keep a daily log on a form approved by the Ministry. The log shall be made at least in duplicate. One copy shall be filed at the licensee's office in Norway. The other copy shall at all times be retained at the platform and there be available for inspectors appointed by the Ministry.

Section 20
During operations whereby the platform is raised or lowered, only the essential personnel shall be present on the platform. Personnel remaining onboard shall, as far as possible, be stationed on deck and be equipped with approved life vests. Suitable means for safe and immediate removal of personnel from the platform shall remain in readiness during the entire operation. In addition, a stand-by vessel with sufficient capacity and equipment shall be kept ready in the immediate vicinity of the platform.

The manoeuvres mentioned in the first paragraph shall, as far as possible, be undertaken in daylight and only when rendered safe by wind and weather conditions.

The provisions contained in Section 104 shall apply.

Section 21
Towing of drilling platforms in areas mentioned in Section 1, intended for use in these areas, shall not be carried out without prior notification to the Ministry or anyone authorized by it. The towing must be carried out in accordance with the international and Norwegian regulations and rules in force at all times. The Ministry or anyone authorized by it may give further provisions for the towing.

Only essential personnel shall remain on the platform during towing. All proper safety measures must be taken.

The towing must be carried out in such a manner that it causes the least possible nuisance in the areas. Special care shall be taken to fishing and shipping in the area.

Section 22
Unauthorized persons must not enter the drilling platform without special permission from the licensee or anyone authorized by him.

During stay on the platform, visitors must comply with the safety rules applicable to the platform. Visitors shall upon arrival be instructed about safety regulations in force. Specific information must be given about areas where smoking is allowed.

Section 23
The licensee shall at all times keep a record of all persons present on board the platform or on their way to and from the platform. The record shall contain the name of the individual and the name of the company or agency by whom he is

employed. This record shall be available for the Ministry, or anyone authorized by it, at the licensee's base in Norway.

Section 24
Detailed safety instructions shall be prepared for each drilling platform with regard to the operations. Special emphasis shall be placed on the safety and wellbeing of the personnel involved. Each employee shall be required to sign a receipt for his individual copy of the safety instructions.

The person in charge shall ascertain that the workers have understood all verbal and written instructions given for the execution of work operations.

Furthermore, general instructions shall be prepared for each drilling platform with regard to measures to be taken in emergencies. These instructions shall likewise be handed to the personnel in the above-mentioned manner. At frequent intervals drill exercises shall be held with a view to coping with emergencies. The daily log shall contain necessary information as to such exercises.

Section 25
Before drilling is commenced, an organization plan shall be submitted to the Ministry or anyone authorized by it. This plan shall clearly stipulate the command set up and the line of command. A responsible chief or his deputy shall always be present on the drilling platform. The plan must expressly stipulate their abilities. The responsible chief must as far as possible have maritime experience. If not, he shall always have an assistant with sufficient maritime experience.

Section 26
The drilling platform shall be marked with the name of the platform and the name of the licensee.

The marking shall be effected in such a manner as to make identification easily possible from vessels as well as from aircraft. The marking shall be easily visible in daylight as well as at night.

Section 27
The drilling platform shall be equipped with approved lights, sound signals, shape and flag signals. Under special circumstances, the Ministry may decide that the platform shall be equipped with light and sound buoys around the platform with lighthouse lanterns, etc.

For the protection of air traffic the platform shall be equipped with approved warning lights. All points on the platform which may endanger helicopter service to and from the platform shall be sufficiently marked.

Section 28
From sunset till sunrise the drilling platform shall be equipped with one or more white lights placed so as to ensure that at least one light is visible upon approaching the platform from any direction. The lights shall be placed not more than 30 metres above sea level and shall be visible – in dark nights with good visibility – from at least 10 nautical miles. The lights shall be equipped with synchronized devices rendering a flashing signal corresponding to the Morse letter U approximately ever 15 seconds. The lenses of the lights must be constructed in such a manner as to ensure that the light – in addition to being visible at the above-

mentioned distance – is visible from any vessel being in the vicinity of the platform.

Section 29
The platform shall be equipped with one or more high-powered, synchronized devices which are so constructed and installed as to emit sound signals audible in all directions. The sound devices shall be placed not more than 30 metres and not less than 6 metres above sea level and shall be audible at a distance of at least 2 nautical miles in calm weather. The character shall be rhythmic blasts – 2 short and 1 long blast – corresponding to the Morse letter U approximately every 30 seconds.

The short blast shall last a minimum of 0.75 seconds. The sound signals shall be in operation when the visibility is less than 2 nautical miles.

Section 30
The drilling platform shall be equipped with an emergency system for light and sound devices which shall be switched on immediately if the ordinary equipment fails.

Section 31
The light and sound systems provided for in Sections 28–30 must be so constructed as to function without special attention in cases where the platform is evacuated for a shorter or longer period of time.

Section 32
The drilling platform shall be equipped with adequate electric lighting to make work and stay onboard as safe as possible.

The drilling platform shall be equipped with an adequate emergency lighting system powered from an independent energy source. The emergency lighting system shall be switched on immediately should the ordinary lighting system fail.

Flash lights of an approved type shall be easily available at appropriate places.

The emergency lights and the flash lights shall be inspected at regular intervals. Note of the inspection shall be made in the log.

Chapter IV

Drilling

Section 33
Drilling shall not commence until the Ministry's written consent has been obtained (see Section 39 in Royal Decree of 9 April 1965 relating to exploration for and exploitation of petroleum in the seabed and its subsoil on the Norwegian Continental Shelf).

Section 34
Before such consent as mentioned in Section 33 is granted, the applicant shall submit to the Ministry a drilling programme which shall contain, *inter alia*, the following information:

(a) The name of the drilling platform, together with a description of the construction and equipment of the platform, as well as information as to whether the drilling shall be carried out by others than the licensee. If the Ministry has previously given its consent to the use of the drilling platform in the areas mentioned in Section 1, all information regarding later changes in construction, installations and equipment, etc. shall be given.

(b) Information on the geographical position of the well.
(c) The estimated total depth of the well.
(d) The geological strata which are expected to be penetrated.
(e) Depth of the ocean at the well-site.

(f) A programme for the installation of casing. The programme shall give the necessary details as to diameter, weight and type of casing, whether new or used casing is to be employed, at what depth the casing is intended to be installed, together with a cementing programme.

The said casing programme shall be in accordance with good oilfield practice. Necessary consideration shall be given to, *inter alia*, the possibility of unknown underground geological structures at the well-site. Necessary consideration shall likewise be given to any pressure which may be anticipated in the well.

(g) Description of blow-out preventers including auxiliary equipment which will be used during the drilling, with information as to make, type, necessary technical details and the manner in which they will be installed. The description shall likewise contain the necessary information as to pressure tests of the blow-out preventers. Details must furthermore be given as to the manner and frequency of pressure tests to be taken during the period of drilling.

(h) Drilling fluid programme.
(i) Programme for pressure tests and other measurements of the well.
(j) Coring programme.
(k) Testing programme for possible petroleum finds.

(l) Four copies of the safety instructions applicable to the platform and the intended operations, whether issued by the licensee or his contractors, shall be enclosed unless these safety instructions have previously been submitted to the Ministry. Information as to changes in, or amendments to, safety instructions previously submitted, must be given.

Section 35

Major changes in the drilling programme must not be made without the Ministry's consent.

In emergencies, the said programme may be departed from without prior consent. The Ministry shall in such cases be notified forthwith of the alterations and of the underlying circumstances.

Section 36

Prior to the placing of a drilling platform in position for drilling, the seabed shall be checked and other necessary safety precautions be taken in accordance with good oilfield practice with a view to ensure that the platform will remain in place during operations.

The result of these investigations shall be transmitted forthwith to the Ministry.

The licensee must constantly check during drilling that the conditions of the seabed, at the places where the legs or anchors of the drilling platform are situated, are not substantially changed.

Section 37

The drilling platform must be placed at a safe distance from other installations for exploitation of petroleum as well as from lighthouses, seabuoys, telegraph and telephone cables, pipelines, etc.

In areas where cables, pipelines and other underwater installations exist, anchoring, jacking up of platforms and drilling cannot be commenced until the licensee has undertaken a thorough bottom survey, which has exactly localized the position of the underwater cable, pipeline or other installation.

Even if permission for placing a platform is granted according to Section 6, special permission from the Ministry or anyone authorized by it is required before anchoring, jacking up or drilling may take place closer than one nautical mile from cables, pipelines or other installations and less than two nautical miles from telephone or telegraph amplifiers.

Damage caused to cables, pipelines or installations, etc., as mentioned in the foregoing paragraphs, shall, regardless of who is to blame, be compensated by the licensee and the contractor whose activity has caused the damage.

Section 38
The drilling platform shall be positioned so as to give maximum protection to the operation performed thereon including mooring of vessels, landing and take-off of helicopters. Particular care should be taken to avoid likely oil or gas leakage from reaching sources of ignition.

Section 39
The lower deck of the drilling platform must be at a safe distance above the sea level.

Section 40
As soon as the drilling platform has been placed in position, the Ministry shall be informed in writing about the exact geographical position of the platform.

Section 41
When circumstances so demand, the licensee shall provide for a stand-by vessel which shall be stationed at the platform during drilling operations. This stand-by vessel shall have sufficient capacity and equipment to take on board and provide for the total crew of the platform in cases of emergencies.

Section 42
On platforms where the derrick has been lowered, the derrick must not be raised until the drilling platform is properly placed on the seabed or properly anchored. Prior to the erection of the derrick, it must be thoroughly checked that the derrick is in proper working order.

The erection or lowering of the derrick must be carried out only when the weather and wind conditions render this safe, and as far as possible only in daylight. The required safety measures for protection of life and health shall be taken, including such measures as mentioned in Sections 20 and 104 of this Decree.

No other work must be carried out below or in the immediate vicinity of the derrick while it is being erected or lowered.

Section 43
By the end of each shift the offgoing crew shall inform the oncoming crew of defects and damages which have occurred or have been detected during the shift, and which have not been repaired.

The oncoming crew shall make certain that the equipment is in a safe condition.

A note shall be made in the daily log about substantial defects, and the manner in which these have been repaired.

Section 44
Special care must be taken during the loading, unloading, handling and racking of drillpipes and casing. Due precaution must be taken to prevent racked pipes and casing from rolling or shifting.

Section 45
Prior to the start of initial drilling operations in a well, the necessary safety devices for the proper control of the well must be present and easily available on the platform. The said devices shall be installed as drilling operations deem them necessary in accordance with good oilfield practice.

During drilling, all necessary steps shall be taken to keep the well under full control against the presence of oil, gas, water, etc., which may cause explosions, blow-outs, pollution or other destruction or accidents.

In the event of explosion, blow-out, etc., in the well, all necessary steps shall immediately be taken in accordance with good oilfield practice to re-establish safe working conditions and bring the well under control. All necessary measures must immediately be taken to repair, as far as possible, all damage sustained.

Section 46
Each well must be equipped with surface casing according to good oilfield practice. The surface casing shall be cemented at a depth justified by the geological conditions and with a view to maintain complete control of the well at any time.

The surface casing shall be properly cemented over its full length. The cement shall be given sufficient time to set prior to the commencement of further drilling.

Section 47
Intermediate casing must be installed and cemented in such a manner, and at such time, as to ensure full control of the well at any time considering, *inter alia*, the geological conditions of the subsurface, the danger of blow-outs, the protection of other resources in the subsurface and the danger of pollution of sea and air.

Section 48
The production casing shall be installed and cemented in a manner to isolate all hydrocarbon-bearing strata.

Section 49
The casing mentioned in Sections 46–48 shall have such diameter, weight and type, and otherwise be so designed and installed, as to withstand any anticipated pressure encountered in the well during drilling or production.

After the casing has been installed and properly cemented, it must be pressure tested according to good oilfield practice before drilling is resumed.

The installation of used casing is not allowed without proper testing of such casing in advance.

Section 50
Apart from drilling for opening the well, drilling must not be carried out before blow-out preventers and the auxiliary equipment have been properly installed in accordance with good oilfield practice. After surface casing has been set, a minimum of one bag-type preventer, one blind-ram preventer and one pipe-ram preventer must be installed.

The blow-out preventers shall have such construction and such capacity as to enable them, together with the casing installed and the drilling fluid, to fully control any pressure which may be anticipated in the well.

The blow-out preventers shall be equipped with hydraulic controls operated by manual remote control from the derrick floor, within easy reach of the driller. The blow-out preventers shall furthermore be equipped with an extra remote control which may be operated independently and placed at a safe distance from the derrick floor, so as to be reached easily and quickly in the event the control-panel at the derrick floor cannot be reached or fails to function.

The control-panel shall plainly indicate whether the blow-out preventers are open or closed.

The accumulator system required for the operation of the hydraulic system of the blow-out preventers shall be of sufficient capacity to operate against maximum pressure conditions to be expected in the well during drilling.

Section 51
Necessary additional blow-out prevention equipment, including a kelly cock and automatic inside blow-out preventer valve (back pressure type), shall be at hand on the platform in accordance with good oilfield practice.

Section 52
During drilling, installation and cementing of casing, the blow-out prevention equipment shall be pressure tested and function tested at regular intervals. Function tests of the blow-out preventers shall be carried out as frequently as necessary, at least once per 24 hours or every time the drill-pipe and drill-bit are pulled out of the borehole. The blow-out preventers shall be pressure tested at regular intervals according to good oilfield practice.

A note shall be made in the daily log concerning such testing.

Section 53
During drilling, drilling fluid of the proper composition shall be kept circulating at all times in the well, in accordance with good oilfield practice. The drilling fluid shall ordinarily be filtered and constantly checked against undesirable elements including gases or liquids which may cause explosions or fire. The drilling fluid shall be of such density and composition as required by the geological conditions and other circumstances at the well-site. While the drilling fluid is in use, proper care must be taken to avoid pollution of the sea.

Shale shakers and drilling fluid tanks shall be provided with suitable and adequate means to remove explosive gases away from the platform. Areas where the shale shakers and drilling fluid tanks are located shall be tested regularly with gas detectors or explosionmeters for explosive gases. The drilling fluid tanks shall be equipped with mud-pit level indicators. The indicator shall be so constructed as to make it possible to read the mud-pit level directly on the control-panel at the drill stand.

Section 54
Drilling which intentionally deviates from the vertical line drawn from the centre of the well on the seabed, shall not be allowed without the written consent of the Ministry. However, such consent is not required for deviations over shorter intervals, deviations to straighten out the well or to overcome difficulties encountered during drilling. The well shall be checked to ensure that it does not deviate substantially from the vertical line.

The written consent of the Ministry is required in cases of drilling multiple holes from the same location.

Section 55
Gas detectors or explosionmeters shall be readily available on the platform.

The platform shall likewise be provided with sufficient apparatus for full breathing protection.

If sulphurous or other poisonous gases are encountered during drilling, all necessary safety precautions shall be taken to prevent accidents. The Ministry shall be notified forthwith.

Section 56
In connection with swabbing, formation testing, shooting, hydraulic fracturing, acidizing or other chemical treatment of a well, all necessary safety measures must be taken. Preferably, such activities must take place by daylight and only when wind and weather conditions render it advisable.

The work must be performed in such a way that the well shall not be damaged and salt water or other alien matter shall not be allowed to penetrate into the well.

Details of the activities mentioned in the first paragraph, together with information on the result achieved, shall be included in the report to the Ministry mentioned in Section 69.

Section 57
Prior to the commencement of the activities mentioned in Section 56, the drilling platform shall be cleared of all unnecessary obstructions. Only the personnel necessary for the operation shall be on or below the drilling floor, or in the immediate vicinity. All necessary precautions against fire shall be taken. The firefighting equipment shall be ready for immediate use.

After termination of the activities mentioned in Section 56, the well and the drilling platform shall immediately be cleaned.

Section 58
During acidizing operations personnel who may come in contact with acid shall be provided with protective clothing including hoods, gloves and boots.

Acid-containers must be handled with care and shall be properly secured during transport and use so as to prevent unnecessary movement, breakage or the inflicting of damage to the surroundings.

A sufficient amount of neutralizing material shall be easily available for neutralizing any spillage of acid.

Section 59
If coal or other natural resources are encountered during drilling, the Ministry shall, within a reasonable time, be informed about the nature and extent of such

deposits. All necessary precautions must be taken to preserve exploitable deposits. The Ministry may issue instructions for the preservation of the discoveries.

Section 60

During drilling operations the necessary logs must be taken according to good oilfield practice. Such logs, together with any analyses made thereof, shall be forwarded without delay to the Ministry.

The Ministry shall receive a composite log of the well within 6 months after the completion or abandonment of a well. Within the same time limit a final report concerning the well shall be transmitted to the Ministry.

Section 61

The finding of any petroleum deposits shall promptly be reported to the Ministry.

Within a reasonable time, complete information relating to the nature of the deposit, and what further steps have been taken to determine the extent of the deposit and the results thereof, shall be submitted in writing to the Ministry. Furthermore, information shall be given as to whether the deposits are considered commercially exploitable. When the plan for exploitation is completed, it shall likewise be furnished to the Ministry.

Section 62

Wells where petroleum finds have been made shall be secured in a proper manner according to good oilfield practice. The security precautions shall be of a type to facilitate production, protect the well against penetration of water and other alien matter, to prevent escape of petroleum from the well and to protect the sea and air against pollution.

Section 63

The Ministry shall be informed at least 24 hours in advance of a discontinuation of extended duration and the resumption of drilling operations.

Chapter V

Abandonment of wells

Section 64

A well cannot be abandoned unless the Ministry has been notified at least 24 hours in advance. The licensee shall explain in the notification the reasons for abandoning the well. He shall furthermore submit a plan for how the well will be plugged, secured and abandoned.

The Ministry may stipulate a time limit within which each installation in or above the well shall be removed.

Section 65

When a well is abandoned, casing strings and cement in the well must not be removed or destroyed – except as provided in Section 67 – without the written consent of the Ministry.

Section 66

An abandoned well shall be plugged – in accordance with good oilfield practice – with top cement plugs and with additional cement plugs in such a number, of such length and with such spacing between the individual plugs as is required in order to maintain complete control of the well and prevent the escape of fluids from the well or penetration of salt water or other alien matter into the well.

The well, including the interval between the cement plugs, shall be filled with drilling fluid or other fluid of sufficient density and with such other properties to safely withstand, together with the plugs, any pressure which may develop within the well.

Section 67

When a well is abandoned, parts of casing strings and other installations protruding from the seabed must – except as provided in Section 64 to 66 – be removed to such a depth that no obstruction remains which may cause danger or impediment to fishing or shipping. Before final abandonment of the well, the licensee must make sure that on the seabed, and on the surface of or in the vicinity of the drilling location, no obstructions of any kind remain, as a result of his operations, which may cause damage or impediment to fishing, shipping or other activities.

Chapter VI

Reports, samples, etc., relating to drilling, finds and abandonment of the well

Section 68

While drilling operations are in progress, the licensee shall keep a daily log containing data on all operations during the day. Such information shall include:

(*a*) Depth of the well at the beginning of the day.

(*b*) Depth of the well at the end of the day.

(*c*) Diameter of the borehole.

(*d*) The geological formations encountered.

(*e*) Characteristics of drilling fluid used.

(*f*) Installation of casing.

(*g*) If casing is installed, all relevant data concerning the installation, indicating the diameter, type and weight, together with information on whether new or used casing is employed and to what depth the casing string has been installed.

(*h*) Patriculars concerning cementing.

(*i*) Water, oil, gas, etc., encountered.

(*j*) Details concerning well-logs.

(*k*) Deviation measurements, formation tests, pressure tests and temperature measurements in the well as well as other tests undertaken.

(*l*) Any other operations carried out, such as the recovery of broken drillpipes from the borehole, shooting, perforating, fracturing or acidizing of the well, completion or abandonment of the well, etc.

(*m*) When the Ministry so decides, what steps have been taken to protect underwater telecables in the area.

The daily log shall further contain information about accidents, damage, injuries and other occurrences and other information which may be deemed of current or future interest to the authorities.

The Ministry may require further information concerning the activities carried out.

Section 69
As long as drilling operations are in progress, the licensee shall transmit to the Ministry a weekly report of the activities. The report shall contain such information as mentioned in Section 68 with regard to the week in question. This report shall be in the possession of the Ministry within the expiry of the following week.

Section 70
The licensee shall, while drilling is in progress, collect from the drilling fluid samples of all rock types in all the geological formations penetrated. When drilling is carried out in geological formations which may be of interest from a petroleum point of view, such samples shall be taken at frequent intervals. In these instances the ordinary intervals shall not exceed 10 metres.

All samples collected by the licensee shall be washed, dried and preserved in bags suited for this purpose. The bag shall be labelled with the name of the well and the date the samples were collected and the depths of origin. The samples or parts thereof shall within three months after the completion or abandonment of the well be dispatched – at the expense of the licensee – to Norges geologiske undersøkelse (the Geological Survey of Norway).

Geologists of the Ministry and of the Geological Survey shall at any time have access to the samples.

Section 71
The licensee shall, when it is deemed necessary, take and keep cores of the various geological formations penetrated. Within three months of the termination of drilling, the licensee shall dispatch, at his own expense, complete longitudinal sections of each core to the Geological Survey. The longitudinal section shall contain not less than one-fourth of the core. The Ministry shall receive copies of descriptions and analyses made of the core.

Geologists of the Ministry and of the Geological Survey shall at any time have access to the cores.

(Chapters VII to XII are omitted)

Chapter XIII

Use of radioactive equipment

Section 112
Due care must be shown during transport, storage, handling and use of radioactive equipment in order to avoid harmful effects to people, animals and plant life.

Section 113
In ample time before radioactive equipment is acquired, the licensee is obliged to submit for approval to the Ministry or anyone authorized by it a complete plan for the transport, storage and use of the radioactive equipment. The plan shall also give a description of the safety measures to be taken.

Section 114
The personnel involved with the transport, storage, handling and use of the radioactive equipment shall be specially trained for the work. The number of persons participating in this work, or persons who otherwise may be exposed to the danger of radioactivity, shall be kept at a minimum.

All necessary precautionary measures must be taken to avoid harmful effects to the persons mentioned above and to the rest of the personnel on board the platform.

Section 115
Radioactive equipment and its wrapping shall be labelled so as to give warning about the danger of radioactivity. The same applies to storage rooms on board the drilling platform and during transport. The labelling will be in accordance with Norwegian standard.

When not in use, radioactive equipment shall be kept in securely locked rooms. Necessary measures shall be taken to prevent such equipment from being lost or misplaced.

Section 116
If radioactive equipment is misplaced or lost, the licensee shall immediately notify the Ministry or anyone authorized by it.

(Chapters XIV and XV are omitted)

ROYAL DECREE OF 31 JANUARY 1969: RULES RELATING TO SCIENTIFIC RESEARCH FOR NATURAL RESOURCES ON THE NORWEGIAN CONTINENTAL SHELF, ETC.

By virtue of Section 3 of the Act of 21 June 1963 relating to exploration for and exploitation of natural resources of the seabed and its subsoil, it is hereby provided:

Section 1
These regulations shall apply to scientific research for the natural resources of the seabed or its subsoil in Norwegian internal waters, in Norwegian territorial waters, and in the part of the Continental Shelf which is under Norwegian sovereignty, but not in areas subject to private property rights.

Section 2
The natural resources referred to in these rules consist of the mineral and other inanimate resources of the seabed and its subsoil together with living organisms belonging to the sedentary species, that is to say, organisms which, at the harvestable stage, either are immobile on or under the seabed or are unable to move except in constant physical contact with the seabed or the subsoil.

Section 3
The Royal Ministry of Industry and Handicrafts (hereinafter referred to as the Ministry) may grant licences for scientific research for natural resources in the seabed or in its subsoil or in limited areas of same. The licence shall be valid for a specified period of time and shall otherwise be in agreement with this Decree. The Ministry may make additional provisions to ensure the implementation of this Decree and may stipulate supplementary conditions in each separate licence.

Section 4
A scientific research licence may be granted to Norwegian or foreign scientific institutions, scientists and others having a need for conducting scientific researches.

Section 5
A written application for a scientific research licence must be filed with the

Ministry at least 30 days prior to the commencement of research activities. If the application is not written in Norwegian, a translation into Norwegian must be enclosed. Appendices to the application should be presented in Norwegian or English.

The application shall contain the following information:

(*a*) Name, address and nationality of the institution, person, etc., on whose behalf the research is to be carried out, together with the name of the person who is to serve as a liaison with the Norwegian authorities.

(*b*) Name, address and nationality of the person or persons, institutions, etc., who are to carry out the research.

(*c*) Information on the nature and objectives of the research, the expected dates of its commencement and termination and the areas in which it will be carried out.

(*d*) A description of the methods of research, including information on ships, aircraft or other floating or airborne vessels, to be used in the research.

(*e*) Whether seismic exploration is contemplated and, if so, a description of the methods and the types of explosives to be used with specification of the size of the charges and of depth of detonation. Information shall likewise be given as to whether the vessels are equipped with radar, echosounder, sonar or other acceptable types of fish-detecting equipment.

(*f*) Indication of the extent to which the research is to be conducted from Norwegian land territory with, as far as possible, indication of Norwegian ports, airfields or other Norwegian areas to be used as bases for the research.

The Ministry may require additional information.

Section 6
A scientific research licence is usually granted for one particular investigation. The licence is free of duty unless otherwise decided in each particular case.

Section 7
Unless otherwise decided, the licence entitles the licensee to carry out the following operations:

(*a*) Magnetic surveys;
(*b*) gravimetric surveys;
(*c*) seismic surveys;
(*d*) thermal conductivity measurements;
(*e*) radiometric measurements;
(*f*) collection of samples from the seabed or its subsoil, provided that drilling is not involved.

The Ministry may, on application, grant permission to use other exploration methods.

Section 8
Any substantial deviation from the research programme submitted (see Section 5 (*c*)), must not be carried out without obtaining the consent of the Ministry in advance.

Section 9
The Ministry may demand in the licence that the Ministry, or anyone authorized by it, shall have the right to participate in or be represented in the research.

Section 10
The scientific research licence does not give any exclusive right to undertake research in the areas covered by the licence. Nor does it give rights or priority to exploit possible natural resources.

The Ministry may at any time grant exploitation licences to others in the areas covered by the granted scientific research licence without incurring liability, to the licensees mentioned in Section 4.

Section 11
At the termination of the research, the holder of a scientific research licence shall, without delay, submit a report to the Ministry concerning the extent and the execution of the research. The Ministry may stipulate in the licence that reports shall also be submitted while the research is in progress.

The holder of a scientific research licence shall, within a reasonable period of time, submit to the Ministry a detailed report on the results of the research.

The Ministry may require additional information and material to supplement the reports mentioned in paragraphs 1 and 2.

The Ministry may decide that the research results shall be published in a recognized scientific publication or in another manner acceptable to the Ministry. A reasonable number of copies of the relevant publication shall be submitted to the Ministry.

Section 12
The scientific research must be carried out in a safe manner and must not interfere, to any unreasonable degree, with other activities. Particular care must be taken to avoid unreasonable impediment or nuisance to fishing, shipping navigation or aviation, damage or risk of damage to marine life, damage or risk of damage to natural resources on the seabed or in its subsoil, or to underwater cables or other underwater installations, pollution or risk of pollution to the seabed, its subsoil, the sea or the air.

Section 13
The scientific research must be carried out in accordance with the safety regulations in force at any time. The provisions of the Royal Decree of 25 August 1967 relating to safe practice, etc., in exploration and drilling for submarine petroleum resources shall be valid in as far they are applicable.

Section 14
The Ministry may, under special circumstances, grant dispensations, wholly or in part, from the provisions laid down in this Decree.

Section 15
This Decree enters into force immediately.

ROYAL DECREE OF 12 JUNE 1970 RELATING TO PROVISIONAL RULES CONCERNING EXPLORATION FOR CERTAIN SUBMARINE NATURAL RESOURCES OTHER THAN PETROLEUM ON THE NORWEGIAN CONTINENTAL SHELF, ETC.

Pursuant to Section 3 of Act No. 12 of 21 June 1963 relating to Exploration and Exploitation of Submarine Natural Resources, the following rules are provided:

Section 1
These rules shall apply to exploration for certain submarine natural resources other than petroleum – see the definition of petroleum in Section 2 of the Royal Decree of 9 April 1965 – on the seabed or in its subsoil in Norwegian internal waters, in Norwegian territorial waters and in the part of the Continental Shelf which is under Norwegian sovereignty, but not in areas subject to private property rights.

Any exploration in Norwegian internal waters and in Norwegian territorial waters is subject to the Royal Decree of 9 February 1968 relating to "Prohibited sea areas" and "Rules regarding the access of foreign non-military vessels to any part of Norwegian territory in peacetime".

Section 2
For the purpose of this Decree, submarine natural resources mean mineral resources other than petroleum, inorganic resources, and coal on the seabed and in its subsoil.

Section 3
The Ministry of Industry may grant licences to explore (reconnaissance licences) for certain submarine natural resources on the seabed or in its subsoil or in defined parts thereof. Such licences are granted for a period of up to two years.

Section 4
Reconnaissance licences may be granted to Norwegian citizens, corporations, foundations or other associations. The licence is nontransferable.

Section 5
Written application for a reconnaissance licence must be filed with the Ministry at least 30 days prior to the intended commencement of the exploration.

The application shall contain the following information:

(a) Name and address of the person or persons or corporations, etc., on whose behalf the exploration is to be carried out, with the name of the person who is to serve as liaison with the Norwegian authorities.

(b) Name, address and nationality of the person or persons or corporations, etc., who will conduct the exploration.

(c) A description of the exploration to be carried out, the purpose of the exploration, with indication of the dates of the intended commencement and termination thereof, and with indication of the areas in which the exploration will be carried out. The exploration area shall be drawn on a separate map attached to the application.

(d) Description of exploration methods including information with regard to ships, aircraft or other floating or airborne objects to be used in the exploration.

(e) Indication of the extent to which the exploration will be conducted from Norwegian land territory, if possible with indication of Norwegian ports, airfields or other Norwegian areas to be used as bases for the exploration.

The Ministry of Industry may require additional information.

(Section 6 is omitted)

Section 7
Except as otherwise provided in the licence, it entitles the licensee to carry out the following explorations:

(*a*) geological and geophysical surveys for the purpose of examining the upper strata of the subsoil;

(*b*) sampling of the seabed or its subsoil, but not exploratory drilling to a greater depth than 25 metres.

The Ministry may, upon special application stating the reasons therefore, permit the use of other exploration methods.

(Sections 8 to 11 are omitted)

Section 12
The exploration shall be conducted in a proper and safe manner and, in so far as possible, must not interfere with other activities. Particular care must be taken in the exploration, as far as possible, to avoid creating any difficulty or obstacle to shipping, fishing or aviation, to avoid any harm or hazard to marine fauna or flora, to natural resources on the seabed or in its subsoil, including petroleum resources, or to submarine cables or other submarine installations, and to avoid contamination or risk of contamination of the seabed, its subsoil, the sea or the air.

The licensee is obliged to comply with instructions regarding safety measures issued by the maritime and port authorities. The costs of such measures will be paid by the licensee.

(Sections 13 to 17 are omitted)

Section 18
If damage or inconvenience is caused, the Norwegian law of torts is applicable. The tort feasor, his employer and the holder of the reconnaissance licence are jointly and severally liable for the claim.

The fact that the Ministry of Industry has approved or permitted the act or device which has caused the damage or inconvenience, does not exempt from liability.

(Sections 19 and 20 are omitted)

Section 21
The Oslo City Court shall be the proper legal venue in any dispute which can be brought before the courts of law, unless another venue is mandatory under Norwegian law or has been explicitly agreed.

(Section 22 is omitted)

ROYAL DECREE OF 8 DECEMBER 1972 RELATING TO EXPLORATION FOR AND EXPLOITATION OF PETROLEUM IN THE SEABED AND SUBSTRATA OF THE NORWEGIAN CONTINENTAL SHELF

Pursuant to Act No. 12 of 21 June 1963 relating to Exploration for and Exploitation of Submarine Natural Resources, Section 3, it is herewith decreed:

Chapter 1

Introductory provisions

Section 1

The provisions of this Decree shall apply to all activities pertaining to exploration for and exploitation of petroleum in the seabed and in substrata of the Norwegian inner coastal waters, in Norwegian territorial waters and on that part of the Continental Shelf which is subject to Norwegian sovereignty, but not in areas subject to private property rights.

Section 2 (part)

As used in this Decree, the term petroleum shall be understood to mean and include all liquid and gaseous hydrocarbons existing in their natural state in the substrata as well as all other substances, including sulphur, produced as a by-product in extraction of such hydrocarbons.

Section 3

Licences of the following types may be granted pursuant to the provisions of this Royal Decree as well as pursuant to such additional conditions as are specified in the licence:

(1) Licence for the exploration for petroleum on the seabed or in its substrata or in specific areas thereof, such licence conveying no exclusive right to the licensee (Reconnaissance licence).

(2) Licence providing exclusive right to exploration for and exploitation of petroleum in specific areas (Production licence).

(3) Licence for the placing of installations other than production facilities, such as storage installations, liquefaction installations, installations for production of electricity, pipelines, shipment installations and electric cables on, in or above the areas mentioned in Section 1.

Chapter 2

Reconnaissance licence

(Sections 4 and 5 are omitted)

Section 6

A reconnaissance licence shall be valid for a period of three calendar years. A licence fee of 20,000 kroner per calendar year shall be paid annually in advance. The licence shall be considered to have been relinquished if the licensee has not paid the fee due for the coming calendar year by 31 December.

Section 7

A reconnaissance licence entitles the licensee to carry out the following types of exploration surveys:

(a) Magnetic surveys;
(b) gravimetric surveys;
(c) seismic surveys;
(d) heat-flow measurements;
(e) radio-metric measurements;
(f) bottom sampling, drilling excluded;

(g) geochemical surveys, excluding sampling deeper than 25 metres below the seabed.

Upon application the Ministry may permit the use of other types of exploration methods.

Section 8

The reconnaissance licence shall stipulate the areas to which it shall be applicable. Such licence neither gives an exclusive right for exploration in the areas to which the licence is applicable, nor does it convey a right or priority for the exploitation of possible petroleum deposits, or natural resources other than petroleum.

The licence does not entitle the licensee to engage in exploration in areas covered by a production licence or in areas covered by a licence for the production of natural resources other than petroleum with such exceptions as provided for in Section 15, third paragraph.

The Ministry may at any time grant a production licence to other applicants for areas to which a reconnaissance licence is applicable, without incurring liability on its part or without resulting in any obligation on the part of the Ministry to repay the licence fee.

The Ministry may stipulate further conditions in the reconnaissance licence.

(Section 9 is omitted)

Section 10 (part)

Copies of all essential field data and interpretations, as well as such samples as are obtained, shall be forwarded to the Ministry when each survey is completed. So shall all other results derived from the survey such as geological maps, structural maps, cross-sections, etc.

Chapter 3

Production licence

Section 11

The King may grant a production licence to companies, foundations or other organizations established in conformity with Norwegian law and having their principal seat of business in Norway.

If special circumstances so require, the Ministry may approve that an agreement is entered into between a Norwegian subsidiary company and its foreign parent company as to the manner in which the exploration for and exploitation of petroleum is to be performed.

If special circumstances so require, the Ministry may grant a licence to foreign companies, etc., having established a branch in Norway with permanent representation which is fully authorized to act for such corporation, etc., and to enter into binding commitments in its name, to the same extent as such authority is vested in the board of a Norwegian joint stock company. The Ministry may at any time establish further conditions as to the organization of the branch.

Two or more corporations, etc., separately fulfilling the requirements described in the preceding part of this section, may be granted a joint production licence.

(Sections 12 to 14 are omitted)

Section 15
A production licence shall be valid for a period of six years. As provided by this Decree or as otherwise stipulated by the licence granted, the licensee may demand that the period of validity be extended with respect to a part of the area.

The licence gives the licensee exclusive right to exploration for and exploitation of petroleum deposits in the areas to which the licence is applicable.

Under special circumstances, the Ministry may authorize the holder of a reconnaissance or production licence applicable to adjacent areas, to engage in such limited exploration in the licenced area as may be deemed necessary to obtain sufficient knowledge as to the geological conditions in said adjacent areas. After the licensee has had an opportunity to present his view, the Ministry may determine what survey(s) may be carried out, in which areas and over what period of time such exploration shall be permitted.

The production licence shall not preclude others than the licensee from obtaining permission to engage in exploration for and exploitation of natural resources other than petroleum, to the extent that such operations do not cause significant inconvenience to the activity conducted by a licensee under the provisions of a production licence.

In the event that a discovery of both petroleum and of submarine natural resources other than petroleum is made in an area, and it is impossible to exploit both discoveries at the same time, the Ministry shall decide which activity shall have priority. In so deciding, the Ministry shall take into consideration which discovery was made first, the importance of the discovery to the Norwegian economy, the possible duration of the activity and any other significant factors.

The Ministry may determine that the licensee who is permitted to engage in exploitation is to pay compensation to the licensee who is required to postpone his activity. The licensee whose activity is postponed may require a prolongation of his licence for a period corresponding to the length of the postponement. During such period he shall not be required to pay any fees stipulated by provisions of this Decree.

Section 16
A production licence may be granted for one block, several blocks or parts of one or several blocks (the licence area). Each licence area shall be regarded as a single unit in relation to the applicability of the provisions of this Decree, except as otherwise provided or specifically decided in individual cases.

Section 17
No production licence may be granted until the Ministry, after consultation with the applicant, has approved a work programme for the licence area applicable to the six-year period. The work programme may provide for further exploration, including seismic surveys, etc., and drilling of an agreed number of wells to specified depths or geological formations.

If the work programme as provided for in the preceding paragraph is not fulfilled or if the licensee surrenders his rights, or if the licence for any other reasons should lapse prior to the fulfilment of the programme, the Ministry may demand the payment of an amount equivalent to the estimated cost of execution of any non-fulfilled portion of the programme in conformity with good oilfield practices as applicable within the said area.

The Ministry shall fix the magnitude of such amount. If such amount is unacceptable to the licensee, he must, within 30 days after receipt of a written notification of the Ministry's decision, refer the matter to arbitration as provided by the provisions of Section 55 hereof.

(Section 18 is omitted)

Section 19

A licensee may surrender his rights under the licence for the remaining part of the six-year period by giving three months' written notice.

Surrender of the licence does not exempt the licensee from the financial obligations undertaken by him pursuant to the provisions of this Decree or to other applicable special conditions (see Section 17, second paragraph).

A surrender of a licence shall apply to the entire area to which the licence is applicable. The Ministry may accept surrender of part of the area if the licensee submits a revised work programme acceptable to the Ministry.

Section 20

A licensee, who has fulfilled the work programme and such other conditions as required by the particular production licence, may demand that the licence remain valid for up to one-half of the original licence area, except as provided in Section 21, third paragraph. If the production licence is applicable to several blocks, at least half of the area of each block shall be relinquished unless the Ministry should approve some other relinquishment pattern. A written request for the extension of the valid period of the production licence must be submitted to the Ministry not less than three months prior to the expiration of the six-year period, specifying that part of the original licence area for which an extension of validity is desired. Such area shall be drawn on a map enclosed in the request.

If no such request for extension has been made, the rights of the licensee shall lapse at the expiration of the six-year period.

Section 21

The areas which the licensee must reliquish pursuant to Section 20 shall form one continuous area bounded by lines of parallels of latitude and longitude expressed in whole degrees and whole minutes. No boundary line shall be less than three minutes of latitude and five minutes of longitude.

The retained area of a block shall consist of at least 100 square kilometres, unless otherwise approved by the Ministry.

If discoveries of petroleum are made and such discoveries extend over an area exceeding half a block, the licensee may require that the prolongation shall apply to all deposits, even if this should result in retention of more than half the block by the licensee.

In instances as described in the preceding paragraph, the Ministry shall fix the boundaries when the licensee has had an opportunity to present his view.

Section 22

The extension of the licence as provided in Section 20 shall apply for a period of 30 years after expiration of the six-year period mentioned in Section 15 (see, however, Section 33).

(Sections 23 to 30 are omitted)

Section 31
The Ministry may, as a condition for the granting of a production licence, require state participation.

Furthermore the Ministry may require that, in addition to the fees prescribed in this Decree, a production bonus shall be paid, or stipulate that other conditions may be required for the granting of a production licence.

(Section 32 is omitted)

Section 33
If there is reason to believe that a petroleum deposit will continue to be productive after expiration of the 30-year period (see Section 22), the Ministry may permit the licensee to continue such exploitation. An application requesting such permission should be submitted to the Ministry at least two years prior to the expiration of the licence.

The conditions giving such an extension shall be stipulated by the Ministry after the licensee has had an opportunity to present his view.

Section 34 (part)
Produced petroleum shall be landed in Norway unless the King, upon application, approves some other landing point.

Section 35 (part)
In the case of war, danger of war or in other emergency situations, the King may decide that a licensee shall place all produced petroleum, or any part thereof, at the disposal of the Norwegian authorities.

Chapter 4

Storage installations, liquefaction installations, installations for production of electricity, pipelines, shipment facilities, electric cables, etc.

Section 36 (part)
Storage installations, liquefaction installations, installations for production of electricity, pipelines, shipment facilities, electric cables, etc., may not, except as permitted by the Ministry and subject to such conditions as are stipulated by the Ministry, be placed in, on or above the areas mentioned in Section 1. Further provisions as to the valid period of such permission shall be stipulated in each licence.

A holder of a production licence cannot oppose the laying of pipelines or cables of all kinds in, on or above his licence area. This provision shall also apply to such storage or other facilities as may be required in such area by existence of special circumstances. The installations must not, however, cause damage or unnecessary inconvenience to the holder of the production licence.

(Section 37 is omitted)

Chapter 5

General provisions

Section 38

The Ministry may issue such further rules as may be required in regard to the manner in which exploration for and exploitation of petroleum shall, at any given time, be carried out, including rules regarding:

(*a*) designing, building or siting of installations or facilities in, on or above the areas mentioned in Section 1;

(*b*) drilling, measures relating to production, preparation for production, beginning of production and increases in current production;

(*c*) plugging of wells and preventive measures against pollution;

(*d*) measures intended to protect other activities in the area, including navigation, fishing and any other measures intended to protect animal and plant life;

(*e*) safety measures of all types; and

(*f*) measures intended to further proper exploitation of petroleum deposits (conservation).

(Sections 39 and 40 are omitted)

Section 41

The Ministry may for longer or shorter periods, for special reasons, wholly or in part halt current exploration, prohibit exploration in certain areas or impose special conditions on any continued exploration. When special circumstances so require, the Ministry may also take similar steps with respect to drilling and production.

When any measures as mentioned above result from circumstances not attributable to the licensee, the Ministry may upon application prolong the licence for a period of time and modify the obligations imposed on the licensee.

No claim for compensation may be made against the State as a result of its decisions, pursuant to the first paragraph of this Section.

(Sections 42 and 43 are omitted)

Section 44

Any discovery having historical interest, such as shipwrecks, etc., made during exploration for and exploitation of petroleum, shall immediately be reported to the Ministry. The activity must not damage or destroy any such discovery (see Act of 29 June 1951, No. 3, relating to antiquities).

The Ministry may issue orders as to the procedure to be observed in treatment of such discovery.

(Section 45 is omitted)

Section 46

Temporary and permanent installations and facilities on or above the seabed shall be properly marked in accordance with such provisions as may be stipulated by the Ministry. Platforms and other surface installations shall show the name of the licensee as well as the designation of the well or the production field, in order to facilitiate identification (see Royal Decree of 25 August 1967 relating to safe practice, etc. in exploration and drilling for submarine petroleum resources).

Section 47
A safety zone is to be established around and above any temporary and permanent installations on or above the seabed, including drilling platforms or production platforms, pumps, storage installations and shipment facilities. Such a safety zone shall extend 500 metres from the outermost points of the installation. The Ministry may decide that a shorter distance shall apply.

Vessels, floating objects, aircraft or other appliances constructed to be airborne, but not definable as aircraft, must, if not connected with the operations, keep clear of the safety zone.

The provisions of this Section do not apply to pipelines, electric cables, etc.

(Sections 48 to 50 are omitted)

Section 51
If damage or inconvenience is caused, the Norwegian law of torts shall be applicable. The tort feasor as well as his employer and the licensee shall be jointly and severally liable for any claim for compensation.

The fact that the Ministry has approved of or permitted the action or appliance which has caused the damage or inconvenience does not exonerate from liability.

(Sections 52 and 53 are omitted)

Section 54
The licensee shall carry out his exploration for and exploitation of petroleum from a base in Norway. His organization in Norway shall be sufficient to direct this activity and to make all decisions as to the activity.

The licensee shall use Norwegian goods and services in the activity as far as they are competitive with regard to quality, service, schedule of delivery and price.

Norwegian contractors shall be included in invitations for tenders as far as they produce goods or render services of the kind required.

On evaluating the offers given by Norwegian or foreign bidders, the licensee shall take into account the extent to which the bidders will use Norwegian goods and services.

The licensee is responsible for the observation of these provisions by his contractors and their sub-contractors.

Section 55 (part)
Wherever this Decree, or a licence granted pursuant to it, provides that a dispute shall be settled by arbitration, the code of 13 August 1915, No. 6, relating to judicial procedure in civil cases, Chapter 32, shall be applicable unless another procedure for settlement is expressly provided or agreed upon.

Section 56
The Oslo City Court shall be the proper legal venue in disputes which can be brought before the court unless another venue is prescribed under Norwegian law or is expressly agreed upon.

APPENDIX IV

Section 57 (part)
Any serious or repeated violation of the provisions of this Decree or of the stipulated conditions may cause the Ministry to revoke a licence. If the violation is of less serious character, a licence can be revoked only if the violation in question is not corrected within such reasonable time as stipulated by the Ministry.

(Sections 58 to 60 are omitted)

Index

ACTS (U.K.)
Administration of Justice Act (1956), 164
Coastal Protection Act (1949), 173
Consular Relations Act (1968), 164
Continental Shelf Act (1964), 167-8, 170, 172, 173, 177, 197
Control of Pollution Act (1974), 191-4 *passim*, 226, 239
Crown Proceedings Act (1947), 206
Customs and Excise Act (1952), 166
Dumping at Sea Act (1974), 204, 233
Fishery Limits Act (1964), 178, 179
Fishing Vessels (Safety Provisions) Act (1970), 182
Herring Fishery (Scotland) Act (1889), 181
Marine, etc., Broadcasting (Offences) Act (1967), 207-8
Merchant Shipping Act (1894), 170-1, 182, 185, 186, 187, 206; (1970) 185; (1974) 196, 201
Merchant Shipping (Oil Pollution) Act (1971), 199-201
Mineral Workings (Offshore Installations) Act (1971), 170, 173, 176-7, 218, 226
Nuclear Installations Act (1965), 202-4
Petroleum (Production) Act (1934), 173-4, 197
Petroleum (Regulations) Act (1966), 226
Prevention of Oil Pollution Act (1971), 194, 195, 197-8, 208
Public Health (Drainage of Trade Premises) Act (1937), 193-4
Radioactive Substances Act (1960), 169, 203-4
Radiological Protection Act (1970), 204
Sea Fish (Conservation) Act (1967), 180-1, 184
Sea Fish (Industry) Act (1970), 181
Sea Fisheries Act (1968), 179, 181-2
Sea Fisheries Regulation Act (1966), 180, 181
Sea Fisheries (Scotland) (Amendment) Act (1885), 181
Sea Fisheries (Shellfish) Act (1967), 183-4
Town and Country Planning Act (1971), 237
Water Act (1973), 191, 226
Admiralty, 160, 187, 189, 190, 206-7
Advisory Committee on Oil Pollution of the Sea, 33
Africa, 44
Agreements, *see* Treaties
Agricultural waste, 24, 82-3
Air pollution, 36-40
Amsterdam, 45, 46, 48
Anhydrite, 18, 19
Aquaculture, 15-6
Artificial islands, 151-4
Asia, 44
Atomic Energy Authority, *see* United Kingdom

BALTIC SEA CONVENTION, *see* Treaties
Belgium, 1, 3, 44, 57, 233
container ports, 46
fisheries, 9, 10, 13, 112, 179, 215
legislation, 270-2
pollution, 25, 27, 29-30, 81, 130
zonal jurisdiction, 93, 99, 167
see also Treaties
British Society for the Advancement of Science, 81

CANADA, 119
Clyde, River, 31
Coal, 18, 30, 74, 173, 226
Coastguard Service, 64, 182, 232, 245
Common Market, *see* European Communities
Container ports, 46
Contiguous Zone, 88, 89, 95-6

317

INDEX

Continental Shelf,
  Act, see Acts (U.K.)
  Convention, see Treaties
  international law on, 88, 89, 91–5, 103
  national (U.K.) law on, 167–72, 190
  regulation of mineral workings, 172, 173, 175, 177, 225–6
Conventions, see Treaties
Council of Europe, 144–5, 156, 234, 242
CRISTAL, 133
Crown Estate Commissioners, 74, 173, 183, 226

DEEP SEA DRILLING PROJECT (U.S.A.), 51
Denmark, 44, 57, 60
  container ports, 46
  fisheries, 4, 9, 111, 112, 225
  legislation, 272–7
  mineral extraction, 21, 268
  pollution, 25, 27, 30, 130, 131
  zonal jurisdiction, 92, 97, 99
  see also Treaties
Department of Agriculture and Fisheries for Scotland, 39, 181
Department of Employment, 65
Department of Energy, 65, 218, 226, 231
Department of the Environment, 173, 231, 233, 237
Department of Industry, 39
Department of Trade, 65, 74, 190, 219, 231, 237
Diving, 64–5
Dover Strait, see Strait of Dover
Drilling-rigs, see Oil, Natural Gas
Dumping at sea, 29–33 passim, 79
  international law on, 137–41, 228
  national (U.K.) law on, 204
  see also Treaties

ELBE, RIVER, 36, 47, 117
English Channel, 2, 45, 47, 50, 81, 89, 130, 231, 237
  see also Strait of Dover
European Communities, 95, 109, 113, 144, 145
  Commission, 95, 138

EEC, 16, 21, 22, 59, 83, 109–13, 146, 217, 225, 233, 234, 235, 241, 242;
  Common Fisheries Policy, 109–10, 112, 178, 183
European Fisheries Convention, see Treaties
Europoort (Rotterdam), 45, 48, 49, 81, 117, 229

FAEROE ISLANDS, 4, 9, 11
Finland, 131, 249
  see also Treaties
Fisheries, 3–17, 90, 215–7
  international conflict, 70–3
  international law on, 103–14, 225
  management, 14–5
  national (U.K.) law on, 177–85, 225
  pollution, 77–8
  see also Treaties
Flag jurisdiction, 87–8
Food and Agriculture Organization (FAO), 68
Forth, River, 31, 259
France, 44, 233
  fisheries, 9, 11, 13
  pollution, 19, 25, 30, 35, 130

GAS, see Natural Gas
German Democratic Republic, 35, 241
Germany, Federal Republic of, 3, 65, 218, 233
  container ports, 46
  fisheries, 4, 9, 11, 12, 13, 16, 109, 179
  mineral extraction, 268–9
  pollution, 25, 27, 30, 35–6, 130
  zonal jurisdiction, 92, 96, 97, 99
  see also Treaties
Great Britain, see United Kingdom

HERRING INDUSTRY BOARD, 183, 225
High Seas,
  Convention, see Treaties
  international law on, 88, 89, 90–6, 104–5
  national (U.K.) law on, 165–72
Holland, see Netherlands
Humber, River, 18, 26, 31, 45, 49

ICELAND, 9, 10, 17, 72, 113, 136, 216
Industrial waste, 29–33, 79, 80–2

318

INDEX

Institute for Marine Environmental Research (Oceanographic Laboratory), 2, 3
Institute of Geological Sciences, 61
Inter-Governmental Maritime Consultative Organization (IMCO), 43, 47, 84, 115, 116, 117, 123, 125, 129, 130, 135, 136, 143, 220, 228
Internal waters,
    international law on, 88, 89, 101-2
    national (U.K.) law on, 159-61
International Agreements, Conventions, see Treaties
International Atomic Energy Agency (IAEA), 135, 137
International Civil Aviation Organization (ICAO), 220
International Commission on Radiological Protection, 137
International Conventions, see Treaties
International Council for the Exploration of the Sea (ICES), 10, 15, 62, 66, 79, 84, 215, 234, 243
    Working Group on Pollution of the North Sea, 1, 4, 25, 29, 106
International Court of Justice, 92, 96, 118
International Hydrographic Organization, 119
International Labour Office (ILO), 47
Ireland, 46, 111, 136, 225, 241
Italy, 241

Japan, 80
Jeger Committee (1970), 25, 239

Law of the Sea Conferences, see United Nations
Legislation, see Acts (U.K.), Treaties; see also names of countries
Liberia, 47
Lighthouses, see Trinity House
Load Lines Convention, see Treaties
London, Port of, 44, 237
Luxembourg, 241

Maas, River, 59
Magnesium, 18

Merchant Shipping Acts, see Acts (U.K.)
Meteorological Office, 39, 62
Milford Haven, 45, 48, 77
Military use of the North Sea, 146-50, 205-7, 223-5, 231
Mining, 74-5
    see also Coal, Natural Gas, Oil
Ministry of Agriculture, Fisheries and Food (MAFF), 39, 173, 204, 231, 237, 239

National Waters, 88, 89, 96-102, 104, 161-5
NATO, 234
    Science Committee on the North Sea, 39-40
Natural Gas,
    drilling rigs, 50, 51-3
    extraction, 18, 20-1, 75-6, 226
    fields, 254-69 *passim*; Amethyst, 260; Ann, 260; Cod, 21, 254; Ekofisk, 21, 261, 262-3, 264; Frigg, 21, 254, 260-1, 266; Heimdall, 254, 266; Hewett, 259; Indefatigable, 259, 260; Leman Bank, 20, 52, 54, 259; Lomond, 260; Rough, 261; Sean, 260; Slochteren, 267; Statfjord, 21; Viking, 259, 261; West Sole, 259, 261
    liquids, 20
    national (U.K.) law on, 173-7
    pipelines and storage, 53-5
Navigation,
    international law on, 114-9, 220, 228-9
    national (U.K.) law on, 185-90
Netherlands, 3, 44, 56, 57, 59, 153, 179, 241
    container ports, 46
    fisheries, 9, 11, 12, 13, 15, 112, 217
    legislation, 277-86
    oil and gas extraction, 21, 266-8
    pollution, 23, 25, 27, 31-2, 130, 144
    surveying, 60, 61
    zonal jurisdiction, 92, 96, 99
    see also Treaties

319

Netherlands—continued
Nordic Council, 234
North Atlantic Treaty Organization, see NATO
North-East Atlantic Fisheries Commission (NEAFC), 15, 106-7, 114, 215-6, 225, 230, 243
North-East Atlantic Fisheries Convention, see Treaties
North Sea Hydrographic Commission, 60
Norway, 44, 57, 60, 218, 221, 233, 241
  container ports, 46
  fisheries, 4, 9, 11, 12, 13, 111, 113, 179, 225
  legislation, 287-315
  oil and gas extraction, 18, 21, 262-6
  pollution, 25, 27, 32-3, 130, 131
  zonal jurisdiction, 99, 109
  see also Treaties
Norwegian Institute for Air Research, 39
Nuclear Test Ban Treaty, see Treaties

OCEAN FORECASTING, 62-4
Oceania, 44
OECD, 39, 45, 136, 234, 235
Oil,
  drilling-rigs, 50, 51-3, 217-9, 231
  extraction, 18, 20, 21-2, 75-6, 226
  pipelines and storage, 53-5, 219
  pollution, 33-4, 77-8; international law on, 20-34, 143, 227-8; national (U.K.) law on, 173-7, 194-202
  see also Oilfields, Treaties
Oil Development Council for Scotland, 66
Oilfields, 253-69 passim
  Albuskjell, 254, 265, 266
  Alwyn, 254, 257-8, 259, 260
  Argyll, 254, 255, 256
  Auk, 254, 255, 256
  Beryl, 254, 255, 256-7, 258
  Brent, 21, 56, 254, 255, 256, 259, 264, 266
  Claymore, 254, 258
  Cormorant, 254, 259

  Dan, 21, 254, 268
  Dunlin, 254, 255, 257, 259
  Edda, 265, 266
  Ekofisk, 21, 53, 54, 55, 254, 262, 263, 264, 265, 266, 268
  Eldfisk, 265
  Ergofisk, 265
  Forties, 22, 52, 55, 254, 255, 256, 258, 259
  Hutton, 254, 257, 259
  Josephine, 254, 258
  Magnus, 258
  Maureen, 254, 257
  Montrose, 55, 254, 255, 256, 259
  Ninian, 254, 258, 259
  Piper, 254, 255, 257, 259
  Thistle, 254, 256, 259
Oosterschelde, 9, 13, 15
Organisation for Economic Co-operation and Development, see OECD

PETROLEUM, see Oil
Pirate broadcasting, 154-6, 207-8
Poland, 9, 10, 230, 241, 248
Pollution, 22-40, 223, 226-9, 235-6
  international law on, 119-46, 226-9
  national (U.K.) law on, 190-205, 226
  see also Acts (U.K.), Agricultural waste, Air pollution, Industrial waste, Oil, Radioactive pollution, Rivers, Sewage, Thermal waste, Treaties
Potash, 18, 19-20
Project Jonsnap, 62

RADIOACTIVE POLLUTION, 24, 34, 82, 135-8, 202-4, 228
Rhine, River, 56, 59
  International Commission for the Protection of, 144
  pollution, 19, 30, 31, 35-6, 82, 144
Rivers, pollution of, 24-33 passim
  see also names of rivers
Royal Commission on Environmental Pollution, see United Kingdom
Royal National Lifeboat Institution (RNLI), 64, 231, 232
Royal Navy, 205, 219, 231, 232, 237

SALT, 18, 19, 84
Salvage, 64–5
Sand and gravel, 18, 73–4, 173, 213, 226
Schelde, River, 29, 31, 59
Scotland,
 fisheries, 13, 16, 70
 oil and gas, 20, 21, 52, 56, 59, 76, 254–62 *passim*
 pollution, 25, 26, 27, 28, 34, 82
Sea-birds, 29, 68, 70, 77, 78, 212
Sewage, 22–9, 79–80
Shellfisheries, 9–14, 79, 80, 83, 183, 184
Shore bases, 65–6
SOLAS Convention, *see* Treaties
South America, 44
Storm Tide Warning Service (STWS), 63
Strait of Dover, 43, 47, 62, 76, 178, 188, 231
 see also English Channel
Surveying and Charting, 60–2
Sweden, 60, 211
 container ports, 46
 fisheries, 9, 10
 pollution, 28, 32–3, 36, 39, 130, 131
 see also Treaties

TANKERS, 41–2, 45, 47, 48, 76, 81, 127, 194–6, 220
Tees, River, 19, 26, 30, 48
Territorial Sea,
 Convention, *see* Treaties
 international law on, 88, 89, 98–101, 102, 103, 224
 national (U.K.) law on, 161–5
Thames, River, 18, 28, 189
 Estuary, 26, 27, 31
 Water Board, 236, 237
Thermal waste, 34–6, 82
Tilbury, 44
TOVALOP, *see* Treaties
Traffic, 43–50
 congestion, 76, 231
Treaties,
 Agreement for Co-operation in Dealing with Pollution of the North Sea by Oil (Bonn, 1969), 130–1, 134 n.187, 227, 249
 Agreement on the Implementation of a European Project on Pollution on the Topic of "Sewage Sludge Processing" (Brussels, 1971), 144, 250
 Convention relating to Civil Liability in the Field of Maritime Carriage of Nuclear Material (Brussels, 1971), 136 n.197, 249
 Convention on Civil Liability for Nuclear Damage (Vienna, 1963), 135–6, 249
 Convention on the Conduct of Fishing Operations in the North Atlantic (1967), 114, 139, 182, 248
 Convention on the Continental Shelf (Geneva, 1958), 91, 94, 104–5, 120, 134, 138 n.206, 143, 149, 151, 152, 153, 167, 168, 169, 170, 172, 225, 226, 231, 247
 Convention on the Facilitation of Maritime Traffic (London, 1965), 118 n.138, 251
 Convention on Fishing and Conservation of the Living Resources of the High Seas (Geneva, 1958), 105–6, 248
 Convention on the High Seas (Geneva, 1958), 87, 90, 120, 134, 135, 137, 138 n.206, 149, 154 n.257, 167, 247
 Convention on the International Regulations for Preventing Collisions at Sea (London, 1972), 117, 228, 251
 Convention on the Liability of Operators of Nuclear Ships (Brussels, 1962), 136, 148, 250
 Convention for the Prevention of Marine Pollution by Dumping from Ships and Aircraft (Oslo, 1972), 79, 84, 137, 139–40, 141, 145, 152 n.247, 204, 228, 250
 Convention on the Prevention of Marine Pollution by Dumping of Wastes and other Matter (Lon-

Treaties—continued
   don, 1972), 137, 141, 149, 204, 228, 250
   Convention for the Prevention of Marine Pollution from Land-based Sources (Paris, 1974), 138, 145–6, 226, 228, 250
   Convention on the Protection of the Environment between Denmark, Finland, Norway and Sweden (Stockholm, 1974), 28, 251
   Convention on the Protection of the Marine Environment of the Baltic Sea Area (Helsinki, 1974), 28, 251
   Convention for the Protection of Submarine Cables (Paris, 1884), 94 n.30, 150 n.238, 251
   Convention and Statute on Freedom of Transit (Barcelona, 1921), 102 67, 251
   Convention and Statute on the International Regime of Maritime Ports (Geneva, 1923), 102, 118 n.138, 251
   Convention on the Territorial Sea and the Contiguous Zone (Geneva, 1958), 92—102 *passim*, 108, 116 n.126, 150, 151, 152, 158 n.3, 159, 160, 161–2, 165, 166, 224, 247
   Convention on Third Party Liability in the Field of Nuclear Energy (Paris, 1960), 135–6, 249
   Denmark/Finland/Norway/Sweden Agreement concerning Co-operation in Taking Measures against Pollution of the Sea by Oil (Copenhagen, 1971), 131, 249
   Denmark/Finland/Norway/Sweden Agreement concerning Uniform Rules for the Marking of Navigable Waters (Helsinki, 1962), 116 n.126, 251
   Denmark/Federal Republic of Germany Agreement and Protocol concerning the Delimitation in Coastal Areas of the Continental Shelf of the North Sea (Bonn, 1965), 93 n.28, 247
   Denmark/Federal Republic of Germany/Netherlands Protocol to the Agreements Delimiting the Continental Shelf in the North Sea (Copenhagen, 1971), 93 n.27, 248
   Denmark/Federal Republic of Germany Treaty relating to the Delimitation of the Continental Shelf under the North Sea (Copenhagen, 1971), 93 n.27, 247
   Denmark/Norway Agreement on the Delimitation of the Continental Shelf between the Two Countries (Oslo, 1965), 93 n.28, 248
   Denmark/Norway/Sweden Agreement concerning Measures for the Protection of the Stock of Deep Sea Prawns, European Lobsters, Norway Lobsters and Crabs (Oslo, 1952), 106 n.88, 249
   Denmark/U.K. Agreement relating to the Delimitation of the Continental Shelf between the Two Countries (London, 1971), 93 n.28, 247
   European Agreement for the Prevention of Broadcasts Transmitted from Stations outside National Territories (Strasbourg, 1965), 155–6, 207, 240
   European Agreement on the Restriction on the Use of Certain Detergents in Washing and Cleaning Products (Strasbourg, 1968), 144, 250
   European Fisheries Convention (London, 1964), 105, 107–9, 111–14, 177–8, 225, 248
   Federal Republic of Germany/Netherlands Treaty relating to the Delimitation of the Continental Shelf under the North Sea (Copenhagen, 1971), 93 n.27, 248
   Federal Republic of Germany/Netherlands Treaty concerning the Lateral Delimitation of the Continental Shelf in the Vicinity

INDEX

Treaties—continued
   of the Coast (Bonn, 1964), 93 n.28, 248
   Federal Republic of Germany/ U.K. Agreement relating to the Delimitation of the Continental Shelf under the North Sea between the Two Countries (London, 1971), 93 n.28, 247
   International Convention relating to the Arrest of Sea-going Ships (Brussels, 1952), 101 n.61, 118, 165, 251
   International Convention on Certain Rules concerning Civil Jurisdiction in Matters of Collision, 118, 164, 250
   International Convention on Civil Liability for Oil Pollution Damage (Brussels, 1969), 128, 131–3, 199–200, 227, 249
   International Convention on the Establishment of an International Fund for Compensation for Oil Pollution Damage (Brussels, 1971), 131–3, 200–1, 227, 249
   International Convention relating to Intervention on the High Seas in Cases of Oil Pollution Casualties (Brussels, 1969), 127–9, 134 n.187, 143, 148, 197–8, 227, 228, 249
   International Convention relating to the Limitation of Liability of Owners of Sea-going Ships (Brussels, 1957), 118 n.140, 251
   International Convention on Load Lines (London, 1966), 116, 132, 228, 251
   International Convention for the Prevention of Pollution of the Sea by Oil (London, 1954), 120–4, 127, 128, 132, 148, 194, 195, 196, 227, 249
   International Convention for the Prevention of Pollution from Ships (1974), 124–7, 134 n.187, 142–3, 227, 228, 229, 231, 249
   International Convention for the Safety of Life at Sea (London, 1960), 43, 115, 116, 117, 132, 135, 136, 148, 187, 202, 228, 250
   International Convention for the Unification of Certain Rules relating to Penal Jurisdiction in Matters of Collision or other Incidents of Navigation (Brussels, 1952), 117–8, 250
   International Regulations for Preventing Collisions at Sea (London, 1960), 47, 116, 117, 132, 251
   Netherlands/U.K. Agreement relating to the Delimitation of the Continental Shelf under the North Sea between the Two Countries (London, 1965), 93 n.28, 247
   Netherlands/U.K. Agreement relating to the Exploitation of Single Geological Structures Extending across the Dividing Line on the Continental Shelf under the North Sea (London, 1965), 93 n.28, 247
   North-East Atlantic Fisheries Convention (London, 1959), 106, 215, 248
   Norway/Sweden Agreement on the Delimitation of the Continental Shelf (Stockholm, 1968), 93 n.28, 248
   Norway/U.K. Agreement relating to the Delimitation of the North Sea between the Two Countries (London, 1965), 93 n.28, 247
   Norway/U.K. Agreement relating to the Transmission of Petroleum from the Ekofisk Field and Neighbouring Areas to the U.K. (Oslo, 1973), 93 n.28, 249
   Norway/U.S.S.R. Agreement concerning the Handling of Claims in Connection with Damage to Fishing Gear (Moscow, 1959), 114 n.119, 249
   Tanker Owners' Voluntary Agreement concerning Liability for Oil

Treaties—continued
   Pollution (TOVALOP) (1969), 133, 249
   Treaty Banning Nuclear Weapon Tests in the Atmosphere, in Outer Space and Under Water (Moscow, 1963), 148, 250
   Treaty on the Prohibition of the Emplacement of Nuclear Weapons and Other Weapons of Mass Destruction on the Seabed and the Ocean Floor and in the Subsoil thereof (Moscow, 1971), 148-9, 224, 250
   U.K./Norway Agreement for the Continuance of Fishing by Norwegian Vessels within the Fishery Limits of the U.K. (London, 1964), 113 n.113, 248
   U.K./Norway Fishery Agreement (Oslo, 1960), 113 n.115, 114 n.119, 248
   U.K./U.S.A. Exchange of Notes constituting an Agreement relating to the Use of U.K. Ports and Territorial Waters by the Nuclear Ship *Savannah* (London, 1964), 136 n.200, 250
   U.K./U.S.S.R. Exchange of Notes constituting an Agreement on Matters arising from the Establishment by the U.K. of a Fishery Regime provided for by the Fishery Limits Act, 1964 (Moscow, 1964), 113 n.113, 248
Trinity House, 187, 189, 231, 232, 237
Tyne, River, 26, 28, 30

UNITED KINGDOM, 64, 65, 69, 74, 149, 231-41 *passim*, 243, 245
   Acts, *see* Acts (U.K.)
   Atomic Energy Authority, 34
   coastal development, 56-9
   container ports, 46
   fisheries, 9-16 *passim*, 72, 103, 111, 112, 114, 177-85, 216, 217, 225
   legislation, *see* Acts (U.K.) and U.K. national law

   mineral extraction, 18-21 *passim*, 172-7, 226, 253-62
   national law, 158-209, 218-9, 225-30 *passim*
   North Sea traffic, 44-9 *passim*
   Offshore Installations (Construction and Survey) Regulations (1974), 226
   oil, 217-19, 221
   Petroleum (Production) Regulations (1966), 174
   pollution, 24, 25-7, 30-1, 34, 35, 37-9, 78, 130, 148, 190-205
   Royal Commission on Environmental Pollution, 236, 239
   Scotland, *see* Scotland
   surveying, 60, 61
   zonal jurisdiction, 93, 96, 98, 99, 159-172
   see also Treaties
United Nations,
   Conference on the Human Environment (1972), 39, 211
   Conference on the Law of the Sea (First, 1958) 98, (Second, 1960) 98-9, (Third, in progress) 85, 141, 147, 154, 161, 219, 243
   Economic Commission for Europe, 234
   General Assembly Resolution 2574D, 224
   Political Committee, 224
U.S.A., 44, 56, 57, 64, 68, 95, 98, 119, 129, 136, 218, 222, 236, 240
   President's Council on Environmental Quality, 222, 240
   see also Treaties
U.S.S.R., 3, 9, 11, 44, 108, 136, 230, 241
   see also Treaties

WADDENZEE, 13, 15, 82, 217
Warren Spring Laboratory, 39
Wear, River, 26, 30
White Fish Authority, 13, 16, 183, 225
World Court, *see* International Court of Justice

ZONAL JURISDICTION,
   international law on, 88-102
   national (U.K.) law on, 159-172